PERFORMING ARTISTS

REVISED AND ENLARGED

WITHDRAWN

THE BACK STAGE HANDBOOK FOR

PERFORMING ARTISTS

REVISED AND ENLARGED EDITION

The how-to and who-to-contact reference
for actors, singers, and dancers

Compiled and Edited by Sherry Eaker

BACK STAGE BOOKS
An imprint of Watson-Guptill Publications/New York

Sherry Eaker is the editor of *Back Stage*, the national trade publication geared to the performing artist in both the commercial and non-profit theater arenas. As editor since 1977, she has overseen the growth of the paper, which was founded in 1960, to its present form as a national performing arts weekly. She serves on the board of the League of Professional Theater Women, and is both a Tony Award and Drama Desk Award voter. She is a member of the National Theater Conference, and the Manhattan Association of Cabarets and Clubs. She frequently serves on panels focusing on the working actor.

Jacket design: Jay Anning
Book design: Bob Fillie, Graphiti Graphics

Copyright © 1991 BPI Communications, Inc.

This edition first published 1991 by Back Stage Books, an imprint of Watson-Guptill Publications, a division of BPI Communications, Inc., 1515 Broadway, New York, NY 10036

Library of Congress Cataloging-in-Publication Data
The Back stage handbook for performing artists : the how-to and who-to
  contact reference for actors, singers, and dancers / compiled and
  edited by Sherry Eaker. — Rev. and enl. ed.
     p. cm.
   Includes index.
   ISBN 0-8230-7569-9
    1. Acting—Vocational guidance—United States—Directories.
   2. Performing arts—Vocational guidance—United States—Directories.
   I. Eaker, Sherry.
   PN2055.B27 1991
   792'.028'02573—dc20   91-29379
                                              CIP

Manufactured in United States of America

First Printing, 1991

1 2 3 4 5 6 7 8 9 / 96 95 94 93 92 91

To my father,
who raised the curtain
for me and made it all possible,
and to my mother,
who's been coaching me along the way

A special thank you to Michele LaRue and Bruce Peterson for their invaluable assistance and persistence on this project. Many thanks as well to other *Back Stage* staffers—Ben Alexander, Therese Aylward, and Gayle Stahlhuth, and to columnist Rob Stevens. My gratitude to Actors' Equity Association, Screen Actors Guild, and the League of Chicago Theatres for their cooperation. Finally, a sincere acknowledgement to all the freelance feature writers, columnists, and reviewers who have made valuable contributions to *Back Stage* throughout the years.

CONTENTS

INTRODUCTION

BY SHERRY EAKER

know two performers who are both equally talented. However, one is constantly getting callbacks and landing jobs while the other isn't. What's the secret of the working performer? Actually, it isn't really a secret at all. She knows that to survive in this business she's got to treat her career as a business. She's learned that there's a lot more to an acting, singing, and dancing career than just training and performing, and that much of her energy is going to be devoted to finding and getting the work. She has defined her "type," and knows how to "sell herself" at an audition. She also hasn't restricted herself to one segment of the entertainment industry; she auditions for film, TV, commercial print, and voice-overs—in addition to stage work, the one medium that she's spent years training for. She knows full well that "Work begets work," and that she'll eventually get to do what she really wants to do.

The other performer is still waiting for the "ideal" role to come along, and will probably have to leave the business before the opportunity ever presents itself.

The working performer's attitude about her career is, in essence, what this book is all about: helping the artist discover the wide range of opportunities that exist in the performing field and learning how to make the necessary contacts in order to pursue them.

This is also the focus of *Back Stage*, the weekly trade paper geared to the performing artist. Each week, aside from carrying audition information for film and stage productions going on in New York and across the country, *Back Stage* features "how-to" articles designed to help actors, singers, dancers, directors, playwrights, and other creative staff to move ahead in their careers.

The idea of putting all these articles together in book form was the result of the countless requests I receive asking for specific back issues. In response to those requests, the 1989 edition of the *Handbook for Performing Artists* featured almost 30 feature stories, most of which had run in *Back Stage* during that year. Where relevant, these articles were accompanied by trade lists, in keeping with the traditional format of the paper.

The 1989 *Handbook* proved quite successful, and the decision was made in the fall of 1990 to revise it. The original plan was simply to update the chapters and expand the lists to include Los Angeles and Chicago. But when I considered some of the feature stories that I've run in *Back Stage* more recently, I decided to include these as well.

The new chapters include: "Joining the Unions," "Studying Speech and Diction," "Working in Commercial Print," "Auditioning for Shakespeare," "How to Run an Audition," "Working in Los Angeles Theaters," and "Working in Chicago."

All of the chapters—and there are now 35 altogether—fit within the framework of six basic categories: "The Basic Tools," "Training," "Finding the Work," "Getting a Show on the Road," "Working in the Theater," and "Off the Main Stage." There's a progression of information, starting with putting a resume together, going on to choosing a class, finding an agent, producing your own show, and then discovering the various opportunities on stages and before the cameras all across the country.

The first two chapters cover resumes and photos. Since your resume is your number one marketing tool, this chapter details how to put one together to make it most effective, and shows you the most efficient means of sending your resume out. Because a resume is always accompanied by a headshot, learning how to choose the right photographer is the focus of the second chapter.

Play scripts, sheet music, monologue collections, and playwright anthologies are also basics for performing artists, and a complete rundown of performing arts books makes up another section under the "Basic Tools" umbrella.

Joining the performing unions would seem to be a necessary career move. The chapter on unions describes not only *how* to join, but *why* and *when* you should join.

There are hundreds of acting schools, dance studios, and voice teachers in the United States. So, how do you choose one that's right for you? The chapters grouped under the section called "Training" set up some criteria for selecting schools and teachers, are are accompanied by lists that show where to find them.

Now that you've "set up shop" and are busy taking classes, your next step is "Finding the Work." Hopefully, you're already reading the trade papers every week to find out what's being cast. You'll also need to make contact with agents and casting directors since it is they who can help you land a role. Keeping in touch with them on a constant basis, via your headshot-postcard, is necessary, *especially* when you're performing somewhere. They need to be reminded that you are a *working* actor. Included under "Finding the Work" are lists of Equity, SAG, and AFTRA franchised agents, and independent casting directors based in New York, Chicago, and Los Angeles.

There *is* plenty of work to be found in Los Angeles, but adjusting to the city is definite culture shock, especially if you've been living on the East Coast. The final chapter in this section examines ways to cope in the City of Angels.

Suppose you're a playwright or director or actor, and have your hands on a wonderful property and don't want to have to be dependent on others to move it along. What do you do? Produce it yourself! Producing your own show can be a tremendous learning experience, and the chapters designated under "Getting a Show on the Road" tell you specifically what you need to know and do—from creating a budget to hiring a cast, from renting a rehearsal/performance space to doing your own publicity.

I've already mentioned the wide range of opportunities that are available. And there *are* lots of opportunities for performers at all levels of experience on stages all across the country. The section titled "Working in the Theater" features chapters which describe in detail types of theaters, theater companies, booking agents, producers, along with complete contact information. Listed are theater companies in New York, Los Angeles, and Chicago, nonprofit resident theaters across the country, nationwide Equity and non-Equity dinner theaters, and Theater for Young Audiences companies.

"Off the Main Stage" focuses on other opportunities. Theme parks, for example, can offer intense and varied experiences for the young person first getting started. Where these theme parks are, the kind of performers they're seeking, and where and when they hold their audition tours are detailed here.

Performers, as well as staff and technicians, may also take stock in summer stock. Once a year, hundreds of theater producers gather at various sites across the country auditioning performers and interviewing directors, technicians, and staffpersons for the spots that are available at their summer theaters. The chapter on these regional combined auditions informs as to when and where these auditions are held, gives application procedures and deadlines, and tells how to prepare.

Fairly profitable outlets for performers are the industrial shows and films. Coined "business theater," the show is usually a big-budget production using the most advanced technology and offering valuable training and experience—not to mention high salaries—for the artist.

Think you've got what it takes to make people laugh? The chapter on comedy deals with the growing field of stand-up, in clubs and on cable, and what goes into making a successful stand-up comedian.

There are lots of opportunities out there, but not every opportunity offered is a realistic one. Just as phonies and con artists exist in the business world, there are plenty of them around in the show business world. Unfortunately, in such a competitive market, many novice performers fall prey to promises of "stardom" and many end up losing more that just their pride. Based on the many letters and calls that *Back Stage* has received from performers over the years, we put together a comprehensive report on what performers should be aware of and situations they should avoid. This report serves as our concluding chapter.

Show business *is* a business and if you, the performing artist, want to succeed at it you must treat it as such. No one is going to do it for you at the beginning, and the earlier in your career that you start dealing with the business aspects of the business, the greater are your chances of succeeding artistically. Whether or not you get to Broadway, there are audiences waiting for you. There are outlets for your performance skills where you can act, sing, dance, entertain, and derive the satisfaction that comes from performing.

PART ONE

THE BASIC TOOLS

RESUMES

BY JILL CHARLES

The picture/resume is the performer's business card, reference letter, portfolio, and certificate of professional standing all rolled into one. It is the marketing tool that will get you work. Putting it together, making it effective, and getting it out should become part of your daily work and should be given the kind of attention you would give to an audition for an important role. Without a good picture/resume (usually abbreviated P/R) you may not even get to audition for that important role. A good photo is essential, but once the picture gets the casting director's attention, remember that it is usually the resume stapled to its back that clinches the audition.

There is no standard format for the resume itself. Each resume is as individual as the performer it represents. Certain data, however, should always be included in a resume, and some information is better left out. The guidelines below will help you determine what to include and what to exclude in your resume.

When organizing your resume, pay careful attention to its overall look. It should be pleasing to look at, well structured and easy to understand. Imagine how many resumes casting people and directors receive. If yours is hard to read and digest, your credits and skills simply will not register with them. One way of making sure that your resume is easy to understand is to organize it into parts or sections.

VITAL STATISTICS AND CONTACT INFORMATION

The top section of your resume should generally include vital statistics and contact information, such as your name, contact phone number, union affiliations, and talent agent's name. It is not necessary, and not necessarily wise, to put a home address or home phone number here. Once you send out a resume, there is no way of knowing what will happen to it (some even turn up on city sidewalks), and for your own protection it is best to list only a service number.

Important vital statistics include height, weight, and the color of your hair and eyes. This information is essential for a casting person. You may include or omit items such as age, vocal range, and measurements. A general rule of thumb is to include information that will help make you stand out, or underscore a special ability. Omit data that will confuse, mislead, or somehow create false impressions.

Measurements need be listed only in modeling or commercial resumes. For their own protection, many actresses prefer to leave measurements to the costume designer after they have the role. You may want to include your social security number—some agents prefer that their clients do so—but this is not essential since it is not needed until you are hired for a job.

Many performers dislike putting an age range on a resume because they do not want to be typecast into a narrow bracket. They theorize that the casting person should decide whether they appear to be the appropriate age for a role. This is an acceptable approach if a photo is a true representation of a performer. If, for example, an actor appears to be in her young 20s in a photo and actually looks 30 at the audition, the casting person will more than likely not be pleased. If you do put an age range on your resume, make it realistic—few can successfully play ages 15 to 40.

Listing vocal range is important if you can sing. If there is no mention of vocal range, and no musical credits on your resume, the assumption may be made that you cannot sing at all. If you can carry a tune and could sing in a chorus or handle a song in a nonmusical play, list your vocal range on your resume. Show anything you have done that might be pertinent to singing ability, including musical roles and training.

EXPERIENCE

The body of the resume will describe your experience and list your credits. This section is usually organized by genre: theater, film, television, and commercials. You do not have to place the categories in this order, however. List the categories according to the emphasis you put on them. If you do more work in one area than another, it is a good idea to compile two or more different resumes, so that your "film" resume lists film credits first, while your "theatrical" resume lists theater credits first. Those who have sufficient experience, may wish to divide their theater credits into subdivisions, such as Broadway, national tours, Off Broadway, showcase, stock, regional, musical plays, and so on.

A variety of approaches may be used when listing your credits, but one basic tenet holds—include the information that makes you look best, *but don't lie* or stretch the truth. Most people who look at resumes see a lot of them and know the tricks performers use to fatten up slim credits. The phrase "representative roles" is a transparent camouflage for "roles I did in scene-study class" or "roles I would like to play." Your resume should describe your actual experience by listing each role, play, and theater where you performed it. An understudy role should be listed as such, with a notation ("performed twice" or whatever) if you actually performed the role. Whether you list all the directors you've worked with or just those who are better-known is a choice you should make based on the impressiveness of the list and the overall look it will give to the layout. Don't crowd the credits with names that probably will not be recognized (the name and location of the theater company is sufficient), but if you have worked with well-known directors, say so. It is not necessary to list playwrights' names, unless you performed a new play and you want to emphasize that.

If you are entering the professional world from a training school, your credits probably will be limited. Make the most of what you *have* done, but don't try to stretch things too far. List professional credits, like summer stock, before school credits. Try to give a positive (but honest) picture of whatever experience you gained in school, and list any guest directors you worked with who might be known outside your school.

TRAINING

The purpose of the Training section is simply to show where and with whom you have trained. This will help those who see it determine the areas and extent of your training in acting, voice, dance, and related theater skills. If you have trained with well-known teachers be sure to include their names. If, however, the names are not well-known and their inclusion makes the resume look cluttered, do not list them; the type and duration of training should be sufficient.

SPECIAL SKILLS

The Special Skills section should list those talents that might be useful in commercial work, or that a theater company might find especially interesting. Start with theater-related skills such as stage combat, acrobatics, the ability to play musical instruments, and accents and dialects. Then include athletic abilities, and whether or not you drive a car (standard and/or automatic). You can add to this list almost anything you do well, such as photography, graphic design, sign language, carpentry, or electronics; these skills can also generate conversation at an interview or audition.

UPDATING RESUMES

Part of the nature of resumes is that they continually need to be updated, and this can create time and money problems. If you do not get around to updating your resume until the handwritten additions threaten to take it over, you might try exercising this option—design your resume with a heading at the bottom titled "Recent Credits." Leave space under this heading to describe your latest projects. Not only will this keep your resume looking neat, but it will also project the idea that you are constantly working. Of course, you will always want to have something written in this space, so when you have your resume printed, exclude your most recent credit and then jot it down in the open space after the resume has been printed. This is also a good way to call special attention to upcoming readings or workshops in which you may be involved.

PRINTING RESUMES

Once your original is prepared, the resume can be printed in quantity. Believe it or not, these days, duplicating resumes costs *less* than it used to. As recently as two years ago, you had the choice of finding a friend with a day job and access to an IBM Selectric III to type your resume, or spending $45–$75 to have it typeset. Now, with the advent of such high-tech breakthroughs as word processors, desktop publishing programs, and laser printers, you can have your resume done for $15–$35—or maybe you have a friend with a Macintosh computer.

On your hunt for a person or establishment to set up your resume, look at samples of their work, noticing especially typefaces, the boldness of headings, lines or borders, and so on. All of these options are easily created on word processors.

You also need to determine exactly how cheap and easy a resume service will make it for you to update your resume. The harder and more expensive it is, the less likely you are to redo your resume as often as you should (which is as often as your credits change significantly, or when you find the handwritten additions threatening to take over). Most services will store your resume on a file in a computer, making updates available at a reasonable price.

Of course, if you own a computer, you can run off your own originals, keeping your resume on file for easy updating. Be sure your printer is capable of turning out high-quality originals. If you are thinking about buying a computer, this should be a major consideration. Letter-quality printers generally cost $100 to $300 more than dot-matrix printers, but if you intend to use the computer for your resumes and cover letters, a good printer is well worth the extra investment. Boldfacing, which can improve the overall appearance of your resume, is possible with almost any printer and word processing software.

Resumes should always be trimmed to 8-by-10-inch sheets. To accommodate this, the layout of the resume must fall within this space. An 8 x 10 resume is essential—otherwise it will overlap your attractive headshot and look unprofessional.

MAILING PICTURES/RESUMES

Now that you have 100 newly composed, attractive, cleanly offset-printed resumes, it is time to put them to work. Organize a system by which you can send out pictures and resumes with cover letters and followup postcards on a regular basis to a targeted group of theaters, casting directors, and agents. If you have the use of a computer with word processing software and a letter-quality printer, or a memory typewriter, this should not be especially difficult. Take care that your letters look businesslike and professional, and at the same time, reflect something of yourself.

You can select your targets from such sources as *Back Stage*, the *Ross Reports*, the *New York Casting & Survival Guide*, and other lists. There are also a number of sources that provide mailing lists on peel-off labels. If you have your own computer, you can put lists from any of these sources into your data base and run off labels to targeted groups at given times, such as regional theaters in the late summer, or summer stock theaters in March. If you are working with a typewriter, labels can still save you the time of hand-addressing each envelope. Lists are available for casting directors in every area of theater, modeling, film and TV, theaters with summer and winter seasons, talent agents, and personal managers—just about anyone you would ever want to send a copy of your picture/resume.

For some actors, this point in the process—sending out P/Rs and postcards, keeping track of who should get them, and when and how often—is the greatest stumbling block in their careers. Shakespeare Theatrical Mailing Service in New York City was created to help actors with this process (the company serves performers anywhere in the country). The company will send out letters, P/Rs, flyers, or whatever a client wishes, to any number of names in their extensive data bank. Prices vary, depending on the number of pieces sent out and the frequency of mailings.

Before choosing between the do-it-yourself approach or the option of hiring a mailing service, you should assess your finances and organizational capabilities. The total cost of preparing your own cover letter and sending it out to a list you have compiled will certainly be less than hiring a service to do the mailings for you. The question is, *will you actually do it*? That perfect P/R won't do your career any good if it's sitting in your desk drawer.

GETTING THE RIGHT PICTURE

BY TONI REINHOLD

O ne of the most effective marketing tools an actor can use is a headshot. Generally accompanied by a resume, a headshot is your proxy at almost all initial meetings with agents, producers, casting directors, and other key industry professionals. No one closes the door on a headshot, puts it on hold for half an hour, fails to return its phone calls, or tells it to go away. A headshot sent by mail usually reaches its target swiftly and at that point either fulfills its mission—which is to create so much interest that you are asked to appear in the flesh—or fails so miserably that the only file it reaches is the circular one under someone's desk.

A headshot is one of the few things over which an actor has so much control. You decide when to have it taken and by whom, how much you will pay for it, whether the quality is acceptable, how soon you need it, what image you wish to project through it, the kind of work you want to attract with it, and to whom it will be sent.

Having a headshot done is one of the first things you should do to get your career rolling. Because a headshot must deliver a very personal message about you, you must choose a photographer who is right for you—someone who can best capture your individual message on film in the most effective way.

Choosing the right photographer is not something you can do with a random phone call. Many photographers offer headshot services and are qualified to take attractive, usable photos. Most professionals will agree that good chemistry must exist between actor and photographer and that the quality of the photographer's work must be A-1. However, more than personality and art enter into this picture. Other factors must be considered. Prices and services included in photographers' fees vary greatly and must be weighed when you make your decision. You should also have an idea of the image you want to present in your headshots, and this must be communicated to photographers. You need someone who can relate to you and to what you are trying to achieve at this stage of your career.

Many photographers understand the needs of performers and are willing to do what is necessary to produce exciting, effective headshots. There are those, however, who offer little more than a few rolls of exposed film. As New York-based photographer Bruce Cahn has noted, "There is a growing tendency for photographers to give the actor exposed rolls of film rather than pictures. This is unfairly taking advantage of the performer. Lab procedures and development times vary so widely that to get a quality image this way, you have to be lucky. And if the picture is sloppily done, every party involved gets to lay the blame elsewhere."

Photographer Ron Berlin distributes printed lists to his prospective New York City customers with information about headshots, fees, and services, along with do's and don'ts that contribute to the success or failure of a photo shoot. Berlin says he encourages potential clients to read his list and to follow-up by asking questions. "You must ask questions of every photographer you interview," he says. "The selection process should not only be fun, but part of educating yourself as an actor. I spend 40 minutes with potential clients when they first come into my studio because there are things they need to talk about, such as posing techniques and lighting. There are subtle differences among pictures that contribute to the overall good appearance of a photograph. You want to have as many of those differences working in your favor as possible. The whole headshot event is designed to produce an advertising photograph and the person in the picture is the product being promoted. Once you see the project that way, the question becomes, What am I advertising? What am I promoting? Just take it from there."

Most photographers feel that it is important to achieve a good rapport with a client. "When actors are being photographed for a headshot, they are letting their hair down and unmasking themselves, or at the very least presenting a different set of masks. They should feel comfortable about doing that," Ron Berlin stresses. "I tell my clients that I can fake almost anything in a photo except a sense of comfort. Photographers shoot in different styles, but I don't think any of us can fake someone looking relaxed and forthright."

THE PHOTOGRAPHER'S PORTFOLIO

You should ask to see the portfolio of each photographer you interview because it reveals the quality of a person's work. "Seeing portfolios is important," says photographer Art Murphy, who works in New York and Philadelphia. "My portfolio, for example, shows the success I've had with other actors and gives a client something to talk about while deciding whether or not we can work together."

New York-based photographer Nick Granito says variety is important in a portfolio. "Is the photographer equally good with men and women?" asks Granito. "Are you getting a commercial and theatrical shot in one session? Commercial shots are brighter, whereas those used for opera or stage are more dramatically lit. Is the photographer able to use lighting to show contouring on the face? Many photographers use one type of flat bright lighting which does not show 'layers' of personality. Agents want to see as many facets of the actor's personality as possible. Does the photographer employ a variety of angles to complement all faces? We all have a better side. Is the photographer equally adept with older and younger types?"

"If properly lit," Granito continues, "the print should show details of the face, rather than washing them out. Are you able to see highlights in the hair? Can you distinguish a blonde from a redhead? Is the retouching moderate or is it plastic surgery? Do the eyes say something or are they vacant? Is the smile warm, engaging, and energetic as opposed to tense, posed or tentative? Do the pictures look like the person in real life? High-fashion glamour shots with makeup and hair styles not worn on a daily basis are useless if you can't generate that look with an hour's notice."

THE PHOTOGRAPHIC IMAGE

We each have a certain image of ourselves which may or may not coincide with the one we actually project. To be effective, your headshot should reflect the way you look to others. It is important, therefore, to have a realistic idea of the image you want to project before interviewing photographers.

"Not everyone should go for a glamour shot," says New York photographer Ralph Lewin, "but everyone wants to look so much better in their photos than they do in real life. You should go for a headshot that reflects what you are. Are you a character type? You should know this. I like to discuss what clients want and know what kind of work they are going after. Many people want to look glamorous in their photos, then they go out for glamour parts and don't get them because they don't look like the person in the photo," says Lewin. "I discuss image and type with clients and tell them if I think they would be better off going for something else. When a photographer has been doing this work for a long time, they develop a good idea of things like this."

Realism also scores high with casting directors and agents, many of whom are aware of how much work goes into finding the right photographer and getting a good headshot.

"Unless you are well schooled in this business, picking a photographer is a tough choice for an actor or actress," says Vicky Vittes, former head of the commercial print department at the Carson-Adler Agency in New York City. "I feel one of the reasons people have agents is so the agents can recommend photographers. But it's kind of a Catch-22. You can't get in to see an agent unless you have a good picture, but it's hard to get a good picture if you don't have someone recommending the right photographers. I feel that as an agent one of my functions is to look at a person, consider their personality, and then recommend a photographer."

Vittes offers these suggestions to help you narrow down the market: "The most important thing about a headshot is that it should look like you. Don't get a 'signature' picture—a headshot about the photographer's style and not a headshot about what you really look like. If you are a character type, don't get a glitzy, glamorous headshot that is airbrushed to extremes, washed out, and doesn't look anything like you. I also look for clarity in the photo, clean lines, good backlighting, and good contrast. And I want to see some life, something going on behind the eyes. I don't like dead, boring smiling shots."

Jerry Saviola, vice president in charge of casting services at Grey Advertising in New York City, says he and his colleagues are also looking for the "real thing." "I look for a headshot that is accurate and honest—and all I mean by honest is that it isn't too artificially posed," he notes. "Sometimes what is attractive is just an expression on the face. It's very important that the picture look like the person. That sounds like not a lot to ask for, but we get pictures that look nothing like the person."

PHOTOGRAPHERS SURVEY

The questions below are from a survey of photographers in the New York City area, conducted by *Back Stage*. The answers help provide an overview of the range of prices, contents of headshot packages, and costs and related services that are generally available. These questions also supply you with a ready-made checklist to be used when you begin your search for a photographer.

How much do you charge for a headshot photo session?
Prices ranged from $150 to $300 on the average, though some photographers quoted a bottom and a top figure. The bottom/top figures ranged from $75 to $260 to $350 to $655. One photo studio offers a $75 package that includes 72 color shots, chrome transparencies, internegs, and an 8 x 10 color enlargement. At least one photographer charges $25 more for women's headshots, while another charges $300 for single-style photos and $350 for two styles of photos, such as commercial and theatrical.

Many photographers base their prices on the number of rolls of film included in the shoot and then add extra charges for additional rolls of film. These charges vary from $5 to $50 per roll. Some photographers said they will shoot extra film at no additional charge if it is warranted. Tax may or may not be included in the price.

How much time do you allocate for each session?
This depends on a variety of factors, including how many rolls of film are shot, how many changes of clothing are allowed, and how much time is put into lighting. Answers varied from one to three hours for 72 shots, with a typical session lasting about two hours. While some photographers stated that a session could last as little as 45 minutes, most said they would give as much time as necessary. There are photographers who book only two shoots a day so clients have time to comfortably work their way through a session. Some photographers take Polaroid photos before each pose to check lighting, hair, and makeup, and this can add on time.

How many shots are included?
A typical photo session can include anywhere from 72 to 180 shots. Some-

times the number depends on how many shots a client wants. The number of shots may also vary according to the size of film used.

The term format refers to the size of film. There is 35mm format and 120mm format, which is the next size up from 35mm. Film in 120mm format comes with several numbers of exposures per roll, such as 8, 10, 12, or 16. This format offers fewer shots per roll than 35mm, and sometimes as few as 40 shots in a session are taken on this size film. This is an important distinction to make, since the price of a session may be greatly increased if a client wants 72 frames shot on 120mm film. One photographer said each sitting includes 72 poses no matter what size film a client chooses. Because of the difference in clarity offered by this size film (many photographers feel that larger format film results in better quality pictures), some photographers suggest clients have photos taken on both 35mm and 120mm film during the same session. When photographers start talking rolls of film, you should be asking the number of shots per roll.

Does the session include negatives and prints in one price?
Do you give negatives to your clients?
About half the photographers who answered said negs are included. Almost all photographers said blowups are included in their fees. Those photographers who keep the negatives say it is their way of controlling the quality of reproductions. Some say it is also a way to bring clients back when they want prints from a particular shoot.

If negatives are not included, how much do you charge a client to purchase them?
Many photographers said they will not sell negatives. Photographers who said they would sell negatives separately to their clients cited these prices: $30 per roll; $30 to $80 per shoot; $25 for headshot negatives or more if the shoot is more complex. Some photographers double their fees when negatives are included. For example, a $175 photo session would be increased to $350 if the negatives were included.

Do you have a portfolio an actor can see?
All photographers answered yes to this question. Several noted that they also have samples of reproductions from sittings and composites, Polaroids, "before" and "after" retouched photos, original and reproduced 8 x 10s, postcards, and contact sheets.

Are hair and makeup included in your fee?
Most photographers said no, but there are those who include makeup in their fee. Several said they assist in makeup and hair styling. Some photographers say that special makeup techniques are needed for black and white photos. While not all photographers agreed with this, many said they do advise clients to have makeup professionally applied for the shoot. Most photographers agreed that men should not use makeup for a photo session, and advise

clients to wear their hair as it is normally worn so photos will look realistic.

If hair and makeup are not included, do you provide these services for an additional fee? How much? If not, do you recommend a hairdresser/makeup artist?

The majority of photographers said they will recommend someone. Flat fees cited for hair and makeup ranged from $45 to $100, with an average price of $75. Fees for makeup ranged from $25 to $65, with an average price of $40. Flat fees for hair averaged $50. Some photographers have a hairstylist/makeup artist on staff who works with clients for an additional fee.

Do you airbrush? Retouch? How much does this cost?

Airbrushing is used to soften or correct large areas of a photo. Retouching is generally used for smaller areas, such as dark circles under eyes. Most photographers only offer retouching. Those who do not perform either of these services usually refer clients to labs or individuals who specialize in such work. Some photographers report that complete retouching is included in their headshot fees, but most say there is an additional airbrushing/retouching charge ranging from an hourly rate of $25 to $50 to a flat rate of $30 per headshot. Several respondents said their fee includes a minimal touchup, but some photographers said you can get a "full retouch" for as little as $10.

What should a man or woman bring to a photo session to be fully prepared?

Almost all photographers who were queried said they discuss this with clients prior to a session. Although answers varied, many cited these things: an average of four changes of clothing with an emphasis on shirts, tops, and jackets; records or tapes that will help you relax; makeup (including a base for women); hair brush and accessories; props as discussed including glasses, hats, hair clips; clean face, clean hair, and a good haircut; understated jewelry including an assortment of earrings; a positive attitude; energy; a sense of humor; curling iron; clean-shaven men should shave closely beforehand and bring shaving gear; self-confidence and a favorite picture of yourself. Photographers warn against clothing that detracts from the face, and white or black garments. Many suggested pastel or rich colors.

"Having your hair cut before a shoot is the worst thing you can do," says photographer Marie Ruggiero. "The hair never looks right. It always looks best a week to 10 days after a cut. And actors and actresses make a mistake by coming in with a fixed idea of the pose they want. They pose for hours figuring it out. If you want natural pictures, it's the worst thing to do. It's up to the photographer to catch that special pose."

How soon after the photo session do you provide proofs?

These are contact sheets from which photos are selected for enlargement. Delivery time to the client varies from one day to a week.

Do you make prints for your clients or must they have them made by

an outside vendor? Do you recommend someone?

Almost all of the photographers in the survey said they make their own enlargements. Most said that they would recommend a lab for volume reproductions.

If you make prints, how soon after proofs are reviewed will a client have them?

Answers ranged from one day to two weeks, and in one instance as little as one and a half hours. Several photographers offer rush service, but they usually charge extra for this.

Do you do location shoots, studio shoots, or both?

Many photographers do both, although one-fourth of those interviewed said they do only studio work.

Do you charge extra for location shoots?

Most photographers charge extra for location shoots. Additional charges ranged from traveling expenses to a general surcharge of $75. Extra costs could run as high as 20 percent of the session fee, or could consist of a $50 travel fee. Some photographers base extra charges upon the whereabouts of the location or the time involved.

Do you provide studio sets for composites?

The majority of the photographers responded yes to this question, although some offer only limited props and sets. There can be an extra charge for the use of sets, but this is not usual. Most said that composites are no longer in vogue.

How far in advance must a photo session be booked?

Responses varied from one day to three weeks. Some photographers did not specify a time limit, while others stated that they would work with emergencies and rush bookings up to the day of the session.

Do you require a deposit at the time the session is booked? How much?

Responses were fairly evenly divided, with deposit requirements ranging from $50 to 50 percent of the photo session price. Deposits may also be demanded for weekend, evening, or holiday shoots.

How far in advance of a session can a person cancel? Do you charge a cancellation fee?

Answers varied from the day of the session to three days' notice; most photographers said they would appreciate a minimum of one day's notice. The majority of photographers said they do not charge a cancellation fee.

Do you refund the deposit or reshoot if a person is unhappy with the results of the shoot?

Although a few photographers did not specify a policy regarding this, most said they would reshoot. Some charge a fee for this, some do not. Generally, photographers are not willing to issue a refund, but it is rare to encounter one who will neither reshoot nor issue a refund. Some photographers replied that they would only consider a reshoot if a client's unhappiness is caused by technical problems or if they had made mistakes.

How many original shots and prints of each are included in your photo session fee?

Answers varied greatly on this question, however a good percentage of photographers surveyed set a standard that includes two 8 x 10 prints—one each of two poses. Some photographers do not include any prints in their price, although this is not usual. Others said the number of enlargements included varied with the number of rolls of film shot.

How much do you charge for each additional original shot a person wants printed and how many prints are included for that charge?

Prices range from $10 to $45 and all were for single enlargements. Photographers who charge $30 to $45 per enlargement stated that prices include retouching.

Do you provide volume reproductions? How much do you charge for 50? 100? 500?

Most photographers said they do not provide volume prints. Among those who do, these prices were cited: $20 to $35 per 50, $34 to $55 per 100, $150 to $230 per 500; $38 per 25, $50 per 50, $62 per 100 with a borderless 8 x 10 negative.

Do you print postcards? How much do you charge for 50? 100? 500?

Most photographers were not equipped to do postcards. Those who were equipped quoted the following prices: $27 per 100, $110 per 500; $72 per 200 with negative.

Do you also photograph children? Are your fees different for these sessions? What are they?

Almost all respondents said yes to this question, and more than half of them charge the same for children as they do for adults. Most of those whose prices differ charge less for photographing children. Some photographers have a sliding scale based on a child's age. Generally, children's packages vary as widely as those for adults.

Do you offer clients a discount if they return for updated photos? How much?

Close to half the photographers surveyed do not offer such a discount. When it is given, it ranges from $25 off to 10 to 25 percent off the session fee to charging an "old fee" rather than an updated one.

How often should headshots be updated?

All photographers agreed that children's photos should be updated annually.

There was little agreement on how often adults should have new photos taken, although on the average photographers thought it should be done every two years. The one point on which they all agreed is that if your look changes drastically, photos should be updated as soon as possible.

EXTRA TIPS

Trends also affect the way your headshot should look. Ms. Vittes notes, for example, that from the '60s to the late '70s and early '80s, glossies were "in." "Now," she points out, "a matte finish is preferred. I think it looks cleaner and has a more tangible texture. But as far as the look of an actor goes, that depends on who the actor is and on his or her type."

Vittes recommends a cautious approach in the search for a photographer. "Just remember to be very selective," she says. "It's a buyers' market and you can choose whom you want. You have the right to go to every photographer you think you might be interested in. You have the right to look at their books. You have the right to say, 'I want to think about it.' You don't have to make a decision on the spot and you should not feel pressured into making a decision right away. Take your time and make sure you are making the right choice. Don't go to somebody who has been recommended by other actors if you don't feel comfortable with them. If you don't feel comfortable with the photographer, you are not going to get a good session. The most important thing is to get the best shot you can."

Don't overlook decisions that are related to your headshots either, such as having postcards printed. Vittes suggests calling agents and asking if they want to receive postcards, because some, like her, do not. "I think postcards serve a purpose for people who cast soap extras, for example, to remind them that you are around," says Vittes. "I don't like postcards. If I'm going to work with you, I'm going to work with you. I don't need to be reminded that you're around. There are other agents who don't like them either. A casting agency here was receiving postcards every week from an actor. He was never called by the agency—a good indication of whether or not your cards are working—but he kept sending postcards. The agency saved all the cards for a year, and then called the actor and said, 'Your postcards are ready. You can pick them up now.' You have to be able to take a clue! It's perfectly acceptable to call an agency and ask if you should send periodic postcards."

These guidelines should help you to locate the best photographers in town and then narrow down the possibilities to the one who is right for you. Choosing a photographer can be time consuming because of the many factors which should enter into your decision. You will discover, however, that it is time well spent on your career when the result of your photo shoot is an effective, attractive headshot that should help you get work.

2A

TEMPORARY SERVICES

BY ANDREA WOLPER

L et's face it: nobody becomes a performer because they long to type and file. However, many performing artists work as temporary office workers while pursuing theatrical careers, because it is an ideal way to keep bills from accumulating into mountains of unpaid debts between engagements. In fact, working as a "temp" can be as near to perfect a solution to the problem of remaining solvent while chasing artistic dreams as you're likely to find. If you know how to type, or take dictation, or use a computer or some other type of office equipment, you can put these skills to good use as a temporary worker. The financial stability gained working as a "temp" can go a long way toward nurturing the spirit of the struggling actor who is out there making the rounds, or standing in an audition line.

Perhaps the best reason for relying on temporary office employment is the flexible time schedule that it offers. For performing artists, this is an invaluable commodity. You have an audition on Monday and a commercial class on Wednesday? So that week you work Tuesday, Thursday, and Friday. Rehearsing a showcase during the day? Fine—you can make some extra money word processing at night or on weekends. Touring for a few weeks, a couple of months, or more? No problem—you can go back to work as soon as you're ready. Need some extra money for new headshots? Work full-time this month and ease up a little the next.

As a temporary employee you work when you want to work, and if you keep your skills up-to-date you shouldn't have a problem getting assignments. Just remember that when you do accept a job, whether it is for one day, one week, or one month, you will be expected to uphold your commitment to complete that assignment.

Along with reasonable-to-excellent hourly wages for skilled workers, quite a few temp services offer a number of bonuses and benefits. You probably won't qualify for these extras if you're not working on a nearly full-time basis. But if you're planning to work pretty steadily (three or more days a week, every week), be sure to sign up with a service that offers the benefits you need. Many offer free training to upgrade skills; some give referral bonuses, paid vacations, and holidays. Some offer medical and/or dental insurance plans, life insurance, even profit-sharing and credit unions. Whenever you interview at a temporary service, ask about benefits and bonuses. Find out exactly how many hours you'll have to log to become eligible and how to take advantage of what's offered once you do.

Even if you don't plan to work often enough to take advantage of the variety of bonuses and benefits, chances are you'll find plenty of other advantages to being a temp. You may simply enjoy the freedom of not being tied to a regular schedule and of remaining detached from corporation politics, or you may find it stimulating to see new walls and new faces when you feel it's time to move on.

To get yourself started, choose the two or three or four services that seem to be right for you. Talk to friends and fellow artists who've done temp work and ask them to recommend good services. Once you've made your choices, telephone those companies and find out when they interview applicants. Some will give you an appointment; many have specified open hours. Next, put on your best audition or interview outfit; you're going to be playing the role of office worker or trade show representative for the time being, so dress the part. You'll want to make the best impression you can on the folks who are going to be thinking of you for jobs.

If you have a job resume, take it with you to the interview, even though you'll probably be asked to fill out an application. Be prepared to be interviewed and to supply checkable references. (Some services check references, some don't.) If you go to the service early in the day, you just might be offered work then and there. You'll probably be tested for any skills you claim to have, such as typing, shorthand, or word processing. Even if you're only qualified to work as a clerk, you may be tested for math and alphabetization ability. Don't be anxious about the tests. Although expectations differ from service to service, they will try to place you if you have any aptitude at all for the requirements of a particular job.

When you register for work be sure to find out exactly what is required of you regarding general procedure. Are you expected to phone that service more than once a day? If you don't understand the procedure you could lose out on jobs.

WORDS ON WORD PROCESSING

A good reason for learning word processing is that insofar as temporary office employment is concerned, word processing is where the money is. Anyone who can type reasonably well can learn word processing. The most convenient way to learn is to qualify for the free training that many temporary services offer, or to be lucky enough to be trained at an office where you are working. But if you're considering paying for training, don't expect to earn top dollars right away. It may take a while to acquire the experience that will earn you a spot as a "regular" with a temp service. "Most clients prefer people with work experience," according to Richard Ackerman of Eastern Office Temps, "but things are changing now. It's true there are some machines on which prior experience is necessary. If our employees are proficient and have experience on one system, they can be cross-trained on others."

A working knowledge of one type of computer doesn't necessarily translate to that of another in the same way that typing on a Silver-Reed means you can just as easily use a Brother or an Olivetti. Some explanation of the unfamiliar machinery is always required. If you haven't learned word processing on one of the more popular machines, you may be out of luck. Some companies, like Kelly Temporary Services in New York City, have a training room stocked with various types of hard- and software. For no charge, employees who have worked for Kelly for 100 or more hours can train themselves on several systems.

To a typist, breaking into word processing might seem as difficult as getting a union card—it can look darn near impossible. But have faith, new word processing operators enter the job market every day, and if you're determined, you can too.

Whether you're a word processing operator, a messenger, proofreader, paralegal professional, caterer-waiter, telemarketer, stenographer, or the best little product demonstrator that ever lived, there's a temporary job out there with your name on it. So what if you can't type—you can pick up a phone and take a message, can't you? So you haven't the faintest idea what CRT means and you never heard of key punch; that's okay—maybe you can be a fragrance model, a customer service representative, a researcher, product demonstrator, or inventory clerk. Some temporary services even send out makeup artists, specialty acts, and industrial workers. At the very least, with all that experience you've had sending out pictures and resumes, you're certainly qualified to stuff envelopes! The bottom line is that if you're reliable, responsible, can dress yourself neatly, and are personable and reasonably articulate, you should be able to find a temp service that will be able to place you.

AN ACTOR'S MOST POWERFUL RESOURCE

EVERY WEEK.

After 32 years, BACK STAGE is still the premiere newsweekly for the performing arts. Every week, BACK STAGE focuses exclusively on the features that have made us the show business bible - major news stories, reviews, previews of upcoming theatre seasons, informative columns, listings of agents, personal managers, acting coaches, casting directors, rehearsal spaces, and of course, notices for stage, television, screen and cabaret performers and staff. In addition, our sixteen 1992 spotlights bring you the most timely and important topics in the performing arts.

Call today for subscription and advertising information!

BACK STAGE
The Performing Arts Weekly

(212) 947-0020
330 West 42nd Street, New York, NY 10036

12A

NEW YORK'S PERFORMING ARTS BOOKSTORES

BY VICTOR GLUCK

ew York is a city that has everything. It should come as no surprise that if you can't find a book in this city it probably can't be found anywhere. In New York's performing arts book stores you can locate a score for a Kurt Weill musical, the Labanotation for a ballet by Balanchine, the collected plays of Eugene O'Neill, and Bette Davis's first autobiography. In addition, you can find *Playbills*, souvenir programs, plays on record, original drawings for set designs, manuscript copies of unpublished plays, first editions, foreign imports, and theater, film, and dance annuals.

Various bookstores have larger collections of special categories or a staff member who is a respected authority on a particular subject. Applause Theater and Cinema Books can certainly boast the largest selection of modern British plays. However, if you're looking for an acting edition of a script, your best bet might be to go immediately to Samuel French, Inc. or the Dramatists' Play Service, which boast that they have their complete in-print catalogs available. The archives of such establishments are not to be forgotten either. Some used bookstores, such as the Gotham Book Mart, have shelves devoted to important authors such as Tennessee Williams, Shaw, and Shakespeare. Targeting your need to the right bookstore is an art in itself.

Whether as a service to their customers or as a publicity idea, many stores offer interesting and unusual activities. Book signing parties, readings by authors of their latest books, demonstrations, classes, and play readings are some of the possible offerings. In addition, many bookstores have mailing lists of free catalogs, publications, or sale items.

Whatever your interest as a performer, you should be able to track down the information you need somewhere in the vast array of New York's performing arts bookshops.

PERFORMING ARTS BOOKSTORES

NEW YORK
THEATER

APPLAUSE THEATRE AND CINEMA BOOKS
211 W. 71st St.
New York, NY 10023
(212) 496-7511

THE DRAMA BOOK SHOP
723 Seventh Ave., 2nd Fl.
New York, NY 10019
(212) 944-0595

DRAMATISTS PLAY SERVICE INC.
440 Park Ave., So., 11th Fl.
New York, NY 10016
(212) 638-8960

SAMUEL FRENCH INC.
45 W. 25th St., 2nd fl.
New York, NY 10010
(212) 206-8990

SHAKESPEARE AND CO. BOOKSELLERS
2259 Broadway
New York, NY 10024
(212) 580-7800
and: 716 Broadway
New York, NY 10003
(212) 529-1300

RICHARD STODDARD
PERFORMING ARTS BOOKS
18 E. 16th St., Rm. 305
New York, NY 10003
(212) 645-9576

THEATRE ARTS BOOK SHOP
405 W. 42nd St.
New York, NY 10036
(212) 564-0402/0403

THEATRE COMMUNICATIONS GROUP
355 Lexington Ave.
New York, NY 10017
(212) 697-5230

THEATREBOOKS
1600 Broadway, Rm 1009
New York, NY 10036
(212) 757-2834

DANCE

THE BALLET SHOP
1887 Broadway
New York, NY 10023
(212) 581-7990

CAPEZIO AT AILEY
211 W. 61st St., 3rd fl.
New York, NY 10023
(212) 767-0940, ext. 352

CAPEZIO EAST
136 E. 61st St.
New York, NY 10021
(212) 758-8833

CAPEZIO AT STEPS
2121 Broadway
New York, NY 10023
(212) 799-7774

DANCE NOTATION BUREAU BOOKSTORE
Princeton Book Company/Dance Horizons
Box 57
Princeton, NJ 08540
(609) 737-8177

TAFFY'S OF NEW YORK, INC.
1776 Broadway, 2nd fl.
New York, NY 10019
(212) 586-5140

MUSIC

BROWN'S MUSIC CO.
61 W. 62nd St.
New York, NY 10023
(212) 541-6236

COLONY RECORD AND TAPE CENTER
1619 Broadway
New York, NY 10019
(212) 265-2050

GRYPHON RECORD SHOP
251 W. 72nd St.
New York, NY 10023
(212) 874-1588

THE MUSIC EXCHANGE INC.
151 W. 46th St., 10th fl.
New York, NY 10036
(212) 354-5858

THE MUSIC STORE AT CARL FISCHER
62 Cooper Sq.
New York, NY 10003
(212) 677-0821

THE JOSEPH PATELSON MUSIC HOUSE
160 W. 56th St.
New York, NY 10019
(212) 582-5840

FILM

JERRY OHLINGER'S MOVIE
MATERIAL STORE INC.
242 W. 14th St.
New York, NY 10011
(212) 989-0869

THE SILVER SCREEN
35 E. 28th St.
New York, NY 10016
(212) 679-8130

USED BOOKS

ARGOSY BOOK STORE INC.
116 E. 59th St.
New York, NY 10022
(212) 753-4455

GOTHAM BOOK MART & GALLERY, INC.
41 W. 47th St.
New York, NY 10036
(212) 719-4448

GRYPHON BOOKSHOPS
(Main Store)
2246 Broadway
New York, NY 10024
(212) 362-0706
(Annex)
246 W. 80th St., 4th fl.
New York, NY 10024
(212) 724-1541

STRAND BOOK STORE, INC.
(Main Store)
828 Broadway
New York, NY 10003
(212) 473-1452
(Strands at the Seaport)
159 John St.
New York, NY 10038
(212) 809-0875

LOS ANGELES BOOKSTORES

BOOK CASTLE
200 N. San Fernando Rd.
Burbank, CA 91502
(818) 845-1563

BOOK CASTLE
3604 W. Magnoira Blvd.
Burbank, CA 91505
(818) 842-6816

COSMOPOLITAN
7007 Melrose Ave.
Los Angeles, CA 90038
(213) 938-7119

LARRY EDMUNDS
6644 Hollywood Blvd.
Los Angeles, CA 90028
(213) 463-3273

SAMUEL FRENCH THEATRE &
FILM BOOKSHOP
7623 Sunset Blvd.
Los Angeles, CA 90046
(213) 876-0570

FRONT ROW CENTER
THEATRE MEMORABILIA
8127 W. 3rd St.
Los Angeles, CA 90048
(213) 852-0149

MOVIE WORLD
212 N. San Fernando Rd.
Burbank, CA 91502
(818) 846-0459

CHICAGO BOOKSTORES

ACT I
2632 N. Lincoln
Chicago, IL 60614
(312) 348-4658

SCENES COFFEEHOUSE AND
DRAMATIST BOOKSTORE
3168 N. Clark
Chicago, IL 60657
(312) 535-1007

JOINING
THE UNIONS

BY MICHELE LARUE

J oining the unions—like any important career move—is no easy task. To the uninitiated, the process is a Catch-22: you can't perform until you get your union card, but you can't get your card until you work a union job. Moreover, joining is an expensive proposition, with initiation fees approaching $1,000 and basic annual dues running between $70 and $90 at Actors' Equity, SAG, and the larger AFTRA locals.

"How do you get in the union?" is a question performers often ask each other at auditions, rehearsals, and over cups of coffee at McDonald's. Certainly, "how" to join is a critical question. But you should also ask "why" and "when." For answers to these basic questions, three of the several performers' unions were interviewed: Actors' Equity Association (AEA), which protects principal actors, chorus members, and stage managers working in the theater; Screen Actors' Guild (SAG), which primarily covers film performers; and the American Federation of Television and Radio Artists (AFTRA), the union for radio, TV, audio and video tape, cable and slide film performers.

WHY JOIN A UNION?

Actors' Equity business representative Peter Harris has several answers, beginning with professionalism. AEA membership assures your potential employers and coworkers that you are serious about the theater, that acting or stage managing is not just your hobby or interim employment, but your profession.

Benefits, too, are valuable. Union contracts set salary minimums which usually are higher than those volunteered by non-union producers. They include benefits almost never offered outside of the union—health insurance coverage and accumulative pension points, for example.

As collective bargaining agencies, unions exist to promote and protect their members' welfare. This charge doesn't end with establishing minimum salaries; unions monitor employers to ensure that agreed-upon monies and benefits are received on time; that performers work in safe and sanitary environments; that they get ample rest; that members are compensated for extra rehearsal and performance time; and makes sure they are respected by their producers, directors, and fellow union members.

For the health of our unions and our profession as a whole, this is a two-way street, says Harris. Unions discipline their own members, too, thereby guaranteeing employers that their investment in union performers will secure professional behavior—no unlearned lines; no late arrivals or no-shows for rehearsals or performances; no physical, drug, or alcohol abuse on the job.

Each union has its own membership "perks," as well. AEA, SAG, and AFTRA communicate with their members via newspapers and magazines, and offer professional seminars throughout the year. The three have credit unions that provide many services offered by banks, but without the usual suspicion or scrutiny of "civilians" unfamiliar with performing artists. Unions support the welfare of the theater community by contributing to organizations like The Actors' Fund of America and Broadway Cares. Several scholarship programs are available to the children of AFTRA members; Equity members frequently are offered complimentary tickets for Broadway shows; and SAG's Film Society administers sizeable discounts on screenings of new features.

WHEN SHOULD YOU JOIN A UNION?

If you're right out of college or conservatory, chances are you dream of quickly validating your talent through union membership. But even if you're precocious—or lucky—enough to get an immediate offer, think twice before you jump into it. The proportion of young performers to roles for which they are suited is exceptionally high. Non-union companies offer a great deal of work, and the more experience you have under your belt before you join a union, the better your chances of employment once you are a member. For a novice ingenue or juvenile, union membership can be more limiting than liberating.

"A student-aged person unfamiliar with the business, even if eligible, should not rush in and join," opines SAG executive administrator Bill Weiner. He recommends that first an actor should "try to get as much exposure in as many ways as possible—in live showcases, in classes, by speaking to as many actors as you can about what it's like trying to make a living in the business. Make sure this is a career choice, not just a hobby." Because joining the unions is an expensive process and a long-term commitment, Weiner advises that you "do your homework before you come to this decision."

Be sure acting is what *you* (not your parents or your Great Aunt Millie) want for you. Before you join, make certain you get high school and college experience. Furthermore, be careful to line up another source of work, Equity's Harris urges young would-be members.

HOW DO YOU JOIN A UNION?

Each union has its own membership qualifications and procedures. These range in complexity. AFTRA has a simple open-door policy allowing anyone to join who wishes to pay the fee. AEA's rules for membership can be a bit more confusing; they have both a "Equity Membership Candidate" (EMC) Program, that allows you gradually to earn points towards Equity membership and something called "Eligible Performer" status, which permits you to audition for union producers without joining AEA.

AFTRA

Founded in 1937, AFTRA represents 70,000 members. They include actors, TV broadcasters, announcers, disk jockeys, sportscasters, panelists, moderators, and specialty acts, who work in radio, on phonographic recordings, or on television on tape. These performers are served by a national board of 115 members from every geographic area and every category of membership— and by 35 autonomous locals throughout the United States.

AFTRA's initiation fee varies per local, ranging from a low of $100 in Peoria, Ill., and Eugene, Ore., to highs of $700 and $800 in New York and Los Angeles; Chicago's $600 fee is the median. Each local also sets its own semi-annual dues. In New York, the minimum, $42.50, is based on annual income of $2,000 or less. An additional 1½ % is assessed on earnings over $2,000, with a $792.50 semi-annual cap. L.A.'s minimum is also $42.50 twice yearly, but its cap is $1,000. Chicagoans pay $30.40 semi-annually; on yearly wages above $10,000, $12 in additional dues are charged for every $5,000 earned.

A performer may join AFTRA, with or without a job offer, by applying to his or her local office (see list at the end of the chapter).

SAG

SAG is a national union that was founded in 1933. It currently represents 73,000 performers working in films (including theatrical, television, industrial/educational, and experimental) and music videos; in some cases, TV shows on tape go to SAG, as well. Upon joining, the eligible performer pays SAG's initiation fee, $862.00, plus its first semi-annual basic dues, $42.50. Subsequent dues are tiered, based on SAG earnings: members are assessed 1½% of their SAG income over $5,000 (to a limit of $150,000). SAG, like Equity and AFTRA, reduces this amount for members who joined through other "parent" unions.

If you satisfy any of the following qualifications, you may join SAG by making an appointment with the New Membership Department at your SAG office.

1. Entering SAG via "Employment as a Principal Performer" requires proof of employment or prospective employment within two weeks by a SAG signatory company, in a principal or speaking role in a SAG film, videotape, TV program, or commercial. Proof of employment may be a signed contract, a payroll check or check stub, or a letter from the company. The document proving employment must include the applicant's name and social security number, the name of the production or commercial, the salary, and the date(s) worked.

2. Entering via "Employment as an Extra" requires proof of employment as a SAG-covered extra player at full SAG rates and conditions for a minimum of three work days. The employer must be a company signed to a SAG Extra Players Agreement, in a SAG film, videotape, TV program, or commercial. Proof of employment is virtually the same as required of principal performers.

3. Alternatively, if you are already a paid-up member of an affiliated performers' union (AFTRA, AEA, American Guild of Variety Artists, American Guild of Musical Artists, Hebrew Actors' Union, Italian Actors' Union, Screen Extras Guild, or Canada's ACTRA) for a period of at least one year *and* have worked at least once as a principal in that unions's jurisdiction, you are SAG eligible.

AEA

The oldest of the three major actors' unions, AEA was founded in 1913. A national union, it represents 40,000 legit principals, chorus members, and stage managers. AEA's initiation fee, $800, is reduced by half for those who are already members of AGMA, AGVA, HAU, IAU, or APATE (Asociacion Puertorriquena de Artistas y Tecnicos del Espectaculo). Annual dues are paid in two $35 installments. You can join Equity in three ways:

1. If offered an AEA standard contract, you are eligible to join the union upon signing it. Standard contracts include all Production (Broadway), LORT (League of Regional Theaters), Stock, and Dinner Theater contracts. Some tiers of Equity's lesser contracts require you to meet length-of-employment and wage earning minimums as well. These include LOA (Letter of Agreement), SPT (Small Professional Theater), TYA (Theater for Young Audiences), and Mini (a scaled-down Off-Broadway contract used only in New York City).

There are two exceptions under which you may work in an Equity production without joining the union: some contracts (including Dinner Theater, LOA, and SPT) allow producers to economize by hiring a small percentage of non-Equity cast members; performers under 13, who will need non-union experience to mature professionally throughout their adolescence, are not required to join AEA even when working under its standard contracts.

2. Participation in Equity's Membership Candidate Program allows non-professional actors to credit their work toward Equity membership. To become an EMC candidate, you must secure a non-professional position at an Equity theatre offering the Program. Next, you complete the registration form provided by the theater and submit it to AEA with a $100 registration fee (which is deducted from your initiation fee when you join).

After 50 weeks of work (which may be nonconsecutive) at one or more accredited theaters, a registered candidate may join Equity. Alternatively, after 40 weeks of work, a candidate may take a written exam and join if he or she passes. Upon completing the Program, you are eligible for five years to join Equity. During that time, you cannot contract with any AEA theater except through Equity. A list of theaters and additional information about the Membership Candidate Program is available at your regional AEA office.

3. Finally, Equity's "open door admissions" policy allows membership applications from those who, for at least a year, have been members of AFTRA, SAG, AGMA, AGVA, HAU, IAU, APATE, or SEG (the former Screen Extras Guild, now part of SAG). Additionally, you must prove yourself to be an active member in good standing of one of these unions and to have worked under union jurisdiction on either one principal, one "under-five," or three days of extra contracts.

Eligible Performers. Until June 1, 1988, you couldn't audition at Equity casting calls unless you were a paid-up AEA member. This made your chances of joining the union via an Equity contract pretty slim. However, a lawsuit by a disgruntled non-union actor resulted in the practice being declared illegal by the National Labor Relations Board. Since June 1988, non-Equity actors have been able to apply to any AEA regional office to participate in union calls.

To qualify as an "eligible performer," you must meet certain criteria which AEA has established to guarantee that everyone brings a minimal level of professionalism to interviews and auditions. Eligibility is based primarily on the number of weeks worked within a given period of time and minimum salary earned as a performer, whether on stage or in other media. Your regional Equity office will have details.

LEAVING THE UNIONS

If, after joining the unions, you decide that professional performance is not for you, there are mechanisms for temporary or permanent withdrawal.

AFTRA makes leaving as easy as getting in. Simply write a letter to your local office stating that you want to retire from active membership (for any reason). You may reactivate your membership at any time (although no union encourages you to bounce in and out of it). You will not be charged dues during your period of withdrawal. Of course, you will not be allowed to work on any AFTRA-contracted production, either. You may continue to perform under the jurisdiction of any other union of which you are an active member in good standing.

SAG has created two means of going on inactive status: "Honorable Withdrawal" and "Suspended Payment." A request must be made by applying in writing to the membership department just prior to either dues period (May 31 or November 30). The applicant must have been a SAG member for at least 18 consecutive months and an active member for at least one year. After becoming inactive, he or she must remain so for at least one year.

Honorable Withdrawal is granted to those who are paid in full at the time of their request. Upon returning to active status, the member need pay only the dues owed for the current period.

Suspended Payment was designed for members in financial distress. It permits withdrawal by those whose dues are not paid up at the time they apply. The applicant may be no more than two dues periods in arrears (excluding the current period). When he or she returns to active membership, the member must pay all outstanding dues in addition to the current period's.

Members choosing either of these options receive a special SAG card which allows them to continue attending SAG calls. The union has no objections to an inactive member pursuing union work—as long as he or she reactivates membership upon being offered employment. However, employers generally want to see only active members at their calls and often will refuse to interview those on withdrawal, stresses SAG's Bill Weiner.

Actors' Equity grants "Temporary Withdrawal" to members who request it in writing. Withdrawal can be for any length of time (although after five years, the member loses first rights to his or her professional name). Return to active status requires a $25 reinstatement fee plus payment of dues for the current period. AEA members are forbidden to work in non-AEA productions while on withdrawal. Resignation from Equity requires special administrative approval from the main office.

If performing is to be your career—and if you're a capable performer—the opportunity to become a union actor will present itself. Understanding what membership means—what it does for you, what it requires of you, and at what point in your artistic growth it is best for you—is as important as understanding how it is obtained.

NATIONAL AND REGIONAL UNION OFFICES

The following is a nationwide list of offices for Actors' Equity, Screen Actors' Guild, and American Federation of Television and Radio Artists. When writing to an office for information, address envelopes to: Attention: Membership Department, c/o of the office for your region.

ACTORS' EQUITY ASSOCIATION

NATIONAL/EASTERN OFFICE
165 W. 46th St.
New York, NY 10036
(212) 869-8530

MIDWESTERN OFFICE
203 N. Wabash Ave.
Chicago, IL 60601
(312) 641-0393

WESTERN OFFICE
6430 Sunset Blvd.
Los Angeles, CA 90028
(213) 462-2334

SAN FRANCISCO OFFICE
235 Pine St., 11th fl.
San Francisco, CA 94104
(415) 391-3838

SCREEN ACTORS GUILD

NATIONAL OFFICE
7065 Hollywood Blvd.
Hollywood, CA 90028
(213) 465-4600

ARIZONA
1616 E. Indian School Rd., #330
Phoenix, AZ 85016
(602) 265-2712

ATLANTA
1627 Peachtree St., N.E., #210
Atlanta, GA 30309
(404) 897-1335

BOSTON
11 Beacon St., #515
Boston, MA 02108
(617) 742-2688

CHICAGO
307 N. Michigan Ave.
Chicago, IL 60601
(312) 372-8081

CLEVELAND
1367 E. 6th St., #229
Cleveland, OH 44114
(216) 579-9305

DALLAS
6060 N. Central Expy, Suite 302,
LB 604, Dallas, TX 75206
(214) 363-8300

DENVER
(region covers NE, NM, and UT)
950 S. Cherry St., #502
Denver, CO 80222
(303) 757-6226

DETROIT
28690 Southfield Rd.
Lathrup Village, MI 48076
(313) 559-9540

FLORIDA
2299 Douglas Rd., Suite 200
Miami, FL 33145
(305) 444-7677

HAWAII
949 Kapiolani Blvd., #105
Honolulu, HI 96814
(808) 538-6122

HOUSTON
2650 Fountainview, #325
Houston, TX 77057
(713) 972-1806

MINNEAPOLIS/ST. PAUL
15 S. 9th St., #400
Minneapolis, MN 55404
(612) 371-9120

NASHVILLE
1108 17th Ave. South
Nashville, TN 37212
(615) 327-2958

NEW YORK
1515 Broadway, 44th fl.
New York, NY 10036
(212) 944-1030

PHILADELPHIA
230 S. Broad St., 10th fl.
Philadelphia, PA 19102
(215) 545-3150

ST. LOUIS
906 Olive St., #1006
St. Louis, MO 63101
(314) 231-8410

SAN DIEGO
7827 Convoy Ct., #400
San Diego, CA 92111
(619) 278-7695

SAN FRANCISCO
235 Pine St., 11th fl.
San Francisco, CA 94104
(415) 391-7510

SEATTLE
601 Valley St., #200,
Seattle, WA 98109
(206) 282-2506

WASHINGTON, D.C.
The Highland House,
5480 Wisconsin Ave., #201,
Chevy Chase, MD 20815
(301) 657-2560

AMERICAN FEDERATION OF TELEVISION AND RADIO ARTISTS

NATIONAL OFFICE
260 Madison Ave.,
New York, NY 10016
(212) 532-0800

ATLANTA
1627 Peachtree St., N.E.
Atlanta, GA 30309
(404) 897-1335

BOSTON
11 Beacon St., #512
Boston, MA 02108
(617) 742-0208/2688

CHICAGO
307 N. Michigan Ave.
Chicago, IL 60601
(312) 372-8081

CINCINNATI-COLUMBUS-DAYTON
1814-16 Carew Tower
Cincinnati, OH 45202
(513) 579-8668

CLEVELAND
1367 E. 6th St., #229
Cleveland, OH 44114
(216) 781-2255

DALLAS-FT. WORTH
6309 N. O'Connor Rd., #111
2 Dallas Communications Complex
Irving, TX 75039
(214) 869-9400

DENVER
950 S. Cherry St., #502
Denver, CO 80222
(303) 757-6226

DETROIT
24901 N. Western Highway
Heritage Plaza Office Bldg., #613A
Southfield, MI 48075
(313) 354-1774

HAWAII
949 Kapiolani Blvd., #105
Honolulu, HI 96814
(808) 533-2652

HOUSTON
2650 Fountainview, #325
Houston, TX 77057
(713) 972-1806

INDIANAPOLIS
2220 N. Meridian St.
Indianapolis, IN 46208
(317) 925-9200

KANSAS CITY
406 W. 34th St., #206
Kansas City, MO 64111
(816) 753-4557

LOS ANGELES
6922 Hollywood Blvd., 8th fl.
Los Angeles, CA 90028-6128
(213) 461-8111

LOUISVILLE
Lincoln Tower, #1025
6100 Dutchman's Lane
Louisville, KY 40205
(502) 459-6931

MIAMI
20401 N.W. 2nd Ave., #102
Miami, FL 33169
(305) 652-4824

NASHVILLE
1108 17th Ave. South
Nashville, TN 37212
(615) 327-2944/2947

NEW ORLEANS
808 St. Anne
New Orleans, LA 70116
(504) 524-9903

NEW YORK
260 Madison Ave.
New York, NY 10016
(212) 532-0800

PHILADELPHIA
230 S. Broad St., 10th fl.
Philadelphia, PN 19102
(215) 732-0507

PHOENIX
5150 N. 16th St., #C-255
Phoenix, AZ 85016
(602) 279-9975

PITTSBURGH
625 Stanwix St., The Penthouse
Pittsburgh, PA 15222
(412) 281-6767

PORTLAND
516 S.E. Morrison, #M-3
Portland, OR 97214
(503) 238-6914

ROCHESTER
1100 Crossroads Office Building
Rochester, NY 14614
(716) 232-3730

SACRAMENTO-STOCKTON
2413 Capitol Ave.
Sacramento, CA 95816
(916) 441-2392

SAN DIEGO
3045 Rosecrans St., #308
San Diego, CA 92110
(619) 222-1161

SAN FRANCISCO
235 Pine St., 11th fl.
San Franciso, CA 94104
(415) 391-7510

SEATTLE
158 Thomas St.
Seattle, WA 98109
(206) 728-9999

ST. LOUIS
906 Olive St., #1006
St. Louis, MO 63101
(314) 231-8410

TWIN CITIES
15 S. 9th St., #400
Minneapolis, MN 55402
(612) 371-9120

WASHINGTON-BALTIMORE
5480 Wisconsin Ave., #201
Chevy Chase, MD 20815
(301) 657-2560

THE BUSINESS OF ACTING

BY DON SNELL

how business is a business. Actors, dancers, singers—all are engaged in the *business* of entertainment. Many artists, however, have difficulty coming to grips with the reality that art is also a business. They feel that what really is important is their art. This may be true. But a little business savvy won't hurt, and it may help get *your show* on the road. So take a moment now and then to give some serious thought to the business side of show business. You may be able to give a boost to your own career.

Show business is a business of name and facial recognition. Recognition is, in fact, one of the most important elements of a successful career. You should establish a professional name as early as possible in your career and stick with it. It is this name that you should register with the trade unions—it is this name that you will want people in the industry to think of when they are searching for talent. And it is important that people associate your name with your face. One way to assure such an association is to get a photograph that looks like you and to use it over and over. Repetition is the key to recognition.

The next order of business is to define your type. In other words, typecast yourself. The easiest way to do this is to look at a *Player's Guide* and look for the *type* that matches you. If you are unsure what type you are, write down all the types listed and then cross off the ones you are not. Try to make an objective appraisal of the *age range* you are right for, too. Performers are cast according to type and age; if you have a clear idea of your type and age range, it wi~ll make it easier for you to be categorized and cast.

Now you are ready to tackle the business end of show business. So the first thing to do is to set yourself up as a business. For this purpose, think of yourself not so much as a performing artist, but as someone who provides entertainment services. This will help you "push" or "sell" yourself. Many performers are reluctant to do this, but it is something worth doing. Self-promotion becomes easier when you are thinking in terms of selling a "service," rather than selling "yourself." Next, set up a space for your office. Put all your office "tools" in order. First and foremost of these are your picture and resume—they must, of course, be first-rate. Then you should have a wall calendar, appointment book, Rolodex, file cabinet, file folders, stationery, business cards, telephone, and so on.

Once your office is set up, you are ready to make contact with the industry. But whom do you contact? To find this out, do a market study—talk to working performers, consult directories (these you can find in performing arts bookshops or in the public library in your city) and find out where the work is and who is involved in its development and production. Investigate television, film, theater, radio, commercials, industrials, voice-overs—whatever. Then make contact. Apply for the job. Let the powers that be know who you are, what you do, and how to reach you. Approach acquiring an agent in the same way. You only need one agent, but contact one hundred. Learn to arrange the information and data that you accumulate into a well-organized filing system. If you do so, you will discover that the entertainment industry is not as overwhelmingly immense as it appears to be at first glance. In New York City, for example, there are not thousands of television agencies. On the contrary, the figure is closer to 150.

After you have done your market study, set your goals. Every business does this; having goals is like having a crystal ball to look into. Make sure, however, that your goals are realistic and obtainable. Companies assess the market by looking at the sales histories of other companies. You can approach show business in the same way by looking at the performance records of other entertainers. Your goals can be charted in a number of ways: short-term, long-term, dollars, and number of days worked, for instance. After you have set your goals, go after them, but keep them flexible and in touch with changing trends in the industry. At the beginning of each week have a "sales meeting" with yourself. Set a goal for the week and strive for it all week long. At the end of each month, monitor your progress with a sales report showing how many auditions you have gone to, how much work you have gotten, and your gross income for the month.

You will have a much better chance of succeeding in show business if you approach it as a business. In the final analysis, of course, success cannot be judged by financial criteria alone, nor by the barometer of fame. Some make it in this business, and some don't, and talent is often enough not the determining factor. What is important is that you use and enjoy your talent and that you give that talent and show business your best shot. With the application of a little business sense, you will be able to create many more opportunities for yourself, and there is greater likelihood that you will succeed.

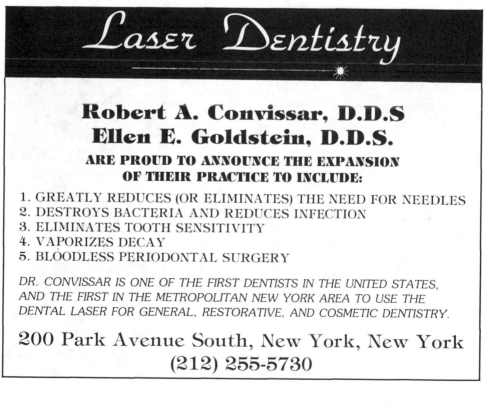

17A

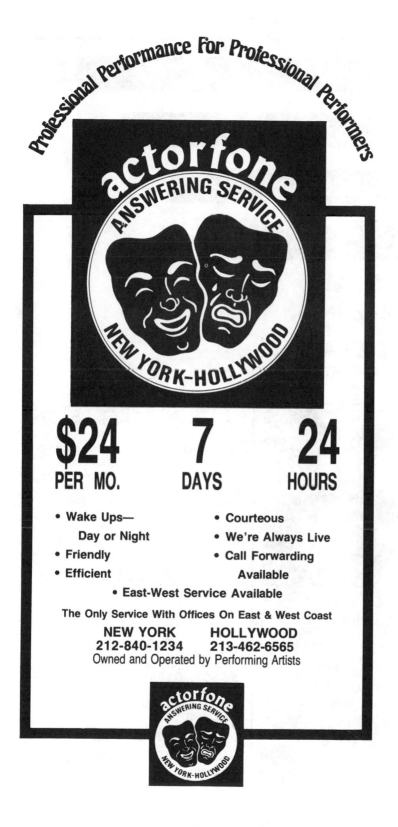

■ TRAINING

■ SOURCES

■ RESOURCES

■ JOBS

IT'S ALL
HERE IN

BACK STAGE ®

THE PERFORMING ARTS WEEKLY

PART TWO

TRAINING

SHOPPING FOR THE RIGHT CLASS

BY FRED SILVER

Many performers who have had careers in show business came to the realization early on that in order to succeed, they must study hard and become well-schooled in their craft. To have any real chance of success, a performer must be prepared. This means that your specialty, whether it be comedy, drama, dance, music—whatever, must be honed and finely polished. If you are wise you will make certain that, if and when that big break does come, you will be ready for it. That is why many hopeful performers enroll in acting schools. In the entertainment industry, there are all kinds of schools and classes, from accredited to non-accredited, from crash courses in "method" acting to degree courses in theater, from scene study to commercial acting, from musical theater auditioning to soap opera performing, from lessons taught by charlatans whose main concern is your pocketbook, to lessons taught by seasoned professionals who have a very real sense of dedication and responsibility to their students. With so many choices out there, it is not always easy to make a selection. Some of the factors that should be considered in choosing a class are discussed below.

One of the first things to ask is: How large is the class? Also, how often does it meet, and if it is a performance class, will you be given plenty of opportunity to perform? Large classes are exciting to be in because of the high energy level they generate. Often the reason they are well-populated, though, is that they are less expensive. The principal drawback to a large class is that you may not get to perform often. Ideally, a performance class should have a maximum of 14 people in it and should last approximately three hours so that everyone has a chance to work.

Does the class provide a safe space? This is a very important question for a performer to ask—safe in this instance meaning psychologically safe. Because performers must feel free to take risks on stage without getting a battered ego. Unfortunately there do exist teachers who delight in humiliating their students. One way to unearth such teachers is to make inquiries among other performers and students in the trade.

One of the best methods of finding out what a teacher is like is to audit a class. Often a fee is charged for auditing, but this is usually applied toward tuition if you decide to take the class. Some teachers, however, do not permit auditing because it threatens the emotional security of those students who are not ready for strangers to see them bare their inner selves.

Tuition and class fees vary. Generally the larger the class, the less it will cost. Private teachers sometimes like to be paid in full before each class. Teachers who allow you to stretch payments may also charge you a higher fee.

Schools usually require you to sign a contract that prohibits refunds. Teachers running their own classes will naturally determine their own refund policies. It is always advisable to inquire about refund policies before enrolling in a class.

In summary, a classroom can be an ideal environment for perfecting the skills that you need in order to better yourself as a performer. There you have an opportunity to assimilate what your teacher has to offer, and you have a chance to learn from your classmates, both by watching them perform and by performing in front of them.

ACTING SCHOOLS, TEACHERS, AND COACHES

The following is a listing of stage, commercial, and film acting schools, teachers, and coaches in New York City, Chicago, and Los Angeles. Although the listing is extensive, it is probably not all-inclusive.

NEW YORK

ACTING FOR CAMERA CLASSES
BY MARIA AND TONY GRECO
CASTING DIRECTORS
630 Ninth Ave., Rm. 702, NYC 10036
(212) 247-2011

ACTING FOR DANCERS
Marlena Lustik
(212) 242-1753

ACTING MANAGEMENT, INC.
182 Fifth Ave., 4th fl.
NYC 10010
(212) 989-8709

THE ACTING STUDIO INC.
29 E. 19th St., NYC 10003
(212) 228-2700

ACTORS ADVENT LTD.
212 W. 29th St., NYC 10001
(212) 242-3900

ACTORS' INFORMATION PROJECT
311 W. 43rd St., NYC 10036
(212) 245-4690

THE ACTORS' INSTITUTE
48 W. 21st St., NYC 10010
(212) 924-8888

ACTORS' MOVEMENT STUDIO
298 Fifth Ave., Box 220, NYC 10001
(212) 736-3309

STELLA ADLER CONSERVATORY OF ACTING
130 W. 56th St., NYC 10019
(212) 246-1195

AIA/THREE OF US STUDIOS
39 W. 19th St., 12th fl., NYC 10011
(212) 645-0030

ELAINE AIKEN
Actors Conservatory, Inc.
750 Eighth Ave., NYC 10036
(212) 764-0543

WILLIAM ALDERSON ACTING STUDIO
276 W. 43rd St., 5th fl., NYC 10036
(212) 924-6627

AMARANTH PRODUCTIONS
250 E. 87th St., NYC 10128
(212) 360-7006

AMERICAN ACADEMY OF DRAMATIC ARTS
120 Madison Ave., NYC 10016
(212) 686-9244

AMERICAN ENSEMBLE STUDIO THEATRE
145 W. 46th St., NYC 10036
(212) 869-9809

AMERICAN GLOBE THEATRE
CONSERVATORY
145 W. 46th St., NYC 10036
(212) 869-9809

THE AMERICAN MIME THEATRE
61 Fourth Ave., NYC 10003
(212) 777-1710

AMERICAN MUSICAL AND DRAMATIC
ACADEMY (AMDA)
2109 Broadway, NYC 10023
(212) 787-5300/800-367-7908

AMERICAN THEATRE OF ACTING
314 W. 54th St., NYC 10019
(212) 581-3044

ATLANTIC THEATER COMPANY
PRACTICAL AESTHETICS WORKSHOP (PAW)
PO Box 1647, Cooper Station, NYC 10276
(212) 529-1646

ELINOR BASESCU ACTING STUDIO
529 W. 42nd St., #8D, NYC 10036
(212) 868-1278

JOHN BASIL
(212) 695-5360

JO ANNA BECKSON
Gushee Studio, Rm. 708
636 Broadway, NYC 10022
(212) 586-6300/353-0114

TERRY BERLAND
1375 Broadway, 11th fl., NYC 10018
(212) 827-2355

JULIE BOVASSO
(212) 807-8303

JERROLD BRODY
AT THE PRODUCERS CLUB THEATRE
358 W. 44th St., Suite 6, NYC 10036

ELIZABETH BROWNING
(212) 541-7600

DAVID BRUNETTI
71 W. 71st St., #1G, NYC 10023
(212) 580-3292

MADELYN J. BURNS SEMINAR
121 W. 27th St., Suite 503, NYC 10001

JON CANTOR
308 W. 30 St., #8E, NYC 10001
(212) 594-4638/840-1234

CENTAUR STAGE/GILLIEN GOLL
(212) 581-6470

JORDON CHARNEY
(212) 734-4463

MICHAEL CHEKHOV STUDIO
226 W. 47th St., 2nd fl., NYC 10036
(212) 768-2711

CIRCLE IN THE SQUARE THEATRE SCHOOL
1633 Broadway, NYC 10019
(212) 307-2732

LORA LEE CLIFF
165 Perry St., #4C, NYC 10014
(212) 627-4670

COLLIER CASTING CENTERS
Actors' Equity Building
1560 Broadway, Suite 509, NYC 10036
(212) 719-9636

COLLIER'S TV SUCCESS SEMINARS
142 E. 16th St., Suite 11A, NYC 10003
(212) 674-2214

LAURENCE CONRO
AIA/ Three of Us Studios
39 W. 39th St., NYC 10010
(212) 645-0030/ 741-1444

CONSERVATORY AT CSC
136 E. 13th St., NYC 10003
(212) 677-4210

CORNER LOFT STUDIOS
99 University Pl., NYC 10013
(212) 228-8728

THE CREATIVE ACTOR'S WORKSHOP
451 W. 43rd St., NYC 10036
(212) 245-1237

DOUBLE IMAGE THEATRE WORKSHOP
John Martello, Artistic Director
445 W. 59th St., NYC 10019
(212) 245-2489

PIERO DUSA
119 W. 23th St., Suite 305, NYC 10011
(212) 727-8455

EMOTIONAL COACHING
Linda Perhach
(212) 382-3535

ENSEMBLE STUDIO THEATRE INSTITUTE
549 W. 52nd St., NYC 10019
(212) 581-9409

WILLIAM ESPER STUDIO
250 Third Ave., NYC 10010
(212) 673-6713

THE FILM ACTING STUDIO
90 Lexington Ave., Suite 1H, NYC 10016
(212) 684-3094

GENE FRANKEL THEATRE WORKSHOP
24 Bond St., NYC 10012
(212) 777-1767

GINGER FRIEDMAN AUDITION
TRAINING INSTITUTE
303 E. 83rd St., #15B, NYC 10028
(212) 472-1714

CATHERINE GAFFIGAN
412 W. 42nd St., NYC 10036
(212) 586-6300

KATHRYN GATELY AND
RICHARD POOLE
442 W. 42nd St., NYC 10036
(212) 517-1677

CHARLES E. GERBER
568 Ninth Ave., #2R, NYC 10036
(212) 244-0435

MIMI GINA/AMERICAN ART THEATRE
Box 212, NYC 10023
(212) 874-4639

MICHAEL GRAVES
127 W. 96th St., #9F, NYC 10025
(212) 663-5133

GAYLE GREENE
20 E. 74 St., NYC 10024
(212) JU2-4240

PHILIP GUSHEE
636 Broadway, Rm. 708, NYC 10012
(212) 353-0114

HB STUDIO
120 Bank St., NYC 10014
(212) 675-2370

MICHAEL HARNEY
(212) 642-5358

KATE HARPER
326 E. 93rd St., 1B, NYC 10128
(212) 410-1906

NICO HARTOS
159 W. 53rd St., NYC 10019
(212) 541-8293

THE HEATHER CO.
55 Bethune St., NYC 10014
(212) 242-5750

PENELOPE HIRSCH
1 Christopher St., NYC 10014
(212) 255-5746

HISPANIC ORGANIZATION
OF LATIN ACTORS (HOLA)
250 W. 65th St., NYC 10023
(212) 595-8286

PRUDENCE HOLMES
255 W. 108th St., #9D,
NYC 10024
(212) 864-6525

MICHAEL HOWARD STUDIO
152 W. 25th St., NYC 10001
(212) 645-1525

THE ITKIN STUDIO OF THE THEATER
251 W. 19th St.,
Studio 5D, NYC 10011
(212) 242-5591

CHARLES KAKATSAKIS
202 W. 80th St., NYC 10024
(212) 362-5757

CHARLES KEBBE
38 E. 85th St., #5D, NYC 10028
(212) 879-3833

RAPHAEL KELLY SHAKESPEARE STUDIO
168 E. 89 St., NYC 10128
(212) 289-1392

ED KOVENS
20 Dongan Pl., #311, NYC 10040
(212) 567-6761

LOUISE LASSER
200 E. 71st St., NYC 10021
(212) 288-5537

SARA LOUISE LAZARUS STUDIO
at the Michael Carson Studios
250 W. 54th St., NYC 10019
(212) 864-7901

LEHNER/STEPHENS STUDIO
333 E. 40th St., Suite 26F, NYC 10016

TIM LEWIS
Impact Studios
612 Eighth Ave., NYC 10018
(212) 391-0418

ROBERT LEWIS
Contact Judd Mathison about
Robert Lewis Theatre Workshop
(212) 986-3594

RICHARD LICHTE
635 Riverside Dr., #10D, NYC 10031
(212) 862-7230

RICK LOMBARDO
111 Hicks St., 5-L
Brooklyn, NY 11201
(718) 834-9331

JUDY MAGEE
401 E. 89th St., NYC 10128
(212) 722-5694

MANHATTAN CLASS COMPANY
Nat Horne Theatre
442 W. 42nd St., NYC 10036
(212) 643-0118

MANHATTAN PUNCH LINE
COMEDY INSTITUTE
410 W. 42nd St., NYC 10036
(212) 239-0827

ERNIE MARTIN STUDIO THEATRE
311 W. 43rd St., 5th fl., NYC 10036
(212) 397-5880

MARGO McKEE'S SOUNDSTAGE
Hotel Consulate
224 W. 49th St., NYC 10019
(212) 757-5436

EDWARD MOOR
(212) 475-3311

SONIA MOORE STUDIO OF THE THEATRE
Office: 485 Park Ave., NYC 10022

NATIONAL SHAKESPEARE CONSERVATORY
591 Broadway, NYC 10012
(212) 219-9874/1-800-472-6667

ANTHONY NAYLOR
(212) 242-5161

NEIGHBORHOOD PLAYHOUSE SCHOOL OF
THE THEATRE
340 E. 54th St., NYC 10022
(212) 688-3770

RUTH NERKEN
52 W. 74th St., NYC 10023
(212) 362-5277

THE NEW ACTORS' WORKSHOP
Mike Nichols, George Morrison, Paul Sills
259 W. 30th St., NYC 10001
(212) 947-1310
NEW CONSERVATORY
THEATRE WORKSHOP
334 Bowery, NYC 10012
(212) 777-1855

ON CAMERA!
3 Milligan Pl., NYC 10011
(212) 255-1208

THE PANARO WORKSHOP
THEATRE COMPANY
c/o Panaro Productions
Box 332, Ansonia Station,
NYC 10023-0332
(212) 840-7788

ROBERT PATTERSON
(212) 840-1234

TODD PETERS
345 W. 85th St., NYC 10024
(212) 873-5836

VINCENT PHILLIP
339 W. 48th St., NYC 10036
(212) 246-3558

PLAYWRIGHTS HORIZONS
416 W. 42nd St., NYC 10036
(212) 967-1481

DANIEL POLLACK
890 West End Ave., NYC 10025
(212) 663-8143

JACK POGGI
880 W. 181 St., NYC 10033
(212) 928-6882/382-3535

CAROL FOX PRESCOTT
221 W. 82nd St., NYC 10024

RAPP THEATRE COMPANY
220 E. 4th St., NYC 10009
(212) 995-2245/529-5921

REED & MELSKY CASTING INC.
928 Broadway, NYC 10010
(212) 505-5000

REED SWEENEY REED
1780 Broadway, NYC 10019
(212) 265-8541

NORMAN RHODES
201 W. 85th St., NYC 10024
(212) 721-0459

JONI ROBBINS VOICEOVER WORKSHOPS
141 W. 73rd St. #9K, NYC 10023
(212) 969-8517

WARREN ROBERTSON
(212) 362-2737

STEVE ROSENFIELD
(212) 838-7239

ROUNDABOUT THEATRE
CONSERVATORY & ENSEMBLE CO.
307 W. 26th St., NYC 10001
(212) 420-1360

DEBORAH SAVADGE
CENTER FOR THE ARTS
West Side YMCA,
5 W. 63rd St., NYC 10023
(212) 787-6557

T. SCHREIBER STUDIO
83 E. 4th St., NYC 10003
(212) 420-1249

CAROL SCHINDLER
(212) 727-7386

MICHAEL SCHULMAN THEATRE WORKSHOP
94 St. Marks Place, NYC (Studio)
28 E. 10th St. NYC (Mail)
(212) 777-3055

JUDITH SETO'S ACTING WORKSHOP
INTERGENERATIONAL ACTORS'
CREATIVE THEATRE.
Gramercy Park
(212) 683-3977

BARRY SHAPIRO
24 W. 25th St., NYC 10010
(212) 807-7706

SANDE SHURIN-BRUCE LEVY
ACTING STUDIO NY
335 W. 38th St., NYC 10018
(212) 563-2298

PAUL SILLS
(212) 222-0620

ROGER HENDRICKS SIMON STUDIO
484 W. 43rd St., NYC 10036
(212) 564-2899

LARRY SINGER
at Michael Howard Studios
152 W. 25th St., 10th fl., NYC 10001
(212) 645-1525

JONATHAN SLAFF
55 Perry St., #1M, NYC 10014
(212) 924-0496.

SUSAN SLAVIN ACTORS &
SINGERS ACADEMY
AT CARNEGIE HALL
154 W. 57th St., NYC 10019
(212) 582-0321

MELODIE SOMERS
118 E. 28th St., Suite 304, NYC 10016
(212) 481-6490

JOANNA C. SPILLER
8 W. 75th St., NYC 10023
(212) 874-5870

ALICE SPIVAK/ THREE OF US STUDIOS
39 W. 19th St., NYC 10011
(212) 924-0561

JOHN STRASBERG, SUSAN GRACE COHEN,
DAVID BLACK & DAVID BERRY
Upper West Side locations.
(212) 678-8515

THE LEE STRASBERG THEATRE INSTITUTE
115 E. 15th St., NYC 10003
(212) 533-5500

STEPHEN STRIMPELL
201 W. 70th St., #20K, NYC 10023
(212) 873-7311

LE STUDIO THEATRE C.A. INC.
(Christian Aubert's Studio Theatre)
853 7th Ave., PH 28, NYC 10019
(212) 956-7267

TALENT VENTURES, INC.
346 E. 63rd St., NYC 10021
(212) 688-0622

MIKHAIL TSOGLIN
1465 E. 45th St., Brooklyn, NY 11234
(718) 338-6555

TOTAL THEATRE LAB
Caroline Thomas
622 Broadway, Suite 4D, NYC 10012
(212) 477-6144

VIDEO ASSOCIATES LTD.
Kim Todd, Gordon Rigsby, owners
311 W. 43rd St., Suite 601, NYC 10036
(212) 397-0018

VIDEO PERSPECTIVES, INC./VPI
165 W. 47th St. NYC
(212) 595-9001

WALTRUDIS
(212) 489-0365

JACK WALTZER
5 Minetta St., NYC 10012
(212) 473-7056/840-1234

STUART WARMFLASH
160 W. 71st St., NYC 10023
(212) 787-1945/541-7600

WEIST-BARRON STUDIOS
35 W. 45th St., NYC 10036
(212) 840-7025

JOAN WHITE ENGLISH THEATRE
SCHOOL, LTD.
153 W. 76th St., #2R, NYC 10023
(212) 787-1575

FLORENCE WINSTON
(212) 541-7600

WALT WITCOVER
40 W. 22nd St., NYC 10010

CATHERINE WOLF
(212) 362-5332

THE WORKSHOP FOR THE THEATRE
160 W. 24th St., Suite 61, NYC 10011
(212) 807-0067/5

MONI YAKIM
220 W. 71st St., NYC 10023
(212) 873-6065

DANA ZELLER-ALEXIS
236 W. 78th St., NYC 10024
(212) 724-4862

GREG ZITTEL
262 Mott St., NYC 10012
(212) 929-6192

TED ZURKOWSKI
840 West End Ave., #B1, NYC 10025
(212) 866-7280

LOS ANGELES

ACADEMY OF PERFORMING &
RELATED ARTS/THEATRE OF ARTS
4128 Wilshire Blvd.
Los Angeles, CA 90010
(213) 380-0511

ACTORS CENTER INTERNATIONAL
12229 Ventura Blvd., North Bldg.
Studio City, CA 91604
(818) 760-1400

ACTORS CONSERVATORY ENSEMBLE
6760 Lexington
Hollywood, CA 90038
(213) 463-6244

THE STELLA ADLER CONSERVATORY
OF ACTING WEST
1651 N. Argyle Ave.
Hollywood, CA 90028
(213) 465-4446
AMERICAN ACADEMY
OF DRAMATIC ARTS
2550 Paloma St.
Pasadena, CA 91107
(818) 798-0777

AMERICAN NATIONAL ACADEMY
OF PERFORMING ARTS
10944 Ventura Blvd.
Studio City, CA 91604
(818) 763-4431

TONY BARR'S FILM ACTORS' WORKSHOP
5004 Vineland Ave.
N. Hollywoood, CA 91601
(818) 766-5108

RICHARD BASEHART PLAYHOUSE
THEATRE CLUB & WORKSHOP
Cynthia Baer, Artistic Director
21028-B Victory Blvd.
Woodland Hills, CA 91367
(818) 704-1845

STANLEY BROCK
(213) 669-1399

CALIFORNIA INSTITUTE OF THE ARTS
24700 W. McBean Parkway
Valencia, CA 91355
(805) 255-1050

VINCENT CHASE
7221 Sunset Blvd.
Los Angeles, CA 90046
(213) 851-4819

MATT CHIAT
6476 Santa Monica Blvd.
Hollywood, CA 90038
(213) 469-5408

JEFF COREY
(213) 456-3319 (service)

CHRIS DE CARLO
SANTA MONICA PLAYHOUSE
1211 4th St.
Santa Monica, CA 90401
(213) 394-9779, ext. 126

BRETT DUNHAM
SCREEN ACTORS WORKSHOP
5342 Laurel Canyon Blvd.
North Hollywood, CA 91607
(818) 766-6425

FILM INDUSTRY WORKSHOPS, INC.
4047 Radford Ave.
Studio City, CA 91604
(818) 769-4146

NINA FOCH
Box 1884
Beverly Hills, CA 90213
(213) 553-5805

KATHLEEN FREEMAN ENTERPRISES
(818) 761-5181/781-5096

THE WILL GEER THEATRICUM BOTANICUM
1419 N. Topanga Canyon Blvd.
Topanga, CA 90290
(213) 455-2322

MARIA GOBETTI AT THE VICTORY THEATRE
THE GOBETTI-ORMENY ACTING STUDIO
3326-24 W. Victory Blvd.
Burbank, CA 91505
(818) 843-9253

ESTELLE HARMAN ACTORS
WORKSHOP, INC.
522 N. La Brea Ave.
Los Angeles, CA 90036
(213) 931-8137

DARRYL HICKMAN
(213) 462-6565

JACQUELYN HYDE ACTING
FOR PROS & BEGINNERS
(213) 650-1067

MILTON KATSELAS WORKSHOPS
AT BEVERLY HILLS PLAYHOUSE
254 S. Robertson Blvd.
Beverly Hills, CA 90211
(213) 855-1556

PAUL KENT AT THE MELROSE THEATRE
733 N. Seward St.
Los Angeles, CA 90038
(213) 465-1885

L.A./ACTOR'S LAB
FREDERICK COMBS
(213) 273-4044

TONY MILLER/FILM INDUSTRY
WORKSHOPS, INC.
4047 Radford Ave.
Studio City, CA 91604
(818) 769-4146

PLAYHOUSE WEST
Robert Carnegie, Jeff Goldblum,
Glenn Vincent
4250 Lankershim Blvd.
North Hollywood, CA 91602
(818)766-3766/506-6345

PROFESSIONAL ARTISTS GROUP, INC.
845 N. Highland Ave.
Hollywood, CA 90038
(213) 871-2222

JOSE QUINTERO
c/o Nick Tsacrios, 4300 Parva Ave.
Los Angeles, CA 90027

TRACY ROBERTS ACTORS STUDIO
141 S. Robertson Blvd.
Los Angeles, CA 90048
(213) 271-2730

AL ROSSI
(818) 902-1538

AVERY SCHREIBER
(818) 989-4775

MICHAEL SHURTLEFF
(213) 469-8745

RON SOSSI AT THE ODYSSEY THEATRE
2055 S. Sepulveda
Los Angeles, CA 90025
(213) 477-2055

SOUTH COAST REPERTORY
655 Town Center Dr.
Costa Mesa, CA 92628
(714) 957-2602

GUY STOCKWELL
(818) 761-8240

THE LEE STRASBERG THEATRE INSTITUTE
7936 Santa Monica Blvd.
Los Angeles, CA 90046
(213) 650-7777

MARK W. TRAVIS
(213) 930-1400

VAN MAR ACADEMY
950 N. Kings Rd., #218
Hollywood, CA 90069

CHICAGO

ACT ONE STUDIO
640 N. LaSalle
Studio 535
Chicago, IL 60610
(312) 787-9384

ACTOR TRAINING INSTITUTE
3300 N. Lake Shore Dr., Suite 14D
Chicago, IL 60657
(312) 871-0349

THE ACTORS' CENTER
1225 W. School St.
Chicago, IL 60657
(312) 549-3303

APPLE TREE THEATRE
593 Elm Pl.
Highland Park, IL 60035
(708) 432-4335

CENTER THEATRE
1346 W. Devon
Chicago, IL 60660
(312) 508-0200

CHICAGO DRAMATISTS WORKSHOP
1105 W. Chicago Ave.
Chicago, IL 60622
(312) 633-0630

ETA CREATIVE ARTS FOUNDATION, INC.
7558 S. Chicago Ave.
Chicago, IL 60619
(312) 752-3955

THE NEW YORK SCHOOL OF ACTING
Theatre Building
1225 W. Belmont
Chicago, IL 60656
(312 262-0438

O'MALLEY THEATRE OF
ROOSEVELT UNIVERSITY
430 S. Michigan
Chicago, IL 60605
(312) 341-3719

ORGANIC THEATRE
3319 N. Clark
Chicago, IL 60657
(312) 327-5507

PIVEN THEATRE AND WORKSHOP
927 Noyes
Evanston, IL 60201
(312) 866-6597

PLAYERS WORKSHOP OF
THE SECOND CITY
2636 N. Lincoln
Chicago, IL 60614
(312) 929-6288

SARANTOS STUDIOS
2857 N. Halsted
Chicago, IL 60657
(312) 528-7114

STAGE LEFT THEATRE
3244 N. Clark
Chicago, IL 60657
(312) 883-8830

TOUCHSTONE THEATRE
Box 458
Lake Forest, IL 60045
(312) 295-7849

VICTORY GARDENS THEATRE
2257 N. Lincoln
Chicago, IL 60614
(312) 549-5788

LAMONT ZENO THEATRE
1512 S. Pulaski Rd.
Chicago, IL 60623
(312) 277-9582

STEPHEN
STRIMPELL

Basic and Advanced
Technique and Scene Study

Admission by interview only

Call: **873-7311**

Mailing address:

**20K, 201 W. 70th St.
NYC, NY 10023**

Private coaching for auditions, roles,

monologue, showcases, etc. is available.

GATELY/POOLE STUDIO

KATHRYN GATELY
RICHARD POOLE

ACTING CLASSES

in The Meisner Technique

442 West 42nd Street

Call 517-1677

ACTING CLASSES

ROBERT PATTERSON

Included among Former Students:
TED DANSON JOBETH WILLIAMS

For Interview Please Call:
(212) 840-1234

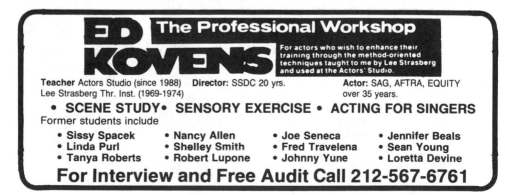

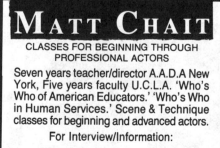

34A

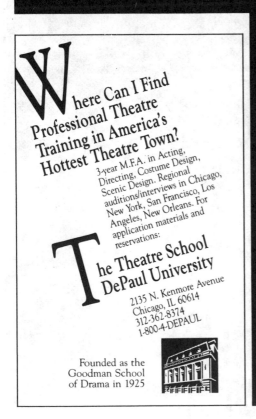

CHOOSING A COLLEGE THEATER PROGRAM

BY JILL CHARLES

choice faced by many theater students about to enroll in college is whether to work toward a Bachelor of Arts or a Bachelor of Fine Arts degree. Equally important is the decision about what kind of school will best provide the skills demanded by the entertainment industry. What are the advantages to enrollment in a private liberal arts school with a small theater department as opposed to matriculation at a state university with a large theater department? And which of these is right for you?

THE BA VERSUS THE BFA DEGREE

The Bachelor of Arts degree is a broad-based, liberal arts program offering courses in all subjects, but with a major in a particular discipline—in this case, theater. The Bachelor of Fine Arts degree, on the other hand, is a more specialized program offering courses in fewer subjects and a major in a particular area of a discipline, for instance, acting, design, directing, and so on. Generally, you have to go through a selection process, such as an audition or an interview, to get into a BFA program even if you have already been accepted into the university. Furthermore, you may be subjected to periodic reviews of your work in which you must meet a certain standard to remain in the program.

One great advantage to the BA degree is the variety of subjects and ideas offered. Studying a broad range of topics and different points of view and philosophies can lead you to a deeper understanding of life, literature, drama, and a better-informed approach to a wide variety of theatrical roles. The BFA program, focusing more specifically on theater, is geared toward helping students acquire professional skills rather than developing a humanistic world view. Even so, a good BFA program will ensure that its students are challenged to think, are well read, and cognizant of the wider points of view that can be found in the study of the humanities. Obviously, when you graduate and go out into the real world, you're going to need to know more than just theater.

DEPARTMENT SIZE

When you begin to investigate various colleges and universities, you can easily determine the size of a theater department from the school's catalog. The number of faculty listed may be as few as three in a small college, and as many as 20 or more in a large university. The question to consider is: What is the optimum size of a theater department? Generally, a department that offers a BFA program will be larger than one offering only a BA degree. Even so, for a small BA program, you should be wary if fewer than five members are on the faculty. A faculty of five is probably the minimum required for a good, solid program; fewer than five means that the courses offered will be limited, and the scope of the department may be narrow. In some cases, where there is a lot of input from other departments (English, dance, or music, for example), a faculty of four could suffice, but with five on the faculty you can be assured of more than one viewpoint in most areas of study. For example, two of the five are more than likely acting/directing people, so this will guarantee some diversity in approach to acting techniques.

FACULTY AND CURRICULUM

When choosing a college, there are, of course, many factors to consider other than what courses to take, or what size school to go to. For example, it is also important to look at the qualifications of the faculty. The catalog will list their degrees, but that won't tell the whole story. How many on the faculty have been or still are working professionals? This factor will tell a great deal about a department: a more academically oriented department will hire MAs and PhDs with the expectation that such a faculty will publish articles, write books, and will be more effective in helping students realize academic goals; a more professionally oriented department will hire MFAs and people without higher degrees who have extensive experience as directors or designers with the expectation that such a faculty will continue to work professionally while associated with the college and will help guide students toward professional careers. The attitude a department takes toward its faculty reflects the attitude it will take toward its students and its philosophy in general. Thus, if you are working toward a degree in theater history or dramatic criticism, find a school with a long list of PhDs on the faculty. *But*, if your main concern is performing or design, or if your goal is to work in the profession as soon as you get out of school, then one of your major considerations should be the amount of practical, professional experience your teachers can bring to the subjects they are teaching.

Many colleges and universities integrate working professionals into their programs by hiring them to teach one or two courses a semester—often top-notch people who are too active to take on heavy teaching loads. A working professional can be invaluable to a college program. The director, designer, or actor who can illustrate a theory with real-life, on-stage examples or anecdotes from a recent live production can bring theater to life in a classroom. Teachers who are active in the industry also provide students with connections that will be helpful in their careers.

COURSE EVALUATION

A typical BA program in general theater should offer a pretty thorough grounding in all liberal arts subjects. One of the first courses you will be required to take will be "Theater 101," which is a general introduction to theater studies. Required courses and electives in theater history and dramatic literature will also be listed; some of the latter courses will probably be offered through the English Department.

A good theater department should offer a variety of courses that teach actual theater skills. Obviously, you will find such a variety in the larger colleges, but even a theater department in a small school should offer more than simply "Acting." Those acting courses that are offered should go beyond the two-semester introductory level, should also cover areas like mime and improvisation, and should offer electives on a more advanced level. There should also be courses in the basics of voice and movement technique. In theater departments in large colleges you will probably be given the option of taking specialized advanced courses like stage combat, commedia dell'arte, period style, non-naturalistic acting, and so on; in BFA programs, such courses are not just electives, but are a part of the degree curriculum.

You will also be required to take a stagecraft or scenography course, including a lab period in the scene shop, where you will work on sets. The BA theater major should also include basic design courses (scenic, costume, and lighting), and a course in directing. Electives in stage management, arts management, and the like should fill out this program. Most departments make an effort to cover special needs of their programs with independent study, advanced seminar, or various catch-all courses that students can tailor to their own needs.

FACILITIES AND PRODUCTIONS

College theaters have some of the best facilities in the country. It is important to remember, however, that the quality of your experience is going to depend more on the faculty and student body than on the facilities. Knowledge of state-of-the-art facilities may be insufficient if you have not learned how to work with more primitive equipment. Production students who are accustomed to pneumatic tools, a welding shop, a computerized lighting board, and a stage full of traps and turntables may be at a total loss when they hit their first Off-Off-Broadway or shoestring summer stock experience. While there is certainly an advantage in the marketplace to being fully aware of and able to work with modern theater technology, there is also much to be said for developing skills that can work miracles with more ingenuity than money.

Look closely at the list of mainstage productions at the college you are interested in. Over the last three or four years has this college presented programs that achieve a balance among contemporary, classical, American, and European theater productions? What about African, Japanese, or Chinese theater? If you see nothing but Shakespeare, Brecht, and Chekhov, where will your exposure to current American playwrights or contemporary drama come from? Is there a studio series for more current work? Has this school ever done a musical? Look out for any discrepancy that may exist between the type of work you will be doing in college and the type of work you want to do when you leave school. Theater history and dramatic literature courses should cover all areas, and theatrical productions should expose you to all styles.

One indication of whether a school offers a well-rounded program may be the student-generated shows. Find out if there is a student drama organization separate from the department, and if so, investigate the relationship between the two. Does the department support, with money and/or enthusiasm, the student group? Or are the two at odds and seen as mutually threatening? Sometimes a student group can be born out of genuine frustration with a department's refusal to deal with contemporary or experimental works; of course, such a venture may merely be the product of frustrated students who weren't cast in a departmental show. In a healthy department, there will be a crossover between student- and faculty-generated projects, with each group respecting and supporting the other's work.

Some programs are connected to a professional summer or regional theater company that shares the college facilities and produces a full season of plays. The Huntington Theater Company at Boston University and Syracuse Stage at Syracuse University are two examples. The benefits of such a connection are obvious—students have a chance to work directly with professionals. The opportunity to observe or take part in a professional company in full swing can give students a very definite advantage when they go out into the theater world later on. Of course, the connection between school and professional company must consist of a real and not just a perceived relationship. Does, in fact, a real interaction exist? Or is the professional company a totally separate entity? Even if the latter instance is true, the situation isn't necessarily all bad—you still have the presence of live regional theater right at home; nevertheless, make sure your expectations are going to be met. Again, the two institutions, school and theater company, should be mutually supportive of each other's activities, not jealously protective of their own interests.

AFTER GRADUATION

The choices commonly open to students after graduation are those of going on to graduate-study programs or going out into the business/professional world. BA students are the more likely candidates for graduate study, because they have not necessarily prepared or trained themselves to enter directly into the theater profession. The unwritten contract with a BA student is that the college will provide a well-rounded education in all areas of theater and that the student will acquire a firm foundation for further study in specific areas.

BA students who decide to pursue a professional career will probably require additional study at the graduate level, at a conservatory, or in private study. Since it is necessary to either audition or present a design portfolio to get into a graduate program, it should be part of the unwritten agreement between students and school that audition and portfolio preparation skills are taught, and that counseling in post-graduate schooling is provided.

The unwritten contract between a college and a BFA student *does* promise that these students will be ready to work upon leaving. Some quotes from school ads are pretty clear about this unstated agreement: "Our Graduates Work . . ."; "Connect with the profession"; "Professional Training for the Actor," and so on. The term "Professional Theater Training Program" has been attached to many BFA as well as graduate programs, and if that is what is claimed and that is what you're buying, then make sure you get it. You should expect a minimum of one full semester course dealing with auditioning, putting together a picture and resume, and learning to approach the *business* of acting. If you're a designer, an equal amount of class time should be devoted to creating a portfolio, learning about union exams, and so forth. If such a course is not listed, inquire if there are guest seminars or workshops that will cover this ground. Enlightened schools, however, will go much farther toward preparing you for the professional world. A school that is connected with a professional theater may enable you to graduate not only with a degree, but with reputable professional credits on your resume. (You may also get a start toward your Equity card, although this is by no means crucial.)

CHECKING OUT THE ALUMNI

A school's alumni can tell you a great deal about that institution. For instance, you should ask: How many recent graduates are now working professionals? Does an alumni "network" exist in a major theater center like New York? Have any alumni theater companies been formed?

An alumni network can form the basis for some of your first (and best) contacts in the profession. Yale, Juilliard, Carnegie-Mellon, and The Theater School (formerly the Goodman), are all examples of institutions that have developed national theater networks. Smaller colleges can and should offer a similar commitment that will last beyond graduation day.

A college or university's overall philosophy can be stated at great length in promotional material, but its real values are going to be obvious in every aspect of the department's activities. What you sense is what you are going to get. A school that creates a milieu where students and faculty can be open and curious also has provided an environment where you can nurture and develop your own creativity. When you evaluate the school where you will be spending four crucial years of your life, look for signs of people working hard in an atmosphere of productivity, self-imposed discipline as a means of achieving quality work, and mutual respect among students, teachers, peers, and colleagues.

STUDENT CHECKLIST

Ask the department:

☐ Who on the faculty is currently working professionally?

☐ Do you bring in guest directors and designers?

☐ Do you run a summer theater, or encourage students to work at other summer theaters?

☐ Do you give credit for summer theater work, or for internships with professional theaters during the school year?

☐ How many productions per semester would I be involved in?

☐ Are there any restrictions to freshman participation in productions?

☐ Are there any restrictions in the departmental casting policy?

☐ Are there opportunities in the department for students to direct, design, or write plays?

☐ Does the department encourage students to do projects on their own?

☐ Are any student productions budgeted by the department?

☐ Are graduates prepared to enter the profession?

☐ Does an alumni network exist?

☐ What are recent graduates doing now? Which grad schools did they get into? How many are currently working in the profession?

Ask the current students:

☐ Is the casting policy fair?

☐ Have you been taught how to audition?
☐ Do you feel that you've been prepared to get work once you graduate?

☐ Which areas do you feel are the strengths of the department? The weaknesses?

☐ Are the faculty members accessible to students?

☐ Did you get to know the guest artists who were brought in?

☐ How many productions have you worked on since you entered the program?

☐ If you were looking for colleges now would you choose to come here again?

Ask the graduates:

☐ Are there any areas taught at this school in which you feel you now have to make up for a lack of training?

☐ Did you apply to any grad schools? Did you get accepted?

☐ Were you well prepared to start your career by the time you graduated?

☐ Has it been any advantage to your career that you're an alumni of this particular school?

Then ask yourself:

☐ Is this the program that will take me where I want to go in four years time?

☐ Can I see myself working well in this environment?

☐ Do I sense positive energy and enthusiasm in these people?

STUDYING DANCE IN NEW YORK

BY PHYLLIS GOLDMAN

New York City is a place where dancers may study, learn to perform with finesse and confidence, and find work. There are schools devoted exclusively to ballet and commercial studios where classes in all kinds of dance are offered. The stages of City Center, Lincoln Center, Broadway, the Joyce Theater, and countless other performing venues where dancers may practice their profession await students who attain the high degree of proficiency required.

Dance schools in New York City operate on a "pay-first, dance-later" basis which simply means a student pays for classes in advance, then has access to any teacher or class on the day of his or her choice. Confusion reigns for the new dancer in town as to where to receive the best training and where to be seen by a working choreographer. The scenario is ever-changing as teachers and choreographers come and go. Therefore, the opportunity to train exclusively with one important teacher—thereby gaining insight into what makes him or her tick—can often disappear in a matter of days. Word-of-mouth is as good a guidepost as anything else, and dressing room chatter can often provide a good lead on teachers.

For the serious ballet student the School of American Ballet, which was founded by George Balanchine and is the home for the New York City Ballet, is first choice. However, students are selected by audition only. They are trained in an atmosphere of seclusion, in a tightly organized curriculum that will eventually produce professional ballet dancers, and in all likelihood, a job. Recently, brand-new dormitories were opened to house out-of-state students. Unfortunately, the possibility of being admitted to SAB is small, and alternative plans should be considered before taking the audition.

There are many other options for study, as is self-evident from the list that follows. Also, with the rapid growth of regional ballet, there are more opportunities for training outside of New York City than ever before. Schools associated with major ballet companies—the San Francisco Ballet School, the Houston Ballet School, the Cleveland Ballet School—are excellent examples. Whatever the choice of school or location, it is certain that dancers forge a career in ballet out of an amalgam of grit, determination, commitment, and love.

"I still think New York is the place a dancer *must* come to during some part of his or her life," says David Howard, director of the David Howard Dance Center. And indeed, most dance students are eager to do so. However, city living expenses are prohibitive and monies for classes keep increasing; therefore, the opportunity is not always feasible. An increasingly attractive alternative to private studio training is the city's university dance departments. The Tisch School of the Arts at New York University and Juilliard School in Lincoln Center are two examples of institutions that offer a combination of high-caliber dance instruction, a complete roster of different dance techniques, plus the possibility of earning a degree—arming the graduate with double insurance for the future.

Broadway shows demand a solid ballet technique—first and foremost. In fact, you won't be able to pass an audition without it. Of course, you must also be proficient in jazz combination, waltz, or soft shoe—whatever the script dictates. Because of the varied demands of professional theater, privately owned studios must offer a full program of classes in order to compete. The variety of dance styles offered for study in New York City is mind-boggling. From funky to flamenco; from aerobics to pointe work; as well as Afro-Cuban, mime, jazz, tap, belly dance, video dance—teachers for all these movement techniques can be found in New York dance studios. Additionally, many studios never close—commercial studios offer classes every hour on the hour, so that Broadway dancers can keep in shape despite a grueling eight-shows-a-week schedule.

Studio directors are eager to make their facilities comfortable. It is also important that a studio be located in a safe, accessible area. Not only should the neighborhood be safe, but also the facilities within the school. Clean dressing rooms, heat, light and security are qualities to look for and to expect when making a choice of which studio to attend.

Be sure to inspect the floor. It should be covered with sponge-like material to absorb the impact of jumping. Look for music or some adequate accompaniment as opposed to a teacher who counts while filing her nails.

In the lofts that once spawned some of the great innovators of modern dance—Martha Graham, Doris Humphrey, Jose Limon and Katharine Dunham—second generation teachers and performers now carry on the same innovative tradition. Many young companies and choreographers have evolved from these sources and today fill the theater spaces with their own eclectic creativity. With such a tradition to draw from, you should be able to find a school or class that will help you fulfill your artistic goals. The diversity of classes offered at the present time is unparalleled in the history of American dance.

DANCE SCHOOLS AND STUDIOS

The following is a listing of dance studios, teachers, instructors, and schools in New York, Los Angeles, and Chicago.

NEW YORK

THE ALVIN AILEY AMERICAN
DANCE CENTER
211 W. 61st St., 3rd fl.
NYC 10023
(212) 767-0940
Denise Jefferson, dir.

ALPHA OMEGA DANCE STUDIOS
711 Amsterdam Ave.,NYC 10019
(212) 749-0095
Andy Torres, dir.

THE AMERICAN DANCE MACHINE
AT STEPS STUDIO
2121 Broadway
NYC 10023
(212) 794-5100
Robert Tucker, dir.

ANDERSON-KASAKOVE STUDIO
2067 Broadway
NYC 10023
(212) 362-3300
Brenda Anderson, Mary Kasakove, dirs.

MARY ANTHONY STUDIO
736 Broadway
NYC 10003
(212) 674-8191

APPLEBY STUDIO FOR CONTEMPORARY
DANCE
579 Broadway
NYC 10012
(212) 431-8489

ASIAN-AMERICAN DANCE THEATRE
26 Bowery
NYC 10013
(212) 233-2154/233-8660

BALLET ACADEMY EAST
1651 Third Ave., 3rd fl.
NYC 10128
(212) 410-9140
Julia Dupno, dir.

BALLET ARTS
City Center, 130 W. 56th St.
NYC 10019
(212) 582-3350

BALLET HISPANICO SCHOOL OF DANCE
167 W. 89th St.
NYC 10024
(212) 362-6710
Tina Ramirez, dir.

BALLET SCHOOL N.Y.
30 E. 31st St.
NYC 10016
(212) 679-0401
Diana Byer, dir.

BROADWAY DANCE CENTER
1733 Broadway
NYC 10019
(212) 582-9304
Robert Nunez, dir.

RITA COLBY—BALLET BASICS
AND DANSARTS STUDIO
300 W. 55th St.
NYC 10019
(212) 245-3605

ELINOR COLEMAN EXERCISE
AND DANCE STUDIO
153 Mercer St., 2nd fl.
NYC 10012
(212) 219-3177

CREATIVE MOVEMENT WITH JACK WIENER
98 Riverside Dr.
NYC 10024
(212) 724-2044

CROSBY STREET STUDIO
56 Crosby St.
NYC 10012
(212) 941-8313
Lesley Howes, dir.

AILEEN CROW SCHOOL
OF ALEXANDER TECHNIQUE
Box 1273
Ansonia Station
NYC 10023
(212) 866-2260

MERCE CUNNINGHAM STUDIO
463 West St.
NYC 10014
(212) 255-8240
Michael Bloom, dir.

RUTH CURRIER DANCE STUDIO
425 Broome St.
NYC 10013
(212) 966-7521
Alan Danielson, dir.

DANCE CENTER OF THE
92ND STREET YM-YWHA
1395 Lexington Ave.
NYC 10128
(212) 415-5552
Cathryn Williams, dir.

DANCE CIRCLE
763 Eighth Ave.
NYC 10036
(212) 541-7986
Alfredo Corvino, dir.

DANCE—JUNE LEWIS AND
COMPANY SCHOOL
48 W. 21st St., 7th fl.
NYC 10010
(212) 741-3044

DANCE SPACE, INC.
622 Broadway, 6th fl.
NYC 10012
(212) 777-8067
Lynn Simonson, dir.

DANCE SPORT
1845 Broadway
NYC 10102
(212) 307-1111
Paul Pellicoro, dir.

DANCE THEATRE OF HARLEM
466 W. 152nd St.
NYC 10031
(212) 690-2800
Arthur Mitchell, dir.

ISADORA DUNCAN DANCE
FOUNDATION
141 W. 26th St., 3rd fl.
NYC 10001
(212) 691-5040
Lon Belilove, dir.

DON EMMONS
45 W. 60th St.
NYC 10023
(212) 581-8916

JERRI GARNER'S DANCE FOR
SINGERS AND ACTORS
124 W. Houston St.
NYC 10012
(212) 254-3951

GELABERT STUDIOS
255 W. 86th St.
NYC 10024
(212) 874-7188

MARTHA GRAHAM SCHOOL
OF CONTEMPORARY DANCE
316 E. 63rd St., NYC 10021
(212) 838-5886
Diane Gray, dir.

ERICK HAWKINS SCHOOL OF DANCE
38 E. 19th St., 8th fl.
NYC 10003
(212) 777-7355
Michael Wright, exec. dir.

THE HEBREW ARTS SCHOOL
Abraham Goodman House
129 W. 67th St., NYC 10023
(212) 362-8060
Lydia Kontos, dir.

NAT HORNE MUSICAL
THEATRE COMPANY
440 W. 42nd St.
NYC 10036
(212) 736-7128

DAVID HOWARD DANCE CENTER
211 W. 61st St.
NYC 10023
(212) 757-9877

JOFFREY BALLET SCHOOL
(American Ballet Center)
434 Ave. of the Americas
NYC 10011
(212) 254-8520
Edith D'Addario, dir.

CATHERINE KINGSLEY BALLET CENTER
244-250 W. 54th St., 4th fl.
NYC 10019
(212) 307-6909

SUSAN KLEIN SCHOOL OF DANCE
48 Beach St., 4th fl.
NYC 10013
(212) 226-6510
Susan Klein, Barbara Mahler, dirs.

BETH KURTZ
915 West End Ave.
NYC 10025
(212) 663-2229

LABAN/BARTENIEFF INSTITUTE
OF MOVEMENT STUDIES
31 W. 27th St., NYC 10001
(212) 689-0740
Suzanne Youngerman, exec. dir.

HENRY LE TANG DANCE STUDIO
109 W. 27th St.
NYC, 10001
(212) 627-1126

THE LIMON INSTITUTE
38 E. 19th St., 9th fl.
NYC 10003
(212) 777-3353
Norton Owen, dir.

LOTUS FINE ARTS
Traditional Arts of India
JAF Box 7784
NYC 10116-4633
(212) 627-1076
Kamala Cesar, art. dir.

LUIGI JAZZ CENTRE
(at Neubert Ballet Institute)
881 Seventh Ave., 8th fl.
NYC 10019
(212) 246-3166

THE MANHATTAN BALLET SCHOOL
1556 Third Ave.
NYC 10028
(212) 369-3369
Elfriede Merman, dir.

MOROCCO ACADEMY
OF MIDEASTERN DANCE
320 W. 15th St.
NYC 10011
(212) 727-8326

MULTIGRAVITATIONAL
AERODANCE GROUP
234 E. 23rd St.
NYC 10010
(212) 696-5274
Barbara Salz, Kay Gainer, co-dirs.

NB CONTEMPORARY DANCE THEATRE
Box 555,Canal Street Station
NYC 10013
(212) 966-6828
Nanette Bearden, dir.

NEUBERT BALLET INSTITUTE
Carnegie Hall Studio, #819
881 Seventh Ave., NYC 10019
(212) 246-3166
Christine Neubert, dir.

THE NEW BALLET SCHOOL
Associate School of Feld Ballets/NY
890 Broadway, 8th fl.
NYC 10003
(212) 777-7710
Eliot Feld, dir.

NEW DANCE GROUP STUDIO
254 W. 47th St.
NYC 10036
(212) 719-2733
Rick Schussel, dir.

NEW YORK CONSERVATORY OF DANCE
30 E. 31st St.
NYC 10016
(212) 725-2855
Vladimir and Patricia Dokoudovsky, dirs.

NIKOLAIS AND LOUIS DANCE LAB
38 E. 19st St., 7th fl.
NYC 10003
(212) 226-7700
Lynn Lesniak Needle, school dir.

PERIDANCE CENTER
33 E. 18th St., 5th fl.
NYC 10003
(212) 505-0886
Igal Perry, dir.

CAROL RIOUX BALLET
Lezly Dance School
622-26 Broadway
NYC 10012
(201) 652-8149

ROD RODGERS DANCE
COMPANY STUDIO
62 E. 4th St.
NYC 10003
(212) 674-9066

SANSON-NAYA DANCE SPOT
446 W. 46th St.
NYC 10036
(212) 541-8003
Kathy Sanson, dir.

SCHOOL OF AMERICAN BALLET
70 Lincoln Center Plaza, 5th fl.
NYC 10023
(212) 877-0600
Nathalia Gleboff, dir.

SPACE PLACE DANCE STUDIOS
303 Park Ave. South
NYC 10010
(212) 677-8075
Myra Hushansky, dir.

STEPPING OUT BALLROOM
DANCE STUDIO
1780 Broadway
NYC 10023
(212) 245-5200
Diane Lachtrupp and
Katharina Mario, co-owners

STEPS STUDIO
2121 Broadway, 3rd fl.
NYC 10023
(212) 874-2410
Carol Paumgarten and
Patrice Soriero, art. dirs.

STUDIO 400
400 Lafayette St., 2nd fl.
NYC 10003
(212) 260-0453
Diane Grumet, art. dir.

PAUL TAYLOR SCHOOL
552 Broadway
NYC 10012
(212) 431-5562
Henry Liles, dir.

THEATRE DANCE
1697 Broadway, 2nd fl.
New York, NY 10019
(212) 247-3755
Lisa Danias, dir.

TOKUNAGA DANCE KO.
1 Sheridan Sq.
NYC 10014
(212) 929-8937
Emiko Tokunaga, dir.

WEST SIDE DANCE PROJECT
162 W. 83rd St.
NYC 10024
(212) 580-0914
John DeBlass and Maria Zannieri, co-dirs.

NINA YOUSHKEVITCH BALLET
WORKSHOP
27 W. 72nd St.
NYC 10023
(212) 873-0455

YWCA DANCE DEPARTMENT
610 Lexington Ave.
NYC 10022
(212) 735-9755
Melettie Abd Leaziz, dance coor.

LOS ANGELES

B & B STUDIOS
13639 Burbank Blvd.
Van Nuys, CA 91401
(818) 787-6421

CALIFORNIA INSTITUTE OF THE ARTS
24700 W. McBean Pkwy.
Valencia, CA 91355
(805) 255-1050

DANCERS STUDIO
5772 W. Pico Blvd.
Los Angeles, CA 90019
(213) 934-0987

DANCEWORKS
7315 Melrose Ave.
Los Angeles, CA 90046
(213) 933-7069

DEBBIE REYNOLDS STUDIOS
6514 Lankershim Blvd.
North Hollywood, CA 91606
(818) 985-3193

THE DOWNTOWN DANCE STUDIO
929 E. 2nd St., #105
Los Angeles, CA 90012
(213) 680-0392

DUPREE DANCE ACADEMY
8115 W. 3rd St.
Los Angeles, CA 90048
(213) 655-0336

GASCON INSTITUTE OF SPORT,
EDUCATION & THE ARTS AT
THE WESTSIDE FENCING CENTER
8735 Washington Blvd.
Culver City, CA 90230
(212) 204-2688

STANLEY HOLDEN DANCE CENTER
10521 W. Pico Blvd.
Los Angeles, CA 90064
(213) 475-1725

STUDIO A DANCE
2306 Hyperion Ave.
Los Angeles, CA 90026
(213) 661-8311

STUDIO F AT DEBBIE REYNOLDS STUDIO
6514 Lankershim Blvd.
North Hollywood, CA 91606
(818) 985-4176

STUDIO OF PERFORMING ARTS
8558 W. 3rd St.
Los Angeles, CA 90048
(213) 275-4683

TREMAINE SLEIGHT/
THE DANCE CENTER
11401 Chandler Blvd.
North Hollywood, CA 91601
(213) 877-2323/(818) 980-3336

CHICAGO*

ABIOGENESIS, INC.
Studio: 606 W. 18th St., Suite 4
Chicago, IL 60616-1003
School: 1065 N. Orleans
Chicago, IL 60610

BALLET ENTRE NOUS
Box 713, Wilmette, IL 60091
(708) 251-3022

BART COLLEGE
Performing Arts Center
700 E. Westleigh Rd.
Lake Forest, IL 60045
(708) 234-3000

BETSEY HERSKIND SCHOOL OF DANCE
2740 W. Touhy Ave.
Chicago, IL 60645
(312) 973-6446

BEVERLY ART CENTER
2153 W. 11th St.
Chicago, IL 60643
(312) 445-3838

BOITSOV CLASSICAL BALLET SCHOOL
410 S. Michigan, Suite 300
Chicago, IL 60605
(312) 663-0844

BOULEVARD ARTS CENTER
1850 W. Garfield Blvd.
Chicago, IL 60609
(312) 476-4900

CHICAGO ACADEMY FOR THE ARTS
1010 W. Chicago Ave.
Chicago, IL 60622
(312) 454-9577

CHICAGO DANCE MEDIUM
410 S. Michigan, Suite 833
Chicago, IL 60605
(312) 939-0181

CHICAGO MOVING COMPANY
1225 W. School St.
Chicago, IL 60657
(312) 880-5402

CHICAGO NATIONAL ASSOCIATION
OF DANCE MASTERS
c/o 936 Cedar Lane
Northbrook, IL 60062
(708) 272-4753

CHI-TOWN JAZZ DANCE
610 Davis St.
Evanston, IL 60201
(708) 864-2623

DANCE CENTER OF COLUMBIA COLLEGE
4730 N. Sheridan
Chicago, IL 60640
(312) 271-7804

DANCESCAPE
203 S. 3rd St.
St. Charles, IL 60174
(708) 377-4955

ELMWOOD PARK CIVIC
BALLET COMPANY
c/o 2128 N. Newland
Chicago, IL 60635
(312) 237-1874

FOLK DANCE COUNCIL OF CHICAGO
714 Reba Pl.
Evanston, IL 60202
(708) 328-6678

GUS GIORDANO JAZZ DANCE CHICAGO
614 Davis St.
Evanston, IL 60201
(708) 866-9442

JOEL HALL DANCE STUDIO
1225 W. School St.
Chicago, IL 60656
(312) 880-1002

JOSPEH HOLMES CHICAGO DANCE
THEATRE STUDIO
1935 S. Halsted
Chicago, IL 60608
(312) 942-0881

LOU CONTE DANCE STUDIO
218 S. Wabash, 3rd fl.
Chicago, IL 60604
(312) 461-0892

LYNDA MARTHA DANCE CO./
THE DANCE INSTITUTE
927 Noyes St.
Evanston, IL 60201
(708) 475-1770

MOMENTA! ACADEMY OF
MOVEMENT AND MUSIC
605 Lake St.
Oak Park, IL 60302
(708) 848-2329

*All Chicago dance school listings are from *Dance Instruction Directory '90-'91*,
published by the Chicago Dance Coalition.

MONTAY FINE ARTS CENTER
3750 W. Peterson Ave.
Chicago, IL 60659
(312) 539-1919

MUNTU DANCE THEATRE
6800 S. Wentworth, Rm. 396E
Chicago, IL 60621
(312) 602-1135

NAJWA DANCE CORPS
414 W. Goethe
Chicago, IL 60610
(312) 664-7943

NORTHWESTERN UNIVERSITY
Dance Center
1979 Sheridan
Evanston, IL 60208
(708) 491-3147

PARTNERS IN MIME, INC.
4753 N. Broadway, Suite 918
Chicago, IL 60640
(312) 907-2187

PUSZH STUDIO
3829 N. Broadway
Chicago, IL 60613
(312) 327-0510

RIVER NORTH DANCE STUDIO
400 W. Erie
Chicago, IL 60610
(312) 337-1567

RUTH PAGE FOUNDATION
SCHOOL OF DANCE
1016 N. Dearborn
Chicago, IL 60610
(312) 337-6543

SACRED DANCE GUILD
2620 N. Hampden Ct.
Chicago, IL 60614
(312) 472-8235

SECOND CITY BALLET
1515 Kingsbury
Chicago, IL 60622
(312) 943-4306

SENTIENCE, INC.
2502 Southport
Chicago, IL 60614
(312) 281-8953

MICHAEL ISAACS

FILM: "A LONGTIME COMPANION"

THEATRE: "LITTLE MURDERS" POWER THEATRE
"ALICIA IN WONDERLAND" INNERVISIONS

TRAINING: DRAMA TREE THEATRE CO.
HEATHER CO.

COMMERCIALS: BOB COLLIER'S PRIVATE COACHING

DANCE TRAINING: LOIGI'S JAZZ
NEUBERT BALLET INSTITUTE

AEROBICS TRAINING: TAUGHT BODIES INC.
MOLLY FOX STUDIOS
SASHA AND CO.

AEROBICS CERTIFICATE OF ACHIEVEMENT AWARD:
NATIONAL AEROBIC CHAMPIONSHIP CHAMP CAMP 1991

FINDING THE RIGHT SINGING TEACHER

BY FRED SILVER

To perform in a musical today requires that performers be able to sing better than their counterparts of 20 or 30 years ago. Just listen to cast albums of Broadway musicals of that era and compare the vocal performances with those of more recent vintage. There was a time when dancers in a Broadway show were rarely required to be able to sing; that's what the chorus was for.

Today all that has changed. As the result of tighter budgets, only a limited number of chorus personnel are hired, and they have to do triple duty. Not only do they have to be able to dance or move; they have to be able to sing and act. Today's chorus people would have been yesteryear's stars. Therefore, to stand any chance of being hired for a musical today, an actor or a dancer must not only be able to sing, but must be able to sing well. To achieve this, many actors seek the services of a singing teacher.

Singing teachers come from varied backgrounds. Some are conservatory-trained and sang opera or lieder before turning to teaching as an occupation. Some were not only classically trained but had careers in the musical theater and have performed in Broadway shows. This is important, because teachers' backgrounds play an important part in how they train their students. Teachers with an operatic background may tend to stress voice placement and tessitura better suited to more classical repertoire, and their teaching of vocal technique may emphasize tone and size at the expense of good diction and ease of singing. Teachers who have had experience acting and who have performed in musical shows tend to be more realistic about the rigors of singing on stage. Giving eight performances a week requires a vocal technique that prevents strain and helps the voice to endure the strenuous demands of today's musical.

How then do you select a singing teacher? Here are some answers to commonly asked questions that should prove useful in helping you find the singing teacher that is right for you.

How long should the duration of the lesson be?
Thirty minutes is the maximum length of time for a beginner and that one lesson per week is the minimum amount of time you will need. After all, a voice

lesson is a vocal workout that is as vigorous, in its own way, as any workout in a gym. By the end of a half-hour there may be some vocal fatigue, but there should not be pain. If there is any pain, burning, or hoarseness, something is very wrong and you are studying with the wrong singing teacher. The end of a good lesson is accompanied by a happy sense of release of tension and relaxation.

Should I study with a teacher of the same gender?

It doesn't really matter. A good singing teacher is able to communicate sound vocal techniques and the theory behind them regardless of gender. Sometimes, if the student is very new to singing and very self-conscious, it may be wise to select a teacher of the same sex if it makes the student feel more comfortable.

How long should it take to develop my voice so that I can be ready to audition and perform?

It depends on several things—how often you have lessons, how frequently you practice your vocal exercises, and how quick you are in absorbing and putting into practice the new techniques you are learning. It could take anywhere from six months to several years before you reach the level of development you need. Voice building is very much like body building. You are developing muscular control through frequency of repetition and resistance.

What can I expect to happen during a lesson?

Your singing teacher will put you through a series of *vocalises* (vocal exercises) that exercise and navigate all ranges of your voice in a way that keeps tension to a minimum and results in a free and honest sound in all vocal registers. The voice teacher will teach you how to stand as well as how to breathe. You will also be learning where to place your tongue so it doesn't get in the way as well as learning how to relax your jaw and facial muscles. Ideally, you will learn through positive reinforcement how to produce the largest and most focused sound you can.

How, and where do I find a good voice teacher?

Ask everyone you know who sings well for recommendations. Often they will have found someone they wanted to stay with after trying out others they didn't like. You can gain from their experience. There are also organizations like NYSTA (New York Singing Teachers Association) and NATS (National Association of Teachers of Singing). Contact them, or your own state organization, for their list of teachers. Also, look in *Back Stage* and other trade magazines and publications in which many singing teachers place ads. Don't be afraid to audition a singing teacher.

What questions should I ask a singing teacher in deciding whether they're the right one for me?

The first question could be: How much are the lessons going to cost? A realistic fee would start between $25 and $45 for a half-hour lesson from a good teacher. Obviously you can't pay more than you can afford. One well-known voice teacher in Los Angeles now gets $500 per hour. Of course, these prices are geared to stars, who can afford such a price. But such prices need not concern you for now. You can certainly find a teacher who will work wonderfully for you at a price you can afford.

Next, ask about the students whom the teacher has trained. It would especially be noteworthy to know how many of his or her students have sung or are singing in Broadway or Off-Broadway shows.

Try to find out what the singing teacher wants to do for you, and make it clear that you are primarily interested in singing the repertoire of the musical theater. Mozart arias may be challenging to sing at lessons but will hardly be suitable when auditioning for a musical.

And finally, make certain that you are getting a voice teacher and not a vocal coach. The voice teacher trains you to develop your vocal instrument whereas the vocal coach helps you select material and teaches you to sing it. Study with a voice teacher first. Later, when your voice is ready, you may begin to look for a vocal coach.

SINGING TEACHERS AND VOCAL COACHES

The following is a representative sampling of voice and sight-singing teachers and vocal coaches in New York City, Los Angeles and Chicago.

NEW YORK

DAVID AND NANCY ADAMS
221 W. 82nd St., Apt. 2D
New York, NY 10024
(212) 595-3324/2886
(voice; vocal coach)

EDWARD ALBANO
Albano Voice Institute
152 W. 72nd St.
New York, NY 10023
(212) 362-2331
(voice; sight-singing)

MME. LENORE ALESSANDRO
Lenore Alessandro Studio
2109 Broadway
New York, NY 10023
(212) 799-7280
(voice; vocal coach)

ELIZABETH ARRIGO
175 W. 76th St., Apt. 2C
New York, NY 10023
(212) 874-0998
(voice)

GEORGE AXILTREE
222 W. 15th St., Apt. 8C
New York, NY 10011
(212) 255-2565
at HB Studio:
(212) 675-2370
(voice; sight-singing)

JOSEPH BAKER
102 W. 75th St., Suite 55
New York, NY 10023
(212) 580-3899
(vocal coach)

BARBARA BLISS
1160 Park Ave.
New York, NY 10128
(212) 860-3896
(voice)

JOE BOUSARD
990 Sixth Ave., Apt. 8A
New York, NY 10018
(212) 594-2249
(voice; vocal coach)

JAMES BROUGH
Soundvision
Box 1031, Village Station
New York, NY 10014
(212) 677-6217
(voice)

DAVID BRUNETTI
71 W. 71st St., #1G
New York, NY 10023
(212) 580-3292
(voice; vocal coach)

JANE BURBANK
Upper West Side Studio
(212) 580-0399
(voice)

LINDA AMIEL BURNS
Director, The Singing
Experience
15 W. 72nd St., 31F
New York, NY 10023
(212) 595-4379
(voice; vocal coach)

TOM BUTLER
442 W. 57th St.
New York, NY 10019
(212) 265-2662
(voice; vocal coach)

SHIRLEY CALLAWAY
59 W. 76th St.
New York, NY 10023
(212) 496-2476
(voice; vocal coach)

ALICE CANNON
(914) 472-2774
(vocal coach)

LANA CANTRELL
300 E. 71st St.
New York, NY 10021
(212) 249-6046
(vocal coach)

PAUL CAPUTO
(212) 661-3766/
(718) 444-7270
(voice; sight-singing coach)

LARRO CHELSI
17 Park Ave.
New York, NY 10016
(212) 689-4596
(voice; vocal coach)

STEPHEN CHENG
Tao of Voice Center
395 Riverside Dr.
New York, NY 10025
(212) 663-6430
(voice; vocal coach)

THE COACHING
COLLECTIVE
Rod Hausen, Bob Lindner
(212) 877-3993
(vocal coach)

C.O.S.I.
Carl Olsen Singers Institute
Manhattan and
Long Island Studios
(516) 543-2325
(voice)

DAVID SORIN COLLYER
50 W. 67th St.
New York, NY 10023
(212) 362-2225
(voice; vocal coach)

ANDREW COOKE
318 W. 100th St., Apt. 4A
New York, NY 10025
(212) 866-8982
(vocal coach)

JON DELFIN
(212) 595-3228
(vocal coach)

CHRISTOPHER DENNY
7 W. 14th St., Apt. 20R
New York, NY 10011
(212) 929-5198
(vocal coach)

ANTHONY DI LEVA
160 W. 73rd St.
New York, NY 10023
(212) 874-0756
(voice; vocal coach)

DR. DAVID FAIRCHILD
(914) 337-6405
(voice)

MARY FEINSINGER
99 E. 4th St., Apt. 5C
New York, NY 10003
Ansonia Hotel
2109 Broadway
Studio 13-131
New York, NY 10023
(voice; vocal coach)

MAURICE FINNELL STUDIOS
Ansonia Hotel
2109 Broadway
Studio 977
New York, NY 10023
(212) 722-6215
(voice; sight-singing)

BOB GERARDI
Sherman Square Studios
160 W. 73rd St.
New York, NY 10023
(212) 874-6436
(voice; vocal coach)

RICHARD L. HILTY
150 W. 80th St., Apt. 4C
New York, NY 10024
(212) 362-5257
(voice)

HELEN HOBBS JORDAN
119 W. 57th St.
New York, NY 10019
(212) 757-3689
(sight-singing)

ELIZABETH HOWELL
Howell Studio
325 Central Park West
New York, NY 10025
(212) 864-6472
(voice)

JANE G. KENNEDY
West 72nd St. Studio
New York, NY 10023
(212) 595-2491
(voice; vocal coach)

JAY KERR
1697 Broadway, Suite 605A
(Ed Sullivan Bldg.)
New York, NY 10019
(212) 582-5118
(voice)

JEFFREY KLITZ
300 E. 40th St.
New York, NY 10016
(212) 867-1799
(vocal coach)

MARTIN LAWRENCE
260 W. 72nd St.
New York, NY 10023
(212) 787-4614
(voice)

SARA LOUISE LAZARUS
(At the Michael Carson
Studios)
250 W. 54th St.
New York, NY 10019
(212) 864-7901
(vocal coach)

ANNIE LEBEAUX
Upper West Side
(212) 580-4460
(vocal coach)

RONA LESLIE
142 West End Ave.
New York, NY 10023
(212) 724-3082
(voice; vocal coach)

CHARLES LOFFREDO
12 Charles St., #4D
New York, NY 10014
(212) 627-3959[IS]
(voice; vocal coach)

ALLEN LOKOS
5 W. 86th St.
New York, NY 10024
(212) 877-4655
(voice)

JEANNETTE LOVETRI
(212) 662-9338
(voice)

SHELLEN LUBIN
170 Claremont Ave., #10
New York, NY 10027-4667
(212) 864-2380
(voice; vocal coach)

JOYCE LYNN
(212) 873-9836
(voice)

BARBARA MAIER
365 W. 28th St.
New York, NY 10001
(voice)

MANHATTAN SCHOOL
OF MUSIC
120 Claremont Ave.
New York, NY 10027
(212) 749-2802
(voice)

ROBERT MARKS
850 Seventh Ave., Suite 804
New York, NY 10019
(212) 664-1654
(vocal coach)

NANCY A. MAYANS
255 W. 23rd St., #4AE
New York, NY 10011
(212) 868-1162
(voice)

MARK McLAREN
419 E. 72nd St.
New York, NY 10021
(212) 861-6231
(voice; vocal coach)

BARBARA IONE MILLER
(212) 787-3362
(voice)

CARLO LIFAVI MENOTTI
160 W. 73rd St.
New York, NY 10023
(212) 874-0867
(voice)

MUSICAL THEATRE WORKS
440 Lafayette St.
New York, NY 10003
(212) 677-0040
Frank Ventura, dir.
(voice; vocal coaching)

YVONNE NAUM
2109 Broadway
New York, NY 10023
(212) 362-4698
(voice)

ALVA NELSON
202 W. 138th St., #13
New York, NY 10030
(212) 690-2407
(vocal coach)

RON PANVINI
Ron Panvini Studio for Singers
160 W. 73rd St.
New York, NY 10023
(212) 595-4952
(voice; vocal coach)

SHARON POWERS
(212) 580-1675
(voice; vocal coach)

KATHLEEN PRUDON
(212) 673-5830
(voice; vocal coach)

KAREN PURCELL
(212) 580-3051
(voice)

ROSAMONDE RITT
Upper West Side
(212) 874-3597
(vocal coach)
ROB RUSHTON
65 W. 95th St., #7F
New York, NY 10025
(212) 749-9428
(voice; vocal coach)

DAVID RUSSELL
Seventh Ave. and 54th St.
(212) 245-0924
(voice)

HAL SCHAEFER
Studio at Greene St.
103 Greene St.
New York, NY 10012
(212) 941-9753
(voice; vocal coach)

TOM SHEPARD
484 W. 43rd St.
New York, NY 10036
(212) 564-1368
(voice; vocal coach)

THE SINGING FACTORY
(212) 243-6889
(voice; vocal coach)

MARY SMALL
165 W. 66th St.
New York, NY 10023
(212) 580-3339
(voice; vocal coach)

ALLYSON STARR
The Singer's Studio
101 W. 57th St.
New York, NY 10019
(212) 582-6448
(voice)

LYNN STARLING
30 Lincoln Plaza
New York, NY 10023-7107
(212) 245-5939
(voice; vocal coach)

ROBERT STECKO
Upper West Side Studio
(212) 580-0399
(voice; vocal coach)

ELLY STONE
(212) 874-7871
(voice; vocal coach)

SUSAN-BETH
The Voice Studio
(212) 460-0034
(voice)

JOYCE SUSKIND
200 W. 70th St., Apt. 9M
New York, NY 10023
(212) 362-0135
(voice)

LUBA TCHERESKY
915 West End Ave.
New York, NY 10025
(212) 222-8585
(voice)

GRACE TESTANI
Grace Notes Enterprises
Box 229
Cathedral Station
New York, NY 10025
(212) 222-6632
(voice; sight-singing)

CARL THOMPSON
(718) 852-1771
(voice)

GREGORY TOROIAN
27 W. 16th St.
New York, NY 10011
(212) 206-1192
(vocal coach)

GUY WAID
(212) 866-3078
(voice)

RICHARD WALL
498 West End Ave.
New York, NY
(212) 580-1750[IS]
(vocal coach)

THOMAS WHITNEY
780 Riverside Dr.
New York, NY 10032
(212) 926-2491
(voice; vocal coach; sight-singing)

FREDERICK WILLARD
234 E. 14th St., #6C
New York, NY 10003
(212) 254-3628
(voice; vocal coach)

WILLIAM YOUNG
(212) 627-1513
(voice)

MARK ZELLER
The Mark Zeller Workshop
236 W. 78th St.
New York, NY 10024
(212) 362-1736
(voice)

WILLIAM T. ZEFFIRO
200 W. 16th St., 3A
New York, NY 10011
(212) 633-1182
(voice)

LOS ANGELES

ED COUPPEE/ONE ON
ONE PRIVATE LESSONS
Santa Monica
(213) 828-1825

BILL ELLIOTT
(213) 876-4461

DEREK GRAYDON
(213) 650-8320

PAMELA HALL
(818) 996-0505

JAN RITSCHEL
(213) 531-0429

KAREN SOROCA
(213) 876-7195

CHICAGO

JILL GABRIELLE
448 Circle
Forest Park, IL 60130
(708) 771-4904

SHARON NORTH JONES
CHICAGO VOICE STUDIO
410 S. Michigan, Suite 929
Chicago, IL 60610
(312) 465-1422

FAYE KAISER
THE VOICE STUDIO
Noyes Cultural Center
927 Noyes Ave.
Evanston, IL 60201
(708) 864-0940

PATRICIA MARTINEZ
560 W. Roscoe, Apt. 3 West
Chicago, IL 60657
(312) 549-1073

DON MILLER
135 S. Cuyler
Oak Park, IL 60302
(708) 848-3245

RICHARD NORBY
1137 W. Columbia
Chicago, IL 60626
(312) 465-5055

JANICE PANTAZELOS
CHICAGO STUDIO OF
PROFESSIONAL SINGING
6253 N. Sheridan
Chicago, IL 60660
(312) 764-5022

WILLIAM RUSH
VOICE CONSULTANTS
320 N. Michigan Ave.
Chicago, IL 60604
(312) 984-1039

SIVS SCHOOL OF MUSIC
722 Lake St.
Oak Park, IL 60301
(708) 848-3008

SHERWOOD
CONSERVATORY OF MUSIC
1014 S. Michigan
Chicago, IL 60605
(312) 427-6267

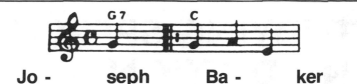

STUDYING SPEECH AND DICTION

BY TONI REINHOLD

With the exception of mimes, SAG extras, and spear-carriers, all actors are in the business of speaking. Although good speech is one of the most important skills for stage performers to have, it is often the most neglected element of their training. An actor who speaks well is generally composed and self-assured, and can compete for a wide range of roles. But actors who carry the name of their hometowns in every vowel they speak are in for some rough going.

Unacceptable accents and speech patterns can cost you work. You may already have suspected that your regional accent has placed you at a disadvantage and affected your choice of auditions. Worries about the way you sound can shake your self-confidence, and that shakiness is automatically communicated to the folks who do the hiring. This can make you reticent about pursuing work in your field. It is a vicious circle that often leads to the unemployment line.

Hometown accents are a problem for many actors. One of the most maligned accents in the world is the one associated with Brooklyn, New York. Called Brooklynese, it changes such sounds as "TH" to "T" and "IR" and "EAR" to "OI" so that *third* becomes "toid", *three* becomes "tree," and *these* is pronounced "dese." If you still cannot place this sound, think of the Bowery Boys—The Dead End Kids of film fame—and you will have a good idea of how some folks in one corner of the world pronounce "Thirty-Third and Third."

Regional accents have their place in the acting game. The Bowery Boys would never have clicked with moviegoers if they had spoken the King's English. And it is laughable to imagine Robin Hood saying that he "hoid de Sheriff of Nottin'ham was deef." But experts say it is better to speak general or standard American English and to use that as a springboard for learning regional accents when they are needed. Once known as Mid-Atlantic speech, this clean sound lacks distortions, like drawls or twangs, which are found in various parts of the country.

PURPOSES OF SPEECH TRAINING

"There are several reasons to study speech and develop good diction," says Sam Chwat of New York Speech Improvement Services. "The most obvious is unintelligiblity. Your accent may differ from your listener's expectations so much that you will not be understood.

"Another reason is stigma. People are often discriminated against because of speech behavior. Also, actors are frequently typecast by the way they speak.

"Distractability is another reason to head to a speech therapist. If a spokesperson in a commercial speaks with an unusual accent, the listener's tendency will be to pay attention to *how* the actor says the commercial's copy and not *what* he or she says.

"A speaker who feels in control of his or her speech tends to be a more self-confident communicator and is more in charge of the page content of his lines," notes Chwat, a licensed speech therapist who specializes in accent elimination and professional speech and voice improvement.

To get the most out of them, speech lessons must be tackled with the same fervor as any other aspect of a performer's training. But experts say that many actors mistakenly believe that speech problems can be completely corrected in a few lessons. Depending upon the specific problem, these studies could take months, even years. However, Chwat notes that "with a competent teacher you should see results with every session." All that is required is that "you must have normal hearing, good instruction from a competent professional, and the ability to imitate particular sounds and sound and inflectional patterns."

Chwat explains his method: "The approach we use is based on learning to produce the correct sounds, but principally on learning to identify what the speaker expects of the general American accent." Unless you have what he calls a "specialized accent," such as Barbara Walters' or Carol Channing's, and "if you are not making a go of it with your native accent, it's time to learn to speak in the most widely acceptable manner, which is Standard American English," advises Chwat. "The movie *Peggy Sue Got Married* is a great example of standard American speech." In contrast, he says, it was "jarring to hear Al Pacino do *Richard III* on Broadway with his very heavy New York accent. Shakespeare did not write for New Yorkers.

"Losing an accent is a mechanical task. Either you can eliminate the sound and monitor yourself or you can't," Chwat continues. "We help students to monitor their speech by ear and motivate them to correct their speech in conversation so they adjust to the new way they are speaking. Through self-monitoring, we help their mouths catch up with their ears," he notes.

New Jersey-based speech instructor Gordon Jacoby points out that an actor or student of acting "should study speech if his or her normal speech calls attention to itself when it is applied to reading text, interferes with the artistic elements the playwright has striven to emphasize, or diminishes the aesthetic qualities of the language of the play.

"An actor from New York City who may have a speech pattern rife with distorted vowels and the absence of an "R" sound would seriously weaken the congruity of a production which isn't about characters for New York, whether it's a play by O'Casey or Inge. In the same light, Midwestern speech would be incongruous in *A View for the Bridge* or any other strongly Eastern play.

"Acting is primarily characterization. Its main task is to realize a character and make him or her believable to an audience," adds Jacoby. "Speech is the most prominent and conspicuous part of characterization, and although speech in the theater is heightened speech, it must nevertheless reflect the speech of people of a particular region or culture.

"One might ask whether speech is really important for an actor in interpreting a role. Doesn't the actor bring life to a role through the control of other more significant manifestations of character? It is clear that characterization is not speech alone. It is also clear that from the way a person speaks, everything else about the person can be determined."

Elise May, who teaches diction, dialects, voice, and movement at Soundstage in New York City, says that once you have the foundation in speech training and control over your voice—something she calls "voice by choice"—you "have the world at your feet as far as acting is concerned." Control includes being able to learn different dialects and accents.

"Sometimes it's beneficial for someone to keep his or her accent but soften it," says May, who has a degree in speech pathology and audiology. "But actors can usually get much more work if they can turn it on and off.

"We often work with actors who want to acquire a dialect for a particular role. The key is consistency and how good an ear one has. I have been hired by directors to teach an entire cast. One of the shows I worked with was George Abbott's *Broadway* in London, teaching Londoners to speak like American gangsters of the 1920s.

"The acumen for learning a dialect differs from person to person. It is a technique that should be learned before the acting process, just like learning how to use a microphone or standing in front of a camera or audience. It is basic work that every actor should know. You can't have every dialect under your belt, but there are shortcuts to learning, such as the International Phonetics Alphabet, that make it much easier to pick up a script and translate it into a dialect," notes May.

Many actors work on dialects or accents as they are needed. Chwat recently worked with Robert De Niro when he had to learn a heavy Appalachian accent for his role in Martin Scorsese's remake of the movie *Cape Fear*. He also worked with Kathleen Turner, Charles Durning, and the rest of the cast of *Cat on a Hot Tin Roof*, because they had to sound as if they were from the same Southern family.

"Changing the way one has spoken since Day One is not something that happens over night," May emphasizes. "A lot of the beauty of acting is discovery, and it is the same with speech. The exercises you use in speech training, such as breath relaxation, will enhance other areas of your art. You develop vocal energy, which helps turn lifeless, dull tones into happy, bright tones. You learn to rid your body of tension and to work [the appropriate] muscles. A basic voice class deals with relaxation, breathing, and body alignment," May points out.

SPEECH TRAINING FOR SINGERS

Experts stress that speech training should not be confused with voice or vocal training, which centers around learning how to sing. But, they say, proper speech training is also crucial for singers, many of whom are also actors.

Steven Cheng, founder of the Tao Voice Center in New York City, says he encourages singers to get speech training. "Many actors and singers don't understand how important this is. Speech training incorporates the correct use of the breath, which is vital to speaking and singing well," he insists. "Correct breathing is important to correct speech because it is the motor. You must have the energy to get your sound out properly, whether you are speaking or singing.

"I emphasize it in my work, where I concentrate on helping actors and singers to transform their voices by improving their vocal quality, and extending their vocal range. I also work with them to enrich their voices by increasing power and developing vocal color, identity, and dynamics," says Cheng, who is an actor, singer, teacher, and Taoist philosopher.

His technique involves more than simply working on the physical aspects of speech: "I use the term 'transformation' because I work on more than improving the technical aspects of speech and voice. It also involves forming a healthy, constructive philosophical attitude because this effects one's emotional and mental health.

"I have developed a system over the years which combines the best of Western vocal techniques and modern psycho-physical approaches with ancient Chinese philosophy and breathing practices," notes Cheng, author of the book *The Tao of Voice, a New East-West Way to Transforming the Singing and Speaking Voice.*

Cheng incorporates a number of exercises into his program, not the least of which is based on the Tao technique of breathing. "It not only relaxes people but has them generate an energy flow without force," explains Cheng, who trained at Columbia University and Juilliard, and teaches at New York University.

Elizabeth McCullough, a native of Mississippi and instructor of voice at the Brooklyn Conservatory of Music, Manhattan's Greenwich House Music School, and the Jewish Community Center Music Institute in Staten Island, New York, agrees that speech training is an important tool in the hands of singers as well as actors.

"Speech training imparts techniques that insure the uninterrupted flow of breath, which is vital for any form of speaking and singing, which many people think of as an extension of the speaking voice," explains McCullough, whose training has virtually eliminated her Southern accent.

"This type of training teaches the free use of the body so the breath will flow properly and muscles will come together correctly. When you speak improperly you create tension. When pressure from that tension is placed on your vocal apparatus, the voice will not function properly. Breath is an integral part of this and the most important aspect of good vocal production.

"Singers often neglect speech training, but singing is really speaking well on pitch," observes McCullough, who has performed with the National Opera Company and American Chamber Opera. "When you are singing, you don't leave the idea that you are speaking. Speech and diction training are necessary so the voice will function well and naturally when you sing." McCullough also advocates use of the Alexander Technique—a way of poising the body so that it is used in the most efficient way possible—as a tool to improve one's speech and diction.

GUIDELINES FOR SEEKING SPEECH TRAINING

Use the following guidelines when seeking professional speech training services.

1. Many experts believe that speech teachers should have anatomical knowledge and an understanding of the body's structure, including all major muscle groups and the speaking apparatus. They also say professionals working with performers should have practical knowledge of what the work of actors and singers entails.

2. You should be afforded a free consultation with a speech teacher or therapist to discuss your specific needs, what your expectations are for your voice, and what can be achieved by working with a specific teacher.

3. Look for a professional who seems enthusiastic about teaching, can help you establish realistic goals, and with whom you will have a rapport.

4. Fees should be a consideration for struggling actors. Compare each teacher's hourly or session rate. Some teachers and schools offer group speech lessons. Some adjust their fees according to a student's ability to pay. Rates vary. One school, for example, told me that eight two-hour group sessions cost $200 and private classes cost $30 and hour.

5. Don't substitute reading about speech training for the real thing. Elise May cautions: "You can read voice books but if you don't take it into correct practice with a teacher, they are just some great books that you've read."

6. Don't be on your best "voice" behavior when you go to a speech teacher for a consultation. And bring a tape recorder with you to tape your session. Many actors who hear themselves on tape for the first time don't believe they sound that way. Be objective about your voice. As how it needs to be changed, what you are doing wrong and what you can do to make it sound better and bring you more work.

7. "You should not go to an acting teacher or voice teacher for accent elimination. They are totally different fields," advises Sam Chwat. A speech therapist has a master's degree and strong experience in correcting pathological and organic speech impediments, such as stuttering, hearing impairment, cleft palate, and muscular problems. "A degree in drama or a bachelor or major in dramatic arts or communications skills in not sufficient," he concludes.

8. Ask for and check a person's credentials before paying or agreeing to work with him or her.

SPEECH AND DICTION TEACHERS

NEW YORK

BONNIE BARTON
Actors Workshop
65 W. 55th St.
New York, NY 10019
(212) 757-2835/ (201) 944-4133

SUSAN BERKFIFY PRODUCTIONS
611 Broadway
New York, NY 10012
(212) 420-9747
(800) 333-8108

MARNER BROOKS
(212) 787-8128

STEPHEN C. CHENG
Tao of Voice Center
395 Riverside Dr.
New York, NY 10025
(212) 663-6430

DR. SAM CHWAT
New York Speech Improvement Services
253 W. 16th St.
New York, NY 10011
(212) 242-8435

BARBARA COLTON
222 W. 83rd St.
New York, NY 10024
(212) 580-4856

STEVE GARRIN'S VOICEWORKS
SIGMA Sound Studios
(212) 245-8389
(215) 969-8835 (in Philadelphia)
JEFF JACOBI
Voice Development
(212) 787-6721

GORDON JACOBY
223 S. Mountain Ave
Montclair, NJ 07042
(201) 783-4528

DORLORES McCULLOUGH
Box 1403
New York, NY 10013-1403
(212) 473-8651

RALPH PROODIAN, Ed.D
Speech Communication Analysis
390 Riverside Dr.
New York, NY 10025
(212) 222-0713

JUTTA ROSE
321 W. 14th St.
New York, NY 10011
(212) 989-7836

JOYCE SARANDON
(212) 245-5625

LOS ANGELES

ROWENA BALOS
(213) 285-8489

FRAN BENNETT
(213) 663-5991

JACKY DE HAVILAND
Los Angeles/Hollywood
(213) 939-7077

ROBERT EASTON
THE DIALECT DOCTOR/
THE HENRY HIGGINS OF
 HOLLYWOOD, INC.
(213) 468-4311

SPEECH MECHANIC
BILL DEARTH
LA Arts Theatre Complex
11305 Magnolia Blvd., #201
North Hollywood, CA 91601
(818) 761-1051

DAN STURDIVANT
(213) 664-4954

CHICAGO

ELLEN ALESHIRE
6600 N. Bosworth
Chicago, IL 60626
(312) 465-7137

JILL GABRIELLE
448 Circle
Forest Park, IL 60130
(708) 771-4904

GILLIAN LANE-PLESCIA
731 W. 18th
Chicago, IL 60616
(312) 829-6155

SHARON NORTH JONES
Chicago Voice Studio
410 S. Michigan, Suite 929
Chicago, IL 60610
(312) 465-1422

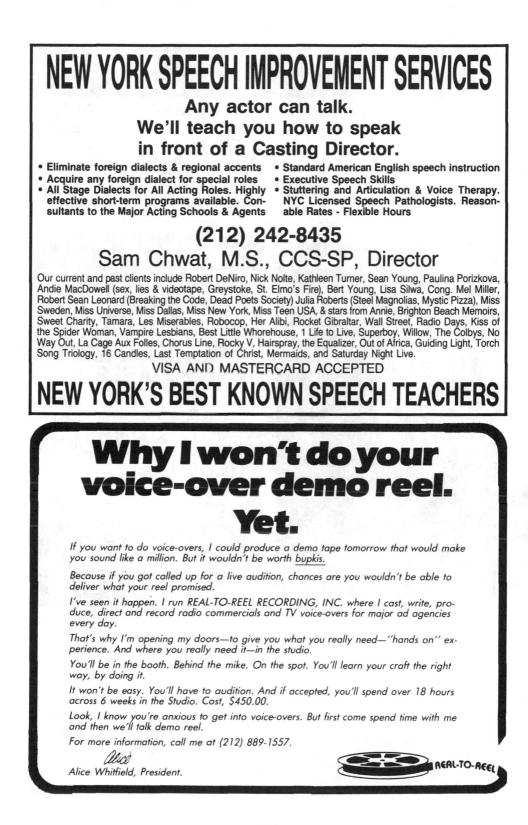
45A

PART THREE

FINDING THE WORK

AEA, AFTRA, AND SAG AGENTS

BY MARJE FIELDS

Talent agencies represent the interests of performing artists in all areas of the entertainment industry. They are the representatives franchised by Actors' Equity (AEA), the Screen Actors Guild (SAG), and the American Federation of Television and Radio Artists (AFTRA) to negotiate contracts for performers. These three trade unions have established a body of regulations that talent agents must abide by. In addition, these representatives are also regulated in New York and California by state laws. These regulations protect the performer in a manner similar to that of other consumer protection legislation. The regulations have been in existence for over 50 years and prescribe a high standard of business ethics and personal behavior for agents. No other performer's representative—lawyer, personal manager, or publicity agent—is so tightly regulated. Armed with your union's assurance that it has investigated an agency, you can set your mind at ease with regard to an agency's reliability and ethics, and can proceed to concentrate on finding the agency that can best develop your talents.

WHAT AN AGENT DOES

It is the agent's business to seek out talented artists and help them develop their careers. It is the agent who can open doors and lead the performer through them, who can give suggestions that advance a career. The agent advises, urges, listens, lectures, negotiates, soothes, worries, and, finally, applauds.

HOW TO APPROACH AN AGENCY

Once you have determined that an agency handles your particular range of talents, send them an 8 x 10 black and white headshot, on the back of which you have attached your resume. If the agency is interested, one of their agents will phone you to come in and see them. At the initial interview, the agent will try to determine whether there is a possibility that the agency can help you develop your career. Of course, no decision can be reached until the agent has seen your work. If, however, the agency is interested, they will ask you to let them know when you are performing in a showcase, a reading, or for a non-union repertory company.

Agents are invited to every showcase and production in town. Many of them see something every evening in order to search out talent. Although there are more actors than agents, and occasionally an agent will seem brusque when turning down your request for an appointment, *they do need you*. An agency's business and reputation is built on the quality of the talent it represents.

HOW TO WORK WITH AN AGENCY

When an agency decides it can work with you (this is a crucial decision because agencies only make money when their clients are employed) the agency will proceed in one of two ways:

Signed Clients: If your talents fall within the range of the agency's expertise, you will be asked to sign one or more of the exclusive management contracts provided by each of the three unions. These contracts establish a legal relationship between you and the agency. Such an agreement can also be considered as a show of faith in your talents. Whatever work you get that is within the union's jurisdiction during the term of this contract (first contracts can be a year with SAG and AFTRA and no more than 18 months with AEA) is commissionable by the agency.

Freelance: If representatives at an agency wish to become further acquainted with your work, and if, in their estimation, there is not enough demand for your type or talent, they may ask if you will work on a freelance basis with them. If you agree to this arrangement, you must sign an agreement that will guarantee that you will pay commission if you get a part that the agent has submitted you for. Many actors with particular specialties work this way and, in fact, prefer a freelance arrangement, wherein they can be submitted for auditions by more than one agent.

AGENCY FEES

Union-franchised agents can charge you 10 percent of your salary for a job they helped you secure. This 10 percent covers costs of sending you out on auditions, bringing casting directors to see you in showcases, advising you, counseling you, and submitting you for work regionally or nationally.

SUMMARY

Agents work primarily with union actors, but they do advise beginning talent on how best to pursue union credentials. Agents work within strict union guidelines. Agencies either ask you to sign union-devised contracts in which they represent you exclusively or as freelancers. All agreements are legally binding and the agency fee is 10 percent.

AEA, AFTRA, AND SAG AGENTS

The following agencies in the New York, Los Angeles, and Chicago metropolitan areas are franchised with Actors' Equity Association, Screen Actors Guild, and/or the American Federation of Television and Radio Artists, indicated by (E) for Equity; (S) for SAG; and (A) for AFTRA.

NEW YORK AREA

ABRAMS ARTISTS & ASSOCIATES
420 Madison Ave., 14th fl.
New York, NY 10017
(212) 935-8980 (E) (S) (A)

ACTORS GROUP OF NEW YORK
157 W. 57th St., Suite 604
New York, NY 10019
(212) 245-2930 (E) (S) (A)

BRET ADAMS
448 W. 44th St.
New York, NY 10036
(212) 765-5630 (E) (S) (A)

AGENCY FOR THE PERFORMING ARTS
888 Seventh Ave., Suite 602
New York, NY 10106
(212) 582-1500 (E) (S) (A)

AGENTS FOR THE ARTS
1650 Broadway, Suite 306
New York, NY 10019
(212) 247-3220 (E) (S) (A)

BONNI ALLEN TALENT
1650 Broadway, Suite 611
New York, NY 10019
(212) 757-7475 (E) (S) (A)

MICHAEL AMATO
THEATRICAL ENTERPRISE
1650 Broadway, Suite 307
New York, NY 10019
(212) 247-4456 (E) (S) (A)

AMBROSIO/MORTIMER & ASSOCIATES
165 W. 46th St., Suite 1109
New York, NY 10036
(212) 719-1677 (E) (S) (A)

AMERICAN INTERNATIONAL TALENT
303 W. 42nd St., Suite 608
New York, NY 10036
(212) 245-8888 (E) (S) (A)

BEVERLY ANDERSON AGENCY
1501 Broadway, Suite 2008
New York, NY 10036
(212) 944-7773 (E) (S) (A)

ANDREADIS TALENT AGENCY
119 W. 57th St., Suite 711
New York, NY 10019
(212) 315-0303 (E) (S) (A)

ARTIST'S AGENCY
230 W. 55th St., #29D
New York, NY 10019
(212) 245-6960 (E) (S) (A)

ARTISTS GROUP EAST
1650 Broadway, Suite 711
New York, NY 10019
(212) 586-1452 (E) (S) (A)

ASSOCIATED BOOKING
1995 Broadway
New York, NY 10023
(212) 874-2400 (E) (S) (A)

RICHARD ASTOR AGENCY
1697 Broadway
New York, NY 10019
(212) 581-1970 (E) (S) (A)

AVENUE TALENT
295 Madison Ave., 46th fl.
New York, NY 10017
(212) 972-9040 (S)

BARRY, HAFT, BROWN
165 W. 46th St., Suite 908
New York, NY 10036
(212) 869-9310 (E) (S) (A)

BAUMAN, HILLER & ASSOCIATES
250 W. 57th St., Suite 2223
New York, NY 10107
(212) 757-0098 (E) (S) (A)

PETER BEILIN AGENCY
230 Park Ave., Rm. 1223
New York, NY 10169
(212) 949-9119 (S) (A)

THE BETHEL AGENCIES
641 W. 59th St., Suite 23
New York, NY 10019
(212) 664-0455/0462 (E) (S)

J. MICHAEL BLOOM & ASSOCIATES
233 Park Ave. South, 10th fl.
New York, NY 10003
(212) 529-5800/529-6500 (E) (S) (A)

J. MICHAEL BLOOM & ASSOCIATES
(at Ford Models—Television)
344 E. 59th St.
New York, NY 10022
(212) 688-8628 (S) (A)

BOOKERS
150 Fifth Ave., #834
New York, NY 10011
(212) 645-9706 (S)

BRESLER, KELLY & KIPPERMAN AGENCY
111 W. 57th St., Suite 1409
New York, NY 10019
(212) 265-1980 (E) (S)

DON BUCHWALD & ASSOCIATES
10 E. 44th St.
New York, NY 10017
(212) 867-1070 (E) (S) (A)

CARRY COMPANY
1501 Broadway, Suite 1408
New York, NY 10036
(212) 768-2793 (E)

CARSON-ADLER AGENCY
250 W. 57th St., #729
New York, NY 10107
(212) 307-1882/6231 (E) (S) (A)

RICHARD CATALDI AGENCY
180 Seventh Ave., #1C
New York, NY 10011
(212) 741-7450 (E) (S) (A)

CELEBRITY TALENT
247 Grand St., 2nd fl.
New York, NY 10011
(212) 741-7450 (S) (A)

CNA & ASSOCIATES
19 W. 44th St., Suite 812
New York, NY (212) 10036
(212) 840-7330 (E) (S)

COLEMAN-ROSENBERG
210 E. 58th St., #2F
New York, NY 10022
(212) 838-0734 (E) (S) (A)

COLUMBIA ARTISTS MANAGEMENT
165 W. 57th St.
New York, NY 10019
(212) 397-6900 (A)

BILL COOPER ASSOCIATES
224 W. 49th St., Suite 411
New York, NY 10019
(212) 307-1100 (A)

CUNNINGHAM, ESCOTT, DIPENE AND
ASSOCIATES
118 E. 25th St., 6th fl.
New York, NY 10010
(212) 477-1666 (E) (S) (A)

CURTIS BROWN LTD.
10 Astor Pl.
New York, NY 10003
(212) 473-5400 (E)

JANE DEACY AGENCY
181 Revolution Rd.
Scarborough, NY 10510
(914) 941-1414 (S) (A)

DESPOINTES/CASEY ARTISTS
75 Varick St., Suite 1407
New York, NY 10013
(212) 334-6023 (S)

DIAMOND ARTISTS
170 West End Ave., #3K
New York, NY 10023
(212) 247-3025 (E) (S) (A)

GINGER DICCE TALENT
1650 Broadway, #714
New York, NY 10019
(212) 974-7455 (E) (S) (A)

DOUGLAS, GORMAN,
ROTHACKER & WILHELM
1501 Broadway, Suite 703
New York, NY 10036
(212) 382-2000 (E) (S) (A)

DAVID DRUMMOND TALENT
REPRESENTATIVES
102 W. 75th St.
New York, NY 10023
(212) 877-6753 (E) (S) (A)

DULCINA EISEN ASSOCIATES
154 E. 61st St.
New York, NY 10021
(212) 355-6617 (E) (S) (A)

ENTERTAINMENT ASSOCIATES
Lakeview Commons, Suite 103
Gibbsboro, NJ 08026
(609) 435-8300 (S)

MARJE FIELDS
165 W. 46th St., Suite 1205
New York, NY 10036
(212) 764-5740 (E) (S) (A)

ALLEN FLANNAGAN AGENCY
1501 Broadway, Suite 404
New York, NY 10036
(212) 840-6868 (E)

FLICK E&W TALENT
881 Seventh Ave., Suite 1110
New York, NY 10019
(212) 307-1850 (S)

FOSTER-FELL TALENT
90 West St., #PH
New York, NY 10006
(212) 571-7400/7834 (E) (S)

FRONTIER BOOKING INTERNATIONAL
1776 Broadway
New York, NY 10019
(212) 246-1505/265-0822 (E) (S) (A)

FTA TALENT AGENCY
401 Park Ave. South, PH
New York, NY 10016
(212) 686-7010 (S) (A)

FUNNYFACE
440 E. 62nd St., Suite 1B
New York, NY 10021
(212) 752-4450 (S)

GAGE GROUP
315 W. 57th St., Suite 4H
New York, NY 10019
(212) 541-5250 (E) (S) (A)

GERSH AGENCY
130 W. 42nd St., Suite 2400
New York, NY 10036
(212) 997-1818 (E) (S) (A)

GILCHRIST TALENT GROUP
310 Madison Ave., Suite 1003
New York, NY 10017
(212) 692-9166 (E) (S) (A)

HV TALENTS
18 E. 53rd St., 6th fl.
New York, NY 10022
(212) 751-3005 (S)

PEGGY HADLEY ENT.
250 W. 57th St., Suite 2317
New York, NY 10019
(212) 246-2166 (E) (S) (A)

HARTER MANNING WOO
111 E. 22nd St.
New York, NY 10010
(212) 529-4555 (E) (S) (A)

HARRIS & GOLDBERG TALENT
& LITERARY AGENCY
130 W. 57th St., Suite 5A
New York, NY 10019 (E)

MICHAEL HARTIG AGENCY
114 E. 28th St., Suite 203
New York, NY 10016
(212) 684-0010 (E) (S) (A)

HENDERSON-HOGAN AGENCY
850 Seventh Ave., Suite 1003
New York, NY 10019
(212) 765-5190 (E) (S) (A)

DIANA HUNT
Royalton Hotel
44 W. 44th St.
New York, NY 10036
(212) 391-4971 (E) (S) (A)

IANNONE-DAY AGENCY
311 W. 43rd St., Suite 1405
New York, NY 10036
(212) 957-9550 (E) (S) (A)

INTERNATIONAL CREATIVE MANAGEMENT
40 W. 57th St.
New York, NY 10019
(212) 556-5600 (E) (S) (A)

MARIAN IVRY
303 W. 66th St.
New York, NY 10023
(212) 877-1297 (E)

JAN J. AGENCY
213 E. 38th St., #3F
New York, NY 10016
(212) 682-0202 (E) (S) (A)

JORDAN, GILL & DORNBAUM AGENCY
156 Fifth Ave., Suite 711
New York, NY 10010
(212) 463-8455 (E) (S) (A)

MARVIN A. JOSEPHSON
16 W. 22nd St., 7th fl.
New York, NY 10010
(212) 727-7280 (E)

KMA ASSOCIATES
211 W. 56th St., #17D
New York, NY 10019
(212) 581-4610 (S)

JERRY KAHN I
853 Seventh Ave., Suite 7C
New York, NY 10019
(212) 245-7317 (E) (S) (A)

CHARLES KERIN ASSOCIATES
360 E. 65th St., #11J
New York, NY 10021
(212) 288-6111 (E) (S) (A)

ARCHER KING
1 Dag Hammarskjold Plaza, 7th fl.
New York, NY 10017
(212) 207-9826 (E) (S) (A)

KINGMAN AGENCY
1501 Broadway, #1808A
New York, NY 10036
(212) 354-6688 (E) (S)

ROSEANNE KIRK AGENCY
730 Fifth Ave., 9th fl.
New York, NY 10019
(212) 315-3487 (E) (S) (A)

LUCY KROLL AGENCY
390 West End Ave.
New York, NY 10024
(212) 877-0556 (E) (S) (A)

KRONICK, KELLY & LAUREN
(a division of Abrams Artists)
420 Madison Ave., 14th fl.
New York, NY 10017
(212) 684-5223/935-8980 (E) (S) (A)

L.B.H. ASSOCIATES
1 Lincoln Plaza
New York, NY 10023
(212) 787-2609 (A)

LALLY/ROGERS & LERMAN
37 E. 28th St.
New York, NY 10016
(212) 889-8284 (E) (S) (A)

THE LANTZ OFFICE
888 Seventh Ave.
New York, NY 10106
(212) 586-0200 (E) (S) (A)

LIONEL LARNER
130 W. 57th St.
New York, NY 10019
(212) 246-3105 (E) (S) (A)

LESTER LEWIS ASSOCIATES
400 E. 52nd St., #11D
New York, NY 10022
(212) 758-2480 (E) (S) (A)

LURE INTERNATIONAL TALENT GROUP
156 Fifth Ave., Suite 210
New York, NY 10010
(212) 675-5454 (E) (S) (A)

LW2
9 E. 37th St.
New York, NY 10016
(212) 779-0490 (S)

MANNEQUIN MODELS
150 E. 58th St., Suite 3500
New York, NY 10155
(212) 755-1456 (S) (A)

JOHN MARTINELLI ATTRACTIONS
888 8th Ave.
New York, NY 10036
(212) 586-0963 (S) (A)

MARGE McDERMOTT ENTERPRISES
216 E. 39th St.
New York, NY 10016
(212) 889-1583 (S) (A)

MEREDITH MODEL MANAGEMENT
10 Furler St.
Iotowa, NJ 07512
(201) 812-0122 (S) (A)

MODELSWEST
38 Chatham Rd.
Short Hills, NJ 07078
(201) 379-3887 (E) (S) (A)

WILLIAM MORRIS AGENCY
1350 Ave. of the Americas
New York, NY 10019
(212) 586-5100 (E) (S) (A)

THE NEW YORK AGENCY
1650 Broadway, Suite 504
New York, NY 10019
(212) 245-8860 (E) (S)

THE NEWS & ENTERTAINMENT CORP.
221 W. 57th St., 9th fl.
New York, NY 10019
(212) 765-5555 (E) (S) (A)

NOBLE TALENT
250 W. 57th St., Suite 1527
New York, NY 10107
(212) 581-3800 (A)

NOUVELLE TALENT
20 Bethune St., Suite 3B
New York, NY 10014
(212) 645-0940 (S)

OMNIPOP
223 Jericho Tpke., Suite 200
Mineola, NY 11501
(516) 248-4019 (S) (A)

OPPENHEIM-CHRISTIE ASSOCIATES
13 E. 37th St.
New York, NY 10016
(212) 213-4330 (E) (S) (A)

FIFI OSCARD ASSOCIATES
24 W. 40th St., 17th fl.
New York, NY 10018
(212) 764-1100 (E) (S) (A)

HARRY PACKWOOD TALENT
250 W. 57th St., Suite 2012
New York, NY 10107
(212) 586-8900 (E) (S) (A)

DOROTHY PALMER TALENT AGENCY
235 W. 56th St.
New York, NY 10019
(212) 765-4280 (E) (S) (A)

PAULINE'S TALENT CORP.
379 W. Broadway, Suite 502
New York, NY 10012
(212) 941-6000 (S)

PHOENIX ARTISTS
311 W. 43rd St., Suite 1401
New York, NY 10036
(212) 586-9110 (E) (S) (A)

PREMIER TALENT ASSOCIATES
3 E. 54th St.
New York, NY 10022
(212) 758-4900 (S) (A)

PROFESSIONAL ARTISTS UNLIMITED
513 W. 54th St.
New York, NY 10019
(212) 247-8770 (E) (S) (A)

PYRAMID ENTERTAINMENT GROUP
89 Fifth Ave.
New York, NY 10003
(212) 241-7274 (E) (S) (A)

RADIOACTIVE TALENT INC.
476 Elmont Rd.
Elmont, NY 11003
(212) 315-1919 (S) (A)

RASCALS UNLTD.
135 E. 65th St.
New York, NY 10021
(212) 517-6500 (S)

EDITH REA AGENCY
1776 Broadway, 14th fl.
New York, NY 10019
(212) 246-3434 (E) (S) (A)

NORMAN REICH AGENCY
65 W. 55th St., Suite 4D
New York, NY 10019
(212) 399-2881 (S) (A)

REVELATION ENTERTAINMENT CO.
601 Halstead Ave.
Mamaroneck, NY 10543
(914) 381-5207 (S)

GILLA ROOS LTD.
16 W. 22nd St., 7th fl.
New York, NY 10010
(212) 727-7280 (S) (A)

CHARLES V. RYAN ENTERPRISES
1841 Broadway, #907
New York, NY 10023
(212) 245-2225 (S) (A)

SAMES & ROLLNICK ASSOCIATES
250 W. 57th St., Rm. 703
New York, NY 10107
(212) 315-4434 (E) (S) (A)

SANDERS AGENCY
1204 Broadway, #306
New York, NY 10001
(212) 779-3737 (E) (S) (A)

SCHIFFMAN, EKMAN,
MORRISON & MARX
156 Fifth Ave., Suite 523
New York, NY 10010
(212) 627-5500 (S) (A)

WILLIAM SCHILL AGENCY
250 W. 57 St., #1429
New York, NY 10107
(212) 315-5919 (E) (S) (A)

SCHULLER TALENT/NY KIDS
276 Fifth Ave.
New York, NY 10001
(212) 532-6005 (E) (S) (A)

DICK SCOTT AGENCY
159 W. 53rd St.
New York, NY 10019
(212) 246-6096 (E)

SELECT ARTISTS' REPRESENTATIVES
337 W. 43rd St., Suite 1B
New York, NY 10036
(212) 586-4300 (E) (S)

SILVER, KASS & MASSETTI/EAST
145 W. 45th St., #1204
New York, NY 10036
(212) 391-4545 (S) (A)

SUSAN SMITH & ASSOCIATES
192 Lexington Ave., Suite 1204
New York, NY 10016
(212) 545-0500 (E) (S) (A)

ANTHONY SOGLIO
423 Madison Ave.
New York, NY 10017
(212) 751-1850 (E) (A)

SPOTLITE ENTERPRISES LTD. OF NY
221 W. 57th St., 9th fl.
New York, NY 10019
(212) 586-6750 (E) (S) (A)

THE STARKMAN AGENCY
1501 Broadway, Rm. 301A
New York, NY 10036
(212) 921-9191 (E) (S) (A)

STE REPRESENTATION
888 Seventh Ave.
New York, NY 10019
(212) 246-1030 (E) (S) (A)

STEWART ARTISTS CORP.
215 E. 81st St.
New York, NY 10028
(212) 249-5540 (S) (A)

PETER STRAIN & ASSOCIATES
1500 Broadway, Suite 2001
New York, NY 10036
(212) 391-0380 (E) (S) (A)

STROUD MANAGEMENT
119 W. 57th St., #1511
New York, NY 10019
(212) 315-3111 (Daytime soap writers only)
(S) (A)

TALENT REPS
20 E. 53rd St.
New York, NY 10022
(212) 752-1835 (E) (S) (A)

MICHAEL THOMAS AGENCY
305 Madison Ave.
New York, NY 10165
(212) 867-0303 (E) (S) (A)

TRANUM, ROBERTSON, HUGHES
2 Dag Hammarskjold Plaza
New York, NY 10017
(212) 371-7500 (S) (A)

TRIAD ARTISTS
888 Seventh Ave., Suite 1602
New York, NY 10106
(212) 489-8100 (E) (S) (A)

GLORIA TROY TALENT AGENCY
34-12 36th St.
Astoria, NY 11106
(718) 392-1290 (E) (S) (A)

UNIQUE SPORTS
ENTERTAINMENT MARKETING
541 Lexington Ave.
New York, NY 10022
(212) 888-0333 (S)

UNIVERSAL TALENT AGENCY
1501 Broadway, Suite 1304
New York, NY 10036
(212) 302-0680 (S)

VAN DER VEER PEOPLE
401 E. 57th St., 2nd fl.
New York, NY 10022
(212) 688-2880 (S)

BOB WATERS AGENCY
1501 Broadway, #705
New York, NY 10036
(212) 302-8787 (E) (S) (A)

RUTH WEBB ENTERPRISES
701 Seventh Ave., #9W
New York, NY 10036
(212) 757-6300 (S)

WILHELMINA ARTISTS' REPRESENTATIVES
9 E. 37th St.
New York, NY 10016
(212) 889-9450 (E) (A)

HANNS WOLTERS THEATRICAL AGENCY
10 W. 37th St.
New York, NY 10018
(212) 714-0100 (S)

ANN WRIGHT REPS.
136 E. 56th St.
New York, NY 10022
(212) 832-0110 (E) (S) (A)

WRITERS & ARTISTS AGENCY
19 W. 44th St., Suite 1000
New York, NY 10036
(212) 391-1112 (E) (S) (A)

BABS ZIMMERMAN PRODS.
305 E. 86th St.
New York, NY 10028
(212) 348-7203 (A) (E)

200 agents

ZOLI MANAGEMENT
3 W. 18th St., 5th fl.
New York, NY 10011
(212) 242-1500/7490 (E) (S) (A)

LOS ANGELES

A SPECIAL TALENT AGENCY
6253 Hollywood Blvd., #830
Los Angeles, CA 90028
(213) 467-7068 (S)

A TOTAL ACTING EXPERIENCE
14621 Titus St., #206
Panorama City, CA 91402
(818) 901-1044 (E) (S) (A)

SALLY AARON
5301 Laurel Canyon, #116
North Hollywood, CA 91607
(818) 980-6719 (E) (S) (A)

#dis conn.

ABRAMS ARTISTS & ASSOCIATES
9200 Sunset Blvd., #625
Los Angeles, CA 90069
(213) 859-0625 (E) (S) (A)

Theatrical dept / commercial dept

ABRAMS-RUBALOFF & LAWRENCE
8075 W. 3rd
Los Angeles, CA 90048
(213) 935-1700 (E) (S) (A)

ACES, A TALENT AGENCY
6565 Sunset Blvd., #300
Los Angeles, CA 90028
(213) 465-8270 (S) (A)

ACTORS GROUP AGENCY
8730 Sunset Blvd., #220
Los Angeles, CA 90069
(213) 657-7113 (E) (S) (A)

not taking

THE AGENCY
10351 Santa Monica Blvd., #211
Los Angeles, CA 90025
(213) 551-3000 (E) (S) (A)

Theatrical / Mr Zeitman / Walter morgen / no name

AGENCY FOR PERFORMING ARTS
9000 Sunset Blvd., #315
Los Angeles, CA 90069
(213) 273-0744 (E) (S) (A)

AGENCY FOR CREATIVE TALENT
8500 Melrose Ave., Suite 210
Los Angeles, CA 90069
(213) 657-5304 (E)

AGENCY II MODEL & TALENT
6525 Sunset Blvd., #303
Los Angeles, CA 90028
(213) 962-7016 (S) (A)

AIMEE ENTERTAINMENT
13743 Victory Blvd.
Van Nuys, CA 91401
(818) 994-9354 (S) (A)

Mr. Ron yates

ALL TALENT AGENCY
2437 E. Washington Blvd.
Pasadena, CA 91104
(818) 797-8202 (E) (S) (A)

ALLEN TALENT AGENCY
10850 Wilshire Blvd., #770
Los Angeles, CA 90024
(213) 936-2095 (E) (A)

CARLOS ALVARADO
8820 Sunset Blvd.
Los Angeles, CA 90069
(213) 652-0272 (S) (A)

AMAREL AGENCY
10000 Riverside Dr., #3
Toluka Lake, CA 91602
(818) 980-1013 (E)

AMBIANCE AGENCY
901 Dove St., #235
Newport Beach, CA 92660
(714) 720-7416 (S)

AMBROSIO/MORTIMER
9000 Sunset Blvd., #702
Los Angeles, CA 90069
(213) 424-4274 (E) (S) (A)

FRED AMSEL
6310 San Vicente, #407
Los Angeles, CA 90048
(213) 939-1188 (E) (S) (A)

no name

ANGEL CITY TALENT
8228 Sunset Blvd., #311
Los Angeles, CA 90046
(213) 650-1930 (S) (A)

APODACA ARTISTS
1720 N. LaBrea Ave.
Los Angeles, CA 90046
(213) 969-8398 (S)

IRVIN ARTHUR ASSOCIATES
9363 Wilshire Blvd., #212
Beverly Hills, CA 90210
(213) 278-5934 (S) (A)

ARTISTIC ENTERPRISES
6290 Sunset Blvd., #403
Los Angeles, CA 90067
(213) 552-1100 (E) (S) (A)

NA taking / 310

sent letter

ARTISTS AGENCY
10000 Santa Monica Blvd., #305
Los Angeles, CA 90067
(213) 277-7779 (E) (S) (A)

ARTISTS ALLIANCE AGENCY
8457 Melrose Pl., Suite 200
Los Angeles, CA 90069
(213) 651-2401 (S)

ARTISTS FIRST
8230 Beverly Blvd.
Los Angeles, CA 90048
(213) 653-5640 (E) (S) (A)

ARTISTS GROUP
1930 Century Park West, Suite 403
Los Angeles, CA 90067
(213) 552-1100 (E) (S) (A)

ARTISTS MANAGEMENT AGENCY
4340 Campus Dr., Suite 210
Newport Beach, CA 92660
(714) 261-7557 (S)

ARTISTS NETWORK
12001 Ventura Pl., Suite 331
Studio City, CA 91604
(818) 508-6397 (S)

ASKEW L.A.
8619 Sunset Blvd.
Los Angeles, CA 90069
(213) 652-1234 (S)

ASSOCIATED TALENT INTL.
9744 Wilshire Blvd., Suite 312
Beverly Hills, CA 90212
(213) 271-4662 (S) (A)

ATKINS & ASSOCIATES
303 S. Crescent Heights Blvd.
Los Angeles, CA 90049
(213) 658-1025 (E) (S) (A)

AVENUE C TALENT
12405 Woodruff Ave.
Downey, CA 90241
(213) 803-5775 (S)

BADGLEY, MCQUENNEY & CONNOR
9229 Sunset Blvd., Suite 206A
Los Angeles, CA 90069
(213) 278-9313 (E) (S) (A)

BALDWIN TALENT
1801 Avenue of the Stars, Suite 640
Los Angeles, CA 90067
(213) 551-3033 (S) (A)

BOBBY BALL TALENT AGENCY
6290 Sunset Blvd., #304
Los Angeles, CA 90028
(213) 465-7522 (E) (S) (A)

RICKEY BARR
Box 69590
Los Angeles, CA 90069
(213) 276-0887 (E) (S) (A)

BARRETT, BENSON, McCARTT & WESTON
10390 Santa Monica Blvd., Suite 310
Los Angeles, CA 90025
(213) 553-2600 (S)

BAUER-BENEDEK AGENCY
9255 Sunset Blvd., Suite 716
Los Angeles, CA 90069
(213) 275-2421 (S)

BAUMAN, HILLER & ASSOCIATES
5750 Wilshire Blvd., Suite 512
Los Angeles, CA 90036
(213) 857-6666 (E) (S) (A)

BDP & ASSOCIATES
10637 Burbank Blvd.
Burbank, CA 91601
(818) 506-7615 (E) (S) (A)

BEAKEL & DEBORO AGENCY
10637 Burbank Blvd.
North Hollywood, CA 91601
(818) 506-7615 (S)

BELSON & KLAUS
144 S. Beverly Dr., Suite 405
Beverly Hills, CA 90212
(213) 274-9169 (E) (S) (A)

DAVID BENDETT AGENCY
9028 Sunset Blvd., #203
Los Angeles, CA 90069 (A)

SARA BENNETT AGENCY
6404 Hollywood Blvd., Suite 323
Los Angeles, CA 90028 (S) (A)

LOIS J. BENSON
518 Toluca Park Dr.
Burbank, CA 91505
(213) 849-5647 (S) (A)

MARIAN BERZON
336 E. 17th St.
Costa Mesa, CA 92627
(714) 631-5936/(213)207-5256 (E) (S) (A)

BEVERLY HILLS SPORTS COUNCIL
9595 Wilshire Blvd., Suite 711
Beverly Hills, CA 90212
(213) 858-1872 (S)

BIGLEY AGENCY
7000 Santa Monica Blvd.
Hollywood, CA 90038
(213) 466-5014 (E)

YVETTE BIKOFF AGENCY
7080 Hollywood Blvd., #1009
Hollywood, CA 90028
(213) 278-7490 (E) (S) (A)

NINA BLANCHARD AGENCY
957 N. Cole Ave.
Los Angeles, CA 90038
(213) 462-7274 (S) (A)

J. MICHAEL BLOOM & ASSOCIATES
9200 Sunset Blvd., Suite 710
Los Angeles, CA 90069
(213) 275-6800 (E) (S) (A)

no name

BORENSTEIN-ORECK-BOGART
8271 Melrose Ave., Suite 110
Los Angeles, CA 90046
(213) 658-7500 (E) (S) (A)

not taking

BRANDON & ASSOCIATES
200 N. Robertson Blvd., #223
Beverly Hills, CA 90211
(213) 273-6173 (S) (A)

NOT ACTING

BRESLER, KELLY & KIPPERMAN
15760 Ventura Blvd., Suite 1730
Encino, CA 91436
(818) 905-1155 (E) (S) (A)

no name

ALEXIS BREWIS
12429 Laurel Terrace Dr.
Studio City, CA 91604
(818) 509-0831 (E) (S) (A)

no name

JIM BRIDGES TALENT AGENCY
1607 N. El Centro, Suite 22
Los Angeles, CA 90028
(213) 874-3274 (S) (A)

BROOKE DUNN & OLIVER
9165 Sunset Blvd., Suite 202
Los Angeles, CA 90069
(213) 859-1405 (E) (S)

BURKETT TALENT AGENCY
1700 E. Garry, Suite 113
Santa Ana, CA 92705
(714) 724-0465 (S) (A)

IRIS BURTON
1450 Belfast Dr.
Los Angeles, CA 90069
(213) 652-0954 (S) (A)

BUSH & ROSS TALENTS
4942 Vineland Ave.
North Hollywood, CA 91601
(818) 762-0096 (S) (A)

C.I. INC.
843 N. Sycamore Ave.
Los Angeles, CA 90038
(213) 461-3971 (S)

CALDER AGENCY
17420 Ventura Blvd., Suite 40
Encino, CA 91316
(818) 906-2825 (S) (A)

CAMDEN ARTISTS
2121 Avenue of the Stars
Los Angeles, CA 90067
(213) 556-2022 (E) (S) (A)

CAREER ARTISTS INTL.
11030 Ventura Blvd., Suite 3
Studio City, CA 91604,
(818) 980-1315/1316 (S) (A)

LESLIE CAROL MANAGEMENT/TALENT
234 Raymond Ave.
Glendale, CA 91201
(818) 246-6260 (S) (A)

WILLIAM CARROLL
120 S. Victory Blvd.
Burbank, CA 91502
(818) 848-9948 (S) (A)

MARY J. CARTER TALENTS
6525 Sunset Blvd., #502
Hollywood, CA 90028
(213) 467-2662 (E) (S) (A)

CASTLE-HILL
1101 S. Orlando Ave.
Los Angeles, CA 90035
(213) 653-3535 (S) (A)

CAVALERI & ASSOCIATES
6605 Hollywood Blvd., Suite 220
Los Angeles, CA 90028
(213) 461-2940 (E) (S) (A)

disconn.

CENTURY ARTISTS LTD.
9744 Wilshire Blvd., Suite 308
Beverly Hills, CA 90212
(213) 273-4366 (E) (S) (A)

not taking

CHARTER MANAGEMENT
9000 Sunset Blvd., Suite 1112
Los Angeles, CA 90069
(213) 278-1690 (E) (A)

CHASIN AGENCY
190 N. Canon, Suite 201
Beverly Hills, CA 90210
(213) 278-7505 (S)

TERRY H. CHIZ
5761 Whitnall Hwy., Suite E
North Hollywood, CA 91601
(818) 506-0994 (S)

JACK CHUTUK & ASSOCIATES
470 S. Beverly Dr.
Beverly Hills, CA 90212
(213) 552-1773 (S)

CIRCLE TALENT
9465 Wilshire Blvd., Suite 725
Beverly Hills, CA 90212
(213) 281-3765 (S) (A)

RANDOLPH W. CLARK
6464 Sunset Blvd., Suite 1050
Los Angeles, CA 90028
(213) 465-7140 (S) (A)

KATHY CLARKE
2030 E. 4th, Suite 102
Santa Ana, CA 92705
(714) 667-0222 (S)

COLLEEN CLER TALENT AGENCY
178 S. Victory Blvd., Suite 108
Burbank, CA 91502
(818) 841-7943 (S)

CNA
1801 Avenue of the Stars, Suite 1250
Los Angeles, CA 90067
(213) 556-4343 (E) (S) (A)

no taking

COAST TO COAST
12307C Ventura Blvd.
Studio City, CA 91604
(E) (S) (A)

KINGSLEY COLTON
16661 Ventura Blvd., Suite 400
Encino, CA 91436
(818) 788-6043 (S)

COMLS UNITD. INC.
(SONJA W. BRANDON'S)
7461 Beverly Blvd.
Los Angeles, CA 90036
(213) 937-2220 (S) (A)

CONTEMPORARY ARTISTS
132 Lasky Dr.
Beverly Hills, CA 90212
(213) 278-8250 (E) (S)

COPPAGE COMPANY
11501 Chandler Blvd.
North Hollywood, CA 91601
(818) 980-1106 (S)

CORALLE JR. _not taking_
4789 Vineland Ave., Suite 100
North Hollywood, CA 91602
(818) 766-9501 (E) (S) (A)

ROBERT COSDEN _not taking_
7080 Hollywood Blvd.
Los Angeles, CA 90028
(213) 856-9000 (E) (S) (A)

COX TALENT AGENCY
6362 Hollywood Blvd., Suite 219
Los Angeles, CA 90028
(213) 467-5340 (S)

CPC & ASSOCIATES
733 N. La Brea Ave., Suite 200
Los Angeles, CA 90038
(213) 662-5672 (S) (A)

CRABEN COMMERCIALS PLUS
1532 Highland Ave.
Duarte, CA 91010
(818) 449-0386 (S)

CRAIG AGENCY _not taking_
8485 Melrose Pl., Suite E
Los Angeles, CA 90069
(213) 655-0236 (E) (S) (A)

CREATIVE ARTISTS AGENCY
9830 Wilshire Blvd.
Beverly Hills, CA 90212
(213) 288-4545 (E) (S) (A)

Referrals

SUSAN CROW & ASSOCIATES
1010 Hammond, Suite 102
West Hollywood, CA 90069
859-9784 (S) (A)

CROWN AGENCY
19454 Ventura Blvd., #100
Tarzana, CA 91356
(818) 343-9199 (A)

LIL CUMBER
6515 Sunset Blvd., Suite 300A
Los Angeles, CA 90028
(213) 469-1919 (E) (S) (A)

CUNNINGHAM, ESCOTT & DIPENE
261 S. Robertson Blvd.
Beverly Hills, CA 90211
(213) 855-1700 (E) (S) (A)

Dianne Seaford.
Commercial Rep.

CURTIS BROWN LTD.
606 N. Larchmont Blvd., Suite 309
Los Angeles, CA 90006
(213) 461-0148 (E)

DADE/ROSEN/SCHULTZ
15010 Ventura Blvd., #219
Sherman Oaks, CA 91403
(818) 907-9877 (E) (S)

DEVROE AGENCY
3365 Cahuenga Blvd.
Los Angeles, CA 90068
(213) 666-2666 (S)

DIAMOND ARTISTS LTD.
9200 Sunset Blvd., Suite 909
Los Angeles, CA 90069
(213) 278-8146 (E) (S) (A)

PATRICIA DOTY & ASSOCIATES
13455 Ventura Blvd., #210
Sherman Oaks, CA 91423
(818) 981-1728 (A)

DOUGLAS, ADDIE J.
1800 Bridgegate St., Suite 107
Westlake Village, CA 91361
(805) 497-3397 (S)

DURKIN ARTISTS
200 N. Robertson Blvd., Suite 218
Beverly Hills, CA 90211
(213) 859-8234 (S)

THOMAS G. ELIAS & ASSOCIATES
23501 Park Sorrento, Suite 218
Calabasas, CA 91302
(818) 888-4608 (E) (S)

ELLIS ARTISTS AGENCY
119 N. San Vicente Blvd., Suite 202
Beverly Hills, CA 90211
(213) 651-3032 (E) (S) (A)

EMERALD ARTISTS
6565 Sunset Blvd., Suite 310
Los Angeles, CA 90028
(213) 465-2974 (S) (A)

ENTERTAINMENT ENTERPRISES
1680 N. Vine, #519
Hollywood, CA 90028
(213) 662-6001 (A)

ESTEPHAN TALENT AGENCY
6018 Greenmeadow Rd.
Lakewood, CA 90713
(213) 421-8048 (S)

EILEEN FARRELL TALENT AGENCY
9744 Wilshire Blvd., Suite 309
Beverly Hills, CA 90212
(213) 271-3400 (E) (S) (A)

FAVORED ARTISTS
8150 Beverly Blvd., Suite 201
Los Angeles, CA 90068
(213) 653-3191 (A) (E)

FEATURED PLAYERS
4051 Radford Ave., #A
Studio City, CA 91604
(818) 508-6691 (A)

WILLIAMS FELBER & ASSOCIATES
2126 Cahuenga Blvd.
Los Angeles, CA 90068
(213) 466-7629 (E) (S) (A)

FIELDS TALENT AGENCY
3325 Wilshire Blvd., Suite 749
Los Angeles, CA 90010
(213) 487-3656 (S)

FILM ARTISTS ASSOCIATES
7080 Hollywood Blvd., Suite 704
Los Angeles, CA 90028
(213) 463-1010 (S) (A)

FIRST ARTISTS AGENCY
10000 Riverside Dr.
Toluca Lake, CA 91602
(818) 509-9292 (S) (A)

FLICK EAST-WEST TALENTS
1608 N. Las Palmas
Los Angeles, CA 90028
(213) 463-6333 (S) (A)

JUDITH FONTAINE AGENCY
1720 N. La Brea Ave., 2nd fl.
Los Angeles, CA 90046
(213) 969-8398 (E) (A)

FOX TALENT AGENCY
4655 Kinsgswell Ave., #203
Hollywood, CA 90027
(213) 661-6347 (A)

BARRY FREED COMPANY
9255 Sunset Blvd., #603
Los Angeles, CA 90069
(213) 274-6898 (A)

THE GAGE GROUP
9255 Sunset Blvd., #1515
Los Angeles, CA 90069
(213) 859-8777 (E) (S) (A)

HELEN GARRETT
6363 Sunset Blvd., #802
Hollywood, CA 90028
(213) 871-8707 (E) (S) (A)

DALE GARRICK
8831 Sunset Blvd.
Los Angeles, CA 90069
(213) 657-2661 (S) (A)

GEDDES AGENCY
8457 Melrose Pl., #200
Los Angeles, CA 90069
(213) 651-2401 (E) (S) (A)

LAYA GELFF AND ASSOCIATES
18075 Ventura Blvd., #225
Encino, CA 91316
(818) 342-7247 (E) (S) (A)

PAUL GERARD TALENT AGENCY
2918 Alta Vista Dr.
Newport Beach, CA 92260
(714) 644-7950 (S)

DON GERLER AND ASSOCIATES
3349 Cahuenga Blvd. West
Los Angeles, CA 90068
(213) 850-7386 (S) (A)

GERRITSON INTERNATIONAL
8721 Sunset Blvd., #203
Los Angeles, CA 90069
(213) 659-8414 (S) (A)

THE GERSH AGENCY
232 N. Canon Dr.
Beverly Hills, CA 90210
(213) 274-6611 (E) (S) (A)

J. CARTER GIBSON
9000 Sunset Blvd., #891
Los Angeles, CA 90069
(213) 247-8813 (S) (A)

GEORGIA GILLY TALENT AGENCY
8721 Sunset Blvd., #103
Los Angeles, CA 90069
(213) 657-5660 (E) (S) (A)

GLOBAL TALENT
12725 Ventura Blvd., #C
Studio City, CA 91604
(818) 766-4441 (E) (S)

HARRY GOLD TALENT AGENCY
3500 W. Olive Dr., #1400
Burbank, CA 91505
(818) 769-5003 (E) (S) (A)

SUE GOLDIN TALENT AGENCY
6380 Wilshire Blvd., #1600
Los Angeles, CA 90048
(213) 852-1441 (E) (S) (A)

ALLEN GOLDSTEIN & ASSOCIATES
15010 Ventura Blvd., Suite 234
Sherman Oaks, CA 91403
(818) 905-7771 (E)

JACK GORDEAN
809 N. Foothill Rd.
Beverly Hills, CA 90210
(213) 273-4195 (E)

GORDON/ROSSON TALENT AGENCY
12700 Ventura Blvd., #350
Studio City, CA 91604
(818) 509-1900 (S) (A)

GORES/FIELDS
10100 Santa Monica Blvd., #700
Los Angeles, CA 90067
(213) 277-4400 (E) (S) (A)

JOSHUA GRAY & ASSOCIATES
6736 Laurel Canyon, #306
North Hollywood, CA 91606
(818) 982-2510 (E) (S) (A)

GRAY/GOODMAN TALENT AGENCY
205 S. Beverly Dr., #210
Beverly Hills, CA 90210
(213) 276-7070 (S) (A)

GREENVINE AGENCY
110 E. 9th St., Suite C-1005
Los Angeles, CA 90068
(213) 662-3016 (E)

MITCHELL J. HAMILBURG
292 S. La Cienega, #212
Beverly Hills, CA 90211
(213) 657-1501 (E) (S) (A)

HANZER HOLDINGS
415 N. Barrington Ave.
Los Angeles, CA 90049
(213) 476-3089 (S) (A)

HARRIS & GOLDBERG
2121 Avenue of the Stars, #950
Los Angeles, CA 90067
(213) 553-5200 (E) (S) (A)

VAUGHN D. HART
200 N. Robertson Blvd., #219
Beverly Hills, CA 90211
(213) 273-7887 (E) (S) (A)

HARTER MANNING WOO
201 N. Robertson Blvd., Suite D
Beverly Hills, CA 90211
(213) 278-7278 (E) (S)

HEACOCK LITERARY AGENCY
1523 6th St., Suite 14
Santa Monica, CA 91401
(213) 393-6227 (S)

BEVERLY HECHT AGENCY
8949 Sunset Blvd.
Los Angeles, CA 90069
(213) 278-3544 (S) (A)

HENDERSON/HOGAN AGENCY
247 S. Beverly Dr.
Beverly Hills, CA 90212
(213) 274-7815 (S) (A)

HOWARD TALENT WEST
3518 Cahuenga Blvd. West, #218
Los Angeles, CA 90068
(818) 766-5300 (S) (A)

GEORGE B. HUNT & ASSOCIATES
121 E. Twin Palms Dr.
Palm Springs, CA 92264
(619) 320-6778 (S) (A)

RAY HUNTER & ASSOCIATES
1901 Avenue of the Stars, #1774
Los Angeles, CA 90067
(213) 277-8161 (S) (A)

GEORGE INGERSOLL
6513 Hollywood Blvd., Suite 217
Los Angeles, CA 90028
(213) 874-6434 (E)

INTERNATIONAL CONTEMPORARY
ARTISTS
19301 Ventura Blvd., #203
Tarzana, CA 91356
(818) 342-3618 (S)

INTERNATIONAL CREATIVE
MANAGEMENT
8899 Beverly Blvd.
Los Angeles, CA 90048
(213) 550-4000 (E) (S) (A)

INTERNATIONAL TALENT
3419 W. Magnolia Blvd.
Burbank, CA 91505
(818) 842-1204 (E) (S) (A)

INTERTALENT
9200 Sunset Blvd., PH25
Los Angeles, CA 90069
(213) 271-0600 (S) (A)

JACKMAN & TAUSSIG
1539 Sawtell Blvd.
Los Angeles, CA 90025
(213) 478-6641 (S) (A)

GEORGE JAY
6269 Selma Ave., #15
Los Angeles, CA 90028
(213) 465-0232 (S)

TOM JENNINGS & ASSOCIATES
28035 Dorothy Dr., #210A
Agoura, CA 91301
(818) 879-1260 (S)

JOSEPH, HELDFOND & RIX
1717 N. Highland Ave., #414
Los Angeles, CA 90028
(213) 466-9111 (E) (S) (A)

JOSEPH/KNIGHT
1680 N. Vine, #726
Los Angeles, CA 90028
(213) 465-5474 (E) (S) (A)

LEN KAPLAN
4717 Laurel Canyon Blvd., #206
North Hollywood, CA 91607
(818) 980-8811 (E) (S) (A)

THE KAPLAN-STAHLER AGENCY
8383 Wilshire Blvd., #923
Beverly Hills, CA 90211
(213) 653-4483 (S) (A)

KARG/WEISSENBACH & ASSOCIATES
329 S. Wetherly Dr., #101
Beverly Hills, CA 90211
(213) 205-0435 (E) (S) (A)

KAYE TALENT AGENCY
1320 W. Alameda Ave.
Burbank, CA 91506
(818) 972-2822 (S) (A)

TONI KELMAN/ARLETTA
7813 Sunset Blvd.
Los Angeles, CA 90046
(213) 851-8822 (E) (S) (A)

WILLIAM KERWIN AGENCY
1605 N. Cahuenga Blvd., #202
Los Angeles, CA 90028
(213) 469-5155 (E) (S) (A)

TYLER KJAR
10653 Riverside Dr.
Toluca Lake, CA 91602
(818) 760-0321 (E) (S) (A)

PAUL KOHNER
9169 Sunset Blvd.
Los Angeles, CA 90069
(213) 550-1060 (E) (S) (A)

not taking

VICTOR KRUGLOV & ASSOCIATES
8537 Sunset Blvd.
Hollywood, CA 90069
(213) 854-3430 (A)

L.A. ARTISTS
2566 Overland Ave., #600
Los Angeles, CA 90064
(213) 202-0254 (E) (S) (A)

no name

L.A. TALENT
8335 Sunset Blvd.
Los Angeles, CA 90069
(213) 656-3722 (S)

LABELLE AGENCY
LaBelle Plaza
1933 Cliff Dr.
Santa Barbara, CA 93109
(805) 965-4575 (S)

MOYA LANE TALENT AGENCY
1589 E. Date St.
San Bernardino, CA 92412
(714) 882-5215 (S) (A)

STACEY LANE
13455 Ventura Blvd., #223
Sherman Oaks, CA 91423
(818) 501-2668 (S) (A)

THE LANTZ OFFICE
9255 Sunset Blvd., #505
Los Angeles, CA 90069
(213) 858-1144 (E) (S) (A)

LAWRENCE AGENCY
3575 Cahuenga Blvd. West, #125-3
Los Angeles, CA 90068
(213) 851-7711 (S) (A)

LEADING ARTISTS
445 N. Bedford
Beverly Hills, CA 90210
(213) 858-1999 (S) (A)

MARK LEVIN ASSOCIATES
208 S. Beverly Dr., Suite 4
Beverly Hills, CA 90212
(213) 278-9933 (E)

SID LEVIN
9255 Sunset Blvd., #401
West Hollywood, CA 90069
(213) 278-5610 (S)

TERRY LICHTMAN
12456 Ventura Blvd., #1
Studio City, CA 91604
(818) 761-4804 (S) (A)

ROBERT LIGHT AGENCY
6404 Wilshire Blvd., #800
Los Angeles, CA 90048
(213) 651-1777 (S) (A)

THE LIGHT COMPANY
901 Bringham Ave.
Los Angeles, CA 90048
(213) 651-1777 (S) (A)

KEN LINDNER & ASSOCIATES
2049 Century Park East, #2717
Los Angeles, CA 90067
(213) 277-9223 (S) (A)

JOHNNY LLOYD TALENT AGENCY
6404 Hollywood Blvd., #219
Los Angeles, CA 90028
(213) 464-2738 (S)

THE LOCKWOOD AGENCY
8217 Beverly Blvd., #5
Los Angeles, CA 90048
(213) 469-3318 (S) (A)

BESSIE LOO AGENCY
8235 Santa Monica Blvd., #202
Los Angeles, CA 90046
(213) 650-1300 (E) (S) (A)

Guy Lee

LOVELL & ASSOCIATES
1350 N. Highland Ave.
Los Angeles, CA 90028
(213) 462-1672 (E) (S) (A)

not taking

LYNNE & REILLY
Toluca Lake Plaza
6735 Forest Lawn Dr., #313
Los Angeles, CA 90068
(213) 850-1984 (S) (A)

MARIS AGENCY
17620 Sherman Way, #8
Van Nuys, CA 91406
(818) 708-2493 (S) (A)

MARSHAK, WYCKOFF & ASSOCIATES
280 S. Beverly Dr., #400
Beverly Hills, CA 90212
(213) 278-7222 (S) (A)

MARTEL AGENCY
1680 N. Vine St., #203
Los Angeles, CA 90028
(213) 874-8131 (E)

M.A.X.
275 S. Beverly Dr., #210
Beverly Hills, CA 90212
(213) 550-8858 (S) (A)

MAXINE'S TALENT AGENCY
4830 Encino Ave.
Encino, CA 91316
(818) 986-2946 (S) (A)

McCARTT, ORECK, BARRETT
10390 Santa Monica Blvd., #310
Los Angeles, CA 90025
(213) 553-2600 (S) (A)

JAMES McHUGH AGENCY
8150 Beverly Blvd., #303
Los Angeles, CA 90048
(213) 651-2770 (E) (S) (A)

HAZEL McMILLAN
8217 Beverly Blvd., #6
Los Angeles, CA 90048
(818) 788-7773 (S)

MEDIA ARTISTS GROUP
6255 Sunset Blvd.
Los Angeles, CA 90028
(213) 463-5610 (S) (A)

M.E.W.
8489 W. 3rd St., #1105
Los Angeles, CA 90048
(213) 653-4731 (S)

PETER MEYER AGENCY
9220 Sunset Blvd., #303
Los Angeles, CA 90048
(213) 278-4766 (E)

MGA/MARY GRADY
150 E. Olive Ave., #111
Burbank, CA 91502
(818) 843-1511 (S)

GILBERT MILLER
21243 Ventura Blvd., #243
Woodland Hills, CA 91364
(818) 888-6363 (S) (A)

LEE MILLER
5000 Lankershim, #5
North Hollywood, CA 91601
(818) 505-0077 (S)

THE MINKOFF AGENCY
12001 Ventura Pl., #339
Studio City, CA 91604
(818) 760-4501 (E) (S) (A)

MIRAMAR TALENT
9157 Sunset Blvd., Suite 300
Los Angeles, CA 90069
(213) 858-1900 (S)

MISHKIN AGENCY
2355 Benedict Canyon
Beverly Hills, CA 90210
(213) 274-5261 (E) (S) (A)

PATTY MITCHELL AGENCY
11425 Moorpark St.
Studio City, CA 91602
(818) 508-6181 (S) (A)

WILLIAM MORRIS
151 El Camino Dr.
Beverly Hills, CA 90212
(213) 274-7451 (E) (S) (A)

BURTON MOSS AGENCY
113 San Vicente Blvd., #202
Beverly Hills, CA 90211
(213) 655-1156 (E) (S) (A)

DAVID H. MOSS & ASSOCIATES
8019 1/2 Melrose, #3
Los Angeles, CA 90046
(213) 653-2900 (E) (S) (A)

MARY MURPHY TALENT AGENCY
6014 Greenbush
Van Nuys, CA 91401
(818) 506-3874 (S) (A)

SUSAN NATHE & ASSOCIATES C.P.C.
8281 Melrose Ave., #200
Los Angeles, CA 90046
(213) 653-7573 (S) (A)

THE NICKLIN GROUP
9478 W. Olympic Blvd., #304
Beverly Hills, CA 90212
(213) 277-5272 (S) (A)

PACIFIC ARTISTS
515 N. LaCienega Blvd.
Los Angeles, CA 90048
(213) 657-5990 (S) (A)

THE PARNESS AGENCY
9220 Sunset Blvd., #204
Los Angeles, CA 90069
(213) 272-2233 (S)

BEN PEARSON AGENCY
606 Wilshire Blvd., #614
Santa Monica, CA 90401
(213) 451-8414 (E) (S)

PECHET, BLANCHARD,
BERMAN AGENCY
1925 Century Park East, #1150
Los Angeles, CA 90067
(213) 556-1971 (E)

VICTOR PERILLO
9229 Sunset Blvd.
Los Angeles, CA 90069
(213) 278-0251 (E)

PRIETO & ASSOCIATES
12001 Ventura Pl., #340
Studio City, CA 91604
(818) 506-4797 (S)

PRIMA ARTISTS
832 N. LaBrea
Los Angeles, CA 90038
(213) 465-8566 (S) (A)

PRIVILEGE TALENT
8344 Beverly Blvd.
Los Angeles, CA 90048
(213) 658-8781 (S) (A)

PROGRESSIVE ARTISTS
400 S. Beverly Dr.
Beverly Hills, CA 90212
(213) 553-8561 (E) (S) (A)

RAINFORD AGENCY
7471 Melrose, Suite 14
Los Angeles, CA 90046
(213) 655-1404 (S) (A)

RAY RAPPA AGENCY
7471 Melrose Ave., Suite 11
Los Angeles, CA 90046
(213) 653-7000 (S) (A)

RISSKY BUSINESS
10966 Le Conte, Suite A
Los Angeles, CA 90024
(213) 208-2335 (S)

THE ROBERTS CO.
9255 Sunset Blvd., Suite 505
Los Angeles, CA 90069
(213) 275-9384(S) (A)

ROBINSON-WEINTRAUB & GROSS
8428 Melrose Pl., Suite C
Los Angeles, CA 90069
(213) 653-5802 (S) (A)

STEPHANIE ROGERS & ASSOCIATES
3855 Lankershim Blvd., Suite 218
North Hollywood, CA 91604
(818) 509-1010 (S)

JACK ROSE AGENCY
9255 Sunset Blvd., Suite 602
Los Angeles, CA 90069
(213) 274-4673 (S) (A)

MARION ROSENBERG OFFICE
8428 Melrose Pl., Suite C
Los Angeles, CA 90069
(213) 653-7383 (A)

NATALIE ROSSON AGENCY
11712 Moorpark St., #204
Studio City, CA 91604
(818) 508-1445 (S) (A)

SAI TALENT AGENCY
4924 1/2 Lankershim Blvd.
North Hollywood, CA 91601
(818) 505-1010 (S)

THE SANDERS AGENCY
8831 Sunset, Suite 304
Los Angeles, CA 90069
(213) 652-1119 (E) (S) (A)

THE SARNOFF COMPANY
8489 W. 3rd St.
Los Angeles, CA 90048
(213) 651-3308 (S) (A)

THE SAVAGE AGENCY
6212 Banner Ave.
Los Angeles, CA 90038
(213) 461-8316 (E) (S) (A)

JACK SCAGNETTI TALENT AGENCY
5330 Lankershim Blvd., #210
North Hollywood, CA 91601
(818) 762-3871 (S) (A)

PEGGY SCHAEFER
10850 Riverside Dr.
North Hollywood, CA 91602
(818) 985-5547 (S) (A)

IRV SCHECHTER CO.
9300 Wilshire Blvd., Suite 410
Beverly Hills, CA 90212
(213) 278-8070 (E) (S) (A)

SCHLOWITZ & ASSOCIATES
8228 Sunset Blvd., Suite 212
West Hollywood, CA 90046
(213) 650-7300 (E) (S) (A)

SANDIE SCHNARR
8281 Melrose Ave., Suite 200
Los Angeles, CA 90046
(213) 653-9479 (S) (A)

JUDY SCHOEN & ASSOCIATES
606 N. Larchmont Blvd., Suite 309
Los Angeles, CA 90004
(213) 962-1950 (E) (S) (A)

BOOH SCHUT AGENCY
11350 Ventura Blvd., Suite 206
Studio City, CA 91604
(818) 760-6669 (S) (A)

DON SCHWARTZ & ASSOCIATES
8749 Sunset Blvd.
Los Angeles, CA 90069
(213) 657-8910 (E) (S)

JOHN SEKURA/A TALENT AGENCY
1680 N. Vine, Suite 1003
Los Angeles, CA 90028
(213) 962-6290 (S) (A)

SELECTED ARTISTS AGENCY
3575 Cahuenga Blvd. West, 2nd fl.
Los Angeles, CA 90068
(213) 905-5744 (S) (A)

DAVID SHAPIRA & ASSOCIATES
5301 Ventura Blvd., #345
Sherman Oaks, CA 91403
(818) 906-0322 (E) (S) (A)

SHAPIRO-LICHTMAN
8827 Beverly Blvd.
Los Angeles, CA 90048
(213) 859-8877 (S)

SHEPHERD AGENCY
9034 Sunset Blvd., Suite 100
Los Angeles, CA 90069
(213) 274-4377 (S) (A)

SHIFFIN ARTISTS
7466 Beverly Blvd., Suite 205
Los Angeles, CA 90036
(213) 937-3937 (E)

THE SHUMAKER AGENCY
6533 Hollywood Blvd., #301
Los Angeles, CA 90028
(213) 464-0745 (E) (S) (A)

SIDELL CANAVAN AGENCY
11530 Sunset Blvd.
Los Angeles, CA 90049
(213) 472-5205 (S) (A)

SILVER ARTISTS
7715 Sunset Blvd.
Los Angeles, CA 90046
(213) 876-9773 (S) (A)

SILVER, KASS & MASSETTI AGENCY
8730 Sunset Blvd., Suite 480
Los Angeles, CA 90069
(213) 289-0909 (E) (S) (A)

S.M. TALENT AGENCY
1408 S. Palm Ave.
San Gabriel, CA 91776
(818) 571-1305 (S) (A)

SUSAN SMITH & ASSOCIATES
121 N. San Vincente Blvd.
Beverly Hills, CA 90211
(213) 852-4777 (E) (S) (A)

CAMILLE SORICE AGENCY
8399 Topanga Canyon Blvd., #204
Canoga Park, CA 91304
(818) 995-1775 (S) (A)

SPECIAL ARTISTS AGENCY
335 N. Maple Dr., #360
Beverly Hills, CA 90210
(213) 859-9688 (S) (A)

SPOTLITE ENTERPRISES
8665 Wilshire Blvd., #208
Beverly Hills, CA 90211
(213) 657-8004 (E) (S) (A)

DOLORES ST. LOUIS TALENT AGENCY
16820 Chatsworth St., #123
Granada Hills, CA 91344
(818) 368-0575 (S) (A)

STAR GLOBE TALENTS
6363 Wilshire Blvd., #500
Los Angeles, CA 90048
(213) 658-6468 (S)

STAR TALENT
1050 N. Maple St.
Burbank, CA 91505
(213) 461-6672 (S) (A)

THE STARS AGENCY
6683 Sunset Blvd., #2
Los Angeles, CA 90028
(213) 962-1800 (E) (S) (A)

STARWIL TALENT AGENCY
6253 Hollywood Blvd., #730
Los Angeles, CA 90028
(213) 874-1239 (S) (A)

STE REPRESENTATION
9301 Wilshire Blvd., #312
Beverly Hills, CA 90210
(213) 550-3982 (E) (S) (A)

CHARLES H. STERN AGENCY
11755 Wilshire Blvd., #2320
Los Angeles, CA 90025
(213) 479-1788 (S) (A)

STONE-MANNERS
9113 Sunset Blvd.
Los Angeles, CA 90069
(213) 275-9599 (E) (S) (A)

STUNT ACTION TALENT AGENCY
21828 Lassen St., #E
Chatsworth, CA 91311
(818) 998-6382 (A)

SUTTER-WALLS AND ASSOCIATES
8322 Beverly Blvd.
Los Angeles, CA 90048
(213) 658-8200 (S) (A)

SUTTON, BARTH & VENNARI
145 S. Fairfax Ave., #310
Los Angeles, CA 90036
(213) 938-6000 (E) (S) (A)

STYLE MODELS & ARTISTS
12377 Lewis St., Suite 101
Garden Grove, CA 92640
(714) 750-4445/
(213) 550-1499 (E) (S) (A)

TALENT BANK
1617 N. El Centro, #14
Los Angeles, CA 90028
(213) 466-7325 (S) (A)

TALENT ENTERPRISES
1607 N. El Centro, #2
Los Angeles, CA 90028
(213) 462-0913 (S)

TALENT GROUP
9250 Wilshire Blvd.
Beverly Hills, CA 90212
(213) 273-9559 (S) (A)

HERB TANNEN & ASSOCIATES
1800 N. Vine St., #120
Los Angeles, CA 90028
(213) 466-6191 (E) (S) (A)

WILLIE THOMPSON
6381 Hollywood Blvd., #450
Los Angeles, CA 90028
(213) 461-6594 (S)

ARLENE THORNTON & ASSOCIATES
5657 Wilshire Blvd., #290
Los Angeles, CA 90036
(213) 939-5757 (S) (A)

TISHERMAN AGENCY
6767 Forest Lawn Dr.
Los Angeles, CA 90068
(213) 850-6767 (S) (A)

TOBIAS-SKOURAS & ASSOCIATES
1901 Avenue of the Stars, #840
Los Angeles, CA 90067
(213) 277-6211 (E) (S) (A)

A TOTAL ACTING EXP.
14621 Titus St., Suite 100
Panorama City, CA 91606
(818) 901-1044 (E)

TRIAD ARTISTS
10100 Santa Monica Blvd., 16th fl.
Los Angeles, CA 90067
(213) 556-2727 (E) (S) (A)

THE TURTLE AGENCY
15010 Ventura Blvd., #219A
Sherman Oaks, CA 91403
(818) 907-9892 (S)

TWENTIETH CENTURY ARTISTS
3800 Barham Blvd., #303
Los Angeles, CA 90068
(213) 850-5516 (E) (S) (A)

VARIETY ARTISTS INTERNATIONAL
9073 Nemo St., 3rd fl.
Los Angeles, CA 90069
(213) 858-7800 (S) (A)

VAUGHN AGENCY
500 Molino St., #213
Los Angeles, CA 90013
(213) 626-7434 (S)

ERIKA WAIN AGENCY
1418 N. Highland Ave., #102
Los Angeles, CA 90028
(213) 460-4224 (S) (A)

WALLACK & ASSOCIATES
1717 N. Highland Ave., #701
Los Angeles, CA 90028
(213) 465-8004 (E) (S) (A)

SANDRA WATT & ASSOCIATES
7551 Melrose, #5
Los Angeles, CA 90046
(213) 653-2339 (S) (A)

ANN WAUGH
4731 Laurel Canyon Rd., #5
North Hollywood, CA 91607
(818) 980-0141 (F) (S) (A)

RUTH WEBB ENT. INC.
7500 Devista Dr.
Los Angeles, CA 90046
(213) 874-1700 (E) (S) (A)

RICHARD WEISS TALENT AGENCY
1680 N. Vine St., #503
Los Angeles, CA 90028
(213) 856-9989 (S)

MARY ELLEN WHITE
151 N. San Vicente, Suite 208
Los Angeles, CA 90211
(213) 653-4731 (E)

THE WILDER AGENCY
3151 Cahuenga Blvd. West, #310
Los Angeles, CA 90068
(213) 969-9641 (S) (A)

WILHELMINA ARTISTS' REPRESENTATIVES
8383 Wilshire Blvd., #954
Beverly Hills, CA 90211
(213) 653-5700 (S) (A)

SHIRLEY WILSON AGENCY
291 S. La Cienega Blvd., #306
Beverly Hills, CA 90211
(213) 659-7030 (S) (A)

WINIFRED STRAND TALENT AGENCY
439 S. La Cienga, Suite 117
Los Angeles, CA 90043
(213) 278-1561 (E)

TED WITZER
1900 Avenue of the Stars, #2850
Los Angeles, CA 90067
(213) 552-9521 (E) (S) (A)

CARTER WRIGHT TALENT AGENCY
6533 Hollywood Blvd., #201
Los Angeles, CA 90028
(213) 469-0944 (E) (S) (A)

WRITERS & ARTISTS AGENCY
11726 San Vicente Blvd., #300
Los Angeles, CA 90049
(213) 820-2240 (E) (S) (A)

STELLA ZADEH & ASSOCIATES
11759 Iowa Ave.
Los Angeles, CA 90025
(213) 207-4114 (S) (A)

THE ZIMRING CO.
9171 Wilshire Blvd., #530
Beverly Hills, CA 90210
(213) 278-8240 (S)

ZOLTAN TALENT
1636 Cahuenga Blvd., #206
Los Angeles, CA 90028
(213) 871-0190 (S) (A)

CHICAGO

A PLUS TALENT
680 N. Lake Shore Dr., #1330
Chicago, IL 60611
(312) 642-8151 (E) (S) (A)

AMBASSADOR TALENT AGENTS
203 N. Wabash Ave., #2212
Chicago, IL 60601
(312) 641-3491 (S)

LARRY BASTIAN
2580 Crestwood Lane
Deerfield Park, IL 60015
(708) 945-9283 (E)

MARY BONCHER MODEL MANAGEMENT
575 W. Madison, #810
Chicago, IL 60606
(312) 902-2400 (E) (S) (A)

DAVID & LEE
70 W. Hubbard St., #200
Chicago, IL 60610
(312) 670-4444 (S)

HARRISE DAVIDSON & ASSOCIATES
65 E. Wacker Pl., Suite #2401
Chicago, IL 60601
(312) 782-4480 (E) (S) (A)

DURKIN TALENT
743 N. La Salle St., #250
Chicago, IL 60610
(312) 664-0045 (E) (S) (A)

ETA
7558 S. Chicago Ave.
Chicago, IL 60619
(312) 752-3955 (S)

FERRER AGENCY
935 W. Chestnut, #520
Chicago, IL, 60622
(312) 243-2388 (E) (S) (A)

GEDDES AGENCY
1925 N. Clybourn, Suite 402
Chicago, IL 60614
(312) 348-3333 (E) (S) (A)

SHIRLEY HAMILTON
333 E. Ontario, Suite B
Chicago, IL 60611
(312) 787-4700 (E) (S) (A)

JEFFERSON & ASSOCIATES
1050 N. State
Chicago, IL 60610
(312) 337-1930 (E) (S) (A)

SUSANNE JOHNSON TALENT
108 W. Oak St.
Chicago, IL 60610
(312) 943-8315 (S)

LILY'S TALENT
650 N. Greenwood
Park Ridge, IL 60068
(708) 698-1044 (E) (S) (A)

EMILIA LORENCE
619 N. Wabash Ave.
Chicago, IL 60611
(312) 787-2033 (E) (S) (A)

CJ MERCURY
1330 Lake Ave.
Whiting, IN 46394
(219) 659-2701 (S)

NATIONAL TALENT NETWORK (NTN)
101 E. Ontario, #760
Chicago, IL 60611
(312) 280-2225 (S)

NOUVELLE TALENT MANAGEMENT
730 N. Franklin St., #304
Chicago, IL 60610
(312) 944-1133 (E) (S) (A)

PHILBIN TALENT
6301 N. Kedvale
Chicago, IL 60646
(312) 777-5394 (3)

PHOENIX TALENT
332 S. Michigan Ave., #1847
Chicago, IL 60605
(312) 785-2024 (S)

SALAZZAR & NAVAS
367 W. Chicago Ave.
Chicago, IL 60610
(312) 751-3419 (S)

NORMAN SCHUCART ENTERPRISES
1417 Green Bay Rd.
Highland Park, IL 60035
(708) 433-1113 (S)

HOWARD SCHULTZ ARTIST REP.
4738 N. Harlem, Suite 5
Harwood Heights, IL 60656
(708) 867-4282 (A)

STEWART TALENT MANAGEMENT
212 W. Superior, #406
Chicago, IL 60610
(312) 943-3131 (E) (S) (A)

VOICES UNLIMITED
680 N. Lake Shore Dr., #1330
Chicago, IL 60611
(312) 642-3262 (S)

ARLENE WILSON TALENT
414 N. Orleans
Chicago, IL 60610
(312) 644-6699 (S)

CASTING DIRECTORS

Casting directors are involved in just about every area of the entertainment industry, from plays and musicals to feature films, and radio and television programs. Their primary function is to bring to the attention of producers and directors those performers whose talents are most suited to the demands of the particular characters in a film, television, radio, or theatrical project. A description and list of requirements for each character is devised through discussions or meetings with the producer along with the director, writer, and other members of the creative staff. Employed by the producer of a play, musical, feature film, commercial, or radio/TV program—including soap operas, pilots, series, mini-series, movies-of-the-week, and specials—casting directors may sometimes cast just one part in a production or they may cast all the roles, from top to bottom, from stars to walk-on parts. To accomplish this purpose, casting directors use a combination of performers they are familiar with, submissions or recommendations from agents, and perhaps, those actors/singers/dancers that impress them at a general audition. Performers who seem most right for each part are then asked to audition for the director and producer.

Not too many years ago the profession of casting director did not exist. It was up to the producer or director to cast a role, but producers tended to use the same performers over and over again. As the performing unions grew stronger—Actors' Equity in particular—hundreds of people *had* to be seen, and it became an unwieldy and time-filling task for the director and producer to handle alone. A new profession was born, and producers put their shows in the hands of a trusted person whose taste and wisdom they could rely upon.

Back Stage contacted some of the top professionals on the Broadway scene in order to define exactly what casting directors do and/or how they choose the actors that they will work with. All agreed that their primary goal is to work for the actor's best interest and to connect it to the director's best interest. Here are some of those responses:

Geoffrey Johnson: "I rely on my knowledge of the actors and actresses that I have seen perform and have liked in the many varieties of theater, film, and television available to me (i.e., showcases, scene nights, soap scenes, and so on). I also go back to the notes I keep on actors who have auditioned for me. However, just because I've liked an actor's work, it does not mean I feel he or she is right for the project I am currently casting.

"Treat every audition you get as a business appointment. Be professional. Try to learn as much as you can beforehand about the project and the people you are auditioning for without being bothersome. The results, even though you may not get the role (next time you will!), will be rewarding to the casting director, the project, and yourself."

Joanna Merlin: "A casting director must use intuition and be imaginative. Often actors may unconsciously limit themselves, whereas when a casting director reads them, he or she can envision them doing something they have never done before. If the casting director can convince the actors to experiment a little, guide them into a new way of thinking, it becomes a creative experience for everyone concerned."

Pat McCorkle: "A casting director is only a funneling system of sorts. You look at a character and you say, 'What do I need to make this come alive? Who do I need?' The creative juices flow and you start searching."

Stuart Howard: "In seeing the hundreds of pictures and resumes that come into the office, I will always give a second look to those who have gone to college... I root for those who are well-prepared and willing. If they don't get my job, I'm sure going to hold on to their name or refer them to someone else."

Julie Hughes: "Objectivity is truly difficult. If asked, our casting firm will give our opinion, and if we have developed a trusting relationship with the producer or director, we can be helpful in pinpointing a problem. Producers are not as experienced as they were in the days of David Merrick and Kermit Bloomgarden. Most are businessmen—we are grateful for their interest, but sometimes they do not have the life experience we have."

Warren Pincus: "Actors should look into themselves as to why they didn't get a particular part. Did they do their homework? Did they dress properly? Do they have an attitude? Will they do things differently next time? Believe me, if I have learned one thing in this business, it's simply keep on trying. You just never know."

NEW YORK, LOS ANGELES, AND CHICAGO CASTING DIRECTORS

NEW YORK CASTING DIRECTORS

The following is a listing of independent New York casting directors. There are many other casting directors who freelance, going from one production office to another and, therefore, do not have an office address that we can include here. Casting directors request that initial contact be made by sending a picture/resume through the mail.

JOSEPH ABALDO CASTING
450 W. 42nd St., Suite 2F
New York, NY 10036
(212) 947-3697

AMERIFILM CASTING
95 Delancey St., Suite 206
New York, NY 10002
(212) 353-3118

DEBORAH AQUILA CASTING
333 W. 52nd St., Suite 1008
New York, NY 10019
(212) 664-5049

BABY WRANGLERS CASTING
201 W. 77th St., #6D
New York, NY 10024
(212) 769-0910

JERRY BEAVER AND ASSOCIATES
215 Park Ave. South, Suite 1704
New York, NY 10003
(212) 979-0909

BREANNA BENJAMIN CASTING
1600 Broadway, Suite 306
New York, NY 10019
(212) 541-9067

JAY BINDER CASTING
513 W. 54th St.
New York, NY 10019
(212) 586-6777

JANE BRINKER CASTING
51 W. 16th St.
New York, NY 10011
(212) 924-3322

DEBORAH BROWN CASTING
250 W. 57th St., Suite 2608
New York, NY 10107
(212) 581-0404

BURNS & RUZAN
121 W. 27th St., Suite 503
New York, NY 10001
(212) 627-0010

KATE BURTON CASTING
39 W. 19th St., 12th fl.
New York, NY 10011
(212) 929-0948

CARROLL & CALANNI CASTING
267 Fifth Ave., #1110
New York, NY 10016
(212) 685-6888

KIT CARTER CASTING
160 W. 95th St., Suite 1D
New York, NY 10025
(212) 864-3147

DONALD CASE CASTING
8 E. 12th St., 5th fl.
New York, NY 10003
(212) 366-1355

CAST-AWAY! CASTING SERVICE
14 Sutton Place South
New York, NY 10022
(212) 755-0960

CENTRAL CASTING OF NY
200 W. 54th St.
New York, NY 10019
(212) 582-4933

COLLIER CASTING CENTER
1560 Broadway, Suite 509
New York, NY 10036
(212) 719-9636

COMPLETE CASTING
(212) 265-7460

CONTEMPORARY CASTING
FDR Station
Box 1844
New York, NY 10022
(212) 838-1818

CREATIVE CASTING GROUP
(INTERNATIONAL)
1375 Broadway
New York, NY 10018
(212) 827-2350

CTP CASTING
22 W. 27th St.
New York, NY 10001
(212) 696-1100

MERRY L. DELMONTE CASTING &
PRODUCTIONS
460 W. 42nd St.
New York, NY 10036
(212) 279-2000

DONNA DE SETA CASTING
525 Broadway, 3rd fl.
New York, NY 10012
(212) 274-9696

LOU DIGIAIMO ASSOCIATES
513 W. 54th St.
New York, NY 10019
(212) 713-1884

SYLVIA FAY
71 Park Ave., Suite 1B
New York, NY 10016
(212) 889-2626

LEONARD FINGER
1501 Broadway
New York, NY 10036
(212) 944-8611

MAUREEN FREMONT CASTING
641 W. 59th St., Room 21
New York, NY 10019
(212) 541-4710/827-5377

GINGER FRIEDMAN
303 E. 83rd St., Suite 115
New York, NY 10028
(212) 472-1714

GODLOVE, SEROW &
SINDLINGER CASTING
151 W. 25th St., 11th fl.
New York, NY 10001
(212) 627-7300

GOLDEN CASTING COMPANY
133 W. 72nd St., Room 601
New York, NY 10023
(212) 496-0146

MARIA & TONY GRECO CASTING
630 Ninth Ave., Suite 702
New York, NY 10036
(212) 247-2011

HANZEL & STARK CASTING
1261 Broadway, Suite 505
New York, NY 10001
(212) 779-0966

HASKINS CASTING
426 Broome St., Suite 5F
New York, NY 10013
(212) 431-8405

JUDY HENDERSON &
ASSOCIATES CASTING
330 W. 89th St.
New York, NY 10024
(212) 877-0225

HERMAN/LIPSON CASTING
24 W. 25th St.
New York, NY 10010
(212) 807-7706

HISPANICAST
(A Division of Riccy Reed Casting)
39 W. 19th St., 12th fl.
New York, NY 10011
(212) 691-7366

STUART HOWARD ASSOCIATES
22 W. 27th St., 10th fl.
New York, NY 10001
(212) 725-7770

HUGHES/MOSS CASTING
311 W. 43rd St., Suite 700
New York, NY 10036
(212) 307-6690

HYDE-HAMLET CASTING
311 W. 43rd St., Room 903
New York, NY 10036
(212) 767-1842

DONNA ISAACSON CASTING
453 W. 16th St., 2nd fl.
New York, NY 10011
(212) 691-8555

JOHNSON-LIFF CASTING ASSOCIATES
1501 Broadway, Suite 1400
New York, NY 10036
(212) 391-2680

KEE CASTING
434 Avenue of the Americas, Box 813
New York, NY 10011
(212) 995-0794

KELLY & CASE CASTING ASSOCIATES
155 W. 13th St.
New York, NY 10011
(212) 463-8630

JODI KIPPERMAN CASTS
39 W. 19th St., 12th fl.
New York, NY 10011
(212) 645-0030

LYNN KRESSELL CASTING
445 Park Ave., 7th fl.
New York, NY 10022
(212) 605-9122

LEHNER/STEPHENS CASTING
300 E. 40th St., Suite 26F
New York, NY 10016

LEWIS/SHEPP CASTING PARTNERS
39 W. 19th St., 12th fl.
New York, NY 10011
(212) 645-1500

WENDY LITWACK CASTING
c/o The Three of Us Studios
39 W. 19th St., 12th fl.
New York, NY 10016
(212) 686-0014

JOAN LYNN CASTING
39 W. 19th St., 12th fl.
New York, NY 10011
(212) 675-5595/750-8865

McCORKLE CASTING
264 W. 40th St., 9th fl.
New York, NY 10018
(212) 840-0992

ABIGAIL McGRATH
1501 Broadway, Suite 1907
New York, NY 10036
(212) 768-3277

METROPOLITAN CASTING
208 W. 20th St., Suite 5A
New York, NY 10011
(212) 255-5037

JULIE MOSSBERG CASTING
1501 Broadway, Room 2605
New York, NY 10036

ELISSA MYERS CASTING
333 W. 52nd St., Suite 1008
New York, NY 10019
(212) 315-4777

NAVARRO/BERTONI CASTING CO.
101 W. 31st St., Room 2112
New York, NY 10001
(212) 736-9272

NURSES ON SET
71 W. 85th St., Suite 3B
New York, NY 10024
(212) 362-8928

MICHELE ORTLIP CASTING
311 W. 43rd St., 4th fl.
New York, NY 10036
(212) 459-9462

JOANNE PASCIUTO
17-08 150th St.
Whitestone, NY 11357

POCO CASTING
Box 628, Radio City Station
New York, NY 10019
(212) 581-5536

REAL SOUND
459 Columbus Ave., Suite 101
New York, NY 10024
(212) 362-6913

RED, WHITE AND BLUE
301 W. 57th St.
New York, NY 10019
(212) 315-5050

RICCY REED CASTING
39 W. 19th St., 12th fl.
New York, NY 10011
(212) 691-7366

SHIRLEY RICH
200 E. 66th St.
New York, NY 10021
(212) 688-9540

REED & MELSKY CASTING
928 Broadway
New York, NY 10010
(212) 505-5000

TONI ROBERTS CASTING
150 Fifth Ave., Suite 521
New York, NY 10011
(212) 627-2250

CHRISTINE ROELFS CASTING
379 West Broadway, 4th fl.
New York, NY 10012
(212) 431-3131

MIKE ROSCOE CASTING
153 E. 37th St., Suite 1B
New York, NY 10016
(212) 725-0014

CHARLES ROSEN CASTING
32 Gramercy Park South, Suite 13K
New York, NY 10003
(212) 254-2080

JUDY ROSENSTEEL CASTING
43 W. 68th St.
New York, NY 10023

SHERIE L. SEFF CASTING
400 W. 43rd St.
New York, NY 10036
(212) 947-7408

SELECTIVE CASTING BY CAROL NADELL
Radio City Station
Box 1538
New York, NY 10101-1538

BARBARA SHAPIRO CASTING
111 W. 57th St., Suite 1420
New York, NY 10019

MEG SIMON CASTING
1600 Broadway, Suite 1005
New York, NY 10019
(212) 245-7670

CAROLINE SINCLAIR CASTING
720 Greenwich St., #75
New York, NY 10014
(212) 675-4094

PAT SWEENEY CASTING
61 E. 8th St., Suite 144
New York, NY 10003
(212) 533-0544

HELYN TAYLOR CASTING
140 W. 58th St.
New York, NY 10019

BERNARD TELSEY CASTING
442 W. 42nd St., 2nd fl.
New York, NY 10036

TODD THALER
130 W. 57th St., Suite 4A
New York, NY 10019
(212) 246-7116

BONNIE TIMMERMANN CASTING
445 Park Ave., 7th fl.
New York, NY 10022
(212) 605-2805

JOY TODD
37 E. 28th St., Suite 700
New York, NY 10016
(212) 685-3537

TRIANGLE CASTING
888 Seventh Ave., 29th fl.
New York, NY 10019
(212) 262-2362
Main Office: (See Los Angeles listing
under Cathy Henderson Associates)

URELL CASTING
641 W. 59th St., Room 10
New York, NY 10019

VOICECASTING/A NO SOAP CO.
161 W. 54th St.
New York, NY 10019
(212) 581-5575

JOY WEBER CASTING
250 W. 57th St.
New York, NY 10019

WEIST-BARRON CASTING
35 W. 45th St.
New York, NY 10036
(212) 840-7025

SUSAN WILLETT CASTING
1170 Broadway, Suite 1008
New York, NY 10001
(212) 725-3588

MARJI CAMNER WOLLIN
& ASSOCIATES
233 E. 69th St.
New York, NY 10021
(212) 472-2528

LIZ WOODMAN
c/o Loving
ABC-TV
320 W. 66th St.
New York, NY 10023

JEFFREY ZEINER
451 W. 43rd St.
New York, NY 10036
(212) 245-1237

LOS ANGELES CASTING DIRECTORS

Since the film industry is the major source of work for actors in Los Angeles, many of the casting directors listed here are associated with the various film and TV studios. Some casting directors work independently and have their own offices; others freelance from project to project and studio to studio, and therefore don't have an office address or phone number that we can include here. Instead, they can be contacted through the Casting Society of America.

JULIE ALTER
8721 Sunset Blvd., #201
Los Angeles, CA 90069
(213) 652-7373

DONNA ANDERSON
c/o Casting Society of America
6565 Sunset Blvd., #306
Los Angeles, CA 90028

MAUREEN A. ARATA
Viacom Productions Inc.
100 Universal City Plaza Bldg. 69, Rm. 103
Universal City, CA 91608
(818) 777-7821

BARBARA BALDAVIN
c/o Casting Society of America
6565 Sunset Blvd., #306
Los Angeles, CA 90028

DEBORAH BARYLSKI
c/o Casting Society of America
6565 Sunset Blvd., #306
Los Angeles, CA 90028

FRAN BASCOM
Columbia Pictures TV
Columbia Plaza East, Rm. 148
Burbank, CA 91505
(818) 972-8332

PAMELA BASKER
1071 N. La Cienega #90025
Los Angeles, CA 90069
(213) 652-8617

FRANK BAYER
Mark Taper Forum
135 N. Grand Ave.
Los Angeles, CA 90012
(213) 972-7374

ANNETTE BENSON
c/o Casting Society of America
6565 Sunset Blvd., #306
Los Angeles, CA 90028
(213) 836-4901

BERGERON/LAWSON CASTING
Box 1489
La Canada, CA 91011
(818) 790-9832

TAMMY BILLIK
1438 N. Gower St., #1407
Los Angeles, CA 90028
(213) 460-7266

SUSAN BLUESTEIN
4063 Radford Ave., #105
Studio City, CA 91604
(818) 505-6636

EUGENE BLYTHE
Disney Studios
500 S. Buena Vista
Burbank, CA 91521
(818) 560-7625

STEVEN BOCHCO PRODUCTIONS
Alice Cassidy
10201 W. Pico Blvd.
Pico Apts. #5
Los Angeles, CA 90035
(213) 203-1127

DEE DEE BRADLEY CASTING
11684 Ventura Blvd., #195
Studio City, CA 91604
(818) 954-2015

RISA BRAMON
183 N. Martel, #210
Los Angeles, CA 90036
(213) 937-0153

MEGAN BRANMAN
Universal
100 Universal City Plaza
Universal City, CA 91608
(818) 777-1744

BRISKEY/CHAMIAN CASTING
3701 W. Oak St., Bldg. 4
Burbank, CA 91505
(618) 954-5418

BUCK/EDELMAN CASTING
4051 Radford Ave.
Studio City, CA 91604
(818) 506-7328

JACKIE BURCH
c/o Casting Society of America
6565 Sunset Blvd., #306
Los Angeles, CA 90028

BURROWS-TILLMAN
15555 Melrose Ave.
Clara Bow Building, #115
Los Angeles, CA 90038
(213) 956-5921

ALICE CASSIDY
Bob Booker Productions
6605 Eleanor Ave.
Hollywood, CA 90038
(213) 465-7877

ELLEN CHENOWETH
c/o Werthemer, Armstrong & Hirsch
1888 Century Park East, #1888
Los Angeles, CA 90067
(213) 333-4552

BARBARA CLAMAN
c/o Casting Society of America
6565 Sunset Blvd., #412
Los Angeles, CA 90028
(213) 466-3400

LORI COBE
10351 Santa Monica Blvd., #410
Los Angeles, CA 90025
(213) 277-5777

ANDREA COHEN
Warner Bros.
4000 Warner Blvd.
Burbank, CA 91522
(818) 954-1621

DAVID COHN CASTING
9060 Santa Monica Blvd., #202
West Hollywood, CA 90069
(213) 859-4812

ANNELISE COLLINS
1103 El Centro Ave.
Los Angeles, CA 90038
(213) 962-9562

RUTH CONFORTE
Box 4795
North Hollywood, CA 91617-4795
(818) 760-8220

ANITA DANN
Box 2041
Beverly Hills, CA 90213
(213) 278-7765

PATRICIA DeOLIVEIRA
c/o Casting Society of America
6565 Sunset Blvd., #306
Los Angeles, CA 90028

DIANE DIMEO & ASSOCIATES
12725 Ventura Blvd.
Studio City, CA 91604
(818) 505-0945

DICK DINMAN
c/o Casting Society of America
6565 Sunset Blvd., #306
Los Angeles, CA 90028
(213) 469-2283

PAM DIXON CASTING
Box 672
Beverly Hills, CA 90213
(213) 271-8064

DONNA DOCKSTADER
Universal Studios
100 Universal Plaza
University City, CA 91608
(818) 777-1961

KIM DORR
The Arthur Co.
100 Universal City Plaza
Building 447
Universal City, CA 91608
(818) 505-1200

NAN DUTTON & ASSOCIATES
5555 Melrose Ave.
Clara Bow Bldg., #217
Los Angeles, CA 90038
(213) 956-1840

PENNY ELLERS CASTING
4063 Radford Ave., #109
Studio City, CA 91604
(818) 505-6660

RACHELLE FARBERMAN
The Kushner Locke Company
11601 Wilshire Blvd., 21st fl.
Los Angeles, CA 90025
(213) 445-1111, ext. 352

FENTON-TAYLOR CASTING
100 Universal City Plaza
Bungalow 477
Universal City, CA 91608
(818) 777-4610

NANCY FOY
Paramount
5555 Melrose Ave.
Dressing Rm. Bldg., #330
Los Angeles, CA 90028
(213) 956-5000

FRAZIER/GINSBERG CASTING
627 11th St., #400
Santa Monica, CA 90402
(213) 273-8507

JEAN SARAH FROST
c/o Casting Society of America
6565 Sunset Blvd., #306
Los Angeles, CA 90028

MELINDA GARTZMAN
Paramount
5555 Melrose Ave.
Von Sternberg, Bldg., #204
Los Angeles, CA 90038
(213) 273-8507

SHANI GINSBERG
c/o Casting Society of America
6565 Sunset Blvd., #306
Los Angeles, CA 90028
(213) 273-8507

JAN GLASER
MGM/UA
1000 W. Washington Blvd.
Culver City, CA 90232
(213) 280-6238

SUSAN GLICKSMAN
12001 Ventura Pl., #400
Studio City, CA 91604
(818) 766-2610

PETER GOLDEN
Cannell Productions
7083 Hollywood Blvd., 1st fl.
Hollywood, CA 90028
(213) 856-7576

CHRISTOPHER GORMAN
CBS
7800 Beverly Blvd.
Los Angeles, CA 90036
(213) 852-2975

DAVID GRAHAM
590 N. Rossmore Ave.
Los Angeles, CA 90004
(213) 871-2012

JEFF GREENBERG
Paramount
5555 Melrose Ave.
Marx Bros Bldg., #102
Los Angeles, CA 90038
(213) 956-4886

PEG HALLIGAN
c/o Casting Society of America
6565 Sunset Blvd., #306
Los Angeles, CA 90028

MILT HAMERMAN
MCA
100 Universal City
Plaza Building 507-4A
University City, CA 91608
(818) 777-1711

THEODORE HANN
Lorimar
300 S. Lorimar Plaza Bldg. 140
Room 139A
Burbank, CA 91505
(818) 954-7642

ROBERT W. HARBIN
20th Century Fox
10201 W. Pico Blvd.
Executive Bldg., #335
Los Angeles, CA 90035
(213) 203-3847

KAREN HENDEL
HBO
2049 Century Park East
Los Angeles, CA 90069
(213) 273-2220

CATHY HENDERSON ASSOCIATES/
TRIANGLE CASTING
9200 Sunset Blvd., #901
Los Angeles, CA 90069
(213) 273-2220

PAULA HEROLD
Hollywood Pictures
500 S. Buena Vista Rm. 160
Burbank, CA 91521
(818) 560-1532

JANET HIRSHENSON
The Casting Company
8925 Venice Blvd.
Los Angeles, CA 90034
(213) 842-7551

BOBBY HOFFMAN
6311 Romaine St., #7327
Los Angeles, CA 90038
(213) 463-7986

JUDITH HOLSTRA CASTING
4043 Radford Ave.
Studio City, CA 91604
(818) 761-9420

VICKI HUFF
962 N. LaCienega Blvd.
Los Angeles, CA 90069
(213) 659-8557

BETH HYMSON
Patrick Hasburgh Productions
11846 Ventura Blvd., #120
Studio City, CA 91604
(818) 509-1070

JUSTINE JACOBY
c/o Auroa Productions
8642 Melrose Ave., #2
Los Angeles, CA 90069
(213) 854-6900*eot

JANE JENKINS
The Casting Company
8925 Venice Blvd.
Los Angeles, CA 90034
(213) 842-7551

CARO JONES CASTING
5858 Hollywood Blvd., #220
Hollywood, CA 90028
(213) 464-9216

RAMSAY KING
c/o Casting Society of America
6565 Sunset Blvd., #306
Los Angeles, CA 90028

MARSHA KLEINMAN & ASSOCIATES
704 N. Gardner St., #2
Los Angeles, CA 90046
(213) 852-1521

ANNA MARIE KOSTURA
NBC
3000 W. Alameda #233
Burbank, CA 91523
(818) 840-4410

WENDY KURTZMAN
20th Century Fox
10201 W. Pico Blvd.
Bldg. 38-#29
Los Angeles, CA 90035
(213) 203-1900

SHANA LANDSBERG
c/o Casting Society of America
6565 Sunset Blvd., #306
Los Angeles, CA 90028
(818) 777-3497

JASON LAPADURA
c/o Casting Society of America
6565 Sunset Blvd., #306
Los Angeles, CA 90028

ELIZABETH LARROQUETTE
Port Street Films
4000 Warner Blvd.
Producers Bldg. 1, Suite 102
Burbank, CA 91522
(818) 954-2605

KATHLEEN LETTERIE
c/o Casting Society of America
6565 Sunset Blvd., #306
Los Angeles, CA 90028

ELISABETH LEUSTIG
1173 N. Ardmore #1
Los Angeles, CA 90029
(213) 973-4114

JOHN LEVEY
Warner Bros.
4000 Warner Blvd., Bldg. 3A-Rm. 26
Burbank, CA 91522
(818) 954-4080

LIBERMAN/HIRSCHFELD CASTING
1438 N. Gower
Los Angeles, CA 90028
(213) 460-7258

TERRY LIEBLING
8407 Coreyell Pl.
Los Angeles, CA 90046
(213) 656-6803

TRACY LILIENFIELD
c/o Casting Society of America
6565 Sunset Blvd., #306
Los Angeles, CA 90028

ROBIN LIPPIN
Disney Studios
500 S. Buena Vista
Zorro 5
Burbank, CA 91521
(818) 560-2700

LAUREN LLOYD
Paramount
5555 Melrose Ave.
Los Angeles, CA 90038
(213) 956-8565

LISA LONDON
c/o Casting Society of America
6565 Sunset Blvd., #306
Los Angeles, CA 90028
(213) 962-8070
MOLLY LOPATA CASTING

4043 Radford Ave.
Studio City, CA 91604
(818) 753-8086

JUNIE LOWRY-JOHNSON
20th Century Fox
10201 W. Pico Blvd.
Los Angeles, CA 90035
(213) 203-3233

MACDONALD-BULLINGTON CASTING
6930 Sunset Blvd., 2nd fl.
Los Angeles, CA 90028
(213) 957-0091

IRENE MARIANO
Lorimar
300 S. Lorimar Plaza Bldg. 140, 1st fl.
Burbank, CA 91505
(818) 954-7643

DODIE MCLEAN & ASSOCIATES
8033 Sunset Blvd., #810
Los Angeles, CA 90046
(213) 876-7999

JEFFREY A. MESHEL
NBC
3000 W. Alameda Ave.
Burbank, CA 91523
(818) 840-4729

ELLEN MEYER
11811 W. Olympic Blvd.
Los Angeles, CA 90064
(213) 444-1818

ADRIANA MICHEL
Saban Entertainment
4000 W. Alameda, 5th fl.
Burbank, CA 91522
(818) 972-4800

BARBARA MILLER
Lorimar
300 S. Lorimar Plaza
Bldg. 140, 1st fl.
Burbank, CA 91505
(818) 954-7645

RICK MILLIKAN
MGM
10000 W. Washington Blvd., #7046
Culver City, CA 90232
(213) 280-6128

LISA MIONIE
c/o Casting Society of America
6565 Sunset Blvd., #306
Los Angeles, CA 90028

PATRICIA MOCK

8489 W. 3rd St.
Los Angeles, CA 90048

BOB MORONES CASTING
733 N. Seward St.
Los Angeles, CA 90038
(213) 467-2834

HELEN MOSSLER
Paramount Television
5555 Melrose Ave.
Los Angeles, CA 90038
(213) 956-5578

ROBIN S. NASSIF
ABC
2040 Ave. of the Stars
Los Angeles, CA 90067
(213) 557-6423

NANCY NAYOR
MCA/Universal
100 Universal City Plaza Bldg. 463-220
Universal City, CA 91608
(818) 777-3566

WALLIS NICITA
Paramount
5555 Melrose Ave.
Dressing Rm. Bldg., #200
Los Angeles, CA 90038
(213) 956-8514

MERYL O'LOUGHLIN
Imagine Entertainment
1925 Century Park East, 23rd fl.
Los Angeles, CA 90067
(213) 277-1665

ONORATO/FRANKS CASTING
1717 N. Highland Ave., #904
Los Angeles, CA 90028
(213) 468-8833

LORI OPENDEN
NBC
3000 W. Alameda Ave., #231
Burbank, CA 91523
(818) 840-3774

FERN ORENSTEIN
12001 Ventura Pl. Suite 400
Studio City, CA 91604
(818) 766-2610

PAT ORSETH
c/o Casting Society of America
6565 Sunset Blvd., #306
Los Angeles, CA 90028
(213) 372-8411

PAGANO/BIALY CASTING

1680 N. Vine St., #904
Hollywood, CA 90028
(213) 871-0051

MARVIN PAIGE
Box 69964
Los Angeles, CA 90069
(818) 760-3040

JENNIFER J. PART
Universal Studios
100 Universal City Plaza
Bldg. 507, Suite 4F
Universal City, CA 91608
(818) 777-5013

CAMI PATTON
c/o Casting Society of America
6565 Sunset Blvd., #306
Los Angeles, CA 90028

JOEY PAUL
The Arthur Co.
100 Universal City Plaza
Building 447
Universal City, CA 91608
(818) 505-1200

DON PEMRICK CASTING
3939 Lankershim Blvd.
Universal City, CA 91604
(818) 505-0555

LINDA PHILLIPS PALO
Raleigh Studios
650 N. Bronson, #142
Hollywood, CA 90004
(213) 396-8328

PAM POLIFRONI
New World TV
3000 W. Alameda, Stage 11
Burbank, CA 91523
(818) 840-4641

HOLLY POWELL
8489 W. 3rd St., #1110
Los Angeles, CA 90048
(213) 653-6633

SALLY G. POWERS
c/o Casting Society of America
6565 Sunset Blvd., #306
Los Angeles, CA 90028

JOHANNA RAY
c/o Propaganda Films
941 N. Mansfield
Los Angeles, CA 90038
(213) 463-9451

KAREN REA

c/o Casting Society of America
6565 Sunset Blvd., #306
Los Angeles, CA 90028

JOE REICH
NBC Productions
3000 W. Alameda, Studio 9
Burbank, CA 91523
(818) 840-3244

BARBARA REMSEN & ASSOCIATES
650 N. Bronson Ave., #124
Los Angeles, CA 90004
(213) 464-7968

STU ROSEN
7631 Lexington Ave.
Los Angeles, CA 90046
(213) 851-1661

VICKI ROSENBERG
Sunset-Gower Studios
1438 N. Gower
Casting Apts. 1406
Hollywood, CA 90028
(213) 460-7593

DONNA ROSENSTEIN
ABC
2040 Avenue of the Stars
Los Angeles, CA 90067
(213) 557-6532

MARCIA ROSS
Warner Bros. TV
4000 Warner Blvd.
North Administration Bldg., #25
Burbank, CA 91522

RENEE ROUSSELOT
Disney Studios
500 S. Buena Vista
Casting Building #6
Burbank, CA 91523

BEN RUBIN
5750 Wilshire Blvd., #276
Los Angeles, CA 90036
(213) 965-1500

DAVID RUBIN CASTING
640 S. San Vicente Blvd., #306
Los Angeles, CA 90048
(213) 278-5816

DEBRA RUBINSTEIN
Culver Studios
9336 W. Washington Blvd.
Culver City, CA 90230
(213) 202-3490

MARK SAKS

Lorimar
300 S. Lorimar Plaza
Building 140, 1st fl.
Burbank, CA 91505
(818) 954-7326

JEAN SCOCCIMARRO CASTING
c/o Casting Society of America
6565 Sunset Blvd., #306
Los Angeles, CA 90028

SUSAN SCUDDER CASTING
7083 Hollywood Blvd.
Los Angeles, CA 90028
(213) 856-7574

DENNISON/SELZER CASTING
3000 Olympic Blvd.
Santa Monica, CA 90404
(213) 315-4850

JULIE SELZER
Gary Shaffer Casting
1502 Queens Rd.
Los Angeles, CA 90069
(213) 656-9498

BILL SHEPARD
c/o Casting Society of America
6565 Sunset Blvd., #306
Los Angeles, CA 90028

TONY SHEPHERD
Aaron Spelling Productions
5700 Wilshire Blvd., 5th fl.
Los Angeles, CA 90028

MARGERY SIMKIN
20th Century Fox
10201 W. Pico Blvd.
Bldg. 88-Rm. 215
Los Angeles, CA 90035
(213) 203-1530

MELISSA SKOEE
11684 Ventura Blvd., #5141
Studio City, CA 91604
(818) 760-2058

MARY JO SLATER
MGM/UA
10000 W. Washington Blvd., #4011
Culver City, CA 90232
(213) 280-6128

STANLEY SOBLE
Mark Taper Forum
135 N. Grand Ave.
Los Angeles, CA 90012
(213) 972-7374

PAMELA SPARKS & ASSOCIATES

6126 Glen Alden
Los Angeles, CA 90068
(805) 266-9671

LYNN STALMASTER
c/o Weiss, Block & Associates
12100 Wilshire Blvd., #200
Los Angeles, CA 90025
(213) 552-0983

RON STEPHENSON
MCA
Universal Studios Bldg. 463-Rm. 106
Universal City, CA 91608
(818) 777-3498

SALLY STINER
12228 Venice Blvd., #503
Los Angeles, CA 90066
(213) 827-9796

STANZI STOKES
c/o Casting Society of America
6565 Sunset Blvd., #306
Los Angeles, CA 90028
(818) 777-4021

GILDA STRATTON
Warner Bros. TV
4000 Warner Blvd.
North Administration-Rm. 18
Burbank, CA 91522
(818) 954-2843

MONICA SWANN
5300 Melrose Ave., #309E
Los Angeles, CA 90038
(213) 856-1702

ROBERT J. ULRICH
Universal Studios
100 Universal City Plaza
Bungalow 466
Universal City, CA 91608
(818) 777-7802

KAREN VICE
MTM/CBS
4024 Radford Evergreen Bldg., #304
Studio City, CA 91604

JOSE VILLAVERDE
c/o Casting Society of America
6565 Sunset Blvd., #306
Los Angeles, CA 90028

APRIL WEBSTER
c/o Casting Society of America
6565 Sunset Blvd., #306
Los Angeles, CA 90028
(818) 954-2321
ROSEMARY WELDEN

c/o Casting Society of America
6565 Sunset Blvd., #306
Los Angeles, CA 90028

GERI WINDSOR & ASSOCIATES
4500 Forman Ave., #1
Toluca Lake, CA 91602
(818) 509-9993

RONNIE YESKEL
10201 W. Pico Blvd. Apts., #6
Los Angeles, CA 90035
(213) 203-2662

DIANE YOUNG
5700 Wilshire Blvd., 5th fl.
Los Angeles, CA 90036
(213) 965-5986

GARY M. ZUCKERBROD
c/o Casting Society of America
6565 Sunset Blvd., #306
Los Angeles, CA 90028

CHICAGO CASTING DIRECTORS

Chicago theaters and commercial production houses are less dependent on casting directors than are their counterparts in New York and L.A., but they are always used in film work.

JANE ALDERMAN CASTING
190 N. State, 7th fl.
Chicago, IL 60601
(312) 899-4250

ALERT CASTING
Roseanne Krevitt, Director
Box 11115
Chicago, IL 60611

JANE BRODY CASTING
20 W. Hubbard
Chicago, IL 60610
(312) 527-0665

CASTING EYE CHICAGO
405 N. Wabash, Suite 3709
Chicago, IL 60611
(312) 661-1128

GEDDES AGENCY
1925 N. Clybourn St., Suite 402
Chicago, IL 60612
(312) 348-333

HEITZ CASTING SERVICES
920 N. Franklin, Suite 205
Chicago, IL 60610
(312) 664-0601

HOLZER, ROCHE & RIDGE CASTING
700 S. Des Plaines
Chicago, IL 60607
(312) 922-9860

KNUTSEN-SATTERLEE CASTING
919 N. Michigan Ave., Suite 3011
Chicago, IL 60611
(312) 649-1167

KORDOS & CHARBONNEAU
430 Hibbard
Wilmette, IL 60091
(708) 251-2072

K.T.'S (Kate Mattson)
Box 4958
Chicago, IL 60680
(312) 525-1126

CHERIE MANN & ASSOCIATES
1540 N. LaSalle, Suite 1004
Chicago, IL 60610
(312) 751-2927

BETH RABEDEAU CASTING
225 W. Ohio, Suite 400
Chicago, IL 60610
(312) 222-0181

SOOZAN TODD CASTING
Box 8197
Chicago, IL 60614
(312) 975-5015

CAROL VERBLEN CASTING
2408 N. Burling
Chicago, IL 60614
(312) 348-0047

NORMAN SCHUCART ENTERPRISES
1417 Green Bay Rd.
Highland Park, IL 60035
(708) 433-1113

JEFFREY LYLE SEGAL
805 W. Randolph St., 2nd fl.
Chicago, IL 60607
(312) 348-4993/421-7550

PERSONAL MANAGERS

BY FRANK MEYER

Quick, name 10 personal managers.

Unless you're a show business veteran or have been actively seeking a manager, odds are you couldn't come up with even five names. And, if you're like most actors, you're not even sure managers are relevant for you.

But let's ask the relevant question: Does an actor need a personal manager?

Long-time personal manager Kevin Hunter, active in Los Angeles, says, "The average Broadway performer doesn't need a personal manager because there aren't that many parts and everyone knows what's available. Agents cover that very well.

"Unless the person has ambitions in all media, and is viable in those, I don't know why they'd need a personal manager. The only value of a manager to an actor would be to work with the agency in finding parts outside the norm."

Charisse Dicks of New York-based Podesoir International Management disagrees. "I feel actors need a personal manager because it makes everything more focused. A manager is different... an agent...is strictly a booking agent whereas a manager is cook and chief. When no one believes in you, we're there.

"We make sure agents are doing their job. We work on long-term goals whether you just want to be an actor, if you want to branch into the music industry, or maybe want help putting a cabaret act together. I feel personal managers are everything to an actor."

Some actors have never considered a personal manager, some have tried to find one and failed, others never thought a manager would bother, still others have worked with a manager—or more than one—and either stopped, fired the person, or kept looking for the right one.

IF THE SITUATION FITS

If you can think of a situation with managers, you can probably find someone it fits.

For example, actress Christine Andreas, says, "I think if you're born with an innate sense of what's right for you, you have the ability to see the big picture in your life and say, this is where I'm going to start. If you have that kind of gift, then I guess you don't need a manager. I haven't cultivated that and it would help very much to have a manager to give me that perspective. An agent sometimes does that, it depends on your relationship with the agent."

New York actor Jonathan Hadary says he hasn't had a manager, adding, "I don't know if I believe in them or not...I once went to see one, just sort of showed up. I was working at the time and he was extremely nice to me—a major manager here in New York—and he said his rule of thumb was, if you're an actor, you don't need one and you should go to California. If you do other things in addition, or are interested in them, whether it be writing or directing or whatever, a manager can be helpful."

Performer Brian Mitchell once had a manager, but he says, "I don't any more because they didn't do anything for me that I couldn't do for myself. I have a real good business sense and a real good sense of where I want my career to go and found I had a better sense of that than a lot of the people I was working with.

"Because it took so much energy for me letting them know what was going on, I thought, why do I pay people to do this? I felt I can do this myself, I can orchestrate a publicist and all the other people.

"I've had three personal managers, they didn't do anything for me but take my money. When you add their 15 percent to your agent's fee, that's 25 percent out of your paycheck. Then Uncle Sam takes his and you're left with about 25 or 30 percent."

A DEFINITION

Joseph Rapp, executive director of the Conference of Personal Managers East, manages, among others, Nipsey Russell and other comedians and composers. He maintains that "a performer has to understand what a personal manager is. What can they do for a career—in the beginning, middle, or star stage? A good personal manager grooms, guides, befriends, and at all times is supposed to break through the frustrations and barriers a performer encounters. The manager is the one who believes in and keeps fighting for his or her client when others give up. A manager has to have broad experience with the many changes occuring in the many facets of the industry."

Rapp insists a personal manager should be an entertainment expert: "Actors today only know the normal areas of the business. It's theater, television, film, but the cable industry is opening wide for actors, so the manager has to have an updated knowledge to benefit the artist."

And as for agents, Rapp sees that they are very necessary, "but an agent is an employment agency. There are exceptions, there are a few agents who do try to help the creative aspect of an artist."

One of the exceptions is Marje Fields, head of the Marje Fields Agency and president of the National Association of Talent Representatives (NATR). She agrees that a manager can play an important part in an actor's career: "If a performer is multi-faceted, is a very busy person in many different areas, a manager serves a useful purpose." But, she continues, if you're not an overextended Barbara Streisand or Bernadette Peters—and "if you choose wisely"—an agent may well be all you need. "Good agents groom and help their performers get jobs and handle themselves correctly. A very good agent can work with you...and take the place of a good manager."

Still, according to Rapp, "It's the manager who breaks down doors to try to get the better agents and better casting directors to see his client. The manager has the knowledge that helps the client prepare for auditions and gets them to meet the better people. This helps an artist to grow. When they're starting, they can't get into an agent's door." But would a top personal manager want to see an unknown? "You can get very good managers. Managers become big because their clients become big."

Dicks says Podesoir will talk to someone who walks in off the street and says, "I want to be an actor."

"Usually someone calls my office and I'll ask them if they have any kind of acting experience or if they're unionized. We work with non-union as well as union actors. They send me a headshot or a snapshot and a resume. If I feel there's any interest, I'll have them write a letter about why they want to be an actor so I can get some type of feel as to whether they're really serious. If I'm interested, I'll meet with my associates. We'll have the person come in and have a conversation about their aspirations, their future goals, what actually it is they want to do. Then we'll tell them about some acting schools, photographers.

"We'll tell them about the business, what the difference is between an agent and a manager, the difference between a casting director and an industrial producer.

"I don't make promises. I tell them what I have done and what connections I have—show them headshots and resumes of actors I work with and tell them what we've done with them, how long we've represented them...a whole history and background."

They give them names of acting or dance schools, depending on the performer's age and experience. "We tell them the type of pictures needed and try to recommend the best photographers. I wouldn't want anyone to leave my office not knowing anything about this industry."

Rapp agrees a performer needs to find someone he can trust. "And someone who knows the business...if you find a good agent who believes in you, that's a plus for your career. If you find a good manager who knows the ins and outs of the business, that can work with agents, they can only help."

Working with a comic or a singer, a manager has the potential for a fairly quick return if he moves him in the right direction. With an actor whose goal is Broadway, the manager may be looking four or five years down the road before he can turn that into decent money.

"That's correct," Rapp says, "but a manager, if he believes in that talent, is going to gamble in building that client for that area. A person who only wants Broadway is still going to want the commercials market, is going to work in other facets of the entertainment business to make a living. They're not going to just wait on tables for five years until they get a Broadway show.

"There are many good managers around that will go out and look for talent knowing it could be a year before they even see a return on their investment. Their investment is sending out photographs, having messengers go to casting directors, agents, setting up appointments, making phone calls.

"There are a lot of managers that love the theater, that don't want to be a part of the variety end of the business. They invest time, money and energy in building these clients."

SELECTING A MANAGER

Outside of going to a reputable source like the Conference of Personal Managers, how does the neophyte performer find out whether this manager's good?

Rapp believes that "it's almost impossible. The best way is word of mouth, check with people, ask questions. For an artist to go to a manager shouldn't cost the artist a nickel."

Rapp says, "The standard fee is 15 percent, but 15 percent of nothing is nothing. An artist might pay 10 percent to an agent, 15 percent to a manager.

"If no one's making any money, no one's making a commission. A manager knows, to justify his fee, he has to do a job, to try to open those doors to bring your income up to where you're not going to complain about the 15 percent."

What about the artist who says, I don't want to pay two commissions, why don't you book me?

"First, a manager is not a licensed booking agent, by law. Except, in New York State where a manager can obtain 'incidental' employment for signed exclusive artists. But that doesn't mean that you go out become a booking agency.

"The best relationship is where a manager can build a client that can be placed with good agents and have a working situation of agent, manager, and artist all working to help the artist."

The Conference of Personal Managers tries to make sure the organization stays clean by policing its members and being tough on people who want to join.

"Just because you're a manager we don't just take you. We might turn down 70 percent of those who apply. To join, your main source of income has to be personal management. You have to be a personal manager for at least one year or have an extensive knowledge of the business.

"We also check references...The main point of our organization is ethics. Not your success ratio, but are you an ethical manager...a smart manager wants to deal with as many agents as needed to cover every area, because no person can cover every area properly for the artist.

"You want to have as many good people as you can putting things together, that's why you'll hire a good p.r. company, a good choreographer. You try to get the best to make the artist look good.

"Within our organization, we network, we pass on knowledge, mistakes as well as successes. Our seminars are done that way, and through that the managers can help their clients."

MAKING A SWITCH

Broadway performer and recording star Rex Smith noted, "I had one manager when I started in rock 'n' roll, which is different from being an actor with a manager. There are certain things a manager can give me that are useful. I look at them just like they look at an artist now—when you take away all the car lot flags and free balloons, you get down to what each of you can do for the other."

Smith wants various things from a manager. "Entry into a more powerful agency or recording company. It depends on their forte and what you want. Maybe it's worthwhile to go into a relationship with a manager who has entree into the level of people and connections you want.

"An agent's responsibility is limited. Their job is to procure work, but they're overloaded. A manager can give you a little more specific attention and an overall look at the longevity of a career.

"It's hard for the artist in the middle of her work and to see past that even to the next job. Sometimes I think a good manager is able to sort of keep her head above water and help you with the decision making.

"They're paid to advise and consent—with me it's always been a three-way phone call with the manager and the agent, everyone gives advice and counsel, then the artist has the last word. It's like having a big brother that's been through it. They're experienced in watching the mistakes other artists made. Perhaps they can help you."

MEMBERS OF NCOPM

The National Conference of Personal Managers is headed up by Gerard W. Purcell, President, 210 E. 51st St., 2nd fl., New York, NY 10022; (212) 421-2670. The following managers are members of the National Conference of Personal Managers. The name of the company is listed first, followed by the owner/manager's name if it's not readily apparent from the company's name. Associate members are listed below the phone number. The numbers below each listing indicate the different fields of entertainment in which a member is engaged. The following list of seven personal management categories serves as a guideline (in some cases, a specific explanation can be found next to a number): (l) actors/actresses; (2) directors, producers, and/or writers; (3) children and/or teenagers; (4) newscasters and/or sports personalities; (5) variety and/or comedy acts; (6) musicians: performers, composers, recording artists, and/or concert, lounge, and/or rock & roll acts; (7) miscellaneous: anything not mentioned above (artists, photographers, and so on).

EAST COAST CHAPTER

The East Coast chapter of the Conference of Personal Managers is headed up by Joseph Rapp, executive director, 1650 Broadway, New York, NY 10019; (212) 265-3366.

ROGER AILES COMMUNICATIONS
440 Park Ave. South
New York, NY 10016
(212) 685-8400
(Judy Laterza)
(1,2,4,5,6)

ADRIENNE ALBERT
Fox-Albert Management Ent.
1697 Broadway, Suite 1210
New York, NY 10019
(212) 581-1011
(Jean T. Fox)
(1,3)

R.J. ALFREDO TALENT MGMT.
320 E. 73rd St.
New York, NY 10021
(212) 628-7683
(1)

MARK HALL AMITIN
World of Culture, Ltd.
463 West St., Suite 509
New York, NY 10014
(212) 243-0292
(1,2,3,5)

DEE ANTHONY
Jemava Inc.
c/o PNFW & Company
1775 Broadway, 7th Fl.
New York, NY 10019
(212) 410-7200
(6,7)

JAMES ARNOLD
Fine Arts Building
410 S. Michigan Ave.
Chicago, IL 60605
(312) 427-2858
(6)

BUD AYERS
Fastbreak Management
70 Clay Hill Rd.
Stamford, CT 06905
(203) 329-7335
(1,5,6)

TINO BARZIE
Tin-Bar Amusement Corp.
11 W. 69th St., Suite 2B
New York, NY 10023
(212) 586-1015
(2,5,6,7)

HARVEY BELLOVIN
410 E. 64th St.
New York, NY 10021
(212) 752-5181
(1,2,6)

VIC BERI
Management VII
1811 N.E. 53rd St.
Ft. Lauderdale, FL. 33308
(305) 776-1004
(1,5,6)

JOANNE BERKMAN
Bennu Talent Management
165 Madison Ave.
New York, NY 10016
(212) 213-8511
(Ron Uva)
(1,6)

BOBBY BERNARD
40 Central Park South
New York, NY 10019
(212) 753-9843
(2,5,6)

CLINTON FORD BILLUPS JR.
101 River Rd., Collinsville, CT 06022
(203) 693-1637
(Wanda T. Rodgers)
(5)

PHIL BOUGHTON
244 W. 54th St., Suite 800
New York, NY 10019
(212) 864-7397
(2)

NYLE BRENNER
20 W. 64th St.
New York, NY 10023
(212) 362-2735
(1,2)

LEONA BUDILOVSKY
2 S. 635 Ave. Vendom
Oak Brook, IL 60521
(312) 963-2611
(1,6)

DREW BURKE
Madison Avenue Management
248 E. 90th St., Suite 1C
New York, NY 10128
(212) 410-1650
(1,3,4)

MICHAEL J. BURRIS
3922 Edidin Dr.
Jacksonville, FL 32202
(904) 745-1739
(6)

ANTONIO CAMACHO
Top Draw Entertainment
108-22 Queens Blvd., Suite 177
Forest Hills, NY 11375
(718) 896-4001
(5)

DAVID CAMPBELL
Campbell Martin Associates
1457 Broadway, Suite 1011
New York, NY 10036
(212)840-4504
(1,2)

JOYCE CHASE
2 Fifth Ave., New York, NY 10011
(212) 645-0858
(1,2)

KEVIN COBB
ESS Management
95 Horatio St., Suite 6W
New York, NY 10014-1520
(212) 645-0858
(1,4,6)

RON COMENZO
320 W. 37th St., 4th fl.
New York, NY 10018
(212) 279-5198
(1)

THOMAS CURRIE
215 E. 29th St., Suite 4
(212) 532-1476
(1,2:directors)

K. CHARISSE DICKS
Podesoir International Management
211 W. 56th St., Suite 4J
New York, NY 10019
(212) 767-0520
(Reginald A. Murray)
(1,3,5,6)

MICHELE DONAY TALENT MGMT.
236 E. 74th St.
New York, NY 10021
(212) 744-9406
(1,3)

JOHN ESSAY
Box 755
Times Square Station
New York NY 10036
(212) 581-0396
(1)

JOEL A. FELTMAN
Think Tank Talent
225 E. 79th St., Suite 5D
New York, NY 10021
(212) 570-9424/(914) 237-7926
(Grace White)
(1,4)

JONATHAN M. FIRST
1370 Avenue of the Americas, 15th fl.
New York, NY 10019
(212) 581-1122
(Marilyn Zitmer)
(1,3,6)

VICTORIA FRANKMANO
250 W. 57th St., Suite 1632
New York, NY 10107
(212) 586-1573
(1,3)

ESTELLE FUSCO
Discovery Talent Management
72 Moriches Rd.
Lake Grove, NY 11755
(212) 877-6670/(516) 467-7574
(1,3)

TOBE GIBSON
Young Talent
301 E. 62nd St., Suite 2C
New York, NY 10021
(212) 308-0930
(1,3,6)

VERNA GILLIS
Soundscape
799 Greenwich St.
New York, NY 10014
(212) 242-3374
(1,6)

AGGIE GOLD
Fresh Faces Management
2911 Carnation Ave.
Baldwin, NY 11510
(516) 223-0034
(1,6:ethnic)

SID GOLD
Goldstar Talent Management
246 Fifth Ave., Suite 202
New York, NY 10001
(212) 213-1707
(Steven M. Gold)
(3,infants)

DICK GRASS
GMS Management
585 Ellsworth St., Suite 2G
Bridgeport, CT 06605
(203) 334-9285
(Danny Scarpone)
(2,5,6,7)

LLOYD GREENFIELD
3 Sussex Ave.
Massapequa, NY 11578
(516) 798-4409
(5,6)

SETH R. GREENKY
Green Key Management
251 W. 89th St., Suite 4A
New York, NY 10024
(212) 874-7373
(1,2,5,6,7)

CAROLINE HIRSCH
Media and Management
19 Fulton St., Suite 401
New York, NY 10039
(212) 393-9400
(Joe Falzarano)
(2,6)

MARC HOFFMAN
119 Langham St., Brooklyn, NY 11235
(718) 332-7147
(1,6)

VAL IRVING
Shandeila Associates
30 Park Ave.
New York, NY 10016
(212) 685-5496
(5,6)

JOHN N. JENNINGS
881 Tenth Ave., Suite 1A
New York, NY 10019
(212) 581-0377/(201) 224-5974
(1,3,5,6)

CATHY KANNER MANAGEMENT
143 W. 81st St., Suite 1
New York, NY 10024
(212) 496-8175
(1)

LAURIE KANNER
Kanner Talent Management
200 Central Park South
New York, NY 10019
(212) 397-3766
(1)

CARROLL L. KNOWLES
220 E. 63rd St.
New York, NY 10021
(212) 866-5877
(1)

LLOYD KOLMER ENTERPRISES
65 W. 55th St.
New York, NY 10019
(212) 582-4735
(1)

JENNIFER LAMBERT
1600 Broadway, Suite 1001
New York, NY 10019
(212) 315-0665/315-0754
(1,3,5,6)

DICK LEE
King's Highway
Bellmawr, NJ 08030
(609) 931-4802
(1,4,6)

ABBIE LEVITON
Leviton Management
159 Madison Ave.
New York, NY 10016
(212) 213-0151
(1,4,6)

JOSEPH LODATO
264 W. 35th St., Suite 1003
New York, NY 10001
(212) 967-3320
(5,6:record producers)

RICK MARTIN PRODUCTIONS
125 Fieldpoint Rd.
Greenwich, CT 06830
(203) 661-1615
(1,5,6:record producers)

LUIS MEDINA
380 Broad Ave.
Leonia, NJ 07605
(201) 947-1800
(1)

SANDI MERLE
101 W. 57th St.
New York, NY 10019
(212) 489-1578
(4,5,6)

BURT MILLER ASSOCIATES
308 Fern St.
West Hartford, CT 06119
(203) 236-1983
(6)

DAVID MILLER
Miller-Silver Management
27 W. 20th St., Suite 302
New York, NY 10011
(212) 243-0024
(Lucy Silver)
(3)

J. MITCHELL MANAGEMENT
161 Ave. of Americas, 14th fl.
New York, NY 10013
(212) 929-4600
(1,3)

FRED J. MONTILLA, JR.
F.J.M. Productions
7305 W. Sample Rd., Suite 101
Coral Springs, FL 33063
(305) 753-8591
(6)

BARBARA MOORE
Moore Entertainment Group
Possum Trail
Upper Saddle River, NJ 07458
(201) 327-3698
(1,2,3,6)

WILL MOTT
481 W. 22nd St., Suite 2
New York, NY 10011
(212) 924-1444
(1)

ARLINE McGOVERN
McGovern/Goodwin
Theatrical Management
9 Layton Ave.
Hicksville, NY 11801
(212) 860-7400; (516) 681-2723
(Lois Goodwin)
(1,3)

DOREEN NAKAMURA
Dee-Mura Enterprises
269 West Shore Dr.
Massapequa, NY 11758
(516) 795-1616
(2,5,6)

ROSELLA OLSON MANAGEMENT
319 W. 105th St., Suite 1F
New York, NY 10025
(1,5,6)

CATHY PARKER MANAGEMENT
Box 716
Voorhees, Twp., NJ 08043
(609) 354-2020
(1,3)

MARIE PASTOR
Morning Star Management
I-B Quaker Ridge Rd., #434
New Rochelle, NY 10804
41(914) 636-8928
(1,2,6:writers)

MARVIN PEARL
21st Century Management
1700 Broadway, Suite 1001
New York, NY 10019
(212) 977-9236
(1)

FRED F. PHILLIPS
912 Park Manor Dr.
Orlando, FL 32825
(407) 277-3753
(1,3)

GERARD W. PURCELL ASSOCIATES
210 E. 51st St.
New York, NY 10022
(212) 421-2670
(Faith Ball)
(2,5,6:TV, records)

VIC RAMOS MANAGEMENT
49 W. 9th St., #5B
New York, NY 10011
(212) 473-2610/673-9191
(1)

HOWARD RAPP
Charles Rapp Enterprises
1650 Broadway, Suite 609
New York, NY 10019
(212) 247-6646
(1,2,4,5)

JOSEPH RAPP ENTERPRISES
1650 Broadway, Suite 705
New York, NY 10019
(212) 265-3366
(5,6:TV, records)

PATRICK REAVES
Reavestock Management
302 W. 79th St., Suite 3D
New York, NY 10024
(212) 580-1130
(1,2)

EDIE ROBB TALENT WORKS
301 W. 53rd St., Suite 4K
New York, NY 10019
(212) 245-3250/(215) 947-5361
(1,3)

PEGGY ADLER ROBOHM
Connections
45 Lawson Dr.
Madison, CT 06443
(203) 245-4448
(1,3)

JACK ROLLINS
130 W. 57th St.
New York, NY 10019
(212) 582-1940
(1,2,5,6:TV, film)

JAMES D. RONANIELLO
James Daniel Entertainment
1650 Broadway, Suite 201
New York, NY 10019
(212) 489-4950
(6)

JOAN M. ROSENBERG
Talent & Comedy Management
145 B. Allen Blvd.
Farmingdale, NY 11735
(718) 343-9530
(1,3,5)

SUSAN SCHACHTER
Suzelle Enterprises
271 Grand Central Pkwy., Penthouse C
Floral Park, NY 11005
(718) 423-1084
(1,3)

TED SCHMIDT & ASSOCIATES
2149 N.E. 63rd St.
Fort Lauderdale, FL 33308
(305) 771-7282/(212) 751-0200
(5,6)

EDIE F. SCHUR
176 E. 71st St., New York, NY 10021
(212) 734-5100
(1,2,3,4,7)

CHERYL SCOTT MANAGEMENT
25 Breezy Hill Rd., Collinsville, CT 06022
(203) 693-0891/8270
(6:rock)

MARY H. SEAMAN
SEA-MANagement
51 E. 42nd St., Rm. 1601
New York, NY 10017
(212) 697-9840
(1,3)

JACK SEGAL ENTERPRISES
10 Park Ave.
W. Orange, NJ 07052
(201) 731-8801
(5)

SID SEIDENBERG
1414 Ave. of the Americas
New York, NY 10019
(212) 421-2021
(6)

MARTIN SIEGEL
Scott Eden Creative Management
4 Vails Lane
Millwood, NY 10546
(914) 941-8684/(212) 953-1379
(1,3)

C. WINSTON SIMONE
No Name Management
1780 Broadway, Suite 1201
New York, NY 10019
(212) 974-5322
(5,6,7:record producers)

HELENE SOKOL
Cuzzins Management
250 W. 57th St., Suite 1632
New York, NY 10019
(212) 586-1573
(1,3)

CHRISTOPHER SPIERER
Christopher Group Prod.
1775 Broadway, 7th fl.
New York, NY 10019
(212) 601-1951
(1,6)

BURT STRATFORD
221 W. 57th St.
New York, NY 10019
(212) 757-2211
(1,2,5)

LARRY TUNNY ENTERPRISES
30 Lincoln Plaza
New York, NY 10023
(212) 582-2023
(6)

SHARLENE TURNEY
484 W. 43rd St., Suite 115
New York, NY 10036
(212) 564-3536
(1,3)

FRANK E. UNDERWOOD, SR.
1547 Westover Ave.
Petersburg, VA 23805
(804) 861-5691
(1)

SALVATORE VASI
114 Lexington Ave.
New York, NY 10016
(212) 532-6843
(1,5,6)

BARTON G. WEISS MANAGEMENT
39 W. 19th St., 3rd Fl.
New York, NY 10011
(212) 807-7625
(1,5,6)

TERRY WHATLEY
315 E. 57th St., New York, NY 10022
(212) 308-9682
(1,2)

FRANK M. ZAZZA
Zazza Talent Management
Astoria Studios
34-12 36th St.
Astoria, NY 11106
(718) 729-9288
(1,2)

WEST COAST CHAPTER

The West Coast chapter of the Conference of Personal Managers is headed up by Stanley Evans, executive director, 10707 Camarillo St., Suite 308, North Hollywood, CA 91602; (818) 762-NCPM.

FRANK CAMPANA
28035 Dorothy Dr., Suite 210
Agoura Hills, CA 91301
(818) 879-0733/0334
(1,2,5,6)

PAUL CANTOR ENTERPRISES
14332 Dickens St., Suite 1
Sherman Oaks, CA 91423
(818) 907-5224
(6)

BULLETS DURGOM
c/o Manor Care 74-350
Country Club Dr.
Palm Desert, CA 92260
(619) 341-0261
(1,5)

HILLARD ELKINS ENTERTAINMENT
8306 Wilshire Blvd., Suite 438
Beverly Hills, CA 90211
(213) 650-8306
(1,2,4,5,6,7)

STANLEY EVANS
Evans Management
10707 Camarillo St., Suite 308
North Hollywood, CA 91602
(818) 766-0114
(1,2,4,5,6)

THEODORE GEKIS
Gekis Management
6671 Sunset Blvd.
Bldg. 1585, Rm. 106
Los Angeles, CA 90028
(213) 466-9966
(1,3)

MICHAEL GLYNN
Mixed Media
4116 Warner Blvd., Suite B
Burbank, CA 91505
(818) 846-2111
(1,5,7)

SEYMOUR HELLER & ASSOCIATES
7060 Hollywood Blvd., Suite 818
Hollywood, CA 90028
(213) 462-7151
(1,2,5,6)

HOWARD HINDERSTEIN PRODUCTIONS
c/o Mark Goodson
5750 Wilshire Blvd., Suite 47
Hollywood, CA 90036
(213) 965-6500
(1,2,3,5)

RICHARD O. LINKE, PERSONAL MGMT.
4445 Cartwright Ave., #305
North Hollywood, CA 91602
(213) 760-4988; (213) 760-2500
(1,5)

SANDRA LORD
Creative Management Network
Box 3225
Hollywood, CA 90078
(213) 275-9898/550-8982
(1,2,3,5,6)

JEFFREY C. LOSEFF
4521 Colfax Ave., Suite 205
North Hollywood, CA 91602
(818) 505-9468

DAVID MARTIN
4370 Tujunga Ave., Suite 150
Studio City, CA 91604
(818) 980-8600
(1,2,4,5,6)

STEPHEN METZ
Rapp-Metz Entertainment
8383 Wilshire Blvd.
Beverly Hills, CA 90211
(213) 655-4036
(1,4,6)

STAN MORESS ORGANIZATION
12424 Wilshire Blvd., Suite 840
Los Angeles, CA 90024
(213) 450-9797
(5,6)

KATHY McCOMB
3666 Barham Blvd., #N307
Oakwood Apartments
Los Angeles, CA 90068
(213) 878-6528
(1,3)

MICHAEL RIBEIRO
Ribeiro Productions
19122 Halsted St.
North Ridge, CA 91324
(818) 349-0334
(1)

BUD ROBINSON PRODUCTIONS
1100 N. Alta Loma Rd., #707
Los Angeles, CA 90069
(213) 652-3242
(1,2,5,6)

JEFF ROSS
4470 Ventura Canyon Ave.
Sherman Oaks, CA 91423
(818) 788-6841
(1,2,5)

JOE SCANDORE
12411 Magnolia Blvd., Suite 311
North Hollywood, CA 91607
(818) 505-8588
(5)

EARL SHANK
520 N. Kings Rd.
West Hollywood, CA 90048
(213) 651-5241
(1,5)

FONDA ST. PAUL MANAGEMENT
3811 Multiview Dr.
Los Angeles, CA 90068
(213) 876-6161
(1)

MIMI WEBER MANAGEMENT
9738 Arby Dr.
Beverly Hills, CA 90210
(213) 278-8440, (818) 954-1736
(1,7:production)

MARCIA WEISSMAN
C.A.NY Management
5750 Wilshire Blvd., Suite 565
Los Angeles, CA 90036
(213) 933-9215

48A

AUDITIONING FOR COMMERCIALS

BY RORRI FEINSTEIN

Acting in commercials can be a very lucrative business. In 1987, according to statistics provided by the Screen Actors Guild, actors across the country earned almost $350 million performing in TV commercials. The question becomes: How can you have your earnings included in that statistic?

Although every commercial spot is different; on the average, 40-50 actors per character are auditioned for on-camera work. This figure is not set in stone. There are some commercials where the client sees every model in the New York area and some where only five actors are seen. So the odds of getting a commercial once you've got the audition are not bad, considering what the odds are of getting a role from an Equity principal audition or an open call.

AUDITION TIPS

The majority of SAG/AFTRA commercial casting is done through agents' submissions to agency or independent casting directors. The casting director videotapes the preliminary auditions and the tape is then reviewed by the production company, the agency creative team (producer, copy writer, art director), and the client. These three parties decide on who gets called back and who gets cast.

When you get a call for a commercial audition, ask your agent for as much information as possible about the character, the product, and what you should wear. Casting people provide this information because they want you to do well. They are on your side! They want to put together the best audition tape possible. The better you look, the better they look to their clients.

Commercial directors are impressed with actors who make an extra effort to dress the part they are up for. If you are reading for a pharmacist, wear a white jacket; if you'll be playing a yuppie, think Brooks Brothers. In general, keep your wardrobe choices simple. Pale to medium shades are best. Try to avoid red, black, and white (except for uniforms), because these colors pose problems to the video camera. Actresses should keep their makeup light, fresh and natural looking.

Arrive at your audition with your picture and resume stapled together, and with enough time to look over the storyboard and the copy. Use your time in the waiting room productively. Don't give a cold reading—give a performance. This is a business and should be treated as such. Casting people like to see performers who are prepared, who know how to ask the right questions, and who can take direction.

Your audition begins the moment you walk through the door, not when you read the first line from the cue card. Project a positive, professional image. If you are late, don't make a big deal of it. Find out from the receptionist if it has upset the schedule; if not, don't mention it.

At some auditions actors aren't given scripts. Some directors like completely spontaneous auditions. They feel that performers do their best and funniest commercial work when they are just being themselves, when they don't try to act, but just enjoy the process and have fun at the audition. Often the copy hasn't been finalized and the original storyboard can be shaped and enriched by the performers who are auditioning.

So how does one have fun at auditions? By approaching every commercial you read for in an original way. Take a sympathetic point of view, and try to be natural and believable. You don't have to go for a hard sell. Instead, be creative; try to establish your character with a single word or gesture. Although it's easier said than done, take the pressure off yourself. Don't think about who you are competing with or whether or not you'll be called back. If you are right for the role, you'll get it. Your job is simply to give a good audition, do the best work possible, and then leave. Casting decisions in commercials are made too whimsically for actors to be concerned with whether they will be chosen. You have to be satisfied with your performance. The casting director determines who gets to audition and be seen on the audition tape, that is all. Rarely does a casting director make the final casting decision. Often it is not the actor who gave the best performance who books the spot anyway. That is because looks are a major consideration, and everyone has a different idea of what kind of mommy, daddy, executive, or grandma the spot calls for. You can give a great reading and the casting director and the director may love you. But you still won't book the spot if the client wants someone else.

ACTING COURSES AND COMMERCIAL TECHNIQUES

If you are new to the commercial world, it probably would be beneficial to take a commercial acting course. What you learn will help you feel comfortable on camera, and you'll get a chance to build a technique that will prepare you for most audition situations. Being familiar with the process can help boost your self-confidence. There are technical things you need to know, such as how to hit a mark, read from a cue card, and hold a product.

There are schools that specialize in helping actors prepare for working in commercials. At these schools actors have the opportunity to work with copy and be videotaped in a professional studio that simulates the audition experience.

Before you sign up for a course in a school, you should audit a few. A good school should have professional quality video equipment and should employ instructors who are professionals in the business (casting directors, commercial actors, directors). Classes must be small so that each student receives personal attention and gets to work in every session.

Some of the staff from a few of the New York commercial schools offered advice on acting in commercials. Ruth Lehner of Lehner/Stephens Studio stresses the importance of being yourself in front of the camera. She notes that a commercial is a one-to-one situation and that you have to make the copy believable and show that you care about the product. In addition to working on technique, Lehner also deals with the business side of commercials. In these classes, the SAG/AFTRA standard contract is explained, so that performers are knowledgeable enough to talk to their agents rather than just to listen to them.

Ed Ferron of the Weist-Barron School of TV Acting stresses the art of communication in his classes and encourages his students to think of sharing information rather than selling. In this way you really can find the "commercials" in your own life. For example, when you tell a friend about a movie you really liked, or about a new restaurant, you employ the same techniques you use in a commercial—you like a product (movie or restaurant), and you want others to use the product.

Teacher Ruth Nerken compares performing for the camera to talking on the telephone. She notes that we are all very comfortable talking to our friends and business associates on the telephone, but we are in fact talking into a mechanical device. She invites actors to find the essence of each advertising spot and make acting choices that illustrate the point at hand. If the commercial is for a time-saving product, she suggests that you present yourself as a brisk businesslike character. If you are advertising perfume, you should present a softer, more sensual image. Above all, says Nerken, project a winning attitude, and at every audition, bring in something that makes you special.

Bob Collier of Bob Collier TV Success Seminars, teaches his students that the secret to success is a positive mental attitude. In his classes a lot of work is done to achieve that goal, including the use of creative visualization and daily affirmations. Students are given a Polaroid of themselves doing a commercial (in the classroom), which is taken from the monitor screen. This helps students see themselves literally and in their minds' eyes to see themselves as working commercial actors.

Wendy Dillon, who teaches at the Collier Casting Centers advises actors to approach the business with the idea that people like you and want you to do well. Because actors are rejected so often, they often expect failure rather than success. Dillon emphasizes the importance of networking and talking about what you are doing in your career with people who have similar goals. She stresses that it is helpful both personally and professionally to exchange information with friends and to look for opportunities for your friends as well as for yourself.

ON THE SET

When you are cast in a commercial, you will have to deal with an entire set of unfamiliar production elements. Camera, sound, lighting, props, and other technical elements have to be perfect, so you may be asked to do take after take even though your reading is just fine.

Because there are so many chiefs on a commercial set, you may get directional input from all sides. This can be a problem. The only person you should take direction from is the director. So nod politely to the client, the agency and production people, and try to tune them out. Your object is to maintain a good relationship with your employers while fulfilling your responsibilities to the director.

SOME CLOSING THOUGHTS

It has often been said that one should never read the reviews of a show while performing in it, because if you believe the good ones you have to believe the bad ones, too. The point here is to trust your own evaluation of your work. What is important is that you feel you have done a good job in an audition or on a shoot, because they may not use your best take, or you may not get the job where you gave a terrific reading. On the other hand, you could book a national spot on an off day.

AD AGENCY
CASTING DIRECTORS

Listed below are only those advertising agencies in New York, Los Angeles, and Chicago that have their own casting departments. Obviously, there are many other advertising agencies, but they either cast through agents or production houses.

NEW YORK

AC & R ADVERTISING
16 E. 32nd St.,
New York, NY 10016
(212) 685-2500
Claire Ward, prod'r.

ALLY & GARGANO
805 Third Ave..
New York, NY 10022
(212) 688-5300
Rhoda M. Karp, casting dir.

N W AYER
Worldwide Plaza
825 Eighth Ave.
New York, NY 10019-7498
(212) 474-5000
Sally Howes Kandle, senior VP/dir. of casting;
Renee Howley, assoc. dir. of casting;
Janet Eisenberg, Emily Elliot, casting dirs.

BACKER SPIELVOGEL BATES
405 Lexington Ave.
New York, NY 10174
(212) 297-7000
Roger Sturtevant, casting dir.

CALET, HIRSCH & SPECTOR
250 Park Ave. South
New York, NY 10003
(212) 777-0666
Margaux Ravis, ass't prod'r.

CAMPBELL-MITHUN-ESTY
405 Lexington Ave., 6th fl.
New York, NY 10174
(212) 856-4500
Janine Minunno, casting dir.

D'ARCY MASIUS BENTON & BOWLES, INC.
1675 Broadway
New York, NY 10019
(212) 468-3622
Linda Ferrara, mgr. of casting; Karen Goldberg, Shirley Sender-Touillon, casting dirs.;
Russ Militello, casting ass't.

GREY ADVERTISING
777 Third Ave.,
New York, NY 10017
(212) 546-2000
Jerry Saviola, VP; Madeline Molnar,
Michael O'Gara, Arista Baltronis,
Ted Sluberski, casting dirs.;
Eli Tray, casting ass't. (extras);
Barbara Bennett, David Cady, casting ass'ts.

HOLLAND & CALLAWAY
767 Third Ave.
New York, NY 10017
(212) 308-2750
Carol Parrino, broadcast mgr., casting;
Arthur Wright, prod'r./casting.

JORDAN, MCGRATH, CASE & TAYLOR
445 Park Ave.
New York, NY 10022
(212) 326-9100
Anita Guerrea, casting dir.

KETCHUM ADVERTISING
220 E. 42nd St.
New York, NY 10017
(212) 370-9600
Susan Cooney, Susan Rafter,
Don Faller Sr., Prod'rs.

LINTAS/NY
1 Dag Hammarskjold Plaza
New York, NY 10017
(212) 605-8290
Steve Schaefer, VP; Barbara Blomberg,
casting supv.; Susan Mattheiss, casting ass't.

LOWE & PARTNERS
1345 Ave. of the Americas
New York, NY 10105
(212) 708-8800
Sharry Sabin, casting dir.

McCANN-ERICKSON USA
750 Third Ave.
New York, NY 10017
(212) 697-6000
Dolores Messina, dir. of casting.

OGILVY & MATHER
309 W. 49th St.
New York, NY 10019
(212) 237-4000
Daisy Sinclair, casting mgr./senior VP;
Barbara Herzog, casting dir.;
J.B. Sutherland, print casting dir.;
Lorna Weiner, ass't.

ROSENFELD, SIROWITZ, HUMPHREY &
STRAUSS, INC.
111 Fifth Ave.
New York, NY 10003
(212) 505-0200
Judy Keller, casting dir.; Bill Perry, Ross Kron-
man, prod'rs.

SAATCHI & SAATCHI ADVERTISING
375 Hudson St.
New York, NY 10014
Tina Sperber, head of casting;
Kirsten Walther, Debi Gochman,
Lori Tesoro, ass'ts.

J. WALTER THOMPSON CO.
466 Lexington Ave.
New York, NY 10017
(212) 210-7000
Evangeline Hayes, casting dir.;
Catherine Cahill, ass't. casting dir.

YOUNG & RUBICAM
285 Madison Ave.
New York, NY 10017
(212) 210-3000
Barbara Badyna, senior VP/dir. of casting;
Ann Batchelder, Sybil Trent, casting dirs.;
Brenda Bareika, talent negotiator;
Sue Barnes, extras;
Lina Jefferson, ass't.

LOS ANGELES

CLUB BEVERLY HILLS
270 N. Canon Dr., #1110
Beverly Hills, CA 90210
(213) 655-6196
Robert and Rose Clements, casting division.

WILLIAM ERICSON AGENCY
1024 Mission St.
South Pasadena, CA 91030
(213) 461-4969/(818) 799-2404
William Ericson, owner/head of casting

FLYNN ADVERTISING
1440 Reeves St., #104
Los Angeles, CA 90035
(213) 203-9486
Elizabeth Flynn, owner/head of casting

HSR ASSOCIATES
7028 Owensmouth Ave., #103
Canoga Park, CA 91303
(818) 884-2945
Steve Goodman, pres.

NEWSOM & CO., INC.
3536 Ocean View Blvd., #250
Glendale, CA 91208
(818) 957-2062
Stephanie Newson, casting dir.

VINOKUR ADVERTISING
1801 Century Park East, #2000
Century City, CA 90067
(213) 203-0605
Dan Vinokur, casting dir.

CHICAGO

BAYER BESS VANDERWALKER
225 N. Michigan Ave.
Chicago, IL 60601
(312) 861-3800
Tony Vanderwalker, chrmn./creative dir.

BBDO CHICAGO
410 N. Michigan Ave.
Chicago, IL 60611
(312) 337-7860
Tom Cronin, Jan Collins, sr. prod'rs.

BENDER, BROWNING, DOLBY &
SANDERSON ADVERTISING
444 N. Michigan Ave.
Chicago, IL 60611
(312) 644-9600
Paulette Cary, broadcast. prodn. mgr.

BOZELL, INC.
625 N. Michigan Ave.
Chicago, IL 60611
(312) 988-2000
Jeanne Orawiec, broadcast prodn. coord.

LEO BURNETT COMPANY
35 W. Wacker Dr.
Chicago, IL 60601
(312) 220-5959
Bonnie Murray, casting dir.

BURRELL ADVERTISING, INC.
20 N. Michigan Ave.
Chicago, IL 60602
(312) 443-8600
Kim Nelson, casting dir.

CAMPBELL-MITHUN-ESTY
737 N. Michigan Ave.
Chicago, IL 60611
(312) 266-5100
Shirley Cross, creative services mgr.

VINCE CULLERS ADVERTISING, INC.
676 St. Clair, Chicago, IL 60611
(312) 649-7777
Terrence Morris, broadcast coord.

D'ARCY MASIUS BENTON & BOWLES
200 E. Randolph
Chicago, IL 60601
(312) 861-5000
Don Hockstein, mgr. TV prodn.

DDB NEEDHAM WORLDWIDE
303 E. Wacker Dr.
Chicago, IL 60601
(312) 861 0200
Peggy Walter, mgr. talent services

FOOTE, CONE & BELDING
101 E. Erie
Chicago, IL 60611
(312) 751-7000
Steve Keierleber, mgr. creative services

KETCHUM ADVERTISING/CHICAGO
111 N. Canal St., Suite 1150
Chicago, IL 60606
(312) 715-9200
Kevin Beauseigneur, casting dir.

OGILVY & MATHER
676 St. Clair
Chicago, IL 60611
(312) 988-2500
Ray Lyle, senior VP/group prodn. dir.

PROCTOR & GARDNER ADVERTISING
111 E. Wacker Dr.
Chicago, IL 60601
(312) 565-5400
Morgan Proctor, prod'r.

STERN WALTERS PARTNERS
NBC Tower
455 N. Cityfront Plaza Dr.
Chicago, IL 60611
(312) 642-4990
Melanie Kill, prodn. coord.

TATHAM - R.S.C.G.
980 N. Michigan Ave.
Chicago, IL 60611
(312) 337-4400
Lisa Andrews, prodn. coord.

J. WALTER THOMPSON/CHIGAGO
900 N. Michigan
Chicago, IL 60611
(312) 951-4000
Vicki Polfer, talent dept.

WELLS RICH GREENE BDDP, INC.
111 E. Wacker Dr.
Chicago, IL: 60601
(312) 938-0900
Bill Werme, VP/exec. art dir.

YOUNG & RUBICAM
1 S. Wacker Dr., Suite 1800
Chicago, IL 60606
(312) 845-4000
Enid Katz, senior VP/dir. broadcast
communications

ZECHMAN & ASSOCIATES
333 N. Michigan Ave., Suite 1305
Chicago, IL 60601
(312) 346-0551
Jan Zechman, pres./creative dir.

ZWIREN AYER
515 N. State St., Suite 2100
Chicago, IL 60610
(312) 644-2937
Robert Carney, exec. prod'r.

WORKING IN COMMERCIAL PRINT

BY MICHAEL SOMMERS

O pen any magazine and see those ads for cars, computers, and hotels. Look at those billboards that pitch beers and soaps and airlines. Observe the subway signs selling sodas and smokes and technical schools. What else do you see?

Performers. Just like you. Playing people just like you in hundreds, even thousands, of advertisements. Welcome to the world of commercial print.

"Commercial print is all about the way you look," says Scott Powers, an actor who has been so successful personally in the field that he runs workshops in New York on the subject.

"It's the same as TV commercials—but in still-life," explains Jeff Hardwick of the New York-based Gilla Roos, Ltd., talent agency. "It's a marketable look." And Sanford Leigh of Funnyface, who was one of the first New York agents to recognize the ad industry's need for print talent back in the 1960s, adds, "Commercial print especially requires performers who look like real people."

No statistics exist to show how many jobs are out there. But page through a few magazines and check for yourself on the number of different actors of all types who are making some extra money by nabbing commercial print work. Exclude the ultra-glamorous ads, which use fashion models, those gorgeous few who command extremely high fees for their unattainably beautiful looks. Actors who are able to do commercial print will usually receive a fee of $250 per hour, plus additional payments depending upon the subsequent use of the ad. If your face appears in a long-term ad campaign placed in major magazines, the negotiable results can be especially lucrative.

"I take a very pragmatic approach—commercial print is a good way to finance your acting career," Scott Powers remarks. Gary Beyer, an actor who types himself as "an upscale kind of guy," is now in his 11th year of steady commercial print work. His recent jobs include ads for Beefeater Gin, Hertz Rent-A-Car, and Just for Men hair coloring. Even with the current ad trend for the ultra-real-people-look working against Beyer's handsome features, his ability to manipulate his type keeps him in demand.

Just like television spots, commercial print jobs come out of the ad agencies, nearly all of which maintain files of photos and resumes, and some of which have their own casting directors just for print work. The calls go out through the grapevine of talent agencies: "Get me a Japanese CEO. Find me an adorable five-year-old girl with freckles, who dances. How are you fixed for upscale, elegant grandmas? I'm looking for a 30-something mustached blue-collar daddy-type."

TALKING TYPE

Type. That's the operative word for commercial print. Without dialogue, without gestures or expressions—except the one caught forever by the photographer—the type of person you are able to depict by looks alone will determine the sort of print jobs you can get. "There's work out there for people who look like they earn a good living," notes Sanford Leigh, adding that the 25-45 age bracket best corresponds with the consumers who are doing the most product-buying. Jeff Hardwick narrows the most lucrative age range to 30-40, with the proviso that family-types of all ages are always in demand. "The family lasts forever," he says.

Ethnic minorities stand a good chance of finding work in the field, asserts Hardwick. Some ads target specific groups of consumers, so the same billboard you see in Manhattan, which features a Caucasian couple, may well be duplicated with Hispanics for the Bronx and African-Americans for Newark. Other ads that feature groups of people often host a rainbow mix of ethnic types.

Whatever type you may be, the experts say, you better be attractive about it. "Everybody has to be appealing in print," Leigh observes. "You can't sell a product by being repulsive."

YOUR BEST TYPE

So what's your type? "Yourself at your best," Hardwick says. "Don't try to be someone you're not." Leigh agrees. "Be you at your best," he echoes. "This is not summer stock, where you have to play different people. In print, you get hired for what you are." The biggest common mistake that print wannabes make, they both say, is when the performer tries to look like too many different types.

Leigh says he sees all too many composite photo cards where the same actor poses as a doctor, a cowboy, a jock, and an executive. "That's Halloween stuff," Leigh groans. "The client should be interested in you—not your get-ups."

Look to the print ads themselves to determine your best type. "Go through the magazines," says Hardwick. "Concentrate on the ads in *People* and *Ladies Home Journal* and the Time-Life magazines," he advises. "Find a marketable image that you identify with and will be comfortable for you."

The next important step, says Leigh, is to create a life for your type. "If you don't like the word "type," call it your character, then," he chuckles. "But think of a day in the life of that person. What will he or she do from the time they get up till they go to bed?" In this manner, he says, you can present your particular type in different activities and garb, but still represent the same person.

SELLING YOUR SELF

Only when performers are secure in their type should they start shopping for photographers. Photography is the biggest expense of them all, and it might well be money thrown away if the performer pursues the wrong type or presents conflicting types.

Many agents and clients want to see both a headshot and a composite photo card of your type in several looks. "The headshot does not always tell what the client needs to know," Leigh believes. Actor Gary Beyer, however, often gets seen on the strength of just his headshot. "Get yourself a good 8x10, and make sure it's a smiling, honest face," Beyer advises. Honest? "Stay away from the airbrush," he explains. And ad agency Ogilvy & Mather print casting director J.B. Sutherland declares, "I can usually go by a headshot—if it's as true to that person as possible and shows me a specific look." The look is all-important, she observes, but there are other things that a wannabe print model should keep in mind.

Perhaps even more so than in theater, fine photography is essential to success in the world of commercial print. Once you decide your best and most marketable character type for print work—no easy decision—it's up to you and your photographer to create the optimum image that gets your body through the door of the ad agencies.

"The people out there are hiring your face," says Sean Kahlil, a photographer who has shot many print ad campaigns.

Everyone knows what a headshot is, of course, and technical aesthetics vary. Glamour headshots and tricky retouching usually backfire. "Your photo should be as close to natural as possible," warns print casting director Sutherland. "If you want to get rid of a mole or a beauty mark," cautions Funnyface agent Sanford Leigh, "you should get a surgeon, not a retoucher. When someone expects to see the same face as the photo, you better not surprise them."

Unless your physical coloring is especially striking—say, red hair and green eyes—most photographers think you should stick to black and white headshots rather than opt for more expensive color headshots.

Composite card photos—composites, for short—are a series of photos that show off your type in various looks. Done with different attire, props, and backgrounds, the composite represents a cross-section of your type or types. The danger here is when a performer tries to create too many different people on the same composite.

If you wish to project a blue-collar type, Leigh suggests you brainstorm up a variety of different situations. "Be the same person," says Leigh. "But show off that person's different activities."

Sean Kahlil, who shoots many composites, says you should research print ads and try to avoid cliches. "De-program yourself," he declares. Right now, he explains, 30-something women keep demanding photos of themselves in tennis whites, wielding a racket. For one actress who wanted the tennis shot, Kahlil steered her into something quite different—washing her dog. "It was warm and personable and appealing," the photographer says. "And it was different."

The photographers note that your photo session for headshot and composite pictures can be an excellent dress-rehearsal for a go-see and the actual print work sessions.

"Be rested, energized, and ready to have fun," Kahlil affirms. "Be vital and alive. Believe that you are the ideal for the type that you are. Those are the images that will make a client want to see you." Whatever you're doing in front of that camera, whoever you're being, photographers say you should feel good about yourself. "Think of it as a gift," says Kahlil. "The gift you have to offer is you."

Sutherland, who has cast print jobs for TWA, AT&T, American Express, and Seagram's, among many others during her nine years in her present post with the advertising giant, says that your personality is a big plus or minus when it comes to getting the job. Be enthusiastic. "Don't tell me you're a great actress and you're just doing this for some quick money," she states. "A cooperative attitude and showing a strong desire to excel at what you're doing is a must." Top-notch professionalism is the name of the print game, she stresses.

BE A GO-SEE PRO

In the parlance of the print industry, the job interview is known as a "go-see." Just as you would probably dress for a theater audition, you should dress in character for the go-see, according to Leigh and Hardwick. "If I tell you that the go-see is for an upscale exec, you go in pinstripes and power tie and polished shoes and carry a briefcase," Leigh declares. "You can't lay it on too thick." Yet you can bet, Leigh adds with a shake of his head, that some performers will show up for that exec go-see in jeans, T-shirt, and a leather jacket. Because the go-see usually involves a quick Polaroid photo shoot for later comparisons, the more appropriately dressed individual often gets the edge.

Professional behavior extends to the go-see as much as the actual job. "Show signs of self-respect and self-esteem from the very first," says Leigh. "Look at your shoes, hair, and hands, and make sure they're neat. Don't make excuses about your clothes. Be reliable. Be early rather than late." And if you happen to be late from some unavoidable accident, Sutherland advises, "take an extra moment before you go in the door, and gather yourself together. Don't bring all your woes in with you." Beyer adds, "And giving people attitude never got anybody a job."

Along with look, personality, and professionalism, your acting talent is another key factor in commercial print. But sometimes the people running the go-see are not that clear about the performer's intentions. Then it's your job, says Beyer, to ask the photographer or casting director about the desired attitude. "Try to find out what the copy in the ad is going to say," Beyer explains. "Find out if you're supposed to be ecstatic, happy, or only mildly happy."

A POSITIVE APPROACH

Finally, as in nearly every successful career, training and persistence usually pay off. Do those initial mailings to print casting directors, urges Sutherland, and then send photo postcards from time to time. Add those casting directors and agents who specialize in print to your mailing list when you get theater roles or land parts in feature films or television. Keep close track of what you sent to whom and when you did so. Keep looking at print ads to see if new types appear on the scene—maybe you'll discover a new type that's perfect for you.

And don't be discouraged. Gary Beyer, for one, maintains a positive attitude about those inevitable turn-downs that even the best of print professionals get. "The word 'no,'" he remarks, "really means 'not now.'"

AUDITIONING FOR SHAKESPEARE

BY MAUREEN CLARKE

Many terrific actors don't do Shakespeare. When asked why, they look as if they were asked why they don't do triple somersaults on the high wire. "Well," they say, "I never learned how." And while one may agree with the adage "acting is acting," acting Shakespeare isn't quite like acting in a modern play—and auditioning for Shakespeare can be a scary experience. In the thousands of Shakespeare auditions I've seen over the years, most actors disqualify themselves for purely technical reasons.

What do you mean, technical reasons?
Auditioning for Shakespeare isn't like auditioning for a contemporary play. It's more like auditioning for a Mozart ensemble: you will, of course, play Mozart for your audition, and the people who hear your audition will, of course, know the piece you play; they can't help but have preconceptions, and their preconceptions can hurt you if you're not prepared.

What kind of preconceptions?
Here's an obvious one—audition with a piece that's right for you. It's true for all auditions, but especially for the classics. Let's say you're eighteen years old and skinny. If this is an audition for a contemporary play, and you come in and say, "I'm gonna do Jummie Slocum's monologue from 'A Pigless Contortion,'" I don't know whether you're right for the part because I don't know the play. But if you say, "I'm gonna do Falstaff," I say to myself, "Whoa...."

So how do I know if it's a good monologue for me?
Ask yourself: Would I realistically be cast in this part? The key word here is *realistically*. Don't audition with the part of your dreams—audition with part we might cast you in.

But can't you tell whether I can handle the language no matter which monologue I do?
Language is not the only criterion. Your monologue choice reveals a great deal about your artistic judgment—or lack of it.

Maybe I need a new Shakespeare monologue. How do I pick one that's right for me?

Cast yourself realistically. Work for a marriage of (a) established stage tradition and (b) your undeniable personal traits, such as age, gender, physique, and voice.

Your vocal quality is essential. Do you know what you sound like? What kind of voice would your character have? Young ladies with deep voices will have more success with Cressida than Ophelia. Tenors might do Lysander or Puck, but probably not Othello.

How long should my Shakespeare piece be?

Short. *Very* short. Please, please, *please*. One minute is plenty for a Shakespearean monologue. Really, truly, honestly. Within 15 seconds, those of us watching the auditions know whether we can use you.

But doesn't a longer monologue show versatility?

No, it just gives you a better chance to hang yourself. If you're good, we'll know it right away. Don't give us time to get restless and pick it apart. Let us discover your versatility at the callback. Short has another advantage...it's easier to find a piece that's seldom done.

You auditors. You all say you make a judgment within the first 15 seconds. How is it possible?

It's extremely possible. As a matter of fact, it's unavoidable. You do it whenever you meet a new person. The only difference is, the audition situation gives us a license to judge you openly. It's our job to evaluate your height, weight, age, clothes, gait, voice, stance, energy—a thousand signals you send out, all of which blend into what I call your "presentational impact."

What's the most important element of my "presentational impact?"

Your mood! It's so refreshing when an actor arrives happy. Show us your spirit and enthusiasm. A joyous attitude is especially important if you're auditioning with a tragic character; we need to see that *you're* not a tragic character.

What else? You mentioned clothes. Can you tell me what to wear to a Shakespeare audition?

Let's start with what you *shouldn't* wear. Ladies, please don't wear mini-skirts. In my opinion, the best skirt length for a classical character is just below the knees. Unless the casting notice specifies that the play will be set in modern dress or in a Martian steambath, it's safer to dress "classically conservative."

Any colors to avoid?

I think wearing black makes actors look unhappy. (Of course, if you're auditioning against black drapes, no one will notice how unhappy you look, because you'll be invisible.)

What should I wear on my feet?

Men, avoid Big Black Boots—unless you're doing one of the warrior princes like Hal, Hotspur, or Richard III. Lysander and Puck types will fare better in sneakers.

For you women, the most flattering shoe color is the color of your legs. It makes your feet seem smaller and more delicate—assuming that's the effect your wish to create. (Please wear Big Black Punk Shoes if you want to look like you're carrying lunchboxes on your feet.)

In general, don't call attention to your feet. Avoid strange or extreme footwear—resist the urge to wear bright colors, cowboy boots, spurs, bells, rollerskates, flippers, cinder blocks...

What about jewelry?
Don't wear anything we'll notice. Women should avoid long, dangly earrings. They're distracting. They'll upstage you. And of course, no jangly bangle bracelets.

Okay. I'm well dressed and I've got a great monologue—what's next?
Your "lobby attitude." Be nice to everyone helping with the audition, including the Equity monitor and the theater cat. They're all incorrigible tattletales, and we encourage them shamelessly.

Great. Now it's my turn to go in... and there you are! Should I run up and shake your hand to show you how excited I am?
No. Be excited from a distance. Don't shake our hands *unless we offer first*. No offense; it's not because we don't love you. If we shook hands with 150 excited actors, our hands would be crippled by the end of the day... and worse, we would've dispensed billions of cold germs amidst a sizeable population of actors.

What next? Should I introduce my monologue?
Depends. Most Shakespearean monologues are familiar; we've probably heard it before, and we'll probably recognize it when you begin speaking. In my opinion, it doesn't matter whether you introduce it or not.

If you decide to introduce it, a casual introduction is better than a formal one. (Never announce the act and scene numbers—nobody cares.) Make the intro short and unceremonious. All you need say is something like, "I'm going to do a little Helena" or "I'd like to do Helena for you." This sounds confident and familiar. It's not really even necessary to announce the title of the play. As soon as you begin, we'll figure out whether it's Helena from *Midsummer Night's Dream* or *All's Well That Ends Well*.

Since this is Shakespeare, we're extremely interested in your vocal tonalities. If you choose to introduce your piece, use your best, clearest voice. Please don't ask, "Do you wanna know what piece I'm gonna do?" Don't waffle. Either introduce the piece or don't.

Is there a benefit to not introducing the piece—to jumping right in?
Maybe. Consider this: if you come in and say to me, "I'm going to do Sebastian," several things happen. I instantly decide whether Sebastian is a good

choice for your type; I start to compare you to all the other Sebastians I've ever seen; I think of the possible Violas and whether you could be her twin; finally, my mind drops a nickel into the monologue jukebox, and "This is the air..." begins to play. And this all happens before you've said a word of the monologue.

Here's a secret. Now and then, Shakespeare auditors like to play a silent game of "Name That Monologue." I can name that monologue in three words! "Now is the..." *WINTER! From Richard III, right? Do I win the dinette set?* Only joking...sort of. But doesn't it point up the importance of choosing lesser-done pieces?

Speaking of which, what are the most overdone Shakespearean monologues?

Tough question. I'm reluctant to publish a "hate list," because I think if you love the piece and if it's right for you (and it's short), you should do it. Besides, fashions change.

Any pieces I should avoid?

Most of the pieces in any of the books of *Fifty Favorite Shakespearean Monologues* are overdone. In general, it's best to abstain from any of the "well-known" Shakespearean set-pieces.

How can I tell if my monologue is a set-piece?

Quote the first four words. If every other actor standing in line can identify it, you probably qualify.

Any characters I should avoid?

Here's a controversial opinion: I think some Shakespearean characters are less suitable for auditions than others. For example, I think Hamlet and Richard II are hardly ever successful as audition characters. I don't really know why; maybe because they're such ruminative, self-involved, unhappy characters, they engender listless, pause-filled, moody auditions.

Is it okay to use a chair?

If there's a chair handy—which means a chair obviously intended for your use—yes. If you're even slightly doubtful, ask first.

Please don't ever touch anything on stage. *Ever.* Don't touch furniture, curtains, props, anything. I remember, several years ago, watching auditions for a theater company that used a church as its space. One impassioned young actor got so carried away, he ran screaming up the stairs and snatched the red velvet cloth off the altar. God knows what he intended to do with it; we never found out. When the poor guy realized what he'd done, he dropped the cloth, turned white, forgot his lines, and backed out of the room gibbering and apologizing.

But I need a chair. What if there isn't one?

You should always be prepared to do your monologue standing up. Most of

Shakespeare is done standing up anyhow. As someone—I forget who—said, "The King is the best part in Shakespeare: he's the only one who gets to sit down."

If you must use a chair, make sure you get up and move around. Shakespeare's characters are so physical, it's a mistake to trap them in the furniture—and the language will appreciate the support of a standing diaphragm.

But when I'm standing up, I often feel like I don't know what to do with my hands.

Once upon a time, the art of gesture was considered an essential part of actor training. I think it still is. Unfortunately, most actors never learn the vocal and gestural technique needed to fill a big space.

Why aren't there more brilliant classical actors in New York? I blame it partly on the real estate market. If acting schools could afford bigger spaces, they could train bigger actors. And you must be a big actor to do Shakespeare—I don't mean physically big, of course—I mean a big soul and big thoughts. I believe actors are like goldfish—they grow to fill the space they're given. If you've been working in a 99-seater, or in a classroom, or in your shower, be aware that you're learning to be small. If you want to be bigger, find a bigger place to practice in. In the meantime, the most important thing to remember about Shakespearean characters is their athleticism. Keep your gestures clean and muscular. Two large, confident gestures are better than a dozen small, vague ones.

What about props? Can I use a prop?

Bad idea. An audition prop is never the actor's friend. Fans, flowers, cups, daggers, sceptres, swords—they'll always upstage you. If you have a fan in your hand, we'll watch the fan. Wouldn't you rather we watch you?

Okay, here I stand onstage with my face in the light, well-dressed and completely propless. I've decided to introduce my well-chosen piece (and I do so in a clear, strong voice)... Now what? How much time can I take to "prepare"?

None. Zero. Zilch. Please don't "prepare" onstage. Do you want us to think that acting is so difficult for you? Train yourself out of this classroom habit. Even three seconds of "preparation" is too long. Just walk onstage, introduce your piece (or not), come to a fully focused stop, take a deep breath, and begin.

Begin *speaking*, that is. Please don't do any "silent acting" before your monologue. This is Shakespeare; we want to hear how you use the words. If you want to show us how well you move, fine—but move *on* the words.

Can I go off into the wings to make an entrance?

Bad idea. Two reasons: first, we worry that you'll hurt yourself backstage. Second, we've been sitting there long enough to know what the empty stage looks like. We want to see *you*. You have so little time, don't waste it. Remember, this isn't a play, it's an audition. A wise actor knows the difference.

In my monologue, I talk to another character. How should I indicate where that character is?

If you *must* talk to an imaginary character, place him/her out front, somewhere above the auditors' heads. Focus your eyes up and out.

Can I put that other character in an empty chair?

Once more: this isn't a play, it's an audition. Acting to an empty chair might be a good exercise for acting class, but in an audition, we want to see your eyes. If you focus on the chair, so will we.

Do I need any kind of standard English accent to do Shakespeare?

The current fashion (and a healthy one it is) seems to favor Americanized English. But not *too* Americanized. If you have any kind of a regional accent—especially a New Yawk accent—please get rid of it.

If you have a lisp, get speech therapy.

If you don't know whether you have an accent of a lisp, ask someone. (Not your mother; ask an expert.) Sorry if this sounds harsh, but your speech defines you as much as your height, weight, and age. It's those preconceptions again.

Moreover, if you do your monologue with a British accent, be prepared to prove that you were born with it.

I know that the words are really important in Shakespeare...

Oh, yes. Learn the words correctly. Obvious, but essential. You can fudge Shepard and maybe Shaw, but not Shakespeare. If you misplace a word, we'll notice it. Sorry, we can't help it; we've heard the "top 40" speeches so often, we know them by heart.

But what about the technical verse stuff—the iambic pentameter and all that—do you listen for that?

We don't listen for it, but we notice if it's wrong. For example, if you've learned your stresses incorrectly, you'll probably disqualify yourself. It's as obvious as a wrong note in a Mozart audition.

My stresses? How can I find out if they're wrong?

Don't panic. It's not necessary to take a scansion class; just go to the library and find an edition that has the stressed accents marked (G.B. Harrison's edition is a good one). Look up your monologue and find out whether you should be saying *purged* or *purgED*, *disturbed* or *disturbED*. Don't take anything for granted! Just because you've been reciting the words since high school, it doesn't mean you've got them right. Missing a stressed accent won't wreck your career, but it will strain your credibility.

Also, beware of pauses. Shakespeare didn't write any. Shaw said it best: "In playing Shakespeare, play to the lines, through the lines, on the lines, but never between the lines. There simply isn't time for it. You would not stick a five-bar rest into a Beethoven symphony to pick up your drumsticks; and you must not stop the Shakespeare orchestra for business." Frequent pauses produce shallow breathing, and shallow breathing saps your energy.

Okay, it's almost over—I'm coming to the end of my monologue. Any tips?

When the words are over, the audition is over. After you speak the last word, hold for a count of two. (No more.) Then break, give us a big smile (to show us you're happy with your life as an actor), give us a cheerful "Thank you!" and go merrily on to your next audition. No matter how badly you think the audition went, don't let us see it. After all, maybe we thought it was great; if you burst into tears, we might change our minds. From the moment you enter until the moment you exit, it's all acting, right? So act happy.

Any words of wisdom for next time?

Be ready. Practice. Practice in big spaces. And practice every day.

ACTING IN LOS ANGELES

BY PAT HILTON

For a New Yorker, Los Angeles is definite culture shock. "There is no there there," Gertrude Stein once declared about San Francisco, but to newcomers, the phrase seems a more appropriate description of L.A. There is no downtown, for example. (Geographically there is, but despite its theater centers, no one—well, practically no one—goes there to live, shop, or hang out.) Transplanted New Yorkers miss Broadway, cultural opportunities, and public transportation.

But there are ways to cope. Those who've made the jump—directors, casting directors, agents—advise knowing the odds before you come. There is a lot of work in Los Angeles because of television and film, but there is also a lot of competition.

L.A.'s lifestyle is significally different from the East Coast's. "It is difficult for anyone in the creative side of the business to come to a place as socially disorganized as Los Angeles," says film director Martha Coolidge. "Los Angeles does not have meeting places. It is a city of interiors where connections are made in private places, such as at somebody's pool party. You can't hang out and meet people."

TV producer/writer Carmen Finestra agrees that L.A. is rootless, but he has observed that once people make the adjustment, they enjoy its lifestyle, finding the weather and slower pace civilizing attributes.

As for *when* to come, there is still a pilot season—January to May. However, it's best to arrive well ahead of time, so you can take care of life-style decisions: finding a home, job, and so on.

New Yorkers are often tempted to keep one foot in each city. However, casting directors generally advise against bi-coastal living; finding an actor too often out of town may cause his or her name to be dropped from their lists.

LAYING THE GROUNDWORK

You'll need a resume and photographs. And of course the resume will include your training, experience, and strongest credits. Your theater experience, all agree, is a big plus. As for photos, make sure they look like you. Casting directors don't like to be surprised. In addition, a tape is practically mandatory. "Any tape is better than nothing," says agent Laurie Apelian. If you make a commercial, use that—or if you have even a small part on a television show, call the network and ask for a copy. Workshops offer another means of getting a tape of your work.

Prepare for dry spells. Don't come without money. Unless you are financially independent, money concerns will drain energy best poured into your work. If you need to work in non-acting jobs, TV director John Whitesell advises "lowering your monthly nut" so you can spend more time on your acting career. He also suggests choosing a job that lets you make the most money in the shortest time—while avoiding such favorites as bartending. Bartending, he says, "is a false lifestyle because you're up when everybody else is asleep; and you're working weekends, trying to keep your weekdays free to pursue your career."

Consider other jobs in the industry, concludes Whitesell. "Look at the casting directors, agents, directors, studio execs. The majority have come from the acting ranks."

Get a support system. One's emotional and mental health is essential, states director Martha Coolidge, who believes you should "spend as much time putting together a support system as pursuing professional goals. L.A. is fantastically competitive, and anybody in the creative side of the business faces enormous rejection. On the positive side, you see people come here and thrive, and on the negative side, you see them spin down into depression, drugs, and alcohol."

Classes, whether in physical training, improv, or scene study, are a means of building such a system. "They give you somewhere to go, and any form you can give your life here helps," says Finestra.

"There *is* plenty going on—if you look for it," Finestra notes. "There are certainly intelligent, politically concerned people in Los Angeles, but you have to work harder at finding them."

Learn to drive. A car is a must. Managing without one is expensive and inconvenient—if not impossible. Whitesell recommends initially purchasing a cheap auto, "then, when it doesn't run anymore, or the repairs are more than $150, dump it." Don't worry about your image, he advises. "When you go to see a casting agent, nobody sees you in that car except the studio guard."

Get to know the territory. "Become a part of the community," suggests agent Harry Gold. "Hang around actors; become part of the loop of information. Read the trades, and learn how the system works." And to see how the film industry works behind the scenes, he believes *Indecent Exposure* (the David Begelman story), *Final Cut* (the *Heaven's Gate* story), and *Adventures in the Screen Trade* by William Goldman are required reading.

GETTING AN AGENT—AND ALTERNATIVES

Let's face it: it's tough to get an agent in Los Angeles; many claim it's impossible. So, if you have a New York agent with a sister agreement in L.A., you're already a leg up.

But if you are seeking new representation, do your research. Part of being realistic is to sign with an agency that will work for you. Ask questions: Is this the sort of agency that gets involved with new talent? What is its relationship with casting directors?

When Martha Coolidge moved to Los Angeles, she says she asked every person she talked to for the name of an agent, then called those agents and asked them to view her tapes. TV casting director Jeff Greenberg advocates making a lot of contacts. "There's that one chance in a million that you may spark their interest, that they don't have anybody like you," he says.

Agent Harry Gold, on the other hand, is not high on a shotgun approach. "Don't just take meetings, hoping someone will have a gut reaction to you. That's not the way to do it. Make your first order of business to get into something. Act anywhere, everywhere possible. If you are good, you will get signed."

Get involved with theater. That advice cannot be repeated too often. Most casting agents make it their business to see plays in order to find talent, so when you do get into a good production, send a mass mailing to casting directors and agents.

Another means of being seen is through student films done at USC, UCLA, and the American Film Institute. Casting director Cheryl Bayer endorses them as being "often brilliant writing pieces with wonderful, rich characters."

Take classes and workshops. Continuing to study is not only good for your craft, but it is an excellent way to make contacts. Classes are also valuable in helping the stage actor adjust to television and film techniques—learning to work out of sequence, modulating your performance, as well as discovering other necessary adjustments.

Consider a manager. A relationship with a manager is sometimes a possible substitute for having an agent. Some managers do not demand written commitments, so it is possible to have a much looser relationship. Just as in seeking an agent, however, ask questions. What is the manager's reputation? Does he have contacts who will be helpful to your goals? Don't go with just anyone out of desperation.

Seek out casting directors. The importance of casting directors in the life of an actor who is breaking in cannot be exaggerated. More accessible than agents, many encourage you to send them your photo, resume, and a note. "I look at every piece of mail that comes in the office," says Greenberg. Casting directors are supportive of their finds, often helping their discoveries to get established with agents.

THE AUDITION

Once you've gotten an audition for a TV role—and your chance to do what you came for—do your homework. Take time to work on the character. This is not a frivolous admonition. "It's amazing how many people show up for shows they've never seen," marvels Greenberg, who recommends spending some time watching television, so you can audition for a show in the right style.

Be prepared for the difference between auditioning for film and television. "In feature work, there is much more emphasis on what the finished product will be," says TV director Stewart A. Lyons. "In television, the emphasis is on the process. You look for the guest actor who gives you something you didn't expect and yet is completely appropriate."

TV director Barnet Kellman recommends that the New York theater actor approach a television audition as if it were summer stock, meaning, "This is a fast process. At a New York audition you look for the seed and expect it to grow. Those kinds of auditions don't do as well out here. Very often we have an hour to cast a part that will go into next week's show. You have to audition in more of a performance mode."

"Don't play it safe," advises casting director Ronnie Yeskel. "Most people like actors who aren't afraid of making fools of themselves." On the other hand, don't try too hard in your audition. "Actors who try too hard embarrass themselves," says Whitesell. Coming in and saying, "Hey, howya doing?" and shaking hands with everybody is wasted, he says. You want them to remember you "because you're good, not for glad-handing."

"If you have a question about the role or the character, ask it and then do your audition," recommends Whitesell. "Don't become Freud. The words are not a test to see if you can find the hidden meaning."

It's also okay to stop and ask to start over if the audition is not going well. Just do it early—not when you're halfway through.

"Casting directors and producers and directors want you to be good," Whitesell explains. "If they seem tired or short, it's because they've already seen 100 people and they haven't found what they want. Think of them as your friends, and you'll do better."

MAKING IT

To those actors who at one time or another heed the cliched advice to go west, Finestra offers an encouraging word. "Don't be discouraged. People are always looking for new talent."

Finestra observes that, for some reason, in L.A. things happen either immediately or not for two or three years. Meanwhile, "getting little spurts of work here and there builds into recognition."

"The most important thing in making it is tenacity," Whitesell adds. "A lot of actors are not acting today—not because they weren't talented—but because they didn't have the drive. If you feel, 'This is the only thing I want to do no matter how long it takes me,' eventually it will happen."

Greenberg agrees that you must be willing to make a commitment and invest time before expecting anything to happen. "When a casting director finally sees you, then you are in that casting director's vocabulary of actors. It may take a long time—years—before the right thing comes up. It's a matter of planting seeds and doing good work."

Indeed, initially it may be easier for the newly arrived actor to get work than for a Los Angeles regular, says Barnet Kellman, emphasizing the "initially." "There is always interest in faces that have not been seen again and again from one series to another."

PART FOUR

GETTING A SHOW ON THE ROAD

PRODUCING YOUR OWN SHOW

BY BILL ERVOLINO

laywrights struggling to have their plays produced have one course of action they can always fall back upon—they can produce their work themselves. Similarly, actors in search of a stage on which to show their talents can find a dramatist's play or a script in public domain that has juicy roles and produce it themselves. And one of the best options open to those artists who are willing to shoulder the responsibilities of a self-produced venture is an Equity-Approved Showcase.

An Equity-Approved Showcase production must meet the standards set by the AEA Showcase Code and must be approved by AEA. (Although Equity Showcase productions are unique to New York City, there are similar opportunities in other communities throughout the United States. Those who would like to undertake such a production outside of New York should contact an AEA liaison person in their area.) There are, of course, many factors to consider before beginning such an undertaking, such as time, money, energy, organizational ability, and business acumen. Some of the obstacles facing producers of plays are described below, and the requirements of an Equity Showcase production are outlined.

SHOULD YOU OR SHOULDN'T YOU?

The golden rule in show business has always been: Never use your own money. Film director Francis Coppola found that out the hard way and lost his empire in the process. Countless others who have produced their own films, plays, and record albums have learned the same lesson. Certainly it's admirable to believe so strongly in something that you are willing to put yourself on the line for it, financially speaking. But there are risks involved. One danger in producing your own show is that it could be identified as a "vanity production"; this could cause others not to take your show seriously.

Many ask whether it is possible to be creative and also have a good business sense. It is very possible—and also very preferable! The costs of Broadway and Off-Broadway productions are astronomical, but it is possible to mount your own small-cast Equity Showcase production for around $8,000. Although this is for a limited run (16 performances maximum), and the chances of recovering your investment are slim, there are, nevertheless, still advantages to undertaking such a production yourself.

First off, the very fact that you are doing an Equity Showcase lends a certain amount of prestige to your project. A reading is one thing, but a showcase lets those people you've invited know that someone is serious enough about your work to put real money into it, even if that someone is you. (And no one has to know that, unless you tell them.) "Those people" includes potential backers, producers, casting directors, agents, as well as critics. And good reviews from New York critics can only help your chances of luring even more potential backers and producers.

Producing a play is also a bit like spending a summer doing rep. You probably won't be painting scenery, but you'll more than likely be doing everything else. And, what you don't know, you'll learn. Very quickly. Finally—and this may be the toughest lesson of all—you may discover that despite what your friends have been telling you, your play, or the one you've chosen to perform in, really isn't as marvelous as you thought. Audiences may not respond to it, critics may not respond to it, and producers may not respond to it. If you can be objective enough to accept this, then your showcase can save you a lot of time, aggravation, postage, and misery.

All of which brings us back to our basic question: "Should you or shouldn't you produce your own work?" As with so many of life's basic questions, the only person who can decide this is you. There are, however, a few other questions which should be considered before producing a show of your own. They are:

Can you come up with the money to mount the production? And, most importantly, can you afford to lose that money?

If you cannot answer in the affirmative to both of these questions, you may be well advised to postpone a self-produced show. It could be very frustrating to be forced to abandon a project in midstream or to have to overlook aesthetic considerations because of budgetary pressures.

Is the play ready to be produced?

If the play is your own or a new one by someone else, one way to find out is to try a staged reading. If you have already staged a reading and have gotten a positive response, then a showcase could be the next logical step.

Do you have the right director? And the right actors?

Never underestimate the importance of these factors. A theatrical showcase, just like a department store showcase, is a sales tool—it should be as attractive as possible. Don't ruin your chance to have your work finally seen—and then rejected because of the poor quality of some of the other participants' work.

Do you have a space?

A space could mean anything from a loft in the SoHo district in New York City to the Radio City Music Hall. And booking it could turn out to be the toughest part of the entire project.

Do you have the time to devote to producing?

If your time is already at a premium, producing a showcase could be extremely trying. Perhaps you already have a demanding job. Maybe you're even juggling two. Are your hours flexible? Could you take off from work if you were needed at the theater? Will your boss complain about the inevitable phone calls you'll be making and receiving on company time?

FURTHER CONSIDERATIONS

As you probably already know, the ability to visualize a finished work is 50 percent of the battle. This same skill that makes you a competent theater artist can also make you a competent producer. Your ability to come up with ideas, to visualize a finished product, and to organize your thoughts effectively will serve you well during the preproduction period, when you are called upon to carry out certain steps, often simultaneously, and pull them all together.

As a producer you have many responsibilities. You have to hire a cast. You have to hire a director. You have to find a space. You have to work with the landlord. You have to consult an attorney. You have to sign contracts. You have to purchase insurance. You have to arrange for publicity. You have to hire a ticket agent. You have to arrange for rehearsal time. You have to put together a comp list (a list of people who will receive complimentary tickets). You have to make sure all the right people are invited. You have to contact critics. You have to have programs made. And that's before you even open!

Once you do open, you have to deal with your cast. Then you have to deal with your director. Then you have to deal with problems between your cast and your director. And problems between your director and your landlord. And problems between your landlord and your audience.

WHERE TO BEGIN?

Since many things have to be done at the same time and you probably won't have much help doing any of it, you have a dilemma. You need a cast. You need a space. And, you need a cast that's available when the space is available. So you're going to have to find a way to bring all these elements together.

If you've already done a reading of the play, chances are you already have a cast and director in mind. If you haven't done a reading, then you should do one. A reading of your play will allow you to see and hear the work performed, assess dialogue and structure, and get some feedback from an audience as well as the performers and director. (Often, on new plays, playwrights will direct this kind of reading themselves, but having someone else involved will free the writer to observe audience response.)

In preparation for the reading, find someone you think might be a good director. Allow that person a few days to read and digest the play and then sit down and talk it over. Listen to this person's ideas and see if the two of you are in accord over interpretation, key characters, and the situations you have placed them in. Make sure this is not just some idle chat over coffee. When your meeting is over, you should be able to walk away from it with some idea of whether or not this is the person you want to be your director. Just as importantly, how do the two of you get along? Is this someone you can work with, someone who inspires confidence, and who shares your enthusiasm for the work? Your relationship with your director is crucial. Don't select someone simply because you can't find anyone else.

When you've found a director you're comfortable with, discuss casting possibilities together. Between the two of you, you will have to come up with actors for the reading. Many actors who are between projects will gladly give their time for a reading. All you have to do is find them. You must also find someone to read stage directions.

Once you have assembled your director and cast, set a date, find a place, and do the reading. Two or maybe three rehearsals should be sufficient for this type of informal reading— actors with books in hand and an audience of your friends. Often directors will have the actors sit in chairs and read the script; other times some rough blocking is introduced to liven things up a bit, but don't go crazy. You're looking for feedback here, not a Tony Award.

On the night of the reading, pay close attention to how your audience is responding. There's going to be a lot of visualization going on, but the essence of the play should come across loud and clear. When the reading is over, discuss the play with the audience, the director, and the actors, and take notes. How did it sound? How did it feel? (A tape recording of the reading might be a good idea, too.)

At this point you'll have to decide whether the time is right to attempt your showcase. If the script is new, perhaps you'd like more time to work on the play. Perhaps you'd rather put together a *workshop production*. Get as much feedback as you can and give the matter plenty of thought. If you don't feel totally comfortable with the work, then a workshop—in which the actors are fully blocked, off-book, and working with major props—will probably be the best way to go. When you feel that the play is ready (either before or after a staged reading) it is time to move on to the next phase of production.

SETTING A DATE

It's going to be necessary for you to set a target date for your showcase. If your work has a seasonal theme, you may wish to have it performed during that particular season. Summer is generally a bad time for a play to open because so many people are out of town, but, for whatever reasons, summer may be best for your play. (For one thing, theaters are generally easier to book in the summer.) Weigh your decision carefully and then start looking for a space.

Call anyone you know who has ever been involved in an Equity showcase and find out where it was produced. Keep in mind that the Equity Showcase Code states that "AEA members may not rehearse or perform on any premises which lack adequate sanitary facilities or which do not comply with New York City and State fire codes." Also bear in mind that productions mounted under the terms of this code shall not be presented in any theater, auditorium, or hall which is listed by AEA as a contract house. This eliminates large theaters from your list of possibilities. Seating for your showcase may not exceed 99, and that number is firm.

Speak to as many theater owners or managers as you can and ask them what their spaces go for and when they are available. And don't be shy about it. If the rental seems steep to you, try to negotiate. Find out what it will cost per week, and whether it is possible for you to get a discounted per-week rate should you opt for a rental of more than a couple weeks. (Equity will allow your showcase to run for 12 performances with the option of adding another four. These performances need not be held on 16 consecutive evenings. Your total run, however, may not exceed a four-week period.)

You will need answers to the following questions from your prospective landlord: Does this space rent by the evening, the week, or by the hour? What equipment is included with the space—blacks, flats, a light board and instruments? Is the theater yours all day? Will any other party have use of the space during your run? Will it be necessary to strike the set every night?

When you have found a space that looks right, ask to inspect the premises. Take along your director and one or two members of your cast. Check out the dressing rooms for size and sanitary conditions. Walk across the stage and try to visualize your play on it. Look at the backstage area. Is there enough room for the sets and props you need? What is the seating like? Are the chairs in decent condition or are they broken and uncomfortable? How are the sightlines? If a lightboard is included, ask for a demonstration. If you aren't technically adept, bring someone with you who is.

There's no way you'll think of everything when you walk into an unknown theater, but be prepared to experience the space from the standpoint of your actors as well as your audience. Ask plenty of questions, but try to keep your meeting cordial and professional. If the landlord is interested in theater and proud of what he or she has to offer you, chances are you'll be offered a grand tour of the place. If the manager or owner's cold and indifferent, think twice before entering into an agreement with him or her. Ask to see a sample contract, and if there is anything you don't understand, ask the theater manager or owner to explain it to you. *Sign nothing.* If the landlord wants a deposit, make sure it is refundable. If it isn't, speak to an attorney first and get back to the landlord as soon as possible. If you're getting a hard-sell ("I have someone else who wants to rent it on the same days you want it") proceed with caution. If you're sure you want the space and are afraid you might lose it, go with your instincts.

EXAMINING YOUR CONTRACT

No matter what the landlord tells you, there is no standard rental agreement for what you are doing, so don't assume that everything's going to be okay just because it looks good to you on paper. If you don't have a lawyer, find one who has a background in theater.

Yes, your agreement lists performance dates—but what about rehearsal dates? You're going to want the cast to have at least some rehearsal time in the theater. What will that cost? And how will it be paid? In advance? Per night? If the landlord offers a certain amount of rehearsal time at no cost, make sure this appears in the final agreement you sign. When renting by the hour make sure that the times your cast may enter and must leave the theater are clearly stated. And this, of course, goes for rehearsal days and performance days. If you're planning on an eight o'clock curtain, make sure your cast and stage manager are allowed at least an hour to prepare.

Also find out what is included in the rent. If there is a fee for lights or electricity make sure you're aware of it. If you are running during summer months, you are most probably going to want air conditioning. Is there any in the theater? Will it be automatically turned on or do you have to pay for that too?

The rental contract should outline terms of payment. Your landlord may want the entire amount in advance, plus security. If that is going to present a problem to you, try to negotiate the matter. Chances are if you're doing the full 16 performances Equity allows, you're going to have to lay out a hefty amount of cash.

A few other things that must be in the contract are: time involved for you to vacate the premises at the end of your run and to restore the space to its original condition; your responsibility for damages; policies concerning cancellation of any performances, including the entire run. Whatever you do, don't sign away the rights to your play; your landlord has no right to future percentages or options.

EQUITY APPROVAL

Now that you have your cast, your director, your space, and your dates, it is time to seek AEA approval for your showcase production. The AEA Showcase Code, available by contacting Actors' Equity Association, is an 11-page document that spells out certain provisions you *must* follow. For a copy, contact the union at 165 West 46th Street, New York, NY 10036 or call (212) 869-8530. Louise Foisy is the business representative in charge of showcase productions.

As stated within the code, an application must be made to AEA 14 days prior to casting (or rehearsals—whichever comes first) and must include the producer's name, the title of the production, the type of production (musical revue, dramatic play, and so on), and information concerning previous productions. In the application you must also include basic information about the theater, a statement of financial backing, and a proposed production budget.

(For what Equity deems "a one-shot producer," the total budget must be under $15,000.)

Prior to casting, the producer must furnish Equity with a copy of the cast breakdown indicating the roles available, the dates of rehearsals and performances, and the address at which pictures and resumes will be accepted; these will be posted at the Equity offices. At least half of the total number of performances must be presented on a weekday (Monday through Friday) with no more than one two-performance day per week. The producer may not cut the number of performances without the unanimous written consent of the AEA members in the production.

Equity's Showcase Code requires that AEA cast members be reimbursed at $5 per member for each optional performance beyond the initial 12. The theater may not seat more than 99 people and admission can be no more than $10 per ticket. All AEA members are to be comped, on a standby basis, upon presentation of a membership card.

Your cast and crew are working for reimbursement of their expenses, and what is commonly defined as public transportation for each rehearsal and performance. Keep in mind that this is *their* showcase, too. Their photos must be prominently displayed in the lobby of the theater. Their bios must appear in the program. And their professional theater guests—casting agents, other producers, anyone in a position to cast them in something else—are automatically comped. (As a courtesy, you should make a certain number of personal comps available to the cast as well. Four is a nice, round number.)

THE COST OF AN EQUITY SHOWCASE

No matter how hard you try to keep costs down, you're going to find new expenses every day as you get closer to opening night. Keep track of everything!

The following is a sample budget, like the one you must send to Equity, for a five-character show (with minimal—as in "bring your own"—sets, props, and costumes) running the full 16 performances:

Theater rental (performances)	$5,000
Theater rental (rehearsals)	$ 900
Security	$ 100
Insurance	$ 750
Ticket agent	$ 100
Postage	$ 150
Printed Cards/Flyers	$ 75
Set/props/costumes	$ 300
Carfare for cast, director, and stage manager	$ 672
Miscellaneous paper	$ 30
Equity/LORT Trust Fund (when in effect)	$ 150
Total	$ 8,227

As new expenses are incurred, add them to your list. You'll need adequate records for tax purposes. Accordingly, make sure that your reservations book is legible and accurate.

WHO'S IN CHARGE HERE?

As your production comes together, problems are bound to come up. As producer, you will have to recognize when you should be involved, when you should keep your mouth shut, and when you should step in and resolve something.

In the center of your production is the director, who is supposed to be the person guiding the creative end. If you undermine the director's authority you're going to have a major mess on your hands, one that is going to get worse and worse as you approach the opening. Once rehearsals have commenced (and you can rehearse your cast a maximum of four weeks), if you feel that the play is moving in the wrong direction, speak to the director privately and try to correct it.

There are also bound to be problems between the theater owner and resident theater staff, if one exists, and your cast and crew. Props may have been moved onstage. Personal items may be missing from the dressing room. Whatever the problem, it's bound to fall in your lap sooner or later. Be prepared, and do your best to handle whatever comes up as painlessly and diplomatically as possible.

TICKET AGENTS

You can hire a ticket agent for all four weeks of your run for about $100. And, while you could just as easily handle it yourself, a ticket agent does offer certain advantages. A ticket agent will have representatives on staff who have all the information in front of them that a caller might request; they will provide you with the names and numbers of callers every evening before you go to the theater. What's easier than that?

Unless you're completely strapped, and have no other options available, don't use your own phone number. It won't look good for you and it won't look good for the production.

ARE YOU IN GOOD HANDS?

Regardless of what kind of insurance your theater landlord may have on the building, you are probably going to wind up purchasing your own. Concerning this matter, the AEA Showcase Code reads as follows:

"The producer shall cause to be provided liability insurance at all interviews, auditions, rehearsals, and performances. He shall make the name of the insurance carrier available to the actors at the place of the interview, audition, rehearsal, and performance. In the event of an injury, the producer shall advise the actor of the procedure for filing a claim." Without the proper insurance, Equity can close down your production. That's nowhere near the loss you could face, however, if one of the actors is injured and you are held responsible. (If the landlord insists that his or her coverage will apply to your actors, consult your attorney. Generally, the landlord's policy will apply to members of your audience who may fall on a stairway or trip getting into their seats. Make sure this is clear, approved by your attorney, and approved by Equity!)

MISCELLANY

Here are some miscellaneous pointers relating to expenses and production:

1. In the past, the Equity Showcase Code has required a contribution from the producer to the Equity-LORT Subsidiary Rights Trust Fund in the amount of $150 per play ($350 maximum per season—July 1 to June 30). The Fund's trustees decide yearly whether to enforce or suspend this requirement. When the Fund's balance is substantial, the contribution is waived.

2. To keep from being labeled a vanity production—"John Smith presents: *Saturdays at Seven* starring John Smith,"—it's a good idea to come up with a name for your company—"Sentinel Productions presents: *Saturdays at Seven* featuring John Smith." Use your production company name in publicity announcements, on the program, and when you apply for insurance.

3. No taping, filming, or recording of any rehearsal or performance of an Equity Showcase production may be made without the written permission of Equity.

4. Equity defines a performance as "any presentation before an audience, invited or paid, including previews and or rehearsals." If you are planning a special performance of some kind, remember that it must be included in the performance schedule you agreed to.

5. Like Equity, the Society of Stage Directors and Choreographers, Inc. (SSDC) has created a contract which governs showcase productions. SSDC requires any of its members who are directing or choreographing a showcase to file this simple "Special Agreement" with the Society. The agreement allows members and their producers either to plug into one of SSDC's existing standard contracts or to use a special Rider which contains protection clauses standard to all SSDC contracts and appropriate to showcases.

In keeping with the favored-nations clause of Equity's Showcase Code, SSDC does not require payments for showcase productions, and fees received by SSDC members must be no less than those received by any AEA cast member or stage manager.

SSDC's one-page Rider states simple terms covering: extensions of the run, property rights, right of first refusal, subsidiary rights participation, arbitration, and recognition.

Contact SSDC for additional information and for samples of the Special Agreement and Rider: Special Contracts Administrator, SSDC, 1501 Broadway, New York, NY 10036, (212) 391-1070.

6. If you've written the play, don't forget to copyright it. Contact Information and Publications Section, LM-455, Copyright Office, Library of Congress, Washington, DC 20559, and ask for application form PA. The form is free, but you'll be charged $20 to file it. The effective date of your registration begins on the date your papers are received in the copyright office.

7. Opening nights and closing nights are the responsibility of the producer. You don't need to plan anything too fancy, of course, unless you have the money, but some champagne would be nice. If you can't afford to take the whole gang out on closing night, an inexpensive house party will suffice.

8. You're going to require some kind of house staff: someone who can take the money at the door, a coat-room person (if the theater has a coat room), and an usher, depending on whether or not you have designated seating. For these tasks enlist your friends—don't do these jobs yourself.

9. Make sure you purchase two notebooks at the beginning of your run—one for reservations, the other for your guest list. All guests should sign in with their addresses, so you can add them to your ever-growing mailing list.

PROGRAMS

You will undoubtedly want the people who come to see your play to receive a program. But, whether you want to do it or not, Equity says you have to, so start typing.

Certainly, if you have the money, a slick, printed program isn't going to turn anybody off. If you are on a tight budget, however, you'll probably wind up doing what most showcase producers do: Type it all up on a typewriter or word processor and make photocopies on colored paper. Some things to keep in mind:

1. Don't call your program a Playbill or use the name of any other established publication. There are laws against that—the same kind of laws that protect your work.

2. The most common format consists of: the title of the work and some kind of artwork (page 1); the lists of scenes and characters, as well as the actors playing them (page 2); the "Who's Who in the Cast," consisting of the actors' bios (page 3); bios of the director, tech people, and author (page 4); the AEA program bio and logo, to be supplied by Equity, must also appear somewhere on the program.

3. Some of the actors may wish to have their phone numbers included in their bios. Ask them first before printing this information! Bios should be uniform in structure and the information in them factual.

4. Cast members and tech people who are members of Equity must have an asterisk placed next to their name with the following note: "These actors and stage managers are members of Actors' Equity Association, appearing without benefit of contract or salary. The donation of their professional services is with the special permission of Actors' Equity Association."

5. Make sure that the name of the theater, its address, the telephone number of the ticket agent, and the dates of your run are printed somewhere on the program.

PUBLICITY AND ADVERTISING

Cards and/or flyers are the best way to advertise your production. Mail these out to friends and business acquaintances. If your director or any members of your cast have access to mailing lists, make sure you take advantage of them, too. Then, go to the post office and discuss the different mail sizes you have in mind with a postal agent and ask how much postage will cost. If your production is affiliated with a non-profit corporation you might be able to use its lower-cost bulk mailing privileges to cut down on expenses.

From the post office, go directly to a printer and ask to see some different paper stocks. Discuss your ideas for cards and flyers and get feedback on prices. Make sure you find out how large the paper is to start with. The printer should mention that you can print two or more cards on each piece of paper. Naturally, this would be a savings for you and is something you should consider.

The next person to speak with is an artist, preferably one of your close friends who won't charge you too much to make your cards up. You will require professional typography and perhaps some artwork or a logo incorporating the title of your play. The unfinished product should be easy to read, as sharp-looking as possible and should entice people to call up for reservations. The following information should appear on every card or flyer you make:

1. The name of the play, the names of the director, cast, and crew members.

2. The name and address of the theater, with directions how to get there if it is on some out-of-the-way corner.

3. The number to call for tickets, the price of the tickets, the dates of the run, and the show times.

4. The words "Equity-Approved Showcase," as well as asterisks next to the names of Equity people with a note that they are AEA members.

If you have sufficient funds you may consider hiring a professional publicist (also see chapter on "Creating Your Own Publicity"). Such a person deals with all of the newspapers and magazines on a regular basis and is more likely to be able to get a mention of your play into print.

If you can't afford a publicist, you'll have to create your own publicity. A well-written press release shouldn't be too much of a challenge, as long as you remember to keep it simple and include all the pertinent information.

A press release need be no more than a short blurb which adequately describes your play. For example: *"Hanging from the Chandelier, a new play by Goldie Candlestyx, is the touching and often hilarious story of four ex-college buddies who are unexpectedly reunited while standing on line to buy tickets for Phantom of the Opera."*

You can use such a blurb in all the publicity you send out, from full-sized press releases to tiny column items. You may also try to pitch stories on members of your cast, your director, and the playwright, to local papers, magazines, and radio and TV shows.

Approaching critics is more difficult, but not impossible. Keep in mind that critics receive countless invitations each week and yours is going to go into a pile with all the rest. For that reason, try to make your initial announcement and subsequent invitation as enticing as possible and easy to read, and make sure to include all of the necessary information. A personal note won't hurt either. Critics like to know that you're familiar with their work and that you value their input on your work.

Certain publications may be willing to review your work, even though their reviews won't run until your showcase has ended. Welcome them with open arms, anyway. A review is a review and if it's a good one, it can only help your chances for mounting future productions.

Keep in mind also that photo breaks can work miracles for your show. Arrange to have some good pictures taken and send prints to any publication that prints photos. Make sure the shots you send out are clear, interesting, and tasteful, and whatever you do, don't send every newspaper in town the same picture.

Listings are another way to publicize your production and many of them are free. Send your blurb, plus other pertinent information to any publication that runs play listings and keep your fingers crossed. For best results, write up each listing in the format of that particular publication. As with critics, a short personal note can be helpful.

As far as advertising is concerned, your main consideration is probably going to be financial. Print ads are extremely expensive and could easily inflate your budget beyond your means. Once again, unless someone involved in your production has some name recognition, you're probably better off waiting until you have some reviews to tout. Don't wait until the last minute, though, to plan an advertising strategy. Find out what publications run theatrical advertising, their rates, and their deadlines. If you do receive some positive reviews, an ad can substantially help increase the size of your audience.

IT'S A WRAP!

Well now you know all about producing an Equity-Approved Showcase. Do you still want to produce your own play? Think you're ready for the strain? The headaches? The non-stop aggravation? If you are, then more power to you. Even if the production isn't sensational, even if producers and agents don't start beating your door down, even if the critics don't praise you to the heavens, and even if you lose a couple of thousand dollars, it could be the wisest investment you'll ever make of your time and your money. You'll learn a lot about your work. You'll learn a lot about yourself. And you'll learn a lot about the business—more than any six-month course could possibly teach you. Who knows? Once you have acquired experience as a producer, you may be motivated to go on and produce other works.

HOW TO RUN AN AUDITION

BY ANDREA WOLPER

Many performers produce their own shows these days, and while instruction is offered in audition technique, no book or class offers guidelines for *running* auditions. Since there are no formal ground rules for getting the most from your audition (unless you're producing under a union contract), here are some suggestions.

THE CASTING NOTICE

Often, a well-made casting notice is the key to a successful audition. Placing a notice in the trades may cost money, and keeping it short may keep costs down. But investing in a detailed casting notice may save you time, money, and headaches in the long run. A good casting notice includes:

1. The name or working title of the project and/or production company. You might add the names of the director and writer.

2. A brief description of the project if it's not generally known, e.g., "a staged reading of an original avant-garde musical based on *Hamlet*."

3. A character breakdown. The more open-minded you are, the better, but when there are specific requirements, make them clear. If one character *must* be brunette, if another must belt to high Z, say so, or you'll spend most of your day seeing—or sorting through pictures of—people who don't meet your needs. (You may skip this for very well-known shows, although it can be useful to let potential Hamlets know how you/your director envision the character.) You can indicate a preference for non-traditional casting, e.g., "all races/physically challenged encouraged to attend." And if replacements or understudies are what you're seeking, be sure to say so.

4. The type of audition or procedure. Are you interviewing or auditioning? Do you want to see a monologue? Two? What style? (If you don't specify monologues, auditioners will probably expect to read from the script—and if readings are what you'll be doing, say so!) Do you want people to dance or sing? What style(s)? If you're doing a published show, do you want to hear a song or monologue from that show? Do you want people to improvise, tell a story, juggle? You'll want to see people at their best, so allow them to prepare.

5. Production schedule and location. Include as much information as you have, or you may cast your Hamlet only to find he'll be out of town opening night. If you can, include dates and times of callbacks, rehearsal location(s), whether you'll rehearse days or evenings, where the show runs, when it opens and closes, when and where the film shoots. Double-check dates and addresses, and include anything unusual, i.e., midnight shows, performance on a boat, in a park, and so forth.

6. Have actors schedule an audition. By scheduling appointments in advance, you'll avoid either having so many people show up that you can't see them all, or having so few that it isn't worth your time. You can have people send you pictures and resumes in advance. This allows you to do an initial screening and contact those who interest you. If you've given the necessary information by following the guidelines thus far, you need not include a phone number. Why have people call when you're just going to tell them to send a P/R?

Or you can request that people call you for appointments. Specify when people may begin calling; to give everybody a fair chance, consider starting a day or two after the notice is published. You or someone who knows the pertinent details *must* be available to answer the phone. You will appear unprofessional (and professionals will not care to work with you) if your child, your maid, your lover—in short, anyone who is not well-informed about the project—takes the calls.

7. Pay or salary. If you're producing under a union contract, state which it is. If not, are you paying the cast? Are rehearsals paid? Transportation or meals provided or reimbursed? If you're holding an audition for a workshop or collective for which each performer pays a fee or dues, state the amount.

8. Equity-Approved Showcases. If you're producing under Equity's Showcase Code, you must have an application on file at Equity, and the casting notice must say "approval pending." Eligible performers are to be given priority at open calls; consider scheduling two separate auditions—one for eligibles and one for non-eligibles. Eligibles who show up during the second session must be given priority, according to the code.

9. Nudity requirements. If anybody in the cast will be asked to appear nude— if even for a brief moment—include that information in the notice. No ifs, ands, or—pardon the expression—buts.

FIND AN APPROPRIATE AUDITION SITE

If you can't afford to rent a studio, then beg or borrow a theater, auditorium, or church hall. Avoid places—from the dumpy to the deserted—that might arouse discomfort or suspicion. Apartments, private homes, and especially hotel rooms are out! Your office *may* be appropriate for interviews, but *only during regular business hours* and *if* there are other people present. Wherever you are, be sure there's ample waiting space.

SCHEDULING AND SIGN-UP

When scheduling appointments, be sure to allow enough time per person. Don't expect to see 100 auditions in one eight-hour day. One person every five minutes is unrealistic; you'll certainly fall behind. Ten-minute increments may seem too long, but you'll be grateful for the cushion. When you make appointments, you may tell auditioners how many minutes they have for their songs or monologues. Don't forget to schedule a few breaks for you and your colleagues.

Open calls are completely uncivilized, but if for some reason you decide to hold one, make it as painless as possible. *You* should post the official sign-up sheet, which means your casting notice should say something like "official sign-up posted two hours prior." (If you don't, an early-bird actor will start a sheet that others will sign throughout the day; they'll justifiably be upset if you show up hours later with an "official" sheet.) Consider using time slots instead of numbers to give people a ballpark idea of when to return.

THE DAY ARRIVES

RULE 1: Be on time. No—be early. Allow time to get organized, have a cup of coffee, find extra chairs.

RULE 2: You must have a monitor to keep things running smoothly. Anyone who has a part in the actual casting shouldn't be running the audition as well. The last thing you need is to be distracted by having to keep track of entrances and exits, answer procedural questions, or deal with disgruntled performers.

RULE 3: Try to stay on schedule. Some delays are unavoidable, but do your best. Your monitor will have to work in latecomers and, at open calls, returnees.

If you wish to introduce yourself and your colleagues to each auditioner—a nice touch—keep it brief. Skip the history of the production, the background of the play and the characters, and so on. All that can be posted in the waiting area.

Unless you have tons of down-time, don't have the actors who interest you with their monologues or songs stay to read; people you're seriously considering should have at least overnight to become familiar with the script. That's why callbacks were invented! Don't cast on the spot. Everyone deserves a chance to be seen and considered. And at the end of your final callbacks, don't make everyone wait while you and your colleagues debate, and then announce your decisions. When you've seen all you need to see, send everyone home, take the time you need to decide, and notify your cast by phone.

RULE 4: For singing auditions, hire a qualified accompanist—one who has experience accompanying singers and is familiar with the general repertoire of the style you've asked to hear. Your cousin who plays a little probably isn't qualified.

CONDUCT

The performers are also auditioning you, so professional, courteous behavior is a must. Most performers will go out of their way to please you, but if anyone gets testy, remember that it's not personal; some people feel tremendous pressure when they audition. If there's a genuine gripe, let your monitor handle it.

If you want to give direction, be as clear as possible and allow performers a minute or so to take in your suggestions. If someone reads for one role and you'd like to hear another, let the person study the script in the waiting area; the monitor can work them back in when they're ready.

Brief conferences with your colleagues can take place while one performer exits and another enters, or while singer and accompanist look over the music, but *not* during the actual audition. You may instruct the monitor to give you a minute or two between each audition. And if you haven't scheduled a lunch break, you'll have to eat during those stolen moments.

CASTING

Casting is the most challenging part of the audition process. It can be stressful, but try to stay focused. There'll be no need to feel desperate or rushed if you plan well and keep an open mind. Does a cop or a housewife or a homosexual or a lover always look and talk a particular way? Actors with lesser skills sometimes get cast because they "look the part." Better to find a real talent whose work will make you forget the stereotypes. It might be hard to let go of the character you visualized when you wrote or first read the script or screenplay, but the person you least expect to be right may be the very one who brings a spark of life and originality to the role—if you're open enough to perceive it.

WHEN NOT TO HOLD AN AUDITION

Leaving aside for the moment any contractual requirements, you're under no obligation to hold auditions. So if your project has already been cast, or you're holding auditions for publicity or to see who's in town or because it makes you feel important—don't. You have every right to produce a show starring you, your friends, or the people who were in your last show. Just don't ask people to come in and do their stuff if there aren't any jobs available.

IN CONCLUSION

While auditions are an exciting part of the process of bringing a project to life, they can also provoke a lot of anxiety. Advance planning, including a well-written casting notice, will help minimize tension and stress. Creating a clear structure for your audition will leave you freer to improvise during the audition. Most important, an organized, smooth-running audition process will allow you to make the most of the experience and get the best possible cast for your show.

CREATING YOUR OWN PUBLICITY

BILL ERVOLINO

Performers who are unable to latch on to a publicist should not over-look the do-it-yourself option. Many entertainers have learned how to put together an effective publicity campaign with no previous experience. So if you're willing to do a little leg-work and some research you might want to explore this approach. Obviously, you won't gain the advantages of a full-scale promotional effort mounted by a major press agent, but you can do at least some of the public relations work that is so important to your career. A do-it-yourself PR campaign, if profession-ally prepared and well organized, can produce very positive results.

THE PRESS KIT

Start out by preparing a press kit. It doesn't have to be slick to be effective. In fact, if you're an unknown, too-slick a press kit could wind up turning people off. Your goal primarily is to produce a press kit that looks professional.

An effective press kit should contain a description of your project, bios of the people involved, clips and reviews, photographs of performers (or a scene from the production), and a personal letter.

Make sure that all your PR material is well written. Editors have eyes like eagles when it comes to spotting typos, poor grammar, and rambling sentences. There is nothing worse to send to an editor than a poorly written press kit.

Keep your bio short and sweet. If information is colorful, include it. If it's pertinent to your project, include it. If it incorporates anyone famous, include it! Everyone loves to see names so, if you studied with Uta Hagen, took gym class with Meryl Streep, or shared an apartment with anyone well-known, it will be of interest.

Your photographs are extremely important in publicizing your project and should be the best quality you can afford to buy. Unprofessional photos that are fuzzy or grainy or just plain awful will only hurt your publicity effort. If you're beautiful, make sure that your photos are beautiful. If you're funny, try a funny pose, perhaps with some props. Don't send out photos that are mis-leading.

The most effective cover letter is one that is personal and to the point. It should tell the editor or critic what you are doing, when you are doing it, and why you think it is of interest. If the editor recently wrote an article bemoaning how musicals aren't what they used to be, and you're in the middle of rehearsals for a real old-fashioned musical comedy, be sure to mention it. If you are a cabaret singer by night and a veterinarian by day, include this information in your letter and politely suggest that the publication write a feature on moonlighting professionals.

A personal press agent would sit you down and interrogate you like Elliot Ness for any potential story angle that might emerge. Without a press agent, you'll have to discover these angles on your own. If you think about it long enough you're bound to come up with something interesting.

FINDING OUTLETS

Identifying all of the press outlets that are available to you will take time, patience, and all the resourcefulness you can muster. Start by making a list of all the dailies, weeklies, and monthlies you can think of that carry entertainment items. Then go to the largest newsstand you can find and do some browsing. After this, go to a library and ask for any guides they might have which list metro-area publications. Keep adding to your list and don't rule out the hometown papers. They can be excellent sources of publicity and could provide you with a nice feature you can clip out and stick in your press kit.

Once you have a list of possible outlets, make appropriate notations next to each publication with regard to the types of PR opportunities it offers. Some types of press outlets you may find are as follows:

Listings. Many newspapers and magazines list shows and events in their directories. Readers of these publications generally rely on such listings when planning a night on the town. Your best chance of being included in a directory is to study the format in each publication and then write up a listing that is compatible. Make sure you include all the pertinent information (who, what, where, when) and that your listing is neatly typed. Then call the publication you are interested in, ask for the listings or calendar editor, and inquire about deadline information. Address your listing to that particular editor, unless you are told otherwise. A handwritten note, accompanying the listing, probably won't hurt ("Dear Mr./Ms. Smith: Thanks for the information the other day. Hope you can use this...").

Photo Submissions. Editors and art directors like attractive pictures and many publications use one or more on every page. When sending a photo to a publication, make sure to enclose a caption that contains all necessary information and correctly identifies, from left to right, the people in the photo. Also make sure that the photographer's credit is stamped or written legibly on the back of the photo. Your photo can be arty, comical, or provocative. The best tip concerning the submission of photos, however, is to study the publication you are sending them to and see the type of material they like. Once you're familiar with the publication, use some common sense and forward something appropriate.

Column Items. There are countless publications in which you can publicize your project. Look around, familiarize yourself with what's out there, and then be selective about where you send your material. If you have an especially good item, something involving a "name," for example, you may want to send it to a gossip columnist like Liz Smith at *New York Newsday,* or some of the other better-known columns. Keep in mind, however, that the bigger the column, the warier the columnist is likely to be about taking items from strangers. If you want to take a chance, write up the item in the style of the column, keep it brief, send it off, and follow up with a phone call. Be reminded, though, that major columnists are very busy, so don't tie them up with long-winded conversation. A simple, "Will you be using the item?" will do the job.

Features and Interviews. When pitching yourself as a feature subject, make sure you provide the editor or writer with as much information as possible, written as concisely as possible. Include who you are, what you're doing, and sell, sell, sell. If a prominent critic has said something wonderful about you, include it in your pitch. If you have worked with some famous people in the past, include that too. Perhaps you have a special skill or situation that might prove enticing to the editor. If so, try it, no matter how far out it might seem.

Don't be disappointed if your request for a feature or interview is turned down. Arranging press of this type definitely requires a talent for finding angles and pitching them. It is not unheard of for an unknown to grab this type of coverage, but this occurs rarely. Your best bet is to start with your hometown press and build slowly from there.

TELEVISION BOOKINGS

This one is really tricky. It isn't impossible, but it certainly isn't easy, and it isn't always advisable. If you don't have a press agent, have never appeared on TV before, and don't have a long-term publicity campaign mapped out, you may not be ready for a TV appearance. Of course, such an appearance could lead to all kinds of offers, but if you're not ready to hire an agent, you're probably not ready for David Letterman either.

If you are intent on trying for a TV appearance go right ahead. But without a publicist, your chances are very slim. Sandra Furton, formerly the head talent coordinator for "Late Night with David Letterman," says, "We feel more confident if there's a publicist involved, especially if they have worked with us in the past and recommended someone [who appeared on the show]. You learn to trust certain publicists." Furton offers this advice to performers without publicists: "Send a letter, enclose as much information as you can, and, if you have a videotape, send that along, too. It gives us the opportunity to see you in a TV situation." Furton adds that each request is reviewed by several people in the show's talent office.

As the Letterman show is taped in New York, many guests are local performers. Theater companies are rarely represented, unless an act is particularly unusual. One person who did make it onto the show and was invited back a couple of times, was neither a performer nor an artistic director. She was a Broadway house-usherette, who talked about her 45 years behind a flashlight.

Don't overlook *local* TV shows and cable TV programs. They are always looking for guests. Most prefer to deal with publicists, too, but they are bound to be more receptive than national programs. The local shows can also give you an opportunity to get your feet wet. If you've never been interviewed before on camera, it's best to keep it on the smallest scale possible. To book yourself on one of these shows, you should contact the talent coordinator, ask what the requirements are, and then follow up with a letter. If you have a tape, send that as well. Sell yourself as best you can.

Your chances of obtaining exposure are better if you can do something different or unusual during your segment. If you have successfully dealt with a serious issue in your life, overcome a condition or illness, or have anything else that you wouldn't feel uncomfortable talking about on TV, propose it as a segment. Discussing how you've dealt with dyslexia for example, could get you some exposure and help others in the process. Make absolutely sure that you feel comfortable with an appearance of this sort and that a personal issue does not get exploited.

CULTIVATING THE MEDIA

Without a press agent out there helping to develop a relationship with the media for you, you're going to have to do it yourself. This isn't easy, but it can be done.

Critics and editors are used to pushy people, but that doesn't mean they enjoy dealing with them. The more you socialize with friends in the business, the more likely it is that you will run into various members of the press. It is important for you to cultivate professional relationships with these people, so don't just stand there staring at them. If it's someone you don't know, wait for the right time, and go over and introduce yourself. When you run into writers or critics whom you have already met, by all means walk over and say hello. Mention what you've been up to and, if you happen to recall a recent article they've written, it probably won't hurt to comment on it. Be cordial. Be charming. And be quick about it. Don't be pushy, don't be obnoxious, and don't take up too much of their time—just enough to remind them of who you are and what you are doing.

Other ways to remind the press that you're still alive include occasional notes ("I saw your article on such-and-such and found it very informative...") and cards ("Merry Christmas, Happy Hanukkah, Happy New Year, and hope you can catch my next show at Eighty-Eights"). Also, follow-ups are important. Critics do appreciate thank-you notes for their reviews and, if you point out something they said that you felt was particularly on the mark, that's even better. You can even send a polite note for a negative review, thanking the critic for reviewing you, or for any positive comments or suggestions that were in the review.

In between writing all these notes, don't forget mailings to the people who have already seen you in performance. Many small theater companies and individual performers make an address book available to members of the audience who want to be put on their mailing list. Anyone who came to see you and signed your address book is interested in what you are doing. Don't forget about those people. Send them flyers or newsletters and keep them posted on your present and future projects.

Publicity plays a major role in achieving success as a performer. It is hard work, but well worth the effort. Make the most of whatever PR options are available to you during the engagements for which you are hired. Some clubs and theaters have in-house publicity that could help you. Pay attention to what works and what doesn't and learn to be patient, letting your publicity build over time.

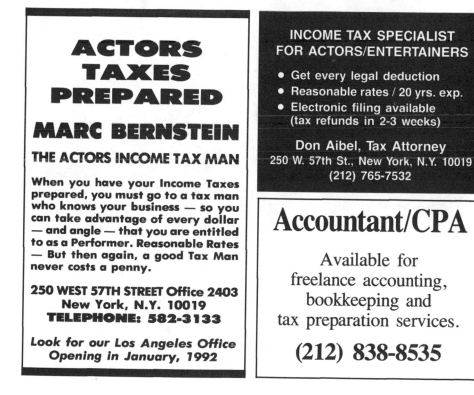
53A

PART FIVE

WORKING IN THE THEATER

OFF- AND OFF-OFF-BROADWAY

BY VICTOR GLUCK

O ff-Broadway theaters have, for about 35 years, offered New York theatergoers an alternative to the fare found on Broadway's stages. Off-Broadway theaters are located all over New York City. Generally intimate spaces, they allow for lower production costs and the presentation of plays with a specialized interest. Although a performer's ultimate goal may be Broadway, the majority of work in the New York theater is actually produced Off- and Off-Off-Broadway. While Broadway theaters' high rents continue to prove prohibitive, hundreds of theater companies away from the Broadway theater district offer more affordable space and endless opportunities to producers, directors, and performers at all levels.

Actors' Equity defines Off-Broadway productions as those presented in a Manhattan theater whose maximum capacity is 499 seats—but which is *not* located within the Broadway (Production Contract) district (defined by Equity as that area bounded by 5th and 9th avenues from 34th to 57th Street and by 5th Avenue to the Hudson River from 55th to 72nd Street). Off-Off-Broadway refers to productions mounted in New York City in theaters under 100 seats, usually under Equity's Showcase Code or Funded Non-Profit Theater Code. Both commercial and non-profit ventures can be found Off-Broadway. Generally, only non-profit productions are mounted Off-Off-Broadway, where often the main point is *showcasing* one's work in exchange for expense reimbursement and/or a minimal stipend.

The Off-Off-Broadway movement began with Caffe Cino (in 1959), the La Mama Experimental Theater Club (in 1962), and a concurrent ferment of creativity that launched the careers of such playwrights as Leonard Melfi, Sam Shepard, Lanford Wilson, John Guare, Israel Horovitz, Robert Patrick, Maria Irene Fornes, and Tom Eyen.

Many well-known stage actors began their careers in Off- or Off-Off-Broadway productions—Meryl Streep, William Hurt, Al Pacino, Robert De Niro, and Richard Dreyfuss are just a few of the stars who, at one time in their careers, were closely linked to the Off-Broadway theater scene. Legends were born Off-Broadway that have permanently changed American theater—talents such as Ellen Stewart, Tom O'Horgan, Charles Ludlam, Julian Beck and Judith Malina, Joseph Chaikin, Harvey Fierstein, and Joseph Papp. The staggering number of plays produced in these and other artists' theaters has provided New York audiences and theater practitioners with hundreds of opportunities that did not previously exist. Countless newcomers to the legitimate stage now gain performance experience in Off-Off-Broadway houses.

The last 30 years has seen the rise of Off-Off-Broadway non-profit theater companies that have become an integral part of New York's cultural life. Because many Off-Off-Broadway companies specialize or host various kinds of theater, they offer newcomers to the acting profession valuable training and experience. Some theaters, like the York Theatre Company, specialize in revivals; others, such as the CSC Repertory Ltd.-The Classic Stage Company, offer new interpretations of the classics. Some theaters are frequently characterized by production style, such as the poetic realism practiced by Circle Repertory Company. Others may offer competitive one-act festivals, as does the Ensemble Studio Theatre, thereby giving an actor a chance to be seen in several different plays at one time.

Often a collective of actors and directors will be formed for the purpose of showcasing the talents of its members. Still other companies, like the Negro Ensemble Company, the Jewish Repertory Theater, or the Pan Asian Repertory Theater, are the home of specific ethnic groups. These companies give work to actors and other theater artists that might not be found elsewhere. The Second Stage specializes in giving a second chance to plays that the company feels have been unjustly neglected, although they've been producing more and more original work of late. Manhattan Punch Line calls itself the "house of comedy" and makes use of actors' and playwrights' comedic gifts, while Soho Repertory Theater's seasons emphasize plays that feature unusual language and theatricality.

The theater space of Off-Off-Broadway may be a church, loft, school, warehouse, or basement. Off-Off-Broadway can, in fact, exist anywhere, from just outside the Broadway theater district to the outer fringes of New York City.

One sign of Off-Broadway's vital contribution to American theater is the fact that, since 1970, the Pulitzer Prize in drama has frequently gone to a work originating in one of these New York theaters. That year the prize went to the New York Shakespeare Festival's production of *No Place to Be Somebody* by Charles Gordone. Since then, two other New York Shakespeare Festival productions have received Pulitzer Prizes as Off-Broadway plays—*That Championship Season* in 1973, and *A Chorus Line* in 1976 (although both of these plays had already moved to Broadway at the time of the awards).

In 1971, Paul Zindel's *The Effect of Gamma Rays on Man-in-the-Moon Marigolds*, which ran Off-Broadway for several years, won the Pulitzer, and went on to become an acclaimed film.

Other theaters honored for initiating Pulitzer Prize-winning plays: Theater for the New City—Sam Shepard's *Buried Child* (1979); Circle Repertory Company—Lanford Wilson's *Talley's Folly* (1980); the Negro Ensemble Company—*A Soldier's Play* by Charles Fuller (1982); and Playwrights Horizons—*Driving Miss Daisy* by Alfred Uhry (1988) and Wendy Wasserstein's *The Heidi Chronicles* (1989).

Major stars of stage and screen as well as big name producers are as likely to be working Off-Broadway as on. Many of Broadway's biggest hits originated at Off-Broadway theaters before risking larger and more expensive venues. Recent Tony winners *Torch Song Trilogy*, *The Elephant Man*, and *I'm Not Rappaport* would not have been possible without the Off-Broadway tryouts that came first. All of these plays kept their original Off-Broadway casts when they moved to Broadway. Hit musicals like *Little Shop of Horrors*, *Joseph and the Amazing Technicolor Dreamcoat*, *The Best Little Whorehouse in Texas*, *Ain't Misbehavin'*, and *Once on This Island* were first mounted in Off-Broadway theaters; many moved uptown.

Many successful Off- and Off-Off-Broadway shows go on to become movies—*Crossing Delancey*, *Fool for Love*, *Key Exchange*, *Little Shop of Horrors*, *A Soldier's Story*, *Orphans*, *Talk Radio*, *Steel Magnolias*, *Driving Miss Daisy*, *Frankie and Johnny in the Clair de Lune*, *Prelude to a Kiss*, and *Other People's Money*. Others have been seen on television: Craig Lucas's *Blue Window*, Terrence McNally's *Andre's Mother*, and Jonathan Marc Sherman's *Women and Wallace*. Sometimes the original actors are signed to recreate their roles in films. Even when not given this opportunity, the very fact that they created the original roles increases their stock with casting agents, directors, and playwrights. For some playwrights, producers, directors, and performers, Off-Broadway is the road to a highly successful career.

OFF- AND OFF-OFF-BROADWAY THEATER COMPANIES

The following is a list of Off- and Off-Off-Broadway theater companies in New York City. Some are non-Equity companies, some produce under Equity's Showcase or Tier Codes, while others may produce under an Equity contract.

THE ABOUT FACE THEATRE COMPANY
Nat Horne Theatre
442 W. 42nd St.
NYC 10036
(212) 268-9638
Sean Burke, art. dir.;
Allison Jones, mng. dir.

ACT NOW THEATRE CO.
286 Clinton St., 1B
Brooklyn, NY 11201
(718) 935-0130
Aaron Ingram, pres.

THE ACTING COMPANY
Box 898
Times Square Station
NYC 10108
(212) 564-3510
Zelda Fichandler, art. dir.;
Margot Harley, exec. prod.

ACTORS' ALLIANCE INC.
JAF Box 7370
NYC 10116
(718) 768-6110
Melanie Sutherland, art. dir.

THE ACTORS COLLECTIVE
145 E. 27th St., Suite 4K
NYC 10016
(212) 779-9885
Warren Manzi, art. dir.;
Catherine Russell, mng. dir.

ACTORS' CREATIVE THEATRE
311 W. 43rd St.
NYC 10036
(212) 397-5880
Ernie Martin, art. dir.

ACTORS THEATRE WORKSHOP
145 W. 28th St.
NYC 10001
(212) 947-1386
Thurman E. Scott, art. dir.

AFRIKAN WOMAN'S REPERTORY
432 W. 42nd St.
NYC 10036
(212) 993-0070
Bonnie Wright, dir.

ALCHEMY THEATRE COMPANY
Box 2408
Times Square Station
NYC 10108
(212) 581-3361
Gita Donovan, Linda Ames Key,
Joseph Purdy, artistic and mng. dirs.

ALLEY CATS PRODUCTIONS
443 W. 43rd St.
NYC 10036
(212) 582-1098
Melanie Webber, gen. mgr.

AMAS REPERTORY THEATRE INC. &
AMAS EUBIE BLAKE YOUTH THEATRE
1 E. 104th St., 3rd fl.
NYC 10029
(212) 369-8000
Rosetta LeNoire, art. dir.;
Jeff Solis, mng. dir.

THE AMERICAN CENTER FOR
STANISLAVSKI THEATRE ART, INC.
485 Park Ave., #6A
NYC 10022
(212) 755-5120
Sonia Moore, art. dir.

AMERICAN ENSEMBLE COMPANY
Box 972, Peck Slip Station
NYC 10272
(212) 571-7594
Robert Petito, art. dir.

AMERICAN INDIAN COMMUNITY
HOUSE THEATRE SPACE
404 Lafayette St., 2nd fl.
NYC 10003
(212) 598-0100
Muriel Miguel, art. dir.

AMERICAN JEWISH THEATRE
307 W. 26th St.
NYC 10001
(212) 633-9797
Stanley Brechner, art. dir.

THE AMERICAN LINE
810 W. 183rd St., #5C
NYC 10033
(212) 740-9277
Richard Hoehler, art. dir.

AMERICAN PLACE THEATRE
111 W. 46th St.
NYC 10036
(212) 840-2960
Wynn Handman, art. dir.;
Stephen Lisner, gen. mgr.

AMERICAN THEATRE OF ACTORS
314 W. 54th St.
NYC 10019
(212) 581-3044
James Jennings, art. dir.

ANY PLACE THEATRE
Box 2467
NYC 10185
Lynn Middleton, art. dir.

APPLE CORPS THEATRE
336 W. 20th St.
NYC 10011
(212) 929-2955
John Raymond, artistic dir.

ART & WORK ENSEMBLE
55 Mercer St.
NYC 10013
(212) 925-3960
Derek Todd, exec. dir.

THE ARTISTS' PERSPECTIVE, INC.
The Master Theatre
310 Riverside Dr.
NYC 10025
(212) 678-6895
Marsha Winstead, art. dir.

ARTS CLUB THEATRE
24 Britton St.
Jersey City, NJ 07306
(201) 451-7278
Linda Pakri, art. dir.

ATLANTIC THEATER COMPANY
336 W. 20th St.
NYC 10011
(212) 546-8015
Scott Zigler, art. dir.

AVALON REPERTORY THEATRE
2744 Broadway
NYC 10025
(212) 316-2668
Lee Gundersheimer, Hilary Six, art. dirs.

BAD NEIGHBORS
336 W. 11th St., #2B
NYC 10014
(212) 989-0788
Michael Yawney, art. dir.

THE BARROW GROUP
Box 2236
NYC 10108
(212) 522-1421
Seth Barrish, art. dir.; Jeffrey Barnes, mng. dir.

THE BASIC THEATRE
Box 1253
Ansonia Station
NYC 10023
(212) 663-5268/397-1511
Sheri Delaine, Jared Hammon, art. dirs.

THE BEACON PROJECT
2130 Broadway, Suite 809
NYC 10023
(212) 362-5777
Stuart Laurence, art. dir.

BILLIE HOLIDAY THEATRE
1368 Fulton St.
Brooklyn, NY 11216
(718) 857-6363
Marjorie Moon, prod'r.

BLACK SPECTRUM THEATRE COMPANY
119th Ave. & Merrick Blvd.
Jamaica, NY 11434
(718) 723-1800
Carl Clay, art. dir.

BLUE DIAMOND PRODUCTIONS
187A 6th Ave., #3
Brooklyn, NY 11217
(718) 789-3984
Wayne Jelks, art. dir.;
J. D. Wyatt, assoc. prod.

BLUE HERON THEATRE
645 West End Ave.
NYC 10025
(212) 745-0422
Ardelle Striker, art. dir.

BOND STREET THEATRE COALITION
2 Bond St.
NYC 10012
(212) 254-4614
Joanna M. Sherman, art. dir.

BREAD AND PUPPET THEATER
c/o George Ashley
310 Greenwich St., #31-A
NYC 10013
(212) 964-0263
Peter Schumann, art. dir.

CHICAGO CITY LIMITS
351 E. 74th St.
NYC 10021
(212) 772-8707
Paul Zuckerman, prod'r.

CIRCLE REPERTORY COMPANY
Office:161 Ave. of the Americas
NYC 10013
(212) 691-3210
Theatre: 99 7th Ave. So., NYC 10014
Tanya Berezin, art. dir.
Terrence Dwyer, mng. dir.

CLASSICWORKS
90 Prince St., Apt. 6N
NYC 10012
Russ Billingsley, art. dir.

COLONY THEATRE
152 W. 71st St.
NYC 10023
(212) 662-6193
Tim Kelleher, art. dir.

COMMON GROUND
210 Forsyth St.
NYC 10002
(212) 505-6047
Norman Taffel, art. dir.

THE COMPANY THEATRE
Box 1874, Old Chelsea Station
NYC 10011
Caymichael Patten, art. dir.

CONEY ISLAND, USA
Boardwalk & W. 12th St.
Coney Island, NY 11224
(718) 372-5159
Dick Zigun, art. dir.

COURTYARD PLAYERS
Office: 426 W. 45th St., Suite 2RW
NYC 10036
Theatre Address: 39 Grove St.
NYC 10014
(212) 496-4288
Bob Stark, art. dir.

CREATION PRODUCTION COMPANY
127 Greene St.
NYC 10012
(212) 674-5593
Matthew Maguire, Susan Mosakowski,
art. dirs.

CSC REPERTORY
The Classic Stage Co.
136 E. 13th St.
NYC 10003
(212) 677-4210
Carey Perloff, art. dir.;
Patricia Taylor, mng. dir.

CUCARACHA THEATRE
(presently looking for new home)
421 W. 22nd St., #3
NYC 10011
(212) 242-5598
Richard Caliban, art. dir.

THE DIRECTORS COMPANY
311 W. 43rd St. #1404
NYC 10036
(212) 246-5877
Michael Parva, Victoria Lanman-Chesshire,
art. dirs.

DOUBLE IMAGE THEATRE
445 W. 59th St., Rm. 1535
NYC 10019
(212) 245-2489
John Martello, art. dir.

DOWNING STREET PRODUCTIONS
496A Hudson St., Suite E23
NYC 10014
(212) 969-0404

DOWNTOWN ART CO.
Office: 280 Broadway, Rm. 412
NYC 10007-1896
(212) 732-1201
Theater address: 64 E. 4th St.
NYC 10003
Ryan Gilliam, Cliff Scott, partners

DRAMATIC RISKS
60 E. 4th St., #19
NYC 10003
Mark Grant Warren, exec./art. dir.

DROGIN PRODUCTIONS
151 E. 31st St.
NYC 10016
(212) 481-0188
Marcy Drogin, prod'r

DUO THEATRE
Box 1200
Cooper Station
NYC 10276
(212) 598-4320
Michael Alasa, exec./art. dir.

ECHO REPERTORY CO.
300 Fort Washington Ave., #31
NYC 10032
(212) 795-3985
Amelia David, art. dir.

ECONOMY TIRES THEATRE
DTW's Bessie Schonberg Theatre
219 W. 19th St.
NYC 10011
(212) 924-0077
David White, exec. dir.

ELYSIUM THEATRE COMPANY
204 E. 6th St.
NYC 10003
(212) 713-5478
Gregori H. von Leitis, art. dir.

EN GARDE ARTS
225 Rector Pl., Suite 3A
NYC 10280
(212) 941-9793
Anne Hamburger, prod'r.

ENSEMBLE STUDIO THEATRE
549 W. 52nd St.
NYC 10019
(212) 247-4982
Curt Dempster, art. dir.

FIRING SQUAD/
COMEDY REP ENSEMBLE
121 E. 12th St., Suite 6C
NYC 10003
(212) 473-0413
David Stamford, writer/prod'r;
Veronique Perrier, art. dir.

FIRST AMENDMENT
COMEDY THEATRE
Box 1796
NYC 10025
(212) 678-0076
Barbara Contardi, art. dir.

FOLKSBIENE THEATRE
(Performances in Yiddish)
123 E. 55th St.
NYC 10022
(212) 755-2231
Ben Schechter, art. dir.

FOUNDATION OF THE DRAMATISTS GUILD/
YOUNG PLAYWRIGHTS FESTIVAL
234 W. 44th St., Rm. 1005
NYC 10036
(212) 575-7796
Sheri M. Goldhirsch, mng. dir.

FOURTH WALL REPERTORY CO.
79 E. 4th St.
NYC 10003
(212) 254-5060
Joan Harvey, art. dir.

GOLDEN FLEECE, LTD.
204 W. 20th St.
NYC 10011
(212) 691-6105
Lu Rodgers, art. dir.

H.A.D.L.E.Y. PLAYERS
207 W. 133rd St.
NYC 10030
(212) 926-0281
Gertrude Jeanette, art. dir.

HERITAGE THEATRE
Pfizer Conference Center
219 E. 42nd St.
NYC 10017
Thomas Luce Summa, art. dir.

HISPANIC ORGANIZATION
OF LATIN ACTORS (HOLA)
250 W. 65th St.
NYC 10023
(212) 595-8286
Francisco Rivela, art. dir.

HOME FOR CONTEMPORARY
THEATRE AND ART
44 Walker St.
NYC 10013
(212) 431-7434
Randy Rollison, art. dir.; Parris Relkin, mng.
dir.

INTAR HISPANIC AMERICAN
ARTS CENTER
Box 788
Times Square Station
NYC 10108
(212) 695-6134
Max Ferra, art. dir.;
Eva Brune, mng. dir.

INTERART THEATRE
549 W. 52nd St.
NYC 10019
(212) 246-1050
Margot Lewitin, art. dir.

IRISH ARTS CENTER
553 W. 51st St.
NYC 10019
(212) 757-3318
Jim Sheridan, art. dir.;
Nye Heron, prod. dir.

IRISH REPERTORY THEATRE
163 W. 17th St.
NYC 10011
(212) 255-0270
Ciaran O'Reilly, prod. dir.

IRONDALE ENSEMBLE PROJECT
782 West End Ave.
NYC 10025
(212) 633-1292
James Nieson, art. dir.

ITALIAN-AMERICAN
REPERTORY THEATRE
496A Hudson St., Suite E-25
NYC 10014
(201) 836-0907
Gene Ruffini, art. dir.

JEAN COCTEAU REPERTORY
330 Bowery
NYC 10012
(212) 677-0060
Robert Hupp, art. dir.;
David Fishelson, mng. dir.

JEWISH REPERTORY THEATRE
344 E. 14th St.
NYC 10003
(212) 674-7200
Ran Avni, art. dir.

LA MAMA ETC.
74-A E. 4th St.
NYC 10003
(212) 475-7710
Ellen Stewart, art. dir.

LAMB'S THEATRE COMPANY
130 W. 44th St.
NYC 10036
(212) 997-0210
Carolyn Rossi Copeland, prod. dir.

LATIN AMERICAN THEATRE ENSEMBLE
Box 18
Radio City Station
NYC 10101
(212) 246-7478/410-4582
Theatre address: 172 E. 104 St.,
NYC 10029
Margarita Toirac, exec. dir.

LINCOLN CENTER THEATER
Mitzi Newhouse Theater
150 W. 65th St.
NYC 10023
(212) 362-7600
Andre Bishop, art. dir. (as of Jan. 1992);
Bernard Gersten, exec. dir.

THE LIVING THEATRE
Box 20180
Tompkins Square Station
NYC 10009
Judith Malina, Hanon Reznikov, art. dirs.

LOVE CREEK THEATRE
325 W. 45th St., 706A
NYC 10036
Philip Galbraith, art. dir.

MABOU MINES
150 First Ave.
NYC 10009
(212) 473-0559
Collective artistic leadership.

MANHATTAN CLASS COMPANY
Box 279, Times Square Station
NYC 10108
(212) 239-9033
Theatre Address: 442 W. 42nd St.,
NYC 10036
Robert LuPone, Bernard Telsey, exec. dirs.

MANHATTAN ENSEMBLE, INC.
RR 2, Box 453, Kerhonkson, NY 12446
Raymond Marciniak, art. dir.

MANHATTAN PUNCH LINE
410 W. 42nd St., 3rd fl.
NYC 10036
(212) 239-0827
Steve Kaplan, art. dir.

MANHATTAN REPERTORY COMPANY
648 Broadway, Suite 701
NYC 10012
(212) 995-5582
Tom Chiodo, Peter DePietro, art. dirs.
(Also owns and operates Murder a la Carte)

MANHATTAN THEATRE CLUB
453 W. 16th St.
NYC 10011
(212) 645-5590
Lynne Meadow, art. dir.

ERNIE MARTIN STUDIO THEATRE
311 W. 43rd St., 5th fl.
NYC, 10036
(212) 397-5880
Ernie Martin, art. dir.;
Michael Hajek, mng. dir.

MEDICINE SHOW THEATRE ENSEMBLE
Box 20240
NYC 10025
(212) 431-9545
Barbara Vann, art. dir.

MIRANDA THEATRE CO.
c/o Valenti Fratti
113 W. 82nd St., Suite BF
NYC 10024

MUSIC THEATRE GROUP
Sept.-May:
735 Washington St.
NYC 10014
(212) 924-3108
June-Aug.:
Box 128
Stockbridge, MA 01262
(413) 298-5122
Lyn Austin, prod. dir.

MUSICAL THEATRE WORKS
440 Lafayette St.
NYC 10003
(212) 677-0040
Anthony J. Slimac, exec. dir.

nada
167 Ludlow St.
NYC 10002
(212) 420-1466
Aaron Beall, art. dir.;
Sara Gaffney, gen. mgr.

NAT HORNE MUSICAL THEATRE
(A membership organization)
440 W. 42nd St.
NYC 10036
(212) 736-7128
Nat Horne, chairman

NATIONAL BLACK THEATRE
2033 Fifth Ave.
NYC 10035
(212) 427-5615
Barbara Ann Teer; chief exec. officer;
Tunde Samuel, mng. prod'r;
Shirley Faison, exec. dir.

NATIONAL IMPROVISATIONAL THEATRE
223 8th Ave.
NYC 10011
(212) 243-7224
Tamara Wilcox, art. dir.

NEGRO ENSEMBLE COMPANY
155 W. 46th St., Suite 500
NYC 10036
(212) 575-5860
Douglas Turner Ward, art. dir.;
Susan Watson Turner, gen. mgr.

NEW ENGLISH STAGE CO.
45 E. 89th St.
NYC 10128
(212) 289-5890

NEW FEDERAL THEATRE
466 Grand St.
NYC 10002
(212) 598-0400
Woodie King, Jr., art. dir.

NEW NINE CO.
352 West End Ave. #5
NYC 10024
(212) 874-6241
Michael C. Mahon, art. dir.

NEW RUDE MECHANICALS
Box 2611, Times Square Station
NYC 10036
(212) 477-2344
Robert Hall, John Pynchon Holmes, art. dirs.

THE NEW STAGECRAFT COMPANY, INC.
553 W. 51st St.
NYC 10019
(212) 757-6300
Daniel P. Quinn, art. dir.

NEW THEATRE ARTS CO.
160 West End Ave., Suite 1C
NYC 10023
(212) 874-6297
Nomi Rubel, dir.

NEW YORK GILBERT & SULLIVAN PLAYERS
251 W. 91st St., 4-C
NYC 10024
(212) 769-1000
Albert Bergeret, art. dir.

NEW YORK REPERTORY THEATRE
COMPANY, INC.
162 W. 83rd St.
NYC 10024
(212) 580-NYRE
Gary Garrison, art. dir.,
Robert North, exec. dir.

NEW YORK SHAKESPEARE FESTIVAL
425 Lafayette St.
NYC 10003
(212) 598-7100
Joseph Papp, art. dir./prod'r.

NEW YORK STAGE & FILM CO.
c/o Cinequest
41 Madison Ave. 38th fl.
NYC 10010
(212) 725-5588
Leslie Urdang, Mark Linn-Baker,
Max Mayer, prod. dirs.

NEW YORK THEATRE STUDIO
130 W. 80th St.
NYC 10024
(802) 388-3318
Joanna Gard, art. dir.

NEW YORK THEATRE WORKSHOP
220 W. 42nd St., 18th fl.
NYC 10036
(212) 302-7737
James C. Nicola, art. dir.;
Nancy Kassak Diekmann, mng. dir.

ODYSSEY THEATRE CO.
2 Bond St.
NYC 10012
(212) 673-5665

ON STAGE PRODUCTIONS CO., LTD.
50 W. 97th St., #8H
NYC 10025
(212) 666-1716
Lee Frank, art. dir.

ONTOLOGICAL-HYSTERIC THEATER
at St. Mark's Church-in-the-Bowery
105 Hudson St., Room 200
NYC 10013
(212) 941-8911
Richard Foreman, art. dir.

THE OPEN EYE: NEW STAGINGS
270 W. 89th St.
NYC 10024
(212) 769-4141
Amie Brockway, art. dir.

OPEN SPACE THEATRE
Box 1018
Cooper Station
NYC 10003
Lynn Michaels, art. dir.

OZ THEATRE CO.
215 W. 101st St.
Suite 6A, NYC 10025
(212) 222-3806
Toko Zelli, dir.

PAN ASIAN REPERTORY THEATRE
47 Great Jones St.
NYC 10012
(212) 505-5655
Tisa Chang, art./prod. dir.

PAPER BAG PLAYERS
50 Riverside Dr.
NYC 10024
(212) 362-0431
Judith Martin, art. dir.

PEARL THEATRE COMPANY
125 W. 22nd St.
NYC 10011
(212) 645-7708
Shepard Sobel, art. dir.

PHOENIX ENSEMBLE
77 W. 15th St., #2P
NYC 10011
(212) 206-9140
Mary Jasperson, art. dir.

PING CHONG & COMPANY
47 Great Jones St.
NYC 10012
(212) 529-1557
Ping Chong, art. dir.;
Bruce Allardice, mng. dir.

PLAYWRIGHTS HORIZONS
416 W. 42nd St.
NYC 10036
(212) 564-1235
Don Scardino, art. dir. (as of Jan. 1992)

POWER THEATRE, INC.
782 West End Ave. #F11122
NYC 10025
(212)866-8922
Nancy Anderson, art. dir.;
Anthony DeRiso, gen. mgr.

PRIMARY STAGES COMPANY
584 9th Ave.
NYC 10036
(212) 333-7471
Casey Childs, art. dir.

PROMETHEAN THEATRE
701 Seventh Ave.
Suite 9W
NYC 10036
(212) 719-9812
Dan Roentsch, art. dir.

PROMETHEUS THEATRE
239 E. 5th St.
NYC 10003
(212) 477-8689
Fred Fondren, art. dir.

PUERTO RICAN TRAVELING THEATRE
141 W. 94th St.
NYC 10025
(212) 354-1293
Miriam Colon Valle, art. dir.

PULSE ENSEMBLE THEATRE
870 6th Ave.
NYC 10001
(212) 213-0231
Alexa Kelly, art. dir.

THE PYRAMID THEATRE ARTS FOUNDATION
159 W. 53rd St., Suite 21F
NYC 10019
(212) 541-8293
Nico Hartos, art. dir.

QUAIGH THEATRE
205 W. 89th St.
NYC 10024
(212) 787-0862
Will Lieberson, art. dir.

RAPP THEATRE COMPANY
220 E. 4th St.
NYC 10009
(212) 529-5921
R. Jeffrey Cohen, art. dir.

RED LIGHT DISTRICT
201 W. 74th St., Suite 7E
NYC 10023
Gregory Reardon, producer

RED EARTH ENSEMBLE
148 W. 76th St.
NYC 10024
(212) 580-5567
Matthew Carnahan, art. dir.

REPERTORIO ESPANOL
Gramercy Arts Theatre
138 E. 27th St. NYC 10016
(212) 889-2850
Rene Buch, art. dir.;
Gilberto Zaldivar, exec. prod'r

THE RICHARD ALLEN CENTER FOR CULTURE
AND ART (RACCA)
550 W. 155th St.
NYC 10032
(212) 281-2220
Shirley Radcliffe, prod'r.

RIDICULOUS THEATRICAL COMPANY
Charles Ludlam Theatre
1 Sheridan Square
NYC 10014
(212) 989-6524
Everett Quinton, art. dir.;
Steve Asher, mng. dir.

RIVERSIDE SHAKESPEARE COMPANY
at Playhouse 91
316 E. 91st St., NYC 10128
(212) 369-BARD
Gus Kaikkonen, art. dir.

ROYAL BUCKINGHAM THEATRE COMPANY
301 E. 29th St.
NYC 10021
(212) 447-5564
Alexandra Jones, prod'r.

RYAN REPERTORY COMPANY
Harry Warren Theatre
2445 Bath Ave.
Brooklyn, NY 11214
(718) 332-5463
John Sannuto, art. dir.;
Barbara Parisi, exec. dir.

SANDCASTLE PLAYERS, INC.
Box 1596
Cathedral Station
NYC 10025
(212) 677-6200
Jeanne Kaplan, art. dir.

THE SECOND STAGE THEATRE
Box 1807, Ansonia Station
NYC 10023
(212) 787-8302
Theatre address: 2162 Broadway
NYC 10023
Robyn Goodman, Carole Rothman, art. dirs.
Dorothy Maffei, mng. dir.

THE SECOND STUDIO FOR ACTORS
163 W. 23rd St.
NYC 10011
(212) 463-7050
Harv Dean, art. dir.

SEVENTH SIGN THEATRE CO.
Box 20467
Park West Finance Station
NYC 10025
(212) 666-3955
Donna Nieman, art. dir.

THE SHALIKO COMPANY
151 2nd Ave., Suite 1-E
NYC 10003
(212) 475-6313
Leonardo Shapiro, art. dir.

SIDEWALKS THEATRE
40 W. 27th St., 3rd fl.
NYC 10001
(212) 481-3077
Gary Beck, art. dir.

ROGER SIMON STUDIO
c/o Barbara Costigan
484 W. 43rd St.
NYC 10036
(212) JU6-6300
Roger Hendricks Simon, founder;
Robert Gregory, studio director

SOHO REP
46 Walker St.
NYC 10013
(212) 977-5955
Marlene Swartz, Julian Webber, co-art. dirs.

SOUPSTONE PROJECT, INC.
309 E. 5th St. #9
NYC 10003
(212) 473-7584
Neile Weissman, dir.

SPECTRUM THEATRE
151 1st Ave., Suite 199
NYC 10003
(212) 475-5529
Benno Hachnel, art. dir.

SPIDERWOMAN THEATER WORKSHOP,
INC.
77 7th Ave., #8S
NYC 10011
(212) 243-6209
Muriel Miguel, art. dir.;
Lisa Mayo, president

SPOTLIGHT REPERTORY THEATRE
Box 368
Parkchester Station
Bronx, NY 10462

THE SPUYTEN DUYVIL THEATRE CO.
22 W. 15th St., #18D
NYC 10011
(212) 255-0054
Collective artistic leadership

SURVIVOR PRODUCTIONS
10 W. 65th St., #2L
NYC 10023
(212) 877-2988
Leslie Sara Carroll, art. dir.

TADA!
120 W. 28th St., 2nd fl.
NYC 10001
(212) 627-1732
Janine Nina Trevens, James Learned, art. dirs.

THALIA SPANISH THEATRE
41-17 Greenpoint Ave.
Box 4368
Sunnyside, NY 11104
Sylvia Brito, art. dir.

THEATER FOR THE NEW CITY
155-157 First Ave.
NYC 10003
(212) 245-1109
George Bartenieff, Crystal Field, art. dirs.
Dante Albertie, administrator

THEATRE OFF PARK
224 Waverly Pl.
NYC 10014
(212) 627-2556
Albert Harris, art. dir.

THEATRE NORTH COLLABORATIVE
336-40 Canal St., Suite 2W
NYC 10013
(212) 517-8564
Bennett I. Windheim,
Christopher D. White, art. dirs.

THEATER 22
54 W. 22nd St.
NYC 10010
(212) 243-2805
Sidney Armus, prod'r.

THEATREWORKS/USA
890 Broadway
NYC 10003
(212) 677-5959
Jay Harnick, art. dir.

THECO
207 Park Pl., #2W
Brooklyn, NY 11238
(718) 398-8189
David Michael Kronick, art. dir.;
Emily Tetzlaff, mng. dir.

THEKOMPANIE INC.
2701 Young Ave., Suite 2
Bronx, NY 10469
(212) 515-4580
J. Michaels, exec. dir.

THIRD STEP THEATRE COMPANY
412 W. 48th St.
NYC 10036
(212) 633-9760
Al D'Andrea, art. dir.;
Melody Brooks, mng. dir.

13TH STREET THEATRE
REPERTORY COMPANY
50 W. 13th St.
NYC 10011
(212) 675-6677
Edith O'Hara, art. dir.;
Ken Terrell, assoc. art. dir.

TINY MYTHIC THEATRE COMPANY
532 LaGuardia Pl., #226
NYC 10012
(212) 274-9807
Maner and Kristen Marting, art. dirs.

TRG PRODUCTIONS
311 W. 43rd St., Suite 1404
NYC 10036
(212) 757-6315
Marvin Kahan, art. dir.

TRIANGLE THEATRE CO.
316 E. 88th St.
NYC 10128
(212) 860-7245
Michael Ramach, prod. dir.;
Molly O'Neil, mng. dir.

TWEED (TheatreWorks: Emerging/
Experimental Directions)
496A Hudson St.
Box G36
NYC 10014
(212) 777-0536
Kevin Maloney, art. dir.

29TH ST. REPERTORY THEATRE
212 W. 29th St.
NYC 10001
(212) 465-0575
Tim Corcoran, art. dir.;
Mallory Morris, mng. dir.

UBU REPERTORY THEATRE
15 W. 28th St.
NYC 10001
(212) 679-7540
Francoise Kourilsky, art. dir

UNDER ONE ROOF
Triplex
Borough of Manhattan Community College
199 Chambers St., #510B
NYC 10007
(212) 618-1900
Wickham Boyle, art. dir.

THE USUAL SUSPECTS THEATRE CO.
2819 W. 12th St., #9P
Brooklyn, NY 11224
(718) 946-4891
Robert Liebowitz, dir.

VIETNAM VETERANS ENSEMBLE
THEATRE COMPANY
1457 Broadway, Suite 1203
NYC 10036
(212) 869-6090
Thomas Bird, art. dir.

VILLAGE THEATRE COMPANY
137 W. 22nd St.
NYC 10011
(212) 627-8411
Susan Farwell, Randy Kelly, Marjorie Feenan,
David McConnell, and Howard Thoresen,
art. dirs.

THE VINEYARD THEATRE
108 E. 15th St.
NYC 10003
(212) 353-3366
Doug Aibel, art. dir.

VORTEX THEATER COMPANY
164 11th Ave.
NYC 10011
(212) 206-1764
Robert Coles, art. dir.

WESTBETH THEATRE CENTER
151 Bank St.
NYC 10014
(212) 691-2272
Arnold Engelman, prod. dir.

WESTSIDE ARTS THEATRE
100 E. 17th St.
NYC 10003
(212) 246-6351
Raymond L. Gaspard, art. dir.

WESTSIDE REPERTORY THEATRE
252 W. 81st St.
NYC 10024
(212) 874-7290

WHITE BIRD PRODUCTIONS
Box 20233
Columbus Circle Station
NYC 10023
(718) 788-5984
Kathryn Dickinson, art. dir.,
Liz Loftus, man. dir.

THE WILLOW CABIN THEATRE CO.
10 Manhattan Ave. #1E
NYC 10025
(212) 662-0077
Edward Berkeley, art. dir.

WINGS THEATRE COMPANY
154 Christopher St.
NYC 10014
(212) 627-2960
Jeff Corrick, art. dir.

WOMEN'S PROJECT AND
PRODUCTIONS, INC.
220 W. 42nd St., 18th fl.
NYC 10036
(212) 382-2750
Julia Miles, art. dir.

WORKING STAGES
316 W. 93rd St.
NYC 10025
(212) 866-5759
Terry Adrian, art. dir.

THE WORKING THEATRE
400 W. 40th St.
NYC 10018
(212) 967-5464
Bill Mitchelson, art. dir.;
Honour Molloy, devel. dir.

WPA THEATRE
519 W. 23rd St.
NYC 10011
(212) 206-0523
Kyle Renick, art. dir.

THE WRITERS THEATRE
145 W. 46th St.
NYC 10036
(212) 869-9770
Linda Laundra, art. dir.

YORK THEATRE COMPANY
2 E. 90th St.
NYC 10128
(212) 534-5366
Janet Hayes Walker, prod. dir.

THE YUEH LUNG SHADOW THEATRE
34-41 74th St.
Jackson Heights, NY 11372
(718) 478-6246
Jo Humphrey, art. dir.

RESIDENT THEATERS

BY VICTOR GLUCK

I n 1986, for the first time in Equity's history, its members clocked more work weeks under the LORT (League of Resident Theatres) contract than any other—including the flagship Broadway (Production) contract. In 1990 the 82 LORT theaters—from Sarasota to Seattle—provided AEA members with 60,000 work weeks. Work in theaters across the country continues to expand as companies offer actors roles under the Small Professional Theatre and Letter of Agreement contracts. The SPT and LOA offer modest, gradually increasing pay scales which encourage newly formed companies to "go Equity" and grow into full-fledged LORT theatres.

While many cite the 1963 founding of the Guthrie Theater in Minneapolis as the start of the resident theater movement, nearly three dozen other companies could challenge that claim, including the Goodman Theatre (Chicago, Ill.), 1925; Barter Theatre (Abingdon, Va.), 1933; Paper Mill Playhouse (Millburn, N.J.), 1934; Oregon Shakespearean Festival (Ashland, Ore.), 1935; Arena Stage (Washington, D.C.), 1950; and Milwaukee Repertory Theater (Milwaukee, Wis.) and the New York Shakespeare Festival (New York City), both 1954.

But the Guthrie's founding is a landmark in its being the first time that a group of major theater artists banded together to create a resident theater company—then looked for a congenial place to put it, and created it virtually overnight. As a result of the Guthrie's success other cities began taking steps to build their own resident theater companies. These companies eventually coalesced into the League of Resident Theatres, all members of which now have a working agreement with Actors' Equity Association. LORT companies provide work and opportunity to performers, directors, and playwrights, and bring the experience of live theater to audiences in almost every state in the union.

LORT companies each have a unique house style and artistic policy. Frequently supported by subscribers, LORT companies often take risks that commercially backed theater ventures dare not attempt. LORT companies may, therefore, run a variety of productions during a typical season, drawing on chestnuts from the repertoire, experimenting with the avant-garde, or presenting works-in-progress. Performers, directors, and playwrights are given not only a chance to hone their crafts while under salary, but are also offered exciting roles and challenges that they might not ordinarily encounter. Casting directors are well aware of the diversified experience that performers gain in resident theater and take special note when they see a LORT company listed on a resume.

In recent years, LORT productions have brightened Broadway and Off-Broadway stages with such comedy and dramatic hits as *The Boys Next Door* (Berkshire Theatre Festival), *Burn This* (Mark Taper Forum), the Tony award-winning adaptation of *The Grapes of Wrath* (Steppenwolf Theatre Company), the Tony- and Pulitzer Prize-winning play *The Heidi Chronicles* (Seattle Repertory Theatre), *Other People's Money* and *Our Country's Good* (Hartford Stage Company), *Rumours* (Old Globe Theatre), and *Speed the Darkness* (Goodman Theatre). Further attesting to the quality of LORT productions are the number of plays that originated in resident theaters and were awarded the Pulitzer Prize for drama since 1977: *The Shadow Box*, *The Gin Game*, *Buried Child*, *Crimes of the Heart*, *'night, Mother*, *Glengarry Glen Ross*, *Fences*, the aforementioned *Heidi Chronicles*, and *The Piano Lesson*.

LEAGUE OF RESIDENT THEATERS

The following is a state-by-state list of theaters operating under Equity's LORT contract. The theaters are listed alphabetically under the state in which they are located. The letter that follows the name of each theater (A, B, B+, C, or D) indicates the level of LORT contract under which that theater operates. These categories are based on the certified actual maximum weekly box office gross of each theater. The breakdown is as follows: D = $15,999.99 and below; C = $16,000-$19,999.99; B = $30,000-$49,999.99; B+ = $50,000 and above. There are no box office gross figures for A theaters. In some instances, theater companies have two or more venues of different sizes so therefore two or more letters might appear next to a company's name. Following the name of the theater is its address, phone number, and the name of its artistic director and/or managing director.

ALABAMA

ALABAMA SHAKESPEARE FESTIVAL (C) (D)
1 Festival Dr.
Montgomery, AL 36117
(205) 272-1640
Kent Thompson, Jim Volz

ARIZONA

ARIZONA THEATRE COMPANY (C)
Box 1631
Tucson, AZ 85702
(602) 884-8210
Gary Gisselman, Robert Alpaugh

CALIFORNIA

AMERICAN CONSERVATORY THEATRE (A)
450 Geary St.
San Francisco, CA 94102
(415) 749-2200
Edward Hastings, John Sullivan

BERKELEY REPERTORY THEATRE (B)
2025 Addison St.
Berkeley, CA 94704
(415) 841-6108
Sharon Ott, Susie Medak

BERKELEY SHAKESPEARE FESTIVAL (D)
Box 969
Berkeley, CA 94701
(415) 548-3422
Michael Addison, Susan Duncan

CALIFORNIA MUSICAL THEATRE (B)
2500 E. Colorado Blvd.
Suite 400
Pasadena, CA 91107
(818) 792-0776
Gary Davis

LA JOLLA PLAYHOUSE (B) (C)
Box 12039
La Jolla, CA 92037
(619) 452-6760
Des McAnuff, Alan Levey

LOS ANGELES THEATRE CENTER (D)
514 South Spring St.
Los Angeles, CA 90013
(213) 627-6500
William Bushnell, Don Hill

MARK TAPER FORUM (A)
135 North Grand Ave.
Los Angeles, CA 90012
(213) 972-0795
Gordon Davidson, Steve Albert

OLD GLOBE THEATRE (B) (B+) (C)
Box 2171
San Diego, CA 92112
(619) 231-1941
Jack O'Brien, Thomas Hall

PASADENA PLAYHOUSE (B)
39 South El Molino
Pasadena, CA 91101
(818) 792-8672
Susan Dietz, Lars Hansen

SAN JOSE REPERTORY COMPANY (C)
Box 2399
San Jose, CA 95109-2399
(408) 995-0733
Timothy Near, John Brown

SOUTH COAST REPERTORY THEATRE (B) (D)
Box 2197, Costa Mesa, CA 92628
(714) 957-2602
David Emmes, Paula Tomei

COLORADO

DENVER CENTER THEATRE COMPANY (C)
1050 13th St.
Denver, CO 80204
(303) 893-4200
Donovan Marley, Kevin K. Maifeld

CONNECTICUT

EUGENE O'NEILL MEMORIAL
THEATER CENTER (D)
National Playwrights Conference
305 Great Neck Rd.
Waterford, CT 06385
(203) 443-5378
Lloyd Richards, George White

GOODSPEED OPERA HOUSE (B+) (D)
East Haddam, CT 06423
(203) 873-8664
Michael Price, Sue Frost

HARTFORD STAGE COMPANY (B)
50 Church St.
Hartford, CT 06103
(203) 525-5601
Mark Lamos, David Hawkanson

LONG WHARF THEATRE (B) (C)
222 Sargent Dr., New Haven, CT 06511
(203) 787-4284
Arvin Brown, M. Edgar Rosenblum

YALE REPERTORY THEATRE (C) (D)
Box 1903A, Yale Station
New Haven, CT 06520
(203) 432-1515
Stan Wojewodski, Jr., Benjamin Mordecai

DISTRICT OF COLUMBIA

ARENA STAGE (B+) (B) (D)
6th & Maine Ave., S.W.
Washington, DC 20024
(202) 554-9066
Douglas C. Wager, Guy Bergquist

SHAKESPEARE THEATRE
AT THE FOLGER (C) (D)
301 E. Capitol St., S.E.
Washington, DC 20003
(202) 547-3230
Michael Kahn, Mary Ann Di Barbieri

FLORIDA

ASOLO THEATRE COMPANY (C)
5555 N. Tamiami Trail
Sarasota, FL 34242
(813) 351-9010
John Ulmer, Linda di Gabriele

CALDWELL THEATRE COMPANY (C)
Box 277
Boca Raton, FL 33432
(407) 368-7509
Michael Hall

COCONUT GROVE PLAYHOUSE (B) (D)
Box 616
Miami, FL 33133
(305) 442-2662
Arnold Mittelman

THE HIPPODROME STATE THEATRE (D)
25 Southeast 2nd Pl.
Gainesville, FL 32601
(904) 373-5968
Mary Hausch

GEORGIA

ALLIANCE THEATRE COMPANY (B) (D)
1280 Peachtree St., N.E.
Atlanta, GA 30309
(404) 898-1119
Kenny Leon, Edith Love

ILLINOIS

GOODMAN THEATRE (B+) (D)
200 S. Columbus Dr.
Chicago, IL 60603
(312) 443-3811
Robert Falls, Roche Schulfer

NORTHLIGHT THEATRE (D)
600 Davis St.
Evanston, IL 60201
(708) 869-7732
Russell Vandenbroucke

INDIANA

INDIANA REPERTORY THEATRE (C) (D)
140 W. Washington St.
Indianapolis, IN 46204
(317) 635-5266
Janet Allen, Victoria Nolan

KENTUCKY

ACTORS THEATRE OF LOUISVILLE (B) (D)
316-320 W. Main St.
Louisville, KY 40202
(502) 584-1265
Jon Jory, Alexander Speer

MAINE

PORTLAND STAGE COMPANY (D)
Box 1458
Portland, ME 04104
(207) 774-1043
Richard Hamburger, Caroline Turner

MARYLAND

CENTER STAGE (B)
700 North Calvert St.
Baltimore, MD 21202
(301) 685-3200
Irene Lewis, Peter Culman

MASSACHUSETTS

AMERICAN REPERTORY THEATRE (B) (D)
Loeb Drama Center
64 Brattle St.
Cambridge, MA 02138
(617) 495-2668
Robert Brustein, Robert Orchard

BERKSHIRE THEATRE FESTIVAL (B)
Main Street
Stockbridge, MA 01262
(413) 298-5536
Richard Dunlop, Chuck Still

THE HUNTINGTON THEATRE COMPANY (B)
Boston University Theatre
264 Huntington Ave.
Boston, MA 02115
(617) 353-3320
Peter Altman, Michael Maso

MERRIMACK REGIONAL THEATRE (D)
Box 228
Lowell, MA 01853
(508) 454-6324
David Kent

STAGEWEST (C) (D)
1 Columbus Center
Springfield, MA 01103
(413) 781-4470
Eric Hill, Martha Richards

MICHIGAN

MEADOW BROOK THEATRE (B)
Oakland University
Rochester, MI 48309
(313) 377-3300
Terence Kilburn, James Spittle

MINNESOTA

THE GUTHRIE THEATER
725 Vineland Pl.
Minneapolis, MN 55403
(612) 347-1100
Garland Wright, Edward A. Martenson

MISSOURI

MISSOURI REPERTORY THEATRE (B)
5100 Rockhill Rd.
Kansas City, MO 64110
(816) 235-1451
George Keathley, Robert Thatch

NEW HAMPSHIRE

AMERICAN STAGE FESTIVAL (C)
Box 225
Milford, NH 03005
(603) 673-4005
Richard Rose, Keith Stevens

NEW JERSEY

GEORGE STREET PLAYHOUSE (C)
9 Livingston Ave.
New Brunswick, NJ 08901
(201) 846-2895
Gregory Hurst, David Edelman

McCARTER THEATRE (B+) (D)
91 University Pl.
Princeton, NJ 08540
(609) 683-9100
Emily Mann, John Herochik

NEW JERSEY SHAKESPEARE FESTIVAL (D)
Science Hall
Drew University, Route 24
Madison, NJ 07940
(201) 377-5330
Bonnie J. Monte

NEW MEXICO

NEW MEXICO REPERTORY THEATRE (D)
Box 789
Albuquerque, NM 87103
(505) 243-4577
Andrew Shea, Steve Fehringer

NEW YORK

THE ACTING COMPANY (B) (C)
Box 898
Times Square Station
New York, NY 10108
(212) 564-3510
Zelda Fichandler, Margot Harley

CAPITAL REPERTORY COMPANY (D)
Box 399
Albany, NY 12201
(518) 462-4531
Bruce Bouchard, Robert Holley

CIRCLE IN THE SQUARE (A)
1633 Broadway
New York, NY 10019
(212) 307-2700
Theodore Mann

GEVA THEATRE (B)
75 Woodbury Blvd.
Rochester, NY 14605
(716) 232-1366
Howard Millman, Chris Kawolsky

LINCOLN CENTER THEATER
COMPANY (A) (B)
Vivian Beaumont and
Mitzi Newhouse Theaters
150 W. 65th St.
New York, NY 10023
(212) 362-7600
Andre Bishop (as of Jan. 1992),
Bernard Gersten

LONG ISLAND STAGE (D)
Box 9001
Rockville Centre, NY 11571
(516) 867-3090
Clint Atkinson, Tom Madden

NEW YORK SHAKESPEARE FESTIVAL (B)
Public Theater
425 Lafayette St.
New York, NY 10003
(212) 598-7100
Joseph Papp, Betsy Gardella, Sally Morse

THE ROUNDABOUT THEATRE
COMPANY (A) (D)
at the Criterion Center
1514 Broadway
New York, NY 10036
(212) 719-9393
Todd Haimes

STUDIO ARENA THEATRE (B)
710 Main St.
Buffalo, NY 14202
(716) 856-8025
David Frank, Raymond Bonnard

SYRACUSE STAGE (C)
John D. Archbold Theatre
820 East Genessee St.
Syracuse, NY 13210
(315) 443-4008
Arthur Storch, James Clark

NORTH CAROLINA

NORTH CAROLINA
SHAKESPEARE FESTIVAL (D)
Box 6066
High Point, NC 27262
(919) 841-6273
Lou Rackoff, Pedro Silva

PLAYMAKERS REPERTORY COMPANY (D)
206 Graham Memorial 052A
Chapel Hill, NC 27514
(919) 962-1122
David Hammond, Regina Lickteig

OHIO

CINCINNATI PLAYHOUSE
IN THE PARK (B)
Box 6537
Cincinnati, OH 45206
(513) 421-5440
Kathleen Norris

CLEVELAND PLAY HOUSE (C) (D)
Box 1989
Cleveland, OH 44106
(216) 795-7010
Josephine Abady, Dean Gladden

GREAT LAKES THEATRE FESTIVAL (B)
1501 Euclid Ave., Suite 250
Cleveland, OH 44115
(216) 241-5490
Gerald Freedman, Mary Bill

OREGON

OREGON SHAKESPEAREAN FESTIVAL (B)
Portland Center of Performing Arts
1111 S.W. Broadway
Portland, OR 97207
(503) 248-4496
Jerry Turner, Paul Nicholson

PENNSYLVANIA

PENNSYLVANIA STAGE COMPANY (D)
J.I. Rodale Theatre
837 Linden St.
Allentown, PA 18101
(215) 434-6110
Peter Wren-Meleck, Betsy Stewart

THE PEOPLE'S LIGHT AND
THEATRE COMPANY (D)
39 Conestoga Rd.
Malvern, PA 19355
(215) 647-1900
Danny Fruchter, Gregory Rowe

PHILADELPHIA DRAMA GUILD (B+)
Robert Morris Building
100 N. 17th St.
Philadelphia, PA 19103
(215) 563-7530
Mary B. Robinson, Daniel Schay

PHILADELPHIA FESTIVAL THEATRE
FOR NEW PLAYS (D)
3900 Chestnut St.
Philadelphia, PA 19104
(215) 222-5000
Carol Rocamora, Steven Charendoff

PITTSBURGH PUBLIC THEATRE (B)
Allegheny Sq.
Pittsburgh, PA 15212-5362
(412) 323-8200
William Gardner, Dan Fallon

WALNUT STREET THEATRE (A) (D)
9th & Walnut Sts.
Philadelphia, PA 19107
(215) 574-3550
Bernard Havard, Ken Wesler

RHODE ISLAND

TRINITY REPERTORY COMPANY (B) (C)
201 Washington St.
Providence, RI 02903
(401) 521-1100
Richard Jenkins

TENNESSEE

CLARENCE BROWN THEATRE (D)
Box 8450
Knoxville, TN 37996
(615) 974-3447
Thomas P. Cooke, Margaret Ferguson

TENNESSEE REP. (D)
427 Chestnut St.
Nashville, TN 37203
(615) 244-4878
Mac Pirkle, Brian Laczko

TEXAS

ALLEY THEATRE (B) (C)
615 Texas Ave.
Houston, TX 77002
(713) 228-9341
Gregory Boyd, Mary Lou Aleskie

DALLAS THEATER CENTER (C) (D)
3636 Turtle Blvd.
Dallas, TX 75219
(214) 526 5671
Ken Bryant, Jeff West

CASA MANANA (C)
3101 W. Lancaster
Fort Worth, TX 76107
(817) 332-9319
Charles Dallinger

HOUSTON SHAKESPEARE FESTIVAL (D)
Drama Dept., Univ. of Houston
Houston, TX 77204-5071
(713) 749-1427
Sidney Berger

THEATRE THREE (D)
2800 Routh St.
Dallas, TX 75201
(214) 871-2933
Chris Harsdorff, Jac Alder

UTAH

PIONEER THEATRE COMPANY (B)
University of Utah
Salt Lake City, UT 84112
(810) 581-4250
Charles Morey

VIRGINIA

BARTER THEATRE (D)
Box 867
Abingdon, VA 24210
(703) 628-2281
Rex Partington

THEATREVIRGINIA (C)
Boulevard & Grove Aves.
Richmond, VA 23221
(804) 367-0840
Terry Burgler

VIRGINIA STAGE COMPANY (C)
Box 3770
254 Granby St.
Norfolk, VA 23514
(804) 627-6988
Carl Mulert

WASHINGTON

A CONTEMPORARY THEATRE (C)
Box 19400
100 W. Roy St.
Seattle, WA 98119
(206) 285-3220
Jeff Steitzer, Phil Schermer

INTIMAN THEATRE COMPANY (D)
Box 19645
Seattle, WA 98109
(206) 624-4541
Elizabeth Huddle, Peter Davis

SEATTLE REPERTORY THEATRE (B+) (D)
Bagley Wright Theatre
155 Mercer St.
Seattle, WA 98109
(206) 443-2210
Daniel Sullivan, Ben Moore

WISCONSIN

MILWAUKEE REPERTORY THEATER (C) (D)
108 E. Wells St.
Milwaukee, WI 53202
(414) 224-1761
John Dillon, Sara O'Connor

DINNER THEATER

BY WILLIAM M. LYNK

The dinner theater industry is based on a relatively new concept. In the summer of 1959, Bill Pullinsi, a university theater freshman on summer vacation, started the Candlelight Theatre Restaurant within the Presidential Arms Hotel in Washington, D.C. Although he called his successful venture a "theater restaurant," it was actually the first dinner theater, because the 600 patrons ate a meal and experienced a live Broadway-type musical in the same room. Ironically, the term "theater restaurant" now defines an operation where dinner service and theatrical presentation are in separate rooms—a subcategory of "dinner theater." In 1960, Pullinsi moved his operation to Chicago and readjusted its name to Candlelight Dinner Playhouse—one of the four Equity dinner theaters in Chicago today.

Entrepreneur Howard Wolfe was intrigued by the dinner theater concept. He went on to build Barn Dinner Theatres in cities across the country from 1963 through 1970. The "Barns" were a franchised business associated with a New York City production company. This tour group traveled easily from theater to theater because the Barns were built similarly. In the Southwest, Tom Eisner started another chain, the Windmill Dinner Theatres, in 1967, and was heavily influenced by Wolf's Barn in Dallas. In the 1960s and 1970s, dinner theaters seemed to be springing up almost everywhere throughout the country. The Carousel, the nation's largest dinner theater, was originally founded in Ravenna, Ohio, in 1973; it relocated to Akron, in 1988.

There are approximately 100 dinner theaters across the United States. Many of the earlier dinner theaters created in the 1960s and 1970s are no longer in operation; some have changed names and locations. New ones are still being created. Approximately 20 are Equity-affiliated, but the balance are non-union. In either case, dinner theater continues to provide patrons with a great night—the convenience of a complete evening of dinner and live entertainment under one roof. It also provides stage actors with a considerable source of income.

THE DINNER THEATER FORMULA

Most dinner theaters have catered to a clientele largely consisting of senior citizens, although the general market seems to be expanding as well and audiences are getting younger. They've also become more demanding. Tom Prather, owner of the Dutch Apple Dinner Theatre in Lancaster, Pennsylvania, says: "As people grow older, the new seniors are becoming more selective in their choices. They want better food, high-quality entertainment, and a clean, fresh facility."

High-quality theatrical productions have always been one of the most attractive features of a night out at a dinner theater. Many employ professional actors who have Broadway, Off-Broadway, national tour, summer stock, and regional theater credits. Monica Wemitt, a union performer from New York City, says that "dinner theater is a very lucrative venue for actors at this point—the money is good and it's great to be able to work with such fine professionals. The experience ranks right under doing Broadway and nationals." Other dinner theaters will employ local actors who are well trained and experienced, providing entertainment at an even more reasonable cost.

The other half of the dinner theater equation is the food. Many operations serve buffet style, although the current trend is toward table service. From fried chicken, green beans, and mashed potatoes to filet mignon and lobster, dinner theater customers expect a good meal out. Bob Stone, director of food services for the Alhambra Dinner Theatre in Jacksonville, Florida, believes the formula for success is simple: "Quality and quantity are what our patrons have come to expect." And, of course, the dinner service must reflect the changing eating habits of Americans. Stone, for instance, observes that "the average age of our patrons is the mid-40s, and we are noticing a trend toward more health-oriented foods."

But the main attraction to dinner theater has always been the low ticket prices. It's a superb package deal—an individual Saturday night ticket price of $29.75, for example, may include dinner, a drink, great entertainment, as well as parking and tax.

THE THEATERS

Dinner theaters vary widely in the type and format of productions presented. The size and physical layout of the facilities run the gamut—arena (in-the-round), proscenium, thrust, and three-quarter-thrust stages are all used. A producer may spend anywhere from $500 to $100,000 for set construction for a single production, creating anything from a small box set to an elaborate multifaceted design.

According to Marc Resnik, associate producer for the Carousel Dinner Theatre in Akron, Ohio, "Both scenery and costumes in today's dinner theaters must be more intricate and exciting than those of 15 or 20 years ago. Audiences today are much more visually oriented, based largely on their conditioning through special effects in movies and on television. Because they expect to see 'spectacles' on stage, the 1950s 'Honeymooners' interior set just won't do." Furthermore, Resnik explains that the general adult attention span has decreased and people need to see more variety in a shorter time span. Whether the stage is an arena or a large proscenium, the sets and costumes must be eye-appealing.

THE SHOWS

The "old war horses" are the productions that seem to be most widely accepted in dinner theater—musicals with tunes that the audience can go home humming. Most were highly successful on Broadway so that audiences at least recognize the titles if not the story lines. Some of these musicals include: *Singin' in the Rain, The Boyfriend, Damn Yankees, Anything Goes, Can Can, Brigadoon, Camelot, Carousel, Fiddler on the Roof, 42nd Street, Guys and Dolls, Hello Dolly!, Mame, I Do! I Do!, The King and I, The Music Man, The Sound of Music, South Pacific, West Side Story, Man of La Mancha, Grease, Evita, Annie, Ain't Misbehavin', A Chorus Line, Cabaret, The Fantasticks, Sugar Babies,* and *Oklahoma!*.

Straight plays, including comedies and new works, are produced less often in dinner theaters, although they are frequently seen in multi-theater facilities like Dinner Playhouses in Kansas City or at Chanhassen outside Minneapolis. But most companies stick to musical productions. When a straight play is produced during a season, it's likely to be something along the lines of *Social Security, Murder at the Howard Johnson's, Everybody Loves Opal, Play It Again Sam,* and Neil Simon comedies like *The Sunshine Boys, God's Favorite, Biloxi Blues, Brighton Beach Memoirs, Barefoot in the Park,* and *Last of the Red Hot Lovers*. Simon's plays work well in the dinner theater circuit because they involve small casts, are easy to produce, can be star vehicles, and are box office draws.

The run for either musicals or straight plays ranges from 4 to 27 weeks, averaging about 8 weeks. It depends, in part, on whether or not the theater has a season subscription plan.

ASSOCIATIONS

Performers frequently hear about the two dinner theater associations and wonder why they're there. Both the American Dinner Theatre Institute (ADTI) and the National Dinner Theatre Association (NDTA) have played important roles within the industry.

The American Dinner Theatre Institute is a trade association mainly consisting of Equity-affiliated dinner theaters. ADTI plays an integral part in negotiating the dinner theater contracts with the actors' union.

Since the first union contract was negotiated with Actors' Equity Association in 1974, ADTI has been involved in negotiating the contracts adhered to by union dinner theaters nationwide. As of May, 1991, the ADTI/AEA contract was Equity's fifth largest, based on the number of work weeks provided to stage actors yearly. AEA's League of Resident Theater contract ranked first—followed by the Production Contract governing Broadway and national tours, the Letter of Agreement, and Small Professional Theatres.

ADTI meets at least once each year to analyze and improve all aspects of the dinner theater industry. Currently, Prescott F. Griffith, owner of the 1,130-seat (Equity) Carousel dinner theater in Akron, Ohio, presides as president.

The National Dinner Theatre Association primarily comprises non-union dinner theaters and meets several times each year to discuss issues pertinent to the industry. Its spring meeting usually involves auditions from which producers and directors can cast upcoming productions. Beckki Jo Schneider is president, as well as co-owner of the 590-seat (non-Equity) Derby Dinner Playhouse in Clarksville, Indiana.

SALARIES

Minimum salaries for union actors range from $261.25 to $412.25 per week. These figures are taken from the ADTI/AEA Agreement, effective 5/6/91 through 1/30/94, and are scaled according to theater size. Keep in mind that this is only a range of minimums, and any actor may receive more per week, depending on past experience and negotiation. The weekly salary can be increased by taking on added responsibilities: acting as dance captain, playing additional parts, performing assistant stage manager duties, and so on. Rehearsal time is compensated by the producer, as are health and pension payments for every actor. The producer is also responsible for roundtrip transportation costs to the theater from the actor's place of residence. Usually, lodging and food are paid for by the performer. A contract is signed by both parties to specify what is expected of the producer and of the performer. A straight play may involve two or more cast members, whereas the average musical includes about 16, all hired on a show-to-show basis.

Non-union performers have no established minimums. Therefore, each dinner theater may set up its own salaries and work expectations. Salaries usually begin at $125 per week, reaching union levels at some of the larger facilities. Salary and other fringes are negotiable. Most non-union dinner theaters do not offer actors health benefits, nor do they pay into a pension plan for actors. Actors' Equity Association does have a Membership Candidate Program that allows non-union actors to eventually become AEA members through a program of monitored work weeks in various Equity theaters.

AUDITIONS

Each week *Back Stage* lists audition notices for numerous dinner theater jobs. Auditions are held in New York City as well as across the country for both union and non-union actors: the union dinner theaters audition in New York, Los Angeles, Chicago, and in other major metropolitan areas; the non-union companies hold local auditions and often join together with NDTA and SETC (Southeastern Theatre Conference—see chapter on "Combined Auditions") for annual regional tryouts. Be prepared to demonstrate singing, dancing, and acting abilities. These auditions are not unlike other acting auditions held throughout the country. The union dinner theaters subscribe to fairness in the audition/hiring process and support affirmative action and equal opportunity rights for all actors.

DOING IT

Often an actor who has never worked in a dinner theater will wonder what the experience is like. "Alan" will serve as an example actor. A union member, he has been hired by a union producer of a medium-to-large dinner theater. After the auditions in New York, the producer contacts Alan to offer him a Chorus contract for the musical *Oliver!*, describing the parts he will be playing. Alan's base salary will be $412.25 per week. Since he is to be hired as an assistant stage manager as well, he'll receive an additional $41.50 per week. Alan will also be playing one extra chorus role at $16.00 extra per week and one principal role (Mr. Sowerberry) at $32.00 more per week. He will understudy one role at no additional compensation and one other role at an additional $20.00 per week. Because Alan will use his own shoes in the musical ($2.50) and his own spectacular overcoat ($5.00)—perfect for the role—he'll receive an extra $7.50 per week. Alan's total weekly income is $529.25.

Alan accepts; the producer mails him the contract, makes the travel arrangements, and sends airline tickets. Alan will be paid to get from his apartment in New York City to LaGuardia Airport. He will be picked up at the local airport and transported to the theater or to his apartment. Several weeks later Alan leaves for the airport, arrives at his destination, and is taken to the cast housing. He shares a two-bedroom apartment with Peter. Rent is $75.00 per week for each actor. Transportation to and from the theater is provided. Alan begins a 10-day rehearsal period to prepare for the show. During a split rehearsal period, Alan is taken to be fitted for the costumes he'll be wearing. The rehearsals are staggered from 10:00 a.m. to 10:00 p.m. during the first week. However, Alan rehearses only seven out of a consecutive eight-and-a-half-hour day.

The show opens on a Wednesday night, with notes given afterwards. The theater opens for patrons at 6:00 p.m., dinner service starts at 6:15 p.m., and the curtain goes up at 8:30 p.m. The performance is over at 10:55 p.m. Call for Thursday night is at 8:00 p.m. Evening shows are Tuesday, Wednesday, Thursday, Friday, Saturday, and Sunday. Matinees are on Wednesday and Saturday, and the day off is Monday. The show runs eight weeks.

Alan and the other cast members often spend their time off sleeping in, running errands, working out, shopping, or socializing. A brush-up rehearsal is scheduled Friday afternoon, and the following Friday a brush-up dance rehearsal starts at 12:00 noon. On Monday night the actors have a "progressive dinner," going to each of their apartments in the complex.

On the sixth week, the producer posts the Notice of Termination to remind the actors that the show will close in two weeks and that scripts and company property must be returned before final paychecks can be distributed. Return transportation arrangements are made by the producer. Sunday night's show is the closing performance and Alan packs his bags and is on his way to the airport Monday afternoon.

INTO THE NINETIES

Dinner theaters have experienced a roller coaster ride of ups and downs during their short three-decade history. During the 1980s it seemed that more dinner theaters were being closed than were being opened. An image problem has also taken its toll on the industry. In many places, dinner theater began as an offshoot of community theater, using only local talent and serving patrons "greasy spoon" buffet food. It was a "bargain package" in the worst sense of the term. Although this isn't a fair assessment of the industry today, this image lingers on.

Many of the union dinner theaters that were thriving in the 1960s and 1970s have either closed or become non-union. In 1978 there were over 70 union dinner theaters; today there are about 20. The main reason: economics.

Another reason for the troubled times is that audiences today have a wider variety of entertainment choices. The competition is fierce: dinner theaters must compete with cable TV and home video rentals. Not withstanding all the visual special effects created by electronic technology, the live theatrical experience can never be replaced.

On the positive side, actors are finding that dinner theater can provide great acting experience. Roles that performers might not play in larger markets, are more readily available on the dinner theater circuit. Actors have also found salary ranges in the union dinner theaters to be competitive with other areas of union work available to them. Patrons, too, are returning to dine and see their favorite shows.

In these difficult economic times, when there are so many entertainment options, it is the bargains that will survive. If costs can be contained, dinner theater should continue to be an important source of income and career experience for the working actor.

DINNER THEATERS

Equity and non-Equity dinner theatres follow, listed alphabetically by state. An asterisk (*) denotes theatres which operate under the Actors' Equity Association Dinner Theatre contract. The designation ADTI or NDTA indicates membership in one of two national dinner theatre organizations: American Dinner Theatre Institute (ADTI) is almost exclusively Equity; National Dinner Theatre Association (NDTA) is almost exclusively non-Equity.

ALABAMA

BLUE MOON DINNER THEATRE
1447 Montgomery Highway
Birmingham, AL 35216
(205) 823-3000
(NDTA)

THE ENTERTAINER DINNER THEATRE
421 Holcombe Dr.
Mobile, AL 36660
(205) 473-8611

ALASKA

ALASKA CABIN NITE
McKinley Chalet Resort
Denali National Park, AK 99755
(907) 683-2215
(NDTA)

ARIZONA

GASLIGHT THEATRE
7000 E. Tanque Verde
Tucson, AZ 85715
(602) 296-0456

ARKANSAS

MURRAY'S DINNER PLAYHOUSE
6323 Asher Avenue
Little Rock, AR 72204
(501) 562-3131
(NDTA)

CALIFORNIA

CANDLELIGHT PAVILION DINNER THEATRE
555 W. Foothill Blvd.
Claremont, CA 91711
(714) 626-2411, ext. 200
(NDTA)

BOULDER'S DINNER THEATRE
5501 Arapahoe
Boulder, CO 80302
(303) 449-6000
(NDTA)

*COUNTRY DINNER PLAYHOUSE
Box 3167
Englewood, CO 80155
(303) 799-0112
Mailing address:
(ADTI, NDTA)

HERITAGE SQUARE MUSIC HALL
No. 5 Heritage Square
Golden, CO 80401
(303) 279-7800

CONNECTICUT

COACHLIGHT DINNER THEATRE
226 Main St.
East Windsor, CT 06088
(203) 623-8227

*CONNECTICUT'S BROADWAY THEATRE/
DARIEN DINNER THEATRE
65 Tokeneke Rd.
Darien, CT 06820
(203) 655-7667
(ADTI)

FLORIDA

*ALHAMBRA DINNER THEATRE
12000 Beach Blvd.
Jacksonville, FL 32216
(904) 641-1212
(ADTI)

*GOLDEN APPLE DINNER THEATRE
Two venues: 25 N. Pineapple Ave.
Sarasota, FL 33577
(813) 366-2646;
447 US 41 Bypass N.
Venice, FL 34292
(ADTI)

*JAN McART'S ROYAL PALM
DINNER THEATRE
*JAN McART'S UPSTAIRS CABARET THEATRE
303 Golfview Dr.
Boca Raton, FL 33432
(305) 426-2211
(ADTI)

*THE JUPITER THEATRE
1001 E. Indiantown Rd.
Jupiter, FL 33477
(407) 747-5261
(NDTA)

MARK TWO DINNER THEATER
3376 Edgewater Dr.
Orlando, FL 32804
(407) 843-6275
(NDTA)

NAPLES DINNER THEATRE
1025 Piper Blvd.
Naples, FL 33942
(813) 597-6031
(NDTA)

*SHOWBOAT DINNER THEATRE
OF TAMPA BAY
3405 Ulmerton Rd.
Clearwater, FL 34622
(813) 573-3777
(ADTI, NDTA)

ILLINOIS

*CANDLELIGHT DINNER PLAYHOUSE
5620 S. Harlem Ave.
Summit, IL 60501
(813) 597-6031
(ADTI)

CIRCA '21 DINNER PLAYHOUSE
1828 3rd Ave., Box 3784
Rock Island, IL 61204
(309) 786-2667
(NDTA)

CONKLIN PLAYERS DINNER THEATRE
Box 301, Conklin Ct.
Goodfield, IL 61742
(309) 965-2545
(ADTI assoc. member, NDTA)
*DRURY LANE DINNER THEATRE
2500 95th St.
Evergreen Park, IL 60642
(708) 422-8000
(ADTI)

*DRURY LANE OAKBROOK THEATRE
100 Drury Lane
Oakbrook Terrace, IL 60181
(708) 530-8300
(ADTI)

*MARRIOTT LINCOLNSHIRE THEATRE
10 Marriott Dr.
Lincolnshire, IL 60069
(708) 634-0204
(ADTI)

PHEASANT RUN DINNER THEATRE
4051 E. Main St.
St. Charles, IL 60174
(708) 584-6342

SUNSHINE DINNER PLAYHOUSE
115 W. Kirby Ave.
Champaign, IL 61820
(217) 359-4503
(NDTA)

INDIANA

*BEEF 'N' BOARDS DINNER THEATRE
9301 N. Michigan Rd.
Indianapolis, IN 46268
(317) 872-9664
(NDTA)

BROADWAY DINNER THEATRE & CABARET
1000 E. 80th Pl., Suite 700 North
Merrillville, IN 46410
(219) 769-6601
(NDTA)

DERBY DINNER PLAYHOUSE
525 Marriott Dr.
Clarksville, IN 47130
(812) 288-2632
(NDTA)

ENCORE DINNER THEATRE
11 W. Iowa St.
Evansville, IN 47710
(812) 422-8899

GOOD TIMES THEATRE
Rt. 1, Box 180B
Bryant, IN 47326
(800) 288-7630
(NDTA)

HOLIDAY STAR
1000 E. 80th Place
Merrillville, IN 46410
(219) 769-6601

IOWA

INGERSOLL DINNER THEATRE
3711 Ingersoll Ave.
Des Moines, IA 50312
(515) 274-5582
(NDTA)

KANSAS

CROWN UPTOWN DINNER THEATRE
3207 E. Douglas
Wichita, KS 67218
(316) 681-1566
(NDTA)

MARYLAND

ACT TWO DINNER THEATRE
8014 Pulaski Hwy.
Baltimore, MD 21237
(301) 686-1126

BURN BRAE DINNER THEATRE
15029 Blackburn Rd.
Burtonsville, MD 20866
(301) 384-5800

HARBORLIGHTS DINNER THEATRE
511 S. Broadway
Baltimore, MD 21231
(301) 522-4126

HARLEQUIN DINNER THEATRE
1330 E. Gude Dr.
Rockville, MD 20850
(301) 340-6813

OREGON RIDGE DINNER THEATRE
13403 Beaver Dam Rd.
Cockysville, MD 21030
(301) 377-6353

PETRUCCI'S DINNER THEATRE
312 Main St.
Laurel, MD 20707
(301) 725-5226
(NDTA)

TOBY'S DINNER THEATRE
Box 1003
Columbia, MD 21044
(301) 730-8311
(NDTA)
TOWSONTOWNE DINNER THEATRE
7800 York Rd.
Towson, MD 21204
(301) 321-6595

MASSACHUSETTS

MEDIEVAL MANOR THEATRE RESTAURANT
246 E. Berkeley St.
Boston, MA 02118
(617) 423-4900

MYSTERY CAFE DINNER THEATRE
288 Berkeley St.
Boston, MA 02116
(617) 262-1826

MICHIGAN

ALPHA THEATRE PROJECT
Box 2218
Saginaw, MI 48605-2218
(517) 790-1005

CORNWELL DINNER THEATRE
Pritchard Productions
Box 734
Marshall, MI 49068
(616) 781-7933
(NDTA)

MINNESOTA

*CHANHASSEN DINNER THEATRE
501 W. 78th Ave.
Chanhassen, MN 55317
(612) 934-1525
(ADTI)

MISSOURI

*AMERICAN HEARTLAND THEATRE
2450 Grand Ave.
Kansas City, MO 64108
(816) 842-9999

*TIFFANY'S ATTIC DINNER PLAYHOUSE
5028 Main St.
Kansas City, MO 64112
Contact:Dinner Playhouse Inc.
1116 W. 25th St.
Kansas City, MO 64108
(816) 221-0677
(ADTI)

NEBRASKA

*FIREHOUSE DINNER THEATRE
514 S. 11th St.
Omaha, NE 68102
(402) 346-6009

UPSTAIRS DINNER THEATRE
221 S. 19th St.
Omaha, NE 68102
(402) 344-7777
(NDTA)

NEW JERSEY

NEIL'S NEW YORKER DINNER THEATRE
Route 46
Mountain Lakes, NJ 07046
(201) 334-0058

NEW YORK

ISLAND SQUIRE DINNER THEATRE
Box 428
Middle Island, NY 11953
(516) 732-2240

*LAKE GEORGE DINNER THEATRE
Box 4623
Queensbury, NY 12804
(518) 761-1092

*WESTCHESTER BROADWAY THEATRE
(Formerly An Evening Dinner Theatre)
11 Clearbrook Rd.
Elmsford, NY 10523
(914) 592-2268
(ADTI)

NORTH CAROLINA

THE BARN DINNER THEATRE
120 Stagecoach Trail
Greensboro, NC 27409
(919) 292-2211

TRIANGLE DINNER THEATRE
Box 12168
Research Triangle Park, NC 27709
(919) 549-8951

OHIO

*CAROUSEL DINNER THEATRE
1275 E. Waterloo Rd.
Akron, OH 44306
(216) 724-9855
(ADTI)

LA COMEDIA DINNER THEATRE
Box 204
Springboro, OH 45066
(213) 746-3114
(NDTA)

SPIRIT DINNER PLAYHOUSE
657 Sinsbury Dr. East
Worthington, OH 43085
(614) 846-2361
(NDTA)

WESTGATE DINNER THEATRE
3301 W. Central Ave.
Toledo, OH 43606
(419) 536-6161
(NDTA)

OREGON

SYLVIA'S DINNER THEATRE
5115 Northeast Sandy Blvd.
Portland, OR 97213
(503) 288-6828

PENNSYLVANIA

ALLENBERRY PLAYHOUSE
Rt. 174, Box 7
Boiling Springs, PA 17007
(717) 258-3211

CONLEY'S DINNER THEATRE
Rt. 30
Irwin, PA 15642
(412) 863-0700

DUTCH APPLE DINNER THEATRE
F11510 Centerville Rd.
Lancaster, PA 17601
(717) 898-1900
(NDTA)

GENETTI DINNER PLAYHOUSE
Rt. 309
Hazelton, PA 18201
(717) 454-2494
(NDTA)

HUNTINGDON VALLEY DINNER THEATRE
2633 Philont Ave.
Huntingdon Valley, PA 19006
(215) 947-6000

PEDDLER'S VILLAGE DINNER THEATRE
Rt. 263, Box 218
Lahaska, PA 18931
(215) 538-3206

RIVERFRONT DINNER THEATRE
Delaware Ave. at Poplar St.
Philadelphia, PA 19123
(215) 925-7000

SHAWNEE PLAYHOUSE
Box 159
Shawnee-on-Delaware, PA 18356
(717) 421-5093

TENNESSEE

CHAFFIN'S BARN DINNER THEATRE
8204 Highway 100
Nashville, TN 37221
(615) 646-9977
(NDTA)

VIRGINIA

BARKSDALE DINNER THEATRE
Box 7
Hanover, VA 23069
(804) 537-5333

OMNI DINNER THEATRE
777 Waterside Dr.
Norfolk, VA 23510
(804) 627-7773

SWIFT CREEK MILL PLAYHOUSE
Box 41
Colonial Heights, VA 23834
(804) 748-5203

TIDEWATER DINNER THEATRE
6270 Northampton Blvd.
Norfolk, VA 23502
(804) 461-2933
(NDTA)

WEST END DINNER THEATRE
4615 Duke St.
Alexandria, VA 22304
(703) 370-2500
(NDTA)

WISCONSIN

CLASSIC ARTS
110 S. Nicolet Rd.
Appleton, WI 54915
(414) 734-2787
(NDTA)

FANNY HILL INN AND DINNER THEATRE
3919 Crescent Ave.
Eau Claire, WI 54703
(715) 836-8184

FIRESIDE DINNER PLAYHOUSE
Box 7
1131 Janesville Ave.
Ft. Atkinson, WI 53538
(414) 563-9505
(NDTA)

NORTHERN LIGHTS PLAYHOUSE
Box 256
Hazelhurst, WI 54531
(715) 356-7173
(NDTA)

THEATER FOR YOUNG AUDIENCES

BY JOSEPH J. SCHWARTZ

Theater for young audiences offers great opportunities to actors searching for experience, credits, and gainful employment. With more than 50 producers regularly mounting Equity children's shows each season (and dozens of non-union producers providing similar opportunities), performers looking to start a professional career would do well to consider acting for younger age groups.

A GATEWAY TO EQUITY

There are a great many more chances for a non-union actor to get into Equity through a TYA (Theater for Young Audiences) contract than any other way. At least that's how Peter Harris, Equity's business representative for TYA, sees it. Harris maintains that producers are often unable to find actors willing to take on the rigors of touring with a TYA contract, which can include long periods of time away from New York, long hours of traveling, and multi-performance days. Therefore, they frequently open TYA auditions to non-union performers, who subsequently become Equity members.

THE TYA CONTRACT

The TYA contract guarantees actors a minimum wage on either a weekly or per-performance basis. In the weekly contract, which guarantees a performer a minimum of two weeks' work, actors must be paid no less than $265 per week. Assistant stage managers who act also receive $276 per week. A first or second assistant stage manager who does not act—and, therefore, has more technical responsibilities—is paid $282 weekly. The salary of a stage manager—who may not act or understudy—is $349 weekly. A per-performance TYA contract guarantees an actor a minimum of $43 per show. The wage is similarly scaled upward, depending upon the stage duty classification.

The TYA workday shall not exceed 10 hours and includes an hour for lunch. Rehearsing, performing, and traveling are all considered part of the 10-hour workday, and actors are guaranteed a 12-hour rest period between days. The standard performance week consists of nine performances. Because shows are brief (no longer than 90 minutes, including any live, educational demonstrations given by performers after a show), producers are allowed to add a tenth, eleventh, or twelfth performance in a given week. For these, each performer must receive no less than $20.00 additional compensation per performance. A $29.25 per night per diem must be paid to performers traveling away from the theater's home base. Overtime is provided at $4.25 per half hour during the workday and $10.50 per hour during the rest period.

To some in the field, the guarantees provided by the TYA contract may not seem overly attractive, but Barbara Colton, formerly Equity's TYA Committee Chair, recalls what children's theater was like before a union contract existed. Colton worked the children's theater circuit in 1961, and remembers working a three-performance day and being paid on a sliding scale: $7 for the first show, $5 for the second, and $3 for the third. "Today the Equity producer can only do a three-performance day twice a week and this must be non-consecutive," she says. "A standard weekly contract with a weekly guarantee and a per diem was absolutely unheard of before 1969. Frequently the actors had to maintain their own costumes, were not paid a rehearsal salary, and were paid only by the performance."

This is not to say that an age of enlightenment has taken over the entire theater establishment. In TYA, actors still have a heavy workload. In Equity companies, technical work is renumerated under the TYA contract's "additional duties rule"—and front-of-house or promotional duties are not allowed.

In non-Equity companies, non-acting duties are not so well controlled or compensated. However, while horror stories are not uncommon in the non-union arena, most performers' experiences of children's theater are positive.

CHILDREN'S THEATER PHOBIA

It may be that some actors shy away from children's theater because they are uncomfortable performing for children. But many theater professionals feel that the reasons have more to do with economic and professional considerations. "Agents will not come to see actors in children's shows," says John Ahearn of the Gingerbread Players and Jack. He believes actors, desperate to advance their careers, stay away from children's productions because of the lack of any critical spotlight. "Actors aren't really investigating children's theater because agents feel the productions are not as good as other shows. But—as with anything else—some *are* as good."

"It's difficult to get actors to leave New York," explains Charles Hull, producer of 30-year-old Theatreworks/USA, one of the nation's oldest professional children's theater companies. "Actors feel that if they are away from New York they will miss something," says Hull. That "something" Hull refers to may be an important audition, a showcase, or a part in a Broadway play. "But for a young actor," he continues, "a national tour provides an invaluable opportunity to develop one's craft. We've seen actors and actresses come back from a tour performing at a higher level than when they went out. There's no substitute for that experience."

Some actors who object to performing in children's theater seem to attach a cultural stigma to the simple act of performing in a show for young audiences. They hold the misconception that what's being done on stage in children's theater is not really legitimate theater, but some kind of simplified bastard version. "I wonder about that," muses actress Amy Butler, a veteran of the children's theater circuit. "I know people who compromise what they are doing all the time, and sometimes they feel better doing a showcase or a 'scene night' for free rather than being paid to do a children's show. I'd rather get paid."

Cultural stigma notwithstanding, many of the country's top performers got their starts performing for the younger set, with many of them supporting themselves through these performances for many years. Among the well-known performers who have appeared in children's theater are Henry Winkler, Kathy Bates, and F. Murray Abraham. In addition, there are numerous examples of established stars coming back to children's theater to do an occasional show or benefit. Elaine Stritch and Richard Kiley are cases in point.

A LIMITED GATE

Money is, of course, at the heart of mounting any successful theatrical production—TYA is no exception. According to Hull, whose Theatreworks/USA company works in agreement with the Equity TYA contract, his cost in mounting a production is approximately $30,000. This does not include the costs incurred while running or maintaining the production. And even though other companies may have fewer costs, one of the common complaints among children's theatrical producers is that the money one can charge is very limited. "There is a very limited gate," says Judith Martin, founder and artistic director of the Paper Bag Players, a 33-year-old company which employs actors under Equity's Guest Artist contract. "The money we take in from tickets sales never meets our expenses. We have to be constantly fundraising," Martin maintains.

Gingerbread's Ahearn agrees. "The labor, the artwork, costumes, scenery, salaries, rent have all gone up. And we always, always have to consider how much organizations are funded to bring in these shows."

The funding that Ahearn refers to are all the budget appropriations, state art council grants, parent/teacher organization donations, and educational cultural monies that usually pay for children's theater when it tours to public and private schools around the country. "In children's theater you can't make a lot of money because people will only pay so much for a seat for a child," Ahearn says.

In the absence of high monetary reward, one can only think that producers who go into mounting children's shows have ulterior motives. "It can be very exhilarating," says Martin. "We feel we make a very interesting kind of theater. It's where our talents lie, and it's a very artistically demanding situation," she adds. For Charles Hull producing theater for young audiences is "fun."

And, finally, Ahearn believes the best reward is the great feeling from having produced quality work.

EQUITY THEATER FOR YOUNG AUDIENCES COMPANIES

The following is a list of TYA companies in the Eastern, Midwestern, and Western regions of the United States. They are listed alphabetically in their appropriate regions, followed by an address, phone number, and the name of the artistic and/or producing director. An asterisk (*) indicates companies which are not currently active on TYA contract.

EASTERN STATES

ALLIANCE THEATRE
Robert W. Woodruff Arts Center
1280 Peachtree St., N.E.
Atlanta, GA 30309
Edith H. Love
(404) 898-1132

AMERICAN STAGE
Box 1560
211 3rd St. South
St. Petersburg, FL 33731
(813) 823- 1600
John Berglund

ARTS POWER
Box 9123
176 Kennedy Ct.
Paramus, NJ 07653
(201) 268-8486
Gary Blackman

ASOLO CENTER FOR THE
PERFORMING ARTS
Linda M. DiGarbriele
5555 N. Tamiami Tr.
Sarasota, FL 34243
(813) 351-9010
Don Creasot

BARTER THEATRE (TYA)
Box 867, Abingdon, VA 24210
(703) 628-2281
Rex Partington

*CHILDREN'S THEATRE OF CHARLOTTE
1017 E. Morehead Street
Charlotte, NC 28204
(704) 376-5745
Steve Umberger

*CHILDREN OF HOPE PROJECT, INC.
247 W. 15th St., #2A
New York, NY 10011
(212) 242-3269
Barbara Tirrell

CLARENCE BROWN THEATRE COMPANY
Box 8450
Knoxville, TN 37996
(615) 974-0964
Dennis Perkins

CLEVELAND PLAY HOUSE (TYA)
Box 1989
Cleveland, OH 44106
(216) 795-7010
Don Roe

*COCONUT GROVE PLAYHOUSE
3500 Main Highway
Miami, FL 33133
(305) 442-2662
Judith Delgado

CYGNET PRODUCTIONS
339 E. 10th St., #4-E
New York, NY 10009
(212) 473-6678
Sterling Swann

CREATIVE STAGES
(Formerly Hippodrome Theatre)
3426 NW 27th St.
Gainesville, FL 32605
(904) 378-1850
Margaret Bachus

CREATIVE THEATRE FOR CHILDREN
30 N. Van Brunt St.
Englewood, NJ 07631
(201) 568-5448

CROSSROADS THEATRE
2044 DeKalb Ave., N.E., #A5
Atlanta, GA 30307
(404) 371-8151
Lon Waitman

DEARKNOWS, LTD
Box 2444
Times Square Station
New York, NY 10108
(212) 921-8968
Jonathan Rosenberg

FANFARE THEATRE ENSEMBLE
100 E. 4th St.
New York, NY 10003
(212) 674-8181
Joan Shepard

*FIRST STAGE COMPANY
216 Ohio Ave.
Wilmington, DE 19805
(302) 998-6020
Peter DeLaurier

FLOATING HOSPITAL CHILDREN'S THEATRE
275 Madison Ave., #1801
New York, NY 10016
(212) 685-0193
Dr. Richard Birrer, Mary Casella

*FOUNDATION THEATRE
Burlington County College
Pemberton, NJ 08068
(609) 894-9311, x423
Julie Ellen Prusinowski

*GEORGIA SHAKESPEARE FESTIVAL
4484 Peachtree Road, N.E.
Atlanta, GA 30319-2797
(404) 264-0020
Lane Anderson

GINGERBREAD PLAYERS & JACK
35-06 88th St.
Jackson Heights, NY 11372
(718) 424-2443
John Ahearn

*HOSPITAL AUDIENCES INC.
220 W. 42nd St.
New York, NY 10036
(212) 575-7660
Max Daniels

IRONDALE ENSEMBLE PROJECT
782 West End Ave.
New York, NY 10025
(212) 633-1292
Josh Broder

*KENNEDY CENTER FOR
THE PERFORMING ARTS
JFK Center Theatre for Young People
Washington, DC 20566
(202) 416-8830
Carole C. Sullivan

LINCOLN CENTER INSTITUTE
140 W. 65th St.
New York, NY 10023
(212) 877-1800
June Dunbar, Mark Schubart

MAXIMILLION PRODUCTIONS
98 Riverside Dr., #7H
New York, NY 10024
(212) 874-3121
Peggy Traktman, Max Traktman

*NATIONAL ASIAN-AMERICAN COMPANY
433 W. 24th St. #1E
New York, NY 10011
(212) 840-1234
Richard Eng

NY STATE THEATRE INSTITUTE
U. Albany PAC, #266
1400 Washington Ave.
Albany, NY 12222
(518) 442-5399
Patricia Snyder

*NORTH CAROLINA SHAKESPEARE
FESTIVAL
305 N. Main St.
High Point, NC 27260
(919) 841-6273
Pedro Silva

*NO LIMITS COMPANY
81 16th St.
Buffalo, NY 14213
(716) 882-1046
Chris O'Neill

*NORTH SHORE MUSIC THEATRE
Box 62
Beverly, MA 01915
(508) 922-8220
Jon Kimbell

OPEN EYE NEW STAGINGS FOR YOUTH
270 W. 89th St.
New York, NY 10024
(212) 769-4143
Amie Brockway

PUSHCART PLAYERS
197 Bloomfield Ave.
Verona, NJ 07044
(201) 857-1115
Ruth Fost, Carole Wechter

*SCHOOLTIME THEATRE INC.
RD 2 Box 289
Irwin, PA 15642
(412) 744-3345
Merle Smith Kuznik

SESAME STREET LIVE/MUPPET BABIES
VEE CORPORATION
Lumber Exchange Bldg., #810
10 S. 5th St.
Minneapolis, MN 55401
(612) 375-9670
Pauline Knight

SHAKESPEARE & COMPANY
The Mount
Lenox, MA 01240
(413) 637-1197
Dennis Krausnick

SHAKESPEARE FOR SCHOOLS
41 Madeline Ave.
Clifton, NJ 07011
(201) 546-5695
Janet Villas

SHOWBOAT DINNER THEATRE (TYA)
3405 Ulmberton Road
Clearwater, FL 34622
(813) 223-2545
Virginia L. Sherwood

SLIM GOODBODY CORP.
27 W. 20th St., #1207
New York, NY 10011
(212) 254-3300
John Burstein

STAGE #4
250 W. 100th St.
New York, NY 10025
(212) 749-7627

STAGE ONE: LOUISVILLE
CHILDREN'S THEATRE
425 W. Market St.
Louisville, KY 40202
(502) 589-5946
Moses Goldberg

STREET THEATRE TOURING COMPANY
228 Fisher Ave. Rm. 226
White Plains, NY 10606
(914) 761-3307
Gray Smith

THEATRE FOR A NEW AUDIENCE
220 E. 4th St., 4th fl.
New York, NY 10009
(212) 505-8345
Jeffrey Horowitz

THEATREWORKS/USA
890 Broadway, 7th fl.
New York, NY 10003
(212) 677-5959
Jay Harnick, Charles Hull

THUNDERBIRD LTD, INC.
(Totem Pole Playhouse)
10290 Golf Course Road
Fayetteville, PA 17222
(717) 352-8811
Carl Schurr, Sue Kocek

TRAVELING PLAYHOUSE
104 Northampton Dr.
White Plains, NY 10603
(914) 946-5289
Kay Rockefeller, Ken Rockefeller

YATES MUSICAL THEATRE FOR CHIILDREN
19 Morse Ave.
East Orange, NJ 07017
(201) 677-0936
Peggy Yates

MIDWESTERN STATES

CLASSICS/ON STAGE
Box 25365
Chicago, IL 60625
(708) 275-6836
Bob Boburka, Michelle Vacca

DRURY LANE CHILDREN'S THEATRE
2500 W. Drury Lane
Evergreen Park, IL 60646
(708) 799-4000
John R. Lazzara

DRURY LANE OAKBROOK
Children's Theatre
100 Drury Lane
Oak Brook Terrace, IL 60181
(708) 530-8300
Anthony DiSantis

FACE TO FACE PRODUCTIONS
2415 N. Kedzie
Chicago, IL 60657
(312) 278-6359
Mark Grimsich

GREAT AMERICAN
CHILDREN'S THEATRE
304 E. Florida
Milwaukee, WI 53204
(414) 276-4230
Teri Mitze

IMAGINARY THEATRE COMPANY
(Repertory Theatre of St. Louis)
130 Edgar Road
St. Louis, MO 63119
(314) 968-0500
Steve Woolf

INDIANA REPERTORY THEATRE
Junior Works
140 W. Washington
Indianapolis, IN 46204
(317) 635-5277
Victoria Nolan

M & W PRODUCTIONS INC.
Box 93910, 925 E. Wells, #416
Milwaukee, WI 53203-0910
(414) 272-7701
Michael Wilson

MARRIOTT CHILDREN'S THEATRE
101 Half Day Road
Lincolnshire, IL 60069
(708) 643-0204
Kary Walker

MUNY/STUDENT THEATRE PROJECT
634 N. Grant, Suite 10-H
St. Louis, MO 63103
(314) 531-1315
William Friemuth

MUSIC THEATRE WORKSHOP
5647 N. Ashland
Chicago, IL 60660
(312) 561-7100
Meade Palidofsky

NATIONAL CHILDREN'S
REPERTORY THEATRE
225 E. St. Paul, Suite 300
Milwaukee, WI 53202
(414) 272-1545
Douglas Love

OLD LOG CHILDREN'S THEATRE
Box 250
Excelsior, MN 55331
(612) 474-5951
Don Stolz

SEEM TO BE PLAYERS
Box 1601
Lawrence, KA 66044
(913) 842-6622
Ric Averill

THEATRE FOR YOUNG AMERICA
7204 W. 80th St.
Overland Park, KA 66204
(913) 648-4600
Gene Mackey

WESTERN STATES

A CONTEMPORARY THEATRE
100 W. Roy St.
Seattle, WA 98119
(206) 285-3220
Philip Schermer

*AMERICAN LIVING HISTORY THEATRE
Box 2677
Hollywood, CA 90028
(213) 876-2202
Dorene Ludwig

BILINGUAL FOUNDATION OF THE ARTS
421 N. Ave. 19
Los Angeles, CA 90032
(213) 225-4044
Carmen Zapata

CABBAGES AND KINGS, INC.
7436 Kenshire Lane
Dallas, TX 75230
(214) 363-7292
Linda Comess

CASA MANANA PLAYHOUSE
Box 9054
Fort Worth, TX 76107
(817) 332-9313
Van Kaplan

DENVER CENTER THEATRE COMPANY
1050 13th St.
Denver, CO 80204
(303) 893-4200
Sarah Lawless

FANTASY THEATRE
Box 19206
Sacramento, CA 95816
(916) 442-5635
Timothy Busfield, Buck Busfield

*LA JOLLA PLAYHOUSE
Box 12039
La Jolla, CA 92037
(619) 534-6760
Alan Levey

*OLD GLOBE THEATRE
Balboa Park
Box 2171
San Diego, CA 92112
(619) 231-1941
Craig Noel, Tom Hall

SEATTLE CHILDREN'S THEATRE
305 Harrison St.
Seattle, WA 98109
(206) 443-0807
Thomas Pecher, Linda Hartzell

SEATTLE REPERTORY THEATRE
Seattle Center
155 Mercer St.
Seattle, WA 98109
(206) 443-2210
Benjamin Moore

SERENDIPITY THEATRE COMPANY
c/o Coronet Theatre
366 N. La Cienega Blvd.
Los Angeles, CA 90048
(213) 652-9199
Jody Johnston-Davidson

SOUTH COAST REPERTORY
655 Town Center Dr.
Box 2197
Costa Mesa, CA 92626-1197
(714) 957-2602
Paula Tomei

*TACOMA ACTORS GUILD
1323 S. Yakima Ave.
Tacoma, WA 98405
(206) 447-4764
Kate Haas

THEATRE WEST
3333 Cahuenga Blvd.
West Los Angeles, CA 90068
(213) 851-4839
Nadine Kalmes

WILL AND COMPANY
7918 Rosewood
Los Angeles, CA 90048
(213) 655-9582
Colin Cox

WORKING IN LOS ANGELES THEATERS

BY ROB STEVENS

When actors speak of Los Angeles—meaning Hollywood—they naturally talk about working in films and television. What about working in the theater? Is there theater work to be found in Los Angeles? The answer is a definite "yes." But can an actor make a living working in the theater in L.A.? Yes and no. Most Los Angeles actors, like their counterparts in New York and elsewhere, earn a living by working in films, television, industrials, and commercials. They use the theater to practice their craft, expand their range, and showcase their acting talents.

According to several theatrical producers, theater is the "bastard child" of L.A.'s entertainment world. Media coverage is mainly focused on film and television in this "industry" town, but a quick look through the theater listings in the *Los Angeles Times* or the *L.A. Weekly* will find nearly 150 productions running in any given week.

There is nothing similar to New York's Broadway theater district in Los Angeles. Theaters are scattered about the landscape much the same as everything else is in this sprawling city. Little clumps of theaters are struggling to become theater districts in places like the Hollywood and Vine intersection in Hollywood, along Melrose Avenue and Santa Monica Boulevard, and in the San Fernando Valley.

The Los Angeles area boasts nearly 20 large commercial houses, with seating capacities ranging from 550 to 3,200—but most of them are empty more than they are booked. The Nederlanders book three venues: the Pantages and Henry Fonda Theatres in Hollywood and the Wilshire Theatre in Beverly Hills. Although the Nederlander houses tend to host national touring productions, an exception is the Los Angeles Civic Light Opera, whose locally mounted productions are being presented by new producers Martin Wiviott and Keith Stava.

The Shuberts have one house in L.A., the Shubert Theatre in Century City, which plays host to long-running attractions such as *Cats* and *Les Miserables*. Much of the casting for these shows has been done locally. The Center Theatre Group/Ahmanson mixes locally produced shows and touring productions in its season.

The Long Beach Civic Light Opera and the California Music Theatre in Pasadena each offer a season of four musicals a year. Stars are cast in the lead roles to attract ticket-buyers, but most of the casting is done through open calls. Other local civic light opera companies—Downey, Fullerton, Whittier-La Mirada, San Gabriel, San Bernardino, and Glendale—usually work with Equity guest artists. Herb Rogers produces a Broadway season of five shows at the La Mirada Theatre for the Performing Arts. Working under a modified stock contract, audience-attracting stars are cast as the leads, with open casting providing for the rest of the roles.

RESIDENT THEATERS IN L.A.

There are four LORT theaters in the area: the Mark Taper Forum, Los Angeles Theatre Center, the Pasadena Playhouse, and South Coast Repertory. The old joke about the Mark Taper is that you had to be born there to be cast in a play. The Taper does tend to use a lot of the same people season after season, and artistic director Gordon Davidson has made several attempts to establish a permanent repertory company. But like most of the theaters in town, the Taper does accept photos and resumes and holds periodic auditions. It also occasionally brings in productions from other regional theaters. South Coast Repertory does have a resident company of actors and the Los Angeles Theatre Center has a group of artistic associates from which it draws frequently to cast its productions.

San Diego lies 100 miles down the freeway from Los Angeles, and the city has a booming theater scene. Its major companies—the Old Globe, San Diego Repertory, La Jolla Playhouse, and Starlight Music Theatre—cast in L.A. and employ a lot of L.A.-based performers in their productions. The Sacramento Music Circus and the PCPA Theatrefest in Santa Maria/Solvang also audition in Los Angeles each year.

MID-SIZE VENUES

The half-dozen mid-size houses in Los Angeles range in capacity from 248 to 498. The Las Palmas, Ivar, and Comedy Store Playhouse in Hollywood, the Canon in Beverly Hills, the Coronet in West Hollywood, and the Westwood Playhouse in Westwood all work under the new Equity Hollywood Area Theatre (HAT) contract. Unfortunately, these houses are dark most of the time except for the occasional rental.

NINETY-NINE-SEAT THEATERS

The majority of theater in Los Angeles takes place in the more than 150 Equity-approved 99-seat theaters. These spaces, which by definition must contain less than 100 seats, are run by theater groups, production companies, or are available for rental. They operate under Equity's "99-Seat Theatre Plan" which has a sliding scale offering reimbursement to the actors from $5 to $15 per performance.

Over a dozen membership theaters dot the Los Angeles area. An actor auditions to join the theater group and then pays monthly dues. Casting for the productions is done primarily from within the company. The procedure for becoming a member of a group theater is fairly standard. First a picture and resume must be submitted, which is filed as to type needed, age range, and so on. Every two to three months auditions are held. Prospective members first go through an interview process; they are told about the group and what would be expected of them if they were to be admitted to the company. When not appearing in a production, members are expected to help out in other capacities, such as stage managing, running the lights, or ushering. Next, candidates audition before a select board of the group. Besides the theater's regular season of productions, many of the groups conduct workshops or mount projects which give those members not cast in a mainstage production a chance to practice their craft. These projects, though not open to review, often are offered as a bonus to the theater's subscribers, giving the actors the opportunity to work in front of an audience.

Theatre West in Hollywood, one of the oldest groups in the city, has dues of $34 a month. Other theater groups in the L.A. area—including Burbank Theatre Guild, Group Repertory Theatre in North Hollywood, Theatre East in Studio City, and Theatre 40 in Beverly Hills—charge monthly dues ranging from $15 to $60.

GETTING INVOLVED

Networking is a major facet in the life of an actor in Los Angeles. It's important to get involved—to be in contact with the principal players, the creative people, the casting directors, writers, producers, directors, or other actors. See as much theater as you can. SAG and Equity offer hotlines that not only list auditions, but announce shows that are giving free tickets to members. Many theaters offer discounts to union members. In order to keep up with industry news, you must read the trades—*Daily Variety*, *The Hollywood Reporter*, and *Drama-Logue*.

Once you get a role, you have to act as your own promoter. You'll need to send flyers or postcards to casting agents and other industry professionals inviting them to come and see your show. If you or the show get good reviews, you should do a second mailing using quotes and follow-up with a phone call. Some casting directors—those who came from the theater—continue to go to the theater to see talent.

More name film and television actors are becoming involved in L.A.'s 99-seat theater scene. They have brought more credence to these theaters, but they have also taken roles away from unknowns. There are fewer open calls now than there used to be. A lot of casting is done through agent submission and through Breakdown Services—a kind of newsletter that casting directors, agents, and managers subscribe to that lists, on a weekly basis, breakdowns of theater, film, and TV roles currently being cast. Since a lot depends not only on what you know, but *who* you know, contacts are vital to a career in Los Angeles. The theater talent pool is much smaller than in New York, so people tend to use people whose work they know or whom they have worked with before.

Can you make a living doing theater in Los Angeles? Most actors still make their living doing other jobs but... Reece Holland spent 18 months in the role of Raoul in *Phantom of the Opera* at the Ahmanson Theatre, after spending the previous 10 months playing Marius in *Les Miserables* at the Shubert Theatre. That's 28 consecutive months of theater work in Los Angeles. It *can* happen here.

LOS ANGELES 99-SEAT THEATERS

The following is a listing of theaters in the Los Angeles area with less than 100 seats. These spaces have been approved by Actors' Equity Association as 99-seat theaters. Members of Equity or its sister unions may only perform in these theaters under the Los Angeles 99-Seat Theatre Plan.

ACTEX STAGES
5051 Klump St.
North Hollywood, CA 91601
(818) 508-1922

ACTORS ALLEY
12135 Riverside Dr.
North Hollywood, CA 91607
(818) 986-2278

ACTORS CENTER THEATRES
11969 Ventura Blvd.
Studio City, CA 91604
(818) 505-9400

ACTORS FORUM
3365 1/2 Cahuenga Blvd.
West
Los Angeles, CA 90068
(213) 850-9016

STELLA ADLER THEATRE
6250 Hollywood Blvd.
Hollywood, CA 90028
(213) 469-6049

ALLIANCE REPERTORY
COMPANY
3204 W. Magnolia Blvd.
Burbank, CA 91505
(818) 566-7935

AN CLIADHEAMN SOLUIS
5651 Hollywood Blvd.
Hollywood, CA 90028
(213) 462-6844

ATTIC THEATRE
656 1/2 Santa Monica Blvd.
Los Angeles, CA 90038
(213) 462-9720

RICHARD BASEHART
21028-B Victory Blvd.
Woodland Hills, CA 91367
(818) 704-1845

BELIEVERS REPERTORY
COMPANY
First Baptist Church
of Beverly Hills
9025 Cynthia St.
West Hollywood, CA 90069
(213) 276-3978

BEVERLY HILLS PLAYHOUSE
254 S. Robertson Blvd.
Beverly Hills, CA 90211
(213) 652-6483

BFA'S LITTLE THEATRE
(Bilingual Foundation
of the Arts)
421 N. Avenue 19
Los Angeles, CA 90031
(213) 225-4044

BURBAGE THEATRE
2330 Sawtelle Blvd.
Los Angeles, CA 90064
(213) 478-0897

BURBANK LITTLE THEATRE
1100 W. Clark Ave.
Burbank, CA 91510
(818) 954-9858

CALIFORNIA COTTAGE
THEATRE
5220 Sylmar Ave.
Van Nuys, CA 91401
(818) 990-5773

CALLBOARD THEATRE
8451 Melrose Pl.
Los Angeles, CA 90029
(213) 852-9205

CAMINITO THEATRE
(Los Angeles City College)
855 N. Velmont Ave.
Los Angeles, CA 90029
(213) 669-4336/669-5528

CARPET COMPANY STAGE
5262 W. Pico Blvd.
Los Angeles, CA 90019
(213) 658-6117

CAST-AT-THE-CIRCLE
800 N. El Centro Ave.
Hollywood, CA 90038
(213) 462-0265/462-9872

CAST THEATRE
804 N. El Centro Ave.
Hollywood, CA 90038
(213) 462-0265/462-9872

CELEBRATION THEATRE
7051 Santa Monica Blvd.
Hollywood, CA 90027
(213) 394-9810

CELEBRITY CENTRE THEATRE
5930 Franklin Ave.
Los Angeles, CA 90028
(213) 464-0411

CENTURY CITY PLAYHOUSE
(Burbage Theatre Ensemble)
10508 W. Pico Blvd.
Los Angeles, CA 90064
(213) 478-0897

CHAMBER THEATRE
3759 Cahuenga Blvd., West
Studio City, CA 91604
(818) 760-9708

CITY HALL THEATRE
(Manhattan Pier Players)
1400 Highland Ave.
Manhattan Beach,
CA 90266
(213) 545-5621/545-9192

COAST PLAYHOUSE
(Catalina Productions)
8325 Santa Monica Blvd.
West Hollywood, CA 90069
(213) 650-8507/664-9657

COMPANY OF ANGELS
2106 Hyperion Ave.
Los Angeles, CA 90027
(213) 666-6989

THE COMPLEX
6476 Santa Monica Blvd.
Los Angeles, CA 90038
(213) 465-0383

COURT THEATRE
722 N. La Cienega Blvd.
West Hollywood, CA 90069
(213) 652-4035

CROSSLEY THEATRE
1st Presbyterian Church
of Hollywood
1760 N. Gower St.
Hollywood, CA 90028
(213) 462-8460

GENE DYNARSKI THEATRE
5600 West Sunset Blvd.
Los Angeles, CA 90028
(213) 465-5600

EAST WEST PLAYERS
4424 Santa Monica Blvd.
Los Angeles, CA 90029
(213) 660-0366

FIG TREE THEATRE
6539 Santa Monica Blvd.
Hollywood, CA 90038
(213) 960-8870

FOUNTAIN THEATRE
5060 Fountain Ave.
Los Angeles, CA 90029
(213) 663-1525

FRIENDS & ARTISTS
THEATRE ENSEMBLE
1761 N. Vermont Ave.
Los Angeles, CA 90027
(213) 664-0680

GARDNER STAGE
1501 N. Gardner Ave.
Los Angeles, CA 90046
(213) 876-2870

GLOBE PLAYHOUSE
(Shakespeare Society of
America)
1107 N. Kings Rd.
Los Angeles, CA 90069
(213) 654-5623

GNU THEATRE
10426 Magnolia Blvd.
Toluca Lake, CA 91601
(818) 508-5344

GOLDEN THEATRE
139 N. San Fernando Blvd.
Burbank, CA 91502
(818) 841-9921

GROUNDLINGS THEATRE
7307 Melrose Ave.
West Hollywood, CA 90046
(213) 934-9700/934-4747

GROUP REPERTORY
THEATRE
10900 Burbank Blvd.
North Hollywood, CA 91601
(818) 760-9368

GYPSY PLAYHOUSE
(Professional Dancers Studio)
3321 W. Olive Ave.
Burbank, CA 91505
(818) 954-8458

HARMON AVENUE
THEATRE
522 N. LaBrea Ave.
Los Angeles, CA 90036
(213) 931-8130

HAUNTED STUDIOS
6419 Hollywood Blvd.
Los Angeles, CA 90028
(213) 465-5224

HELIOTROPE THEATRE
660 S. Heliotrope Dr.
Los Angeles, CA 90004
(213) 660-4247

HIDDEN HILLS PLAYHOUSE
2459 Long Valley Rd.
Hidden Hills, CA 91302
(818) 992-7791

IGLOO THEATRE
6543 Santa Monica Blvd.
East Hollywood, CA 90029
(213) 962-3771

INGLEWOOD PLAYHOUSE
400 West Beach Ave.
Inglewood, CA 90302
(213) 936-7600

INTERNATIONAL CITY
THEATRE
4901 E. Carson St.
Long Beach, CA 90808
(213) 420-4275/420-4128

LANDMARK ALLIANCE
THEATRE
6817 Franklin Ave.
Hollywood, CA 90028
(213) 851-5982

LEX THEATRE
6760 Lexington Ave.
Hollywood, CA 90038
(213) 465-8431

LIBERTY THEATRE
2035 N. Highlands Ave.
Hollywood, CA 90068
(213) 851-3030

LITTLE VICTORY THEATRE
3324 Victory Blvd.
Burbank, CA 91505
(818) 843-9253/841-4404

LOS ANGELES INNER CITY
CULTURAL CENTER
1308 S. New Hampshire Ave.
Los Angeles, CA 90006
(213) 387-1161

MAGNOLIA PLAYHOUSE
11246 Magnolia Blvd.
North Hollywood, CA 91607
(818) 951-1038

MARILYN MONROE
THEATRE
(Lee Strasberg Institute)
7936 Santa Monica Blvd.
Los Angeles, CA 90046
(213) 650-7775

MATRIX THEATRE
(Actors for Themselves)
7657 Melrose Ave.
Los Angeles, CA 90046
(213) 852-1445

McCADDEN PLACE THEATRE
1157 N. McCadden Pl.
Hollywood, CA 90038
(213) 462-9070

MEAN STREET ENSEMBLE
THEATRE
1455 N. Gordon St.
Hollywood, CA 90028
(213) 957-1335

MELROSE THEATRE
733 N. Seward St.
Los Angeles, CA 90038
(213) 465-1885

MET THEATRE
1089 N. Oxford Ave.
Los Angeles, CA 90029
(213) 957-1741/957-1831

NOSOTROS
1314 N. Wilton Pl.
Los Angeles, CA 90028
(213) 465-4167

THE ODDITY THEATRE
5074 W. Pico Blvd.
Los Angeles, CA 90019
(213) 931-7002

ODYSSEY THEATRE
ENSEMBLE
2055 S. Sepulveda Blvd.
West Los Angeles, CA
90025
(213) 477-2055

OFF RAMP THEATRE
1053 N. Cahuenga
Los Angeles, CA 90068
Mail: 6395 Ivarene Ave.
Los Angeles, CA 90068
(213) 469-4343/465-8059

OLIO
3709 Sunset Blvd.
Los Angeles, CA 90026
(213) 667-9556/664-5909

OPEN FIST
1625/27 N. La Brea Ave.
Hollywood, CA 90028
(213) 281-8325

PACIFIC THEATRE
ENSEMBLE
705 1/2 Venice Blvd.
Venice, CA 90291
(213) 306-3943

PLAYBOX THEATRE
1953 Cahuenga Blvd.
Hollywood, CA 90028
(213) 469-9434

POWERHOUSE THEATRE
3116 2nd St.
Santa Monica, CA 90405
(213) 392-6529

ROLAND DUPREE'S
STUDIO THEATRE
8115 W. 3rd St.
Los Angeles, CA 90048
(213) 655-1276/655-6895

ROSE THEATRE
318 Lincoln Blvd.
Venice, CA 90291
(213) 392-4911

SAINT GENESIUS THEATRE
1049 N. Havenhurst Ave.
West Hollywood, CA 90046
(213) 650-8823

SANTA MONICA
PLAYHOUSE
1211 4th St.
Santa Monica, CA 90401
(213) 394-9779

SECOND STAGE THEATRE
6500 Santa Monica Blvd.
Los Angeles, CA 90038
(213) 465-6029

SKYLIGHT THEATRE
(Beverly Hills Playhouse)
1816 1/2 N. Vermont Ave.
Los Angeles, CA 90027
(213) 666-2202

STAGES THEATER CENTER
1540 N. McCadden Pl.
Los Angeles, CA 90028
(213) 465-1010/463-5365

LEE STRASBERG INSTITUTE
7936 Santa Monica Blvd.
Los Angeles, CA 90046
(213) 650-7777

STUDIO JACK KOSSLYN
666 N. Robertson Blvd.
West Hollywood, CA 90069
(213) 855-9242

STUDIO THEATRE
(Long Beach Community
Players)
5021 E. Anaheim St.
Long Beach, CA 90804
(213) 494-1616/494-1014

STUDIO THEATRE
PLAYHOUSE
(at The Colony)
1944 Riverside Dr.
Los Angeles, CA 90039
(213) 665-3011/667-9851

TAMARIND THEATRE
5919 Franklin Ave.
Hollywood, CA 90028
(213) 466-9714

THEATRE EAST
12655 Ventura Blvd.
Studio City, CA 91604
(818) 760-4160

THEATRE EXCHANGE
11855 Hart St.
North Hollywood, CA 91605
(818) 765-9526

THEATRE 40
241 Moreno Dr.
Beverly Hills, CA 90212
Mailing: Box 5401
Beverly Hills, CA 90210
(213) 277-4221

THEATRE OF ARTS
4128 Wilshire Blvd.
Los Angeles, CA 90010
(213) 380-0511

THEATRE OF N.O.T.E.
1705 N. Kenmore Ave.
Los Angeles, CA 90027
(213) 666-5550

THEATRE RAPPORT
1277 N. Wilton Pl.
Los Angeles, CA 90038
(213) 660-0433

THEATRE 6470
6470 Santa Monica Blvd.
Hollywood, CA 90038
(213) 462-7123/487-2112

THEATRE/THEATRE
1713 N. Cahuenga Blvd.
Hollywood, CA 90028
(213) 871-0210/850-6941

THIRD STAGE
2811 W. Magnolia Blvd.
Burbank, CA 91505
(818) 842-4755

TIFFANY THEATRES 1 & 2
8532 Sunset Blvd.
West Hollywood, CA 90069
(213) 289-2999

TRACY ROBERTS THEATRE
141 S. Robertson Blvd.
West Hollywood, CA 90048
(213) 271-2730

TWO ROADS THEATRE
4348 Tujunga Ave.
Studio City, CA 91604
(818) 766-9381

VENTURE THEATRE
Burbank, CA 91505
(818) 846-5323

VICTORY THEATRE
3326 West Victory Blvd.
Burbank, CA 91505
(818) 843-9253/841-4404

WATERFRONT STAGE
250 Santa Monica Pier
Santa Monica, CA
(213) 383-6672 (Fax)

WEST COAST ENSEMBLE
6240 Hollywood Blvd.
Hollywood, CA 90028
(213) 871-1052/871-8673

WEST END PLAYHOUSE
7446 Van Nuys Blvd.
Van Nuys, CA 91405
(818) 904-0444

WHITEFIRE STAGE
13500 Ventura Blvd.
Sherman Oaks, CA 91423
(818) 990-2324

ZEPHYR THEATRE
7456 Melrose Ave.
Los Angeles, CA 90046
(213) 653-4667/852-9069

WORKING IN CHICAGO

BY JONATHAN ABARBANEL

Bottom line—Chicago is *not* where you become rich and famous. It's much better than that—it's where you work. It's where an actor actually can make a living from his or her craft, given a little talent and a little more hustle. A princely living, no. But a living, yes. There's theater all over the place, there's a major commercial industry (in which one *can* become rich), and there's film.

Also, Chicago is an easier place in which to live and work than New York or Los Angeles. All you have to do is enjoy cold winters. Rents are lower than on either coast. Distances are shorter than in L.A., so you don't necessarily need a car. The pace is slower than New York, and the attitude is far less cut-throat and competitive. It's not as homey as it was 10 or 15 years ago, but there's still a family feeling within the theater industry.

Finally, Chicago has become the prime city in the country to be discovered *from*. The strength of its theater industry and the establishment of state and local film offices have been magnets for producers and casting directors from both coasts, who now make Chicago a regular stop. Once known only for its improvisational comedic style, the Chicago School of Acting is now known also for its physically committed, aggressive realism—the so-called "rock 'n' roll" or "scratch and sniff" theater, typified by the work of companies like Steppenwolf and the Remains Ensemble, among others. Having "Chicago" on your resume is the gold standard for any actor today—a credit that will receive instant attention, especially within the film industry. And Chicago *still* is the capital of improv (not to mention the blues).

The "Who's Who" of Chicago theater artists who have made it can go back to Paul Sills, Mike Nichols, Elaine May, Shelly Berman, and others from the pre-Second City days, or it can be as au courant as Joan and John Cusack. In between, consider the fortunes (in random order) of such actors as Michael Gross, Bill Murray, the Belushi brothers, John Malkovich, William L. Petersen, D.W. Moffett, George Wendt, Steven Williams, John Pankow, Holly Fulger, John Herrera, Bruce Norris, Joan Allen, Michael Rooker, Gary Cole, Yvonne Suhor, John Mahoney, Molly Regan, and Joe Mantegna; of such writer/directors as David Mamet, Frank Galati, Stuart Gorden, and Harold Ramis; of such directors as Robert Falls, Michael Maggio, Jonathan Wilson, and Kyle Donnelley.

This is not to suggest that it's easy to make a living as an actor in Chicago. It isn't. But it isn't as impossible as elsewhere. In any given week, one out of every seven Chicago Equity actors is employed under an Equity contract. Not good, but far better than New York's one-in-twenty ratio. The reality is that an actor who loves theater usually must supplement his or her habit with commercial or film work, especially if there is a family to support. But work *is* available, and under conditions more likely to be artistically satisfying than in the industry cauldrons on the coasts. In brief, Chicago may mean less money per mainstage acting job, but more opportunities to work, coupled with far easier access to industry channels.

THEATER OPPORTUNITIES

It is estimated that Chicago and its metropolitan area have some 200 theater companies, of which 125 are members of the League of Chicago Theatres, the principal trade association. They range from large Equity houses like the Shubert, Auditorium, and Goodman to non-union and educational companies. In 1988-89 (the last full year for which there are accurate figures), League members produced 700 shows, giving 12,100 performances attended by nearly three million people.

More than 40 Chicago-area presenters are AEA signatories. The principal contract is CAT: Chicago Area Theatre. While there are only two LORT companies (Goodman and Northlight), four dinner theater contracts, a half-dozen TYA troupes, and a handful of cabaret and special agreements, Chicago has over two dozen CAT companies. This versatile contract is divided into six salary tiers, based on potential gross. Actors' minimums begin at $159 per week for four performances or fewer at Tier I, and scale up to $457 per week for up to eight performances at Tier VI. Unlike New York and Los Angeles, where actors may work under Equity's Showcase Code or 99-Seat Theatre Plan, in Chicago if actors work, they get paid.

If the CAT minimums don't sound like much, remember, this is Chicago. Decent one-bedroom apartments in decent neighborhoods still are available for $500 a month, a monthly pass good for unlimited rides on public transit systems is $60, and two people still can eat out for $20.

The CAT contract is used by commercial and not-for-profit presenters, by subscription companies, and one-timers. Currently in its third three-year term, it will be renegotiated in the summer of 1992. In 1989-1990 (the last complete year on record), there were 5,395 work weeks under CAT, up slightly over the previous year.

Equity's Midwest regional office at 203 N. Wabash Ave., Chicago, IL 60601 (telephone: (312) 641-0393) covers a 13-state area. Headed by Midwestern executive director Tad Currie, it administers all contracts in this region. Paperwork for the Guthrie Theater, Milwaukee and Missouri Repertory Theatres, the Repertory Theatre of St. Louis, and other leading LORT companies flows through Chicago AEA. Many Midwest regionals hold general calls here, as do dinner theaters and theme parks. Clever Midwestern Equity members take advantage of these casting opportunities.

BEYOND CAT

Production contract opportunities, while limited, also exist. National companies of *Les Miserables* and *The Phantom of the Opera* originated in Chicago and held calls here, casting several principal roles, as well as chorus, with local performers (and picking up a musical director). *Les Mis* held a second call on a return visit, too.

Singer/dancers need not wait for national tours, however. Three major musical presenters in town produce lavishly: Candlelight Dinner Playhouse, Drury Lane Oakbrook Terrace, and Marriott's Lincolnshire Theatre. Don't be deceived by their dinner theater contracts: Drury Lane Oakbrook Terrace utilizes a 900-seat proscenium house built within the last 10 years, and once brought in Bob Fosse to stage *Dancin'*, which subsequently went on tour. Marriott's Lincolnshire Theatre regularly spends at least $250,000 to mount its in-the-round shows, with casts of 20 or more and orchestras of up to 13 pieces. Candlelight has salvaged such apparent Broadway failures as *Rags* and *The Human Comedy*, as well as familiar hits, and has launched the odd bus-and-truck tour.

In addition to these three, a half-dozen other presenters usually stage one or more musical projects each season, including the Goodman Theatre, Drury Lane Martinique, New Tuners, and the Pegasus Players (which produced the national bus-and-truck of *Into the Woods*, with Sondheim's blessing).

Limited additional Equity opportunities are offered through live business theater. While this category has severely declined nationwide, Chicago remains as strong a center for live industrials as any.

A final Equity note: nearly a decade ago, Midwest AEA and the League of Chicago Theatres committed themselves actively to non-traditional casting. Statistically, the results have been encouraging. Minorities make up 7 percent of AEA members in the 13-state Midwestern region, but account for approximately 12 percent of AEA contract work weeks.

NON-UNION THEATER

Non-union theater opportunities are, of course, significant. Don't be too New York-ish and dismiss them as amateur. Naturally, Chicago has community theaters of the "weekend warrior" variety, but it also has many award-winning non-union professional companies which have launched successful careers for many performers. A number of professionals hone their acting skills with non-union troupes, while some of the city's best designers, directors, and authors freely move between union and non-union venues. The Society of Stage Directors and Choreographers has no lock on Off-Loop Theater, as the indigenous producing community is called, in contrast to the now mostly dark roadshow houses in the old city center known as The Loop. A substantial number of shows spawned by non-union troupes have enjoyed extended commercial runs.

The best of the non-union companies try to pay actors something—perhaps as little as $10 a show, but possibly as much as $150, for a five- or six-performance week (more if the show should prove to have legs). For an actor, the exposure can be better than the money, because non-union professional shows are as widely and seriously reviewed as Equity productions. Very few of Chicago's most famous companies were born with Equity cards. Steppenwolf, Remains, Organic, Wisdom Bridge, Court, Victory Gardens, and Next Theatre all worked their way up from non-union status with the help of good reviews and good marketing.

Chicago is also an ensemble town. Steppenwolf may be the most famous, but it was not the first. There are Shakespearean ensemble companies and improv ensembles. Few (in fact none that I know of, not even Steppenwolf) can pay ensemble members a living stipend, but that doesn't reduce the commitment to come together at least once or twice a year for specific projects. A significant number (at least seven during the 1990-91 season) are committed to limited rotating repertory, alternating two shows for limited runs.

Finally, Chicago is an original town. There *has* been life for playwrights after Mamet. An actor working here will have ample opportunity to participate in world-premiere productions of plays and musicals by nationally known authors, as well as by local playwrights.

WORKING ON COMMERCIALS

It's surprising to find actors who ignore the commercial market—as if making rounds somehow is less pure, or more demeaning, than cattle call auditions for shows. Obviously, it is time-consuming; you can't make rounds if you're rehearsing days. It also requires the cultivation of commercial acting skills, which are not always the same as "real" acting skills. But the jobs are there, and the income can supplement and even support an actor's theater habit. Furthermore, the commercial market is far more accessible (even for beginners) in Chicago than it is on either coast.

The Chicago production industry in 1990—minus feature films—was a $700 million business, with the lion's share spent on TV commercials. The audio-visual and multi-image business also is huge, accounting for nearly 30 percent of that $700 million. On-camera and voiceover talent took in a $40 million chunk.

THE FILM INDUSTRY

Illinois was the location for 25 feature films in 1990, both theatrical release and made-for-TV. Besides picking up lots of local crews, virtually all of these productions cast extras (non-union), speaking roles, and occasional principals in Chicago. So do the feature films that shoot in Wisconsin, Michigan, Indiana, Iowa, or Kentucky, albeit fewer in number. Just as important to an impending film career are the non-Midwest shoots that come here to scout for fresh faces and "real" actors of the Chicago "school." Remember what we said earlier: Chicago is a regular stop on the casting circuit, no matter where the flick is being made. The soaps come here, too. Chicago agents and casting directors have formed strong alliances with their counterparts on the coasts, and several have their own Los Angeles offices, as well. Each year, more and more Chicago actors spend a few weeks or months in L.A. for pilot season.

In conclusion, Chicago is no longer a film industry wasteland. If you wish to pursue a film/TV career, you actually can do it and still live here (except, perhaps, in the case of a long-run series). John Mahoney and William L. Peterson do okay in Hollywood, but still make Chicago home.

AGENT REPRESENTATION

Assuming you are fully equipped for a professional career—with a good head-shot, an honest resume, a thick skin, a little spunk, and a working knowledge of the telephone—you should be able to do all right on your own, without an agent, certainly in the early stages of a career. Theaters and production houses here do not require that talent be submitted only through agents or casting directors.

You can count on the fingers of one hand the number of times each year that Chicago theaters utilize casting directors. You can get an appointment yourself as easily as an agent can. Just call the theaters directly to inquire about casting policies and auditions. Virtually all have general calls sometime during the year. Watch for casting notices in *Back Stage* and a few other key publications. Check the Equity Hotline (ask AEA for the number); call the privately run Non-Equity Hotline—(312) 976-2278—for $2 per minute; and network among industry people. Film calls also occasionally are reported through these channels.

As for commercials and modeling, Chicago is a town where talent still makes the rounds of ad agencies, production houses, and photographers. It's a chore, to be sure, but it's one an agent cannot do better for you. Voice-over talent almost invariably is selected in-house by ad agency writers or producers. Even on-camera talent is sometimes contacted directly for auditions. This practice is not universal, however, and an agent certainly is practical—though not absolutely essential—in the commercial sector. Commercial and industrial film auditions scheduled by production houses generally are booked through agents, but not casting directors.

Ten years ago, the casting profession really didn't exist in Chicago. Now, there are nearly ten casting houses (agencies sometimes double in casting, too). Some work only with extras, but most cover speaking roles. Their presence in casting theater and commercials is minimal, but in film they are nearly always used. They work with all the agents, and they work directly with talent as well. You need not have an agent to list with one or more casting directors. To reiterate: the Chicago market does not require submissions through agents only. Should you choose to list with an agent or casting service, you will find that multiple agency listings are common. Few will insist that you be exclusive with them, although you may choose to go exclusive once a rapport has been established. A few agents follow theater particularly closely, and have benefitted greatly by signing theater artists. Ask around; your colleagues will know who they are.

A final word on representation: Chicago has talent agents and casting directors, but is not a town of personal and business managers. Beware any lawyer who tells you that he or she is all the representation you need (and that's not just in Chicago).

Chicago is far different from New York in one respect: performers here aren't class crazy. Possibly because it is easier to actually "do it" here, performers are less compulsive about using classes to sharpen their skills. Nonetheless, a range of fine acting and voice classes is available, as well as private scene and vocal coaching. The twice-monthly publication *PerformInk* is a good source of information, as are various callboards, the AEA and SAG/AFTRA offices, and personal recommendations. Dancers have some good options, as well, in both classical and contemporary fields. Particularly notable is the Lou Conte Studio. Conte, a former show dancer/choreographer, is the founder and artistic director of the nationally acclaimed Hubbard Street Dance Company. When you study jazz, tap, or contemporary dance at his studios, you'll be side-by-side with his company (when they're not touring). Classical students should seek out the Ruth Page Foundation, where the ABT takes classes when in town.

WRAPPING IT UP

That, in a large nutshell, is the theater industry in Chicago. Above all—the one thing that actor upon actor, writer after writer, repeats—Chicago is a place where an actor has the freedom to fail. You can work, stretch, bomb, triumph, learn...whatever; it will *not* adversely affect your career. Whatever else you read here, or with regard to the film industry, keep in mind that Chicago theater is isolated from the make-or-break pressures and reviews that dominate theater (and film) in New York and Los Angeles. You can relax here; you can have a life. You can be an artist in Chicago. In a different context, Paul Sills once said, "Come to Chicago. They'll leave you alone here." But it applies to actors, too. You may not make a lot of money, but you will be relatively free to develop yourself.

CHICAGO THEATERS

This list of Chicago-area theaters was compiled by the League of Chicago Theatres. The business phone numbers are listed, as well as names of key artistic and administrative personnel. The listings indicate if the theaters are not-for-profit, commercial, Equity, or non-Equity.

ACTORS CENTER OF
DUPAGE INC.
300 N. Westmore
Villa Park, IL 60181
(708) 530-4802
Norman Engstrom,
Jeff Baumgartner
(not-for-profit, non-Equity)

ALLIED ARTS
ASSOCIATION
Orchestra Hall
220 S. Michigan Ave.
Chicago, IL 60604
(312) 435-8122
Terry Schlender,
Owen Wonders
(not-for-profit, Equity)

AMERICAN BLUES THEATRE
1225 W. Belmont
Chicago, IL 60657
(312) 929-1031
Bill Payne, Mary M. Badger
(not-for-profit, Equity)

AMERICAN RITUAL
THEATRE COMPANY
Box 608516
Chicago, IL 60660
(312) 743-3162
Bill Harper
(not-for-profit, non-Equity)

APOLLO THEATRE
2540 N. Lincoln Ave.
Chicago, IL 60614
(312) 549-1342
Wes Payne, Kearan
Anderson (commercial)

APPLE TREE THEATRE
593 Elm Pl.
Highland Park, IL 60035
(708) 432-4335
Eileen Boevers,
Jane Howard
(not-for-profit, Equity)

AUDITORIUM THEATRE
50 E. Congress Pkwy.
Chicago, IL 60605
(312) 431-2395
Dulcie Gilmore, Barbara
Corrigan (commercial)

AVENUE THEATRE
4223 N. Lincoln Ave.
Chicago, IL 60618
(312) 404-1780
Doug Binkley
(not-for-profit, non-Equity)

BAILIWICK REPERTORY
3212 N. Broadway
Chicago, IL 60657
(312) 883-1090
David Zak, Jackie Ward
(not-for-profit, non-Equity)

BEACON STREET GALLERY
AND THEATRE
4520 N. Beacon
Chicago, IL 60640
(312) 561-3500
Pat Murphy, Susan Field
(not-for-profit, non-Equity)

BLACK ENSEMBLE THEATRE
Box 409323
Chicago, IL 60640
(312) 769-5516
Eboni Puckett, Jackie Taylor
(not-for-profit, Equity)

BLIND PARROT
PRODUCTIONS
1121 N. Ashland
Chicago, IL 60622
(312) 227-5999
Clare Nolan-Long
(not-for-profit, non-Equity)

THE BLUE RIDER THEATRE
1822 S. Halsted
Chicago, IL 60608
(312) 733-4668
Tim Fiori,
Donna Blue Lachman
(not-for-profit, non-Equity)

BODY POLITIC THEATRE
2261 N. Lincoln Ave.
Chicago, IL 60614
(312) 348-7901
Nan Charbonneau,
Albert Pertalion
(not-for-profit, Equity)

BRIAR STREET THEATRE
3133 N. Halsted
Chicago, IL 60657
(312) 348-5996
Phil Eickhoff
(commercial)

BUFFALO THEATRE
ENSEMBLE
Arts Center, College
of DuPage
22nd St. and Lambert Rd.
Glen Ellyn, IL 60137
(708) 858-2800, x2100
Craig Berger
(not-for-profit, Equity)

CACTUS THEATRE
COMPANY
1633 W. Estes, 1E
Chicago, IL 60626
(312) 338-7337
Neil Weiss, Bob Ellerman
(not-for-profit, non-Equity)

CANDLELIGHT DINNER
PLAYHOUSE
5620 S. Harlem Ave.
Summit, IL 60501
(312) 735-7400
Eileen LaCarlo,
William Pullinsi
(commercial, Equity)

CENTER THEATER
1346 West Devon
Chicago, IL 60660
(312) 508-0200
Dan LaMorte, RJ Coleman
(not-for-profit, Equity)

CHAMELEON
PRODUCUTIONS
4753 N. Broadway, Suite 918
Chicago, IL 60640
(312) 907-2188
Lisa Duncan, Bellary Darden
(not-for-profit, non-Equity)

CHICAGO ACTORS
ENSEMBLE
Box 409216,
Chicago, IL 60640
(312) 275-4463
Rick Helweg
(not-for-profit, non-Equity)

CHICAGO CITY THEATRE
1225 W. School
Chicago, IL 60657
(312) 880-1002
Joseph Ehrenberg, Joel Hall
(not-for-profit, non-Equity)

CHICAGO DRAMATISTS
WORKSHOP
1105 W. Chicago Ave.
Chicago, IL 60622
(312) 633-0630
Russ Tutterow, Gary Brichetto
(not-for-profit, Equity)

THE CHICAGO MEDIEVAL
PLAYERS
International House
1414 E. 59th St.
Chicago, IL 60637
(312) 935-0742
Ann Faulkner
(not-for-profit, Equity)

CHICAGO SHAKESPEARE
COMPANY
1800 W. Cornelia
Chicago, IL 60657
(312) 871-8961
Myron Freedman,
Mary Mauro
(not-for-profit, non-Equity)

CHICAGO THEATRE
COMPANY
1801 71st St.
Chicago, IL 60637
(312) 493-0901
Kristin Anderson
(not-for-profit, Equity)

CITY LIT THEATER
COMPANY
4753 N. Broadway, Suite 618
Chicago, IL 60640
(312) 271-1100
Arnold Aprill,
Charles Twichell
(not-for-profit, non-Equity)

CIVIC CENTER FOR
PERFORMING ARTS
20 N. Wacker Dr., Suite 422
Chicago, IL 60606
(312) 346-0270
Fred Solari
(commercial)

CLASSICS ON STAGE!
Box 25365,
Chicago, IL 60625-0532
Bob Boburka, Michele Vacca
(commercial)

THE COMMONS THEATRE
1020 W. Bryn Mawr
Chicago, IL 60660
(312) 769-5009
Morgan McCabe,
Judith Easton
(not-for-profit, non-Equity)

COURT THEATRE
5535 S. Ellis
Chicago, IL 60637
(312) 702-7005
Nicholas Rudall,
Pam Mansfield
(not-for-profit, Equity)

CULLEN, HENAGHAN &
PLATT PRODUCTIONS
1871 N. Clybourn Ave.
Chicago, IL 60614
(312) 404-1200
Sheila Henaghan,
Michael Cullen
(commercial)

DOUGLAS THEATER
CORPORATION
180 E. Pearson, #4602
Chicago, IL 60611
(312) 642-2342
Douglas Bragan
(commercial)

DREISKE PERFORMANCE
COMPANY
1517 W. Fullerton
Chicago, IL 60614
(312) 281-9075
Nicole Dreiske,
Susan Willenbrink
(not-for-profit, non-Equity)

DRURY LANE
DINNER THEATRE
2500 W. 95th St.
Evergreen Park, IL 60642
(708) 422-8000
John R. Lazzara
(commercial, Equity)

DRURY LANE
OAKBROOK THEATRE
100 Drury Lane
Oakbrook Terrace, IL 60181
(708) 530-8300
Sue Linn
(commercial, Equity)

EQUITY LIBRARY THEATRE
Box 14156
Chicago, IL 60614
(312) 528-6033
Darwin R. Apel, Leah Roshal
(not-for-profit, Equity)

ETA CREATIVE ARTS
FOUNDATION
7558 S. Chicago Ave.
Chicago, IL 60619
(312) 752-3955
Abena Joan Brown,
Runako Jahi
(not-for-profit, non-Equity)

FOOTSTEPS THEATRE
COMPANY
6968 N. Clark
Chicago, IL 60626
(312) 764-7164
Yita Dennis
(not-for-profit, non-Equity)

FORUM THEATRE
5620 S. Harlem Ave.
Summit, IL 60501
(312) 735-7400
Tony D'Angelo,
Noreen Herron
(commercial)

GADFLY ETHNIC THEATRE
Box 17076
Chicago, IL 60617
(312) 568-1172
Auggie Lehmann,
Greg Woods
(not-for-profit, non-Equity)

GOODMAN THEATRE
200 S. Columbus Drive
Chicago, IL 60603
(312) 443-3811
Roche Schulfer, Robert Falls
(not-for-profit, Equity)

GRIFFIN THEATRE
COMPANY
2700 N. Elston Ave.
Chicago, IL 60647
(312) 278-2494
William J. Massolia, Richard
Barlena
(not-for-profit, non-Equity)

HALSTED THEATRE CENTER
2700 N. Halsted
Chicago, IL 60614
(312) 348-8455
Michael Frazier
(commercial)

HYSTOPOLIS PUPPET
THEATRE
441 W. North Ave.
Chicago, IL 60610
(312) 787-1524
Michael Schwabe,
Larry Basgall
(not-for-profit, non-Equity)

THE ILLEGITIMATE PLAYERS
1049 W. Altgeld, #3
Chicago, IL 60614
(312) 327-8696
Maureen Fitzpatrick,
Kathy Giblin
(commercial)

ILLINOIS THEATRE CENTER
400 Lakewood Blvd.
Park Forest, IL 60466
(708) 481-3693
Etel Billig, Steve Billig
(not-for-profit, Equity)

THE IMPROV INSTITUTE
2319 W. Belmont
Chicago, IL 60618
(312) 929-2323
Ross Gottstein, Tom Hanigan
(not-for-profit, non-Equity)

INTERPLAY
135 S. Cuyler
Oak Park, IL 60302
(708) 848-3245
David Perkovich,
Donald Miller
(not-for-profit, Equity)

KING'S MANOR
DINNER THEATRE
2122 W. Lawarence Ave.
Chicago, IL 60625
(312) 275-8400
Barbara Velen
(commercial)

KUUMBA THEATRE
c/o Malcolm X City College,
#0515
1900 W. Van Buren
Chicago, IL 60612
(312) 243-2294
Val Gray Ward
(not-for-profit, Equity)

LIFELINE THEATRE
6912 N. Glenwood
Chicago, IL 60626
(312) 791-4477
Meryl Friedman
(not-for-profit, non-Equity)

LIGHT OPERA WORKS
927 Noyes St.
Evanston, IL 60201
(708) 869-6300
Bridget McDonough,
Julianne Barnes
(not-for-profit, non-Equity)

LIVE BAIT THEATRICAL
COMPANY
3914 N. Clark St.
Chicago, IL 60613
(312) 871-1212
Sharon Evans, John Ragir
(not-for-profit, non-Equity)

LIVE THEATRE
1234 Sherman Ave.
Evanston, IL 60202
(708) 475-2570
A.C.Thomas, Marcia Riegel
(not-for-profit, non-Equity)

LOOKINGLASS THEATRE
COMPANY
Box 408487
Chicago, IL 60640-8487
(312) 477-7010
Christine Dunford, Andy White
(not-for-profit, non-Equity)

MARRIOTT'S LINCOLNSHIRE
THEATRE
10 Marriott Dr.
Lincolnshire, IL 60069
(708) 634-0204
Peter Grigsby, Kary Walker
(commercial)

MAVIN PRODUCTIONS II
Box 1262,
Highland Park, IL 60015
(708) 290-8837
Libby Mages, Dan Golman
(commercial)

MAYFAIR THEATRE
Blackstone Hotel,
636 S. Michigan Ave.
Chicago, IL 60605
(312) 786-9317
Kristin Overnl
(commercial)

MUSIC/THEATRE
WORKSHOP
5647 N. Ashland
Chicago, IL 60660
(312) 561-7100
Elbrey Harrell,
Meade Padidofsky
(not-for-profit, Equity)

MYSTERY CAFE
DINNER THEATRE
Essex Inn Hotel
800 S. Michigan Ave.
Chicago, IL 60605
(312) 341-1333
Pam Eckwall, P. Siragusa
(commercial)

NATIONAL JEWISH
THEATER
Horwich/Kaplan JCC
5050 W. Church St.
Skokie, IL 60077
(708) 675-2200
Fran Brunlik,
Arnold Aprill
(not-for-profit, Equity)

NEXT THEATRE COMPANY
127 Noyes
Evanston, IL 60201
(708) 475-6763
Harriet Spizziri,
Chris Barry
(not-for-profit, Equity)

NORTHLIGHT THEATRE
600 Davis St.
Evanston, IL 60201
(708) 869-7732
Russell Vandenbroucke,
Jeffrey Woodward
(not-for-profit, Equity)

OAK PARK FESTIVAL
THEATRE
Box 4114,
Oak Park, IL 60303
(708) 524-2050
Jim Struthers
(not-for-profit, Equity)

ORGANIC THEATER
COMPANY
3319 N. Clark St.
Chicago, IL 60657
(312) 327-2659
Richard Friedman,
Richard Fire
(not-for-profit, Equity)

PASSAGE THEATRE
Box 10730,
Chicago, IL 60613
(312) 975-5939
Scott Guy,
Margaret Scott
(not-for-profit, non-Equity)

THE PAYNE-LEAVITT GROUP
2540 N. Lincoln Ave.
Chicago, IL 60614
(312) 549-1342/472-9263
Wes Payne,
Michael Leavitt
(commercial)

PEGASUS PLAYERS
O'Rourke Center
for Performing Arts
1145 W. Wilson
Chicago, IL 60640
(312) 878-9761
Arlene Crewdson,
David Dillon
(not-for-profit, non-Equity)

PERKINS THEATERS, INC.
DBA/ROYAL GEORGE
THEATRE
1641 N. Halsted
Chicago, IL 60614
(312) 944-5626
Robert Perkins, J
im Jensen
(commercial)

PHEASANT RUN
DINNER THEATRE
4051 E. Main St.
St. Charles, IL 60174
(708) 594-6342
Diana L. Martinez,
Bob Howlett
(commercial)

PIVEN THEATRE
WORKSHOP
927 Noyes
Evanston, IL 60201
Jane Piven, Brian Powell
(not-for-profit, non-Equity)

THE PLAYWRIGHTS' CENTER
c/o Arts Bridge
4753 N. Broadway,
Suite 918
Chicago, IL 60640
(312) 907-2185
Jim MacDowell, Steve Bruce
(not-for-profit, non-Equity)

PROFILES PERFORMANCE
ENSEMBLE
4206 N. Hermitage, 1st fl.
Chicago, IL 60613
(312) 404-8341
Cynthia Jahraus, Joe Jahraus
(not-for-profit, non-Equity)

RAVEN THEATRE COMPANY
6931 N. Clark St.
Chicago, IL 60626
(312) 338-2177
Michael Menendian, JoAnn
Montemurro
(not-for-profit, non-Equity)

REGAL THEATER
1645 E. 79th St.
Chicago, IL 60649
(312) 721-9301
Chuck Gueno
(not-for-profit, Equity)

REMAINS THEATRE
1800 N. Clarkson
Chicago, IL 60614
(312) 335-9595
Jennifer Boznos
(not-for-profit, Equity)

SARANTOS STUDIOS
2857 N. Halsted
Chicago, IL 60657
(708) 848-1100
Ted Sarantos, Pat Taylor
(commercial)

SECOND CITY
1616 N. Wells St.
Chicago, Il 60614
(312) 664-4032
Joyce Sloane,
Cheryl Sloane
(commercial)

SHAKESPEARE REPERTORY
2140 Lincoln Park West
Chicago, IL 60614
(312) 281-2101
Barbara Gaines
(not-for-profit, Equity)

SHUBERT THEATRE
22 W. Monroe, 6th
Chicago, IL 60603
(312) 977-1710
(commercial)

STAGE LEFT THEATRE
3244 N. Clark St.
Chicago, IL 60657
(312) 883-8830
Dennis McCullough,
Debra Rodkin
(not-for-profit, non-Equity)

STEPPENWOLF THEATRE
1650 N. Halsted
Chicago, IL 60614
(312) 335-1888
Stephen Eich,
Randall Arney
(not-for-profit, Equity)

STRAWDOG THEATRE
COMPANY
3829 N. Broadway
Chicago, IL 60613
(312) 528-9889
Larry Novikoff,
Paul Engelhardt
(not-for-profit, non-Equity)

SYNERGY THEATRE
1437 W. Addison
Chicago, IL 60613
(312) 975-1703
Mark Fritts, Annette Lazzara
(not-for-profit, non-Equity)

TALISMAN THEATRE
2074 N. Leavitt
Chicago, IL 60647
(312) 235-7763
Mark Hardiman,
Mary Hatch
(not-for-profit, non-Equity)

THEATRE BUILDING/
NEW TUNERS THEATRE
1225 W. Belmont
Chicago, IL 60657
(312) 929-7367
Ruth Higgins,
Joan Mazzonelli
(not-for-profit, non-Equity)

THEATRE II COMPANY
St. Xavier College,
McGuire Hall
3700 W. 103rd St.
Chicago, IL 60655
(312) 779-3300 x557
JoAnne Fleming, Jim Sherman
(not-for-profit, non-Equity)

TORSO THEATRE
7020 N. Sheridan, #2H
Chicago, IL 60626
(312) 549-3330
Jim Casey,
Billy Bermingham
(not-for-profit, non-Equity)

TOUCHSTONE THEATRE
Box 488
Lake Forest, IL 60045
(708) 295-7849
Ina Marlowe
(not-for-profit, non-Equity)

THE TOURING
CHILDREN'S THEATER OF
THE SECOND CITY
2636 N. Lincoln Ave.
Chicago, IL 60614
(312) 929-6288
Eric Forsberg,
Josephine Forsberg
(not-for-profit, non-Equity)

TRINITY SQUARE ENSEMBLE
927 Noyes, #224
Evanston, IL 60201
(708) 328-0330
Kathleen Martin
(not-for-profit, non-Equity)

VICTORY GARDENS
THEATER
2257 N. Lincoln Ave.
Chicago, IL 60614
(312) 549-5788
Marcelle McVay,
Dennis Zacek,
John Walker
(not-for-profit, Equity)

WELLINGTON THEATER
750 W. Wellington
Chicago, IL 60657
(312) 975-6282
Jim Pappas,
Wes Payne
(commercial)

WISDOM BRIDGE THEATRE
1559 W. Howard
Chicago, IL 60626
(312) 743-0486
Jeffrey Ortmann,
Terry McCabe
(not-for-profit, Equity)

ZEBRA CROSSING THEATRE
4437 N. Ravenswood
Chicago, IL 60640
(312) 728-0082
Bob Buck
(not-for-profit, non-Equity)

PART SIX

OFF THE MAIN STAGE

THEME PARKS

BY THOMAS WALSH

I n terms of sheer quantity of audience, theme parks probably offer the best exposure anywhere for the performing artist. Some 10 million people pass through the gates of a good-sized, year-round theme park. This averages out to over 27,000 audience members a day and offers a performer intense, varied experience.

A handful of the better-known theme parks are open 365 days a year. Most, however, are seasonal operations, generally presenting daily shows from early spring through Labor Day. Nevertheless, audiences at all theme parks are huge. A show may run for 30 seconds, or it can last 20 minutes, an hour, or even all day long. Salaries vary greatly but are generally considered fair, and perks at the theme park are always good. Housing and transportation may be provided. Training, workshops, and internships are usually available and college credits can sometimes be obtained. Additionally, as employees of the theme parks, theater personnel frequently receive unlimited access to the park's multitude of attractions (rides, games, and other shows.

The benefits of working three months, or even a year, in the gorgeous and invigorating outdoor environment that is the setting for most theme parks cannot be overstated. If you compare the pleasures of pushing the sets around at a rep house to the prospect of a summer in Virginia or an autumn in Orlando, you will probably agree.

The following listings contain information about theme parks nationwide. Nearly all theme parks conduct open calls prior to each season for performers, as well as audio engineers, lighting technicians, costumers, dressers, stagehands, and many more. The packages offered to technical personnel are often as attractive as those for performing artists.

ALLAN ALBERT, INC.

The New York-based Albert company serves as a clearing house and central casting headquarters for two large East Coast parks: Hersheypark in Hershey, Pennsylvania, and Action Park in Vernon Valley, New Jersey. This company has been expanding its operations, and in 1987, it presented the first theme park shows in China, before an audience of nearly 50,000 people. Further territorial treks by the Albert company are in the works.

Action Park is one of America's largest water parks. Located just an hour and a quarter from midtown Manhattan, it is a neighbor of the Vernon Valley/Great Gorge ski areas and has been offering theatrical productions since 1981. Its season runs from approximately June 15 to Sept. 2, and presents various showcases that feature a wide variety of entertainers.

Applicants must be at least 17 years old or be high school graduates, and the management prefers that prospective employees be under 30 years of age. On the technical end, stage managers, seamstresses, and a company manager are hired.

Action Park residual benefits are excellent: luxury hotel accommodations with all amenities are available near the park at no cost, and employees have access to the park at all times, including pools and water rides. The weekly pay begins around $320, plus bonuses.

Hersheypark is based in "Chocolatetown, U.S.A.," which is a pretty fair attraction in itself—and more than 30,000 people flock to this park daily. Hersheypark, which has featured live productions since the mid-1970s, is approximately three hours from New York City by car.

Criteria for performers are the same as for Action Park. Additionally, singers must dance and move well, and dancers must be proficient in jazz and tap. Technicians required are stage managers, seamstresses, and sound and lighting technicians.

All applicants are offered a salary package ranging from approximately $275 to $360 weekly, plus bonuses. Employees are provided housing at a subsidized rate (about $45 per week), have free access to park facilities at all times, and may use the employee cafeteria. A limited number of guest passes are available.

ATF ENTERTAINMENT

The ATF company emerged in 1989, its premiere season, as a new contender for theme park talents. Its casts and productions have been seen in a sweeping variety of locations in the U.S., Canada, and Europe, including Playland in Rye, New York, Dorney Park in Allentown, Pennsylvania, Boblo Island in Canada, and Traumland in Germany.

ATF seeks energetic college-age performers: singer/dancers, musicians (trumpet, trombone, tuba), jugglers, magicians, and sound technicians. Salaries start at $250 per week, depending on assignment and experience; housing and transportation are subsidized. Most positions begin in June and end on Labor Day. The company maintains offices in Michigan, Colorado, and Brooklyn, N.Y.; casting information is available only from the Brooklyn office.

THE BUSCH ENTERTAINMENT CORPORATION

The Busch Entertainment Corporation, a subsidiary of Anheuser-Busch Companies, Inc., added a huge new frontier to its empire in November of 1989, when it acquired the four Sea World theme parks plus two other Florida parks — Cypress Gardens and the now-defunct Boardwalk & Baseball — all from Harcourt Brace Jovanovich. The Sea World parks are spread across the map

— Orlando, San Antonio, San Diego, and Aurora, Ohio; and with Busch Gardens—The Dark Continent (Tampa), Busch Gardens—The Old Country (Williamsburg, Va.), Sesame Place (Langhorne, Penn.), and Adventure Island, a water park in Tampa, the Busch family is a thematic conglomerate.

Only two of the Busch Gardens theme parks will be reviewed here, The Dark Continent and The Old Country. Addresses for the other parks are included in the list at the end of this chapter.

The Busch Gardens venues, The Dark Continent and the Old Country, conduct annual safaris to track down singers, dancers, actors, actresses, variety artists, technicians, and stage managers. Busch Gardens theme parks feature Broadway-style variety revues, country and contemporary song-and-dance productions, German and Italian shows, and strolling bands.

Applicants for auditions must be at least 18 years of age and must be available for full-time seasonal employment. A detailed resume is a must. Audition requirements are as follows: Singers are required to perform an up-tempo song and a ballad (bring your own sheet music), and must dance a choreographed piece; dancers must dance and perform a vocal selection; actors must present a comic monologue—improvs and dialects are important; variety artists are required to come up with some type of patter; and musicians must also present vocal material. Auditioners should limit their presentations to two minutes and be prepared to present additional material upon request.

Performers have access to free classes in dance, vocal instruction, and instrumental training, and can participate in choral, band, jazz, and dance concerts.

Busch Gardens—The Dark Continent is a 300-acre representation of yesteryear Africa. It is one of the most popular attractions on Florida's west coast. A year-round showplace, The Dark Continent offers one-year contracts to performers.

Among Dark Continent's attractions are animal shows, strolling performers, Broadway-style shows, thrill rides, exhibits, shops, and games. The Dark Continent hires singer/dancers, musicians, actors, technicians, and others. Wages range from $6 to $10 per hour. Perks include a full medical plan.

Busch Garden—The Old Country is a 360-acre family entertainment park three miles east of historic Williamsburg, Virginia. The Old Country includes eight authentic European hamlets ranging from Oktoberfest (Germany) to Banbury Cross (England). From March to October, the park's strolling performers, magicians, musicians, and storytellers play host to approximately two million visitors.

Salaries range from approximately $278 to $394 weekly, and benefits include free classes and seminars in dance, music, voice, and drama.

The Old Country presents up to 17 hours of live entertainment in 84 to 100 shows daily. Nationwide auditions begin in the fall and are usually completed by mid-December, with others conducted locally during the year.

CEDAR POINT

Over 700 performances are staged annually at Cedar Point, and after nearly 120 years of entertaining America's Midwest, the 364-acre, four-theater park in Ohio can list many alumni who have graduated to Broadway, television, films, major theaters, and concert halls nationwide.

Positions are available for musicians (everything from banjo and bass to trumpet and tuba), singers, singer/dancers, singer/musicians, MCs, specialty acts, and about 20 technicians.

The Cedar Point season runs from early May through Labor Day, with some acts held over for bonus weekends in September. Salaries range from approximately $280 to $305 weekly. Musicians must be members in good standing of the American Federation of Musicians and the minimum age for all live-show employees is 18. Benefits include low-cost housing, free workshops, movies, dances and beach and ride privileges.

WALT DISNEY COMPANY

For the theatrically trained individual seeking big-time exposure and experience, the Disney empire holds some of the most powerful cards in the deck. Applicants may submit resumes throughout the year for any and all positions. Disney's yearly talent search is so wide-spread that company representatives are reluctant to release even a rough estimate of the number of people they hire. Suffice it to say that the annual lineups of professional singers, dancers, musical-theater performers, and orchestra members interning in the Disney Company is huge.

Walt Disney World offers productions featuring old-time vaudeville, contemporary Broadway, country/western, pop, and jazz elements.

Disney World took an historic step in May, 1990, by successfully negotiating a contract with Actors' Equity to cover approximately 400 performers at the site. The deal—the first ever between the union and a theme park—represents a unique collaboration by Equity and a performing venue.

Employment begins in May or June. Hopefuls must attend a preliminary call to be considered for callbacks. Those who are called back will receive written or phone notification. The All American College Band and Orchestra also audition here. They seek musicians who have a flair for jazz and popular music.

Disney World benefits are quite broad, beginning with a base pay for chorus and principal performers of $350 to $488 per week. One-year contracts and summer employment are available; full-timers generally work a 5-day, 40-hour week and are compensated for overtime. Other incentives include relocation assistance, health and dental benefits, paid vacations and sick days, and rehearsals at full salary.

Disney World does not interview technicians, stage managers, or variety acts, but resumes are accepted year-round.

EPCOT Center, the high-tech neighbor to Disney's Magic Kingdom Park, has performance opportunities that are interchanged through both properties, and casting generally happens from the combined singer/dancer/instrumentalist auditions. Additionally, the All American College Show Orchestra is an EPCOT property exclusively, seeking 36 musicians for its ensemble.

Among the incentives for this group are daily workshops and rehearsals in preparation for three nightly shows, with major stars on hand for weekends.

The members of this program are selected during the annual Disney summer instrumentalist audition tour. Benefits and inducements for members include housing and transporation, a weekly stipend of $230, workshops and master classes, and extensive talent and career coaching.

General requirements for auditioners: Each must be at least 18 years old by June 1 and must bring a current picture, resume, and letter of recommendation; all respondents must be willing to make a three-month commitment, and all should know that "talent, versatility, and enthusiasm are essential."

For singers and dancers, audition guidelines are identical to those listed for Disney World. Instrumentalists should bring three music styles for a five-minute presentation (sight-reading material provided); popular music, show band, and jazz experience are preferred, and showmanship and musicianship are important. The musical portions of the auditions will be geared towards recruiting saxophone (all doubles), trumpet, trombone, guitar, electric bass, keyboard/synthesizer, violin, viola, cello, string bass, flute, clarinet, and show-drummer players. All doubles are welcome and movement ability is helpful.

Disney is continually seeking interested professionals for special events and replacements for stage shows.

Disneyland has been operating at Anaheim, California, since 1955. Open 365 days a year, Disneyland's live-entertainment lineups change on an almost constant basis, and talent is recruited nationwide.

New concepts for performers are dreamed up continually at Disneyland, and the entertainment staff chooses the formats and meets the talent needs in shifting patterns. Musical performers dominate Disneyland's roving-entertainment scenario, but all shapes and sizes of talent are sought and staged. The Disneyland Band, a 16- to 17-member ensemble, is among the constants on the park's musical roster; performers are scattered throughout the seven lands of the 76.6-acre Disneyland property.

Disney-MGM Studios was created when the legendary Disney filmmaking unit teamed up with the colossal Metro-Goldwyn-Mayer Studios in a new venue just south of EPCOT Center. The Disney-MGM Studios Theme Park premiered on May 1, 1989, with a star-studded guest list, and after the opening ceremonies, *Newsweek* noted that the place "fulfills Walt Disney's wildest dreams." The 135-acre site is focusing on a diverse set of performers to be recruited for a variety of new productions, with the emphasis of course on the big screeen.

Major attractions include the "Indiana Jones Epic Stunt Spectacular," in a 2,000-seat covered outdoor amphitheater, for which actors and gymnast/tumblers are required, with strong athletic skills and acrobatic routines. Also on the agenda: "Hollywood! Hollywood!," which employs 25 dancers/singers for a musical salute to the movies; "Screen Test," improvisational actors working with park guests in short videotaped comic scenes; and the Streetmosphere Performers, 30 actors taking on the guises of different famous Tinseltown residents (strong improvisatory background necessary).

Performers are screened as part of the Disney World audition tour; technical personnel are encouraged to send resumes to Disney Manpower Planning, c/o MGM Studios at the address noted in the list at the end of this chapter.

Dollywood is a corporation partially owned by country music/film/television star Dolly Parton. Formerly known as Silver Dollar City, this theme park corporation rechristened itself as Dollywood in May of 1986, helping to boost attendance to nearly two million visitors per year. Dollywood runs productions from the last weekend in April to the last weekend in October.

Singers, roving groups, individual performers, and several musical groups entertain throughout the park daily. In April of 1988, a 2,000-seat, three-million-dollar, state-of-the-art theater was unveiled. Gospel, country, and bluegrass music are the main fare at this theater. Performers are paid for a six-day work week. Pay scales range from $300 to $600 weekly.

KINGS PRODUCTIONS

The Kings Entertainment Company of Cincinnati is one of the largest producers of live shows for theme parks in North America. It produces shows for the following theme parks: Kings Dominion in Richmond, Virginia, Carowinds in Charlotte, North Carolina, Great America in Santa Clara, California, Kings Island in Cincinnati, Ohio, and Wonderland in Toronto, Ontario. Shows at Kings Productions sites usually run from March to December and generally are staged from 15 to 30 minutes, five to six times a day.

"Kings" hires over 700 theatrical people for its five theme parks. Actors, singers, dancers, instrumentalists, specialty acts, technicians, backstage personnel, hosts, hostesses, escorts, and others are auditioned during nationwide casting tours throughout the United States and Canada. Applicants must be at least 16 at the time of employment. The weekly pay scale is approximately $270 to $320 for singers, dancers, variety acts, and instrumentalists, and $243 to $282 for technicians, "walkabouts," hosts, hostesses, and escorts. Housing and transportation are not provided.

Kings Productions sponsors free seminars by leading show-business people, industrial shows for corporate clients, and a tour of the Mediterranean and Caribbean in conjunction with the U.S. Department of Defense.

MOLONEY PRODUCTIONS

The Moloney Production company, formed in 1984, has cast and staged theme park shows for venues in New York, Pennsylvania, Arizona, Michigan, and New Hampshire, and has ranged up to Canada and over to Dusseldorf, West Germany. Sites that come under the Moloney banner are negotiated yearly; interested performers can contact the company, and audition information will be sent to them.

Male and female singer/dancers, magicians, jugglers, musicians (wind and percussion), atmosphere characters, technicians, and company managers are needed each year. Salaries are "competitive." Technical personnel need detailed resumes.

OPRYLAND

Over a dozen live musical productions go up at this park. Covering the full spectrum of American music, the multiple scenarios spotlight ballet, jazz, tap, gymnastics, and every conceivable musical motif. Singers, dancers, musicians, specialty acts, and technicians are recruited for shows that are witnessed by an audience of more than two million people per year.

Rehearsals begin in February and productions start in late March and run through early November. The pay scale runs from around $274 (technicians) to $606 (conductor/pianists) for a six-day work week. Rehearsal pay is hourly, and returning employees receive a salary advantage.

Opryland's 30-city audition tour starts in the fall and usually concludes in Nashville around Christmas.

PAUL OSBORNE'S PARK SHOWS

Since 1971, the Paul Osborne company has been keeping dozens of theme parks supplied with everything from scenery and props to small performance groups to full-scale extravaganzas. Osborne-backed shows and technical assistance have been recruited by the Six Flags and Busch Gardens people, as well as in places around the country with names like Deer Forest, Dogpatch U.S.A., and Enchanted Village, plus sites in Canada and Europe. For just about any entertainment idea, Osborne is available to audition, manage, design, produce, consult, anything short of donning a costume and doing a magic show himself, which probably wouldn't be a stretch.

Osborne arranges productions that feature comedy, original scripting, custom costuming, original music, sets, props, and art direction. Complete audition guidelines, dates, locations, and parks to be staffed become available each winter, so talent and others are encouraged to call the Dallas office or fax their interest. Live shows range from Broadway spectaculars to saloon revues and "wagon shows"; magic acts, with themes ranging "from Western to outer space," are a specialty.

The seasons for most of the parks with which Osborne works generally run from late May to early September. Most shows are staged four-six times daily, and performer pay scales roam from $800-$1,500 monthly.

SHOW BIZ INTERNATIONAL, INC.

Show Biz International, Inc. is an independent production company with long experience in coordinating family-style entertainment for theme parks. This Indiana-based group is at the forefront of five theme parks in the U.S. and Canada: Adventureland in Des Moines, Iowa; Cliff's Amusement in Albuquerque, New Mexico; Darien Lake in Darien Center, New York; Geuga Lake in Aurora, Ohio; and Holiday World in Santa Claus, Indiana.

The company hires approximately 400 seasonal employees, including directors, producers, writers, artists, choreographers, arrangers, costumers, designers, magicians, singers, dancers, musicians, and technicians, for a general package of musical extravaganzas, patriotic salutes, and Broadway-style blockbusters.

All those hired are under contract with their respective parks. Length of season is set by each site. Salary at Show Biz International is from about $217 to $378 a week; performers appear four to six times a day during a season that runs from mid-April through Labor Day, with some additional weekends in October.

SIX FLAGS

As one of the country's top five employers of young people, the Six Flags Corporation annually plays host to more than 16 million visitors nationwide. This company has been showcasing live productions since 1961. Six Flags operates seven theme parks featuring musical revues and family-oriented shows. The theme parks are: Astroworld in Houston, Texas; Six Flags Great Adventure in Jackson, New Jersey; Six Flags Great America in Gurnee, Illinois; Six Flags Magic Mountain in Valencia, California; Six Flags Over Georgia in Atlanta; Six Flags Over Mid-America in Eureka, Missouri; and Six Flags Over Texas in Arlington.

The Six Flags Corporation primarily hires singers and dancers, but also hires street entertainers, variety acts, musicians, off-beat vocalists, such as barbershop quartets, etc., and bands specializing in country-western, bluegrass, and ragtime. Pay rates on average can reach $300 weekly. Seasons vary from park to park, though most performers are asked to work five-day work weeks during daily summertime operation and on weekends in the spring and fall.

WORLDS OF FUN

This Missouri theme park has hosted nearly 18 million visitors since its inception in 1973. Worlds of Fun is geared to musical-theater and conducts auditions for singers and dancers each winter, usually through January. Rehearsals begin in mid-March for a season that runs from April through October. Salaries hover around $240-$262 a week, and bonuses can run up to $900 for the season.

THEME PARK
SHOW PRODUCERS

The following is a list of theme parks and theme park show producers. They are listed alphabetically by the name of the park or production company. The names given below the telephone number are the people whom performers and technicians should contact; in most cases, they are the entertainment coordinators at the parks.

ACTION PARK
c/o Allan Albert Productions, Inc.
561 Broadway, Suite 10C
New York, NY 10012
(212) 966-8881
Frank Roth

ALLAN ALBERT PRODUCTIONS, INC.
561 Broadway, Suite 10C
New York, NY 10012
(212) 966-8881
Frank Roth

ASTROWORLD
9001 Kirby Dr.
Houston, TX 77054
(713) 794-3232/799-8404
Michael Svatek

ATF ENTERTAINMENT, LTD.
Box 090039, Brooklyn, NY 11209-0001
(718) 745-4794
Jeff Dailey

BUSCH ENTERTAINMENT CORP.
One Busch Gardens Blvd.
Williamsburg, VA 23187-8785
(804) 253-3300/3301/3304/3345
Entertainment Dept.

BUSCH GARDENS—THE DARK CONTINENT
Box 9158
Tampa, FL 33674-9158
(813) 985-4235
Debbie Baker

BUSCH GARDENS—THE OLD COUNTRY
One Busch Gardens Blvd.
Williamsburg, VA 23187-8785
(804) 253-3300
Entertainment Dept.
CEDAR POINT
Box 5006
Sandusky, OH 44871-8006
(419) 627-0830
Marje Cronenwett

CYPRESS GARDENS
Box 1
Cypress Gardens, FL 33884
(813) 324-2111
Entertainment Dept.

DISNEYLAND
1313 Harbor Blvd.
Anaheim, CA 92803
(714) 490-3126/999-4000
Entertainment Dept.

WALT DISNEY WORLD
Box 10,000
Lake Buena Vista, FL 32830-1000
(407) 345-5701
Ron Rodriguez

WALT DISNEY WORLD/EPCOT CENTER
Box 10,000
Lake Buena Vista, FL 32830-1000
(407) 345-5755
Robert Radock

DISNEY-MGM STUDIOS THEME PARK
Box 10,000
Lake Buena Vista, FL 32830-1000
Talent Booking

DOLLYWOOD
700 Dollywood La.
Pigeon Forge, TN 37863-4101
(615) 428-9433
Entertainment Dept.

HERSHEYPARK
100 W. Hersheypark Dr.
Hershey, PA 17033
(717) 534-3847
Stacy Benson

KINGS PRODUCTIONS
1932 Highland Ave.
Cincinnati, OH 45219
(513) 241-8989
Stephanie Parker

MOLONEY PRODUCTIONS, INC.
2883 Wilder Rd.
Metamora, MI 48455
(313) 667-2811
Theme Park Entertainment

OPRYLAND
2802 Opryland Dr.
Nashville, TN 37214
(615) 871-6656
John Haywood

PAUL OSBORNE'S PARK SHOWS
5118 Goodwin Ave.
Dallas, TX 75206
(214) 824-0128
Paul Osborne

SEA WORLD OF CALIFORNIA
1720 S. Shores Rd.
San Diego, CA 92109
(619) 222-6363
Lurie Pfeffer

SEA WORLD OF FLORIDA
7007 Sea Harbor Dr.
Orlando, FL 32821
(407) 351-3600
Personnel Dept.

SEA WORLD OF OHIO
1100 Sea World Dr.
Aurora, OH 44202
(216) 562-8101
Arthur L. Freeman

SEA WORLD OF TEXAS
10500 Sea World Dr.
San Antonio, TX 78251
(512) 523-3300
Scott Conway

SESAME PLACE
Box L579
Langhorne, PA 19047
(215) 752-7070
Greg Hartley

SHOW BIZ INTERNATIONAL, INC.
5142 Old Boonville Highway
Evansville, IN 47715
(812) 473-0880
Maria A. Rivers

SIX FLAGS CORP. SHOW PRODUCTIONS
1168 113th St.
Grand Prairie, TX 75050
(214) 988-8332
Lynda Doty

SIX FLAGS GREAT ADVENTURE
Box 120
Jackson, NJ 08752
(201) 928-2000
Bob Hoban

SIX FLAGS GREAT AMERICA
Box 1776
Gurnee, IL 60031
(708) 249-1776
David Carter

SIX FLAGS MAGIC MOUNTAIN
Box 5500
Valencia, CA 91385
(805) 255-4100
Scott Sterner

SIX FLAGS OVER GEORGIA
7561 Six Flags Parkway
Mableton, GA 30059
(404) 739-3450, ext. 3309
John Coley

SIX FLAGS OVER MID-AMERICA
Box 60
Eureka, MO 63025
(314) 938-5300
Entertainment Dept.

SIX FLAGS OVER TEXAS
Box 191
Arlington, TX 76004
(817) 640-8900
Show Operations

WORLDS OF FUN
4545 Worlds of Fun Ave.
Kansas City, MO 64161
(816) 454-4545
Gary Noble

CRUISE LINES

BY JOHN ALLEN

t's hard to imagine a more exotic form of theater than working on a cruise ship. Think of spending your summer nights on an open deck, dancing under the stars in port in Bermuda or on the Caribbean. Then think of your colleagues doing one- or two-week stock, rehearsing days and doing eight performances of a full-length show each week!

Although this picture is not 100 percent accurate, there's enough truth in it to make cruise work attractive and desirable—especially for the non-union performer.

THE CRUISES

Most performers are hired for six-month stints. But the cruises that your ship will take can last anywhere from one day to three months. The vast majority fall into the five-day to two-week category.

Generally, short one- or two-day cruises just go out to sea and back as a weekend lark. Cruises of five days or more voyage to the more exotic destinations. Although your ship will go back and forth to one location many times during your six-month contract, often that contract will overlap with a change of itinerary, so you may become familiar with more than one exotic locale.

THE SHOWS

Usually, a ship offers two to four different shows (depending entirely on the length of the cruise), each of which will be performed once during the cruise. On show days, most ships have an early and late performance, so everyone on board can see the production.

Cruise ship shows fall into three categories: (1) a Las Vegas-style revue; (2) a musical revue format; or (3) a complete or tab version of a full-length musical.

Las Vegas-style revues hire self-contained acts: always a comedian and a magician, and usually one or two other novelty acts. Between each act are showgirls with lots of flash, flesh, and feathers.

The musical revues on ships generally run 45 to 60 minutes and use anywhere from 4 to 10 performers. These shows most closely resemble theme park productions: well-produced flash with glitzy costumes. However, few of the family audience restrictions you would find in theme parks apply to ship shows.

PAY

Salaries on ships vary widely, depending on the cruise line and how you are hired. For showgirls and those in musical revues, payment can be as low as $250 or as high as $400 per week.

If you are hired as an individual act, the scale ranges from $300 per week (per person) to $1,000 per week, depending on the line, your experience, and your name.

Pay for performers hired in a book musical will most often fall into the $300-$450 per week range. In all cases, your room and board are free of charge, but the quality of the room will depend on whether you are housed in passenger or crew quarters.

PERFORMANCE SPACES

Some of the nicest and largest ships have theaters on board where the shows play beautifully. Most, however, have less-than-ideal spaces. Ships and Manhattan have one thing in common: space is at a premium! Many ships' performance spaces double as ballrooms, meeting rooms, or game rooms.

Regardless of the quality of the performance space, these shows are anticipated by the passengers, who usually find an enjoyable evening of live performance the perfect conclusion to a relaxing, fun-filled day.

Except on the largest and nicest ships, expect the dressing room areas to be small, because space is precious. On many, it is best to do your makeup in your room.

EXTRA DUTIES ABOARD SHIP

Most actors hired by cruise lines are expected to be part of the cruise staff. As such, you will be assigned some duties in addition to performing. Major exceptions to this are those people hired as an "act." If you have invested time and money in your own costumes, rehearsals, arrangements, and charts, then most cruise lines treat you differently than other performers. Those hired as an act will usually do no cruise staff duties at all.

For example, the first time my wife and I were hired by a cruise line, it was as a song-and-dance team. We had an act—our own costumes, charts, and routine—which fit into 10 minutes of the lines' Vegas-style revue. The ship was doing a five-day cruise to Bermuda followed by a two-day cruise to "nowhere" (over and over again). On the five-day cruise, we performed two evenings: two performances each evening, 10 minutes of our act each time. On the two-day cruise to nowhere, we performed one evening—again with two 10-minute performances. Total work for the week: 60 minutes (two 10-minute performances on three nights). What a life!

The next year, the ship changed its format. Instead of a Las Vegas-style revue, the cruise line produced a musical revue (where it paid for the costumes, the charts, and so on). The revue lasted 45 minutes, but we still did only three days of performances per week. However, we also had cruise staff duties—two hours each day, as a rule. That still averaged out to less than three hours' work daily.

So what are these extra duties? There's *library*. Yes, you may have to spend 30 minutes twice a day in a room containing books, checking them out to the two or three passengers who might want to do a little reading. (This is a great time to catch up on letter-writing.)

Or *bingo*. No, you probably won't call it, but you may have to walk through the crowd and announce the winning card. Or *horseracing* (ship-style), where you might move wooden horses along a "track."

Each ship has its own stash of standard and original games with which you will probably have to help. None of them is taxing or difficult, and if you let yourself go and relax, you will probably enjoy them.

Many ships often require the cruise staff and performers to socialize with the passengers for a certain amount of time every day. As a performer aboard ship, you are always in the public eye and are seen as a representative of the line. As such, you will be required to dress properly at all times, to be helpful and courteous to the passengers, and to be ready to sit and chat with them whenever they want.

ON AND OFF BLUES

Two cruise staff duties which aren't much fun are embarkation and disembarkation. The queues are slow and long when passengers are getting on at the start and off at the end of the cruise. Additionally, with disembarkation, there are customs, rules, and officials to deal with—which means more queues and more waiting.

Frequently, cruise staff must help with this process, and I have found that a pleasant demeanor and "chatting" with the passengers in line is the best way to keep things going smoothly.

LIVING CONDITIONS

If you are hired as an act, you will be given a passenger cabin, with or without a roommate (your choice). If you are hired in a revue or musical, you may be housed in either passenger or crew quarters. Passenger cabins are small, but have a private bathroom. Crew quarters are small and shared; their bathrooms are usually dormitory style.

As an entertainer, you will be encouraged to be in the public areas. Most likely, you will eat in the restaurant with the passengers, but in a staff area. You will have the same choice of food as the passengers—which is usually exceptional. You will also probably have the choice of eating at the many breakfast, lunch, and mid-afternoon buffets.

All cruise ships are owned and operated by foreign companies. On most ships, the vast majority of the crew is not American (although most of the cruise staff, entertainers, and passengers are). Most of the crew (waiters and waitresses, stewards, maintenance workers) speak little English. This exposure to different cultures can be exciting and enjoyable. Just remember that each culture has its own ways of doing things.

SEASICKNESS

If you suffer from motion sickness when in a car or airplane, you will probably get seasick. If Dramamine helps you on land, it will most likely do so on water, too—just remember to take it before the ship starts rocking!

Most people get used to the motion of the ship in just one or two crossings. There is, however, such a thing as chronic seasickness, in which case, you may spend most of your six-month contract on Dramamine!

YOUR CAPTAIN

The person you will answer to directly aboard ship is the cruise director. The cruise director will make up the list of duties you may be required to help with, handle all your complaints, and try to smooth things over if a conflict develops between people.

The cruise director may even be responsible for overseeing the show—especially if it is a Vegas-style revue—and therefore may be giving you notes and suggestions.

AN INTERNATIONAL FAMILY

In the best of circumstances, living on a ship can be like joining a huge family. When a thousand faces change each week (the passengers), those faces which stay the same (the staff and crew) become very important. Wonderful friendships can develop with people from many different cultures.

As in most situations, your own attitude will make a big difference. If you are a picky eater, hate sharing a room, or detest dormitory-style bathrooms, then perhaps cruise line performing is not for you. But if you are easy-going and willing to trade a few comforts, a few hours of work, and socializing each day for good pay, sun time, and trips to exotic or vacation locales—then cruise work could be perfect for you.

CRUISE LINES

CRUISE AGENTS AND PRODUCERS

Many cruise lines hire a booking agent to create an entertainment package for a particular cruise. Some work exclusively with one agent; others use several agents; still others use both booking agents and their own in-house entertainment directors to fill their performance needs. Agents and entertainment directors, in turn, may book revues, acts, or shows produced by an independent production company. Performers interested in cruise work, no matter what their specialty, should introduce themselves to cruise agents *and* producers. The following list is compiled from information gathered from several established cruise agents, producers, and lines.

ALFORD PRODUCTIONS INC.
PABT, Box 21029
New York, NY 10129-0009
Producer/director: Larry Alford;
Casting Director: Ted Hook;
Musical Supervisor: Phil Hall;
Choreographer: Kim Morgan.
Produces song and dance revues for Commodore Cruise Line (Broadway, popular music, 1930s and 1940s revues). Hires strong singers who dance for four-month standard contract. Holds no open calls. Accepts agent submissions, or send picture and resume. Do not send tapes.

BRAMSON ENTERTAINMENT BUREAU
1440 Broadway
New York, NY 10018
(212) 354-9575
President: James Abramson
Largest booking organization for cruise work. Books comedians, big name entertainers, novelty acts, singers, musicians. Books shows, revues from independent producers. Books for such cruise lines as Cunard, Holland America, Ocean Cruise, Seven Seas, SeaEscape, and Royal Cruise. Accepts videotapes, VHS or 3/4-inch format.

ELLIS ISLAND ENTERTAINMENT
1780 Broadway, Suite 101
New York, NY 10019
(212) 974-5322
Producer: Sam Ellis;
Artistic Director: Bill Castellino
Produces original book revues for three Holland America Line ships which cruise to the Caribbean, Alaska, South America, the South Pacific, and Asia. Casts twice yearly in Los Angeles and New York. Seeks strong singers who can move. Accepts pictures, resumes and videotapes.

FIESTA FANTASTICA
230 S.W. 8th St.
Miami, FL 33130
(305) 854-2221
Producer: Marcelo Palacios
Books individual singers and dancers for revues (no variety, specialty, or solo acts) for Holland America, Royal Caribbean, Carnival, and other cruise lines. Holds open calls. Accepts pictures, resumes, and tapes. Send to: Casting Dept.

G&C ENTERTAINMENT
Box 1063
Ansonia Station
New York, NY 10023
Producer: Greg McDonald
Casts for cruise line performers: singers, magicians, specialty acts.

GARRY BROWN ASSOCIATES
27 Downs Side, Cheam, Surrey
SM2 7EH England
011-44-81-643-3991/8375
Agent: Garry Brown
Books variety acts, stars, revues, other entertainment for Cunard and other lines. Holds showcases in New York, other major cities seeking talent. Watch Back Stage for announcements. Accepts pictures, tapes, videos (American, English, European VHS).

HANNA OWEN ENTERTAINMENT AGENCY
22 600 Bella Rita Circle
Boca Raton, FL 33433
(305) 462-3750/(407) 394-3798
Owner/President: Hanna Owen
Books for Cunard and other lines. Interested in many types, including opera singers, Broadway or top 40 singers, novelty acts, comedians. Accepts pictures, resumes, and recent tapes (prefers video).

IMPACT PRODUCTIONS
133 W. 72nd St., Suite 601
New York, NY 10023
(212) 874-0960
Producer: Joyce Flynn;
Artistic Director: Michael Lichtefeld
Produces musical shows, revues for cruise lines and corporate events. Contract is with individual cruise line. Hires dancers and singers for both cruise work and corporate shows. Holds open calls; watch for announcements. Accepts pictures, resumes and tapes. Send Attn: Joyce Flynn.

JEAN ANN RYAN PRODUCTIONS
308 S.E. 14th St.
Fort Lauderdale, FL 33316
(305) 523-6399
Producer: Jean Ann Ryan;
General Manager: Joanne Maiello
Produces revues, Broadway-style productions for Norwegian Cruise Lines. Producing Meet Me in St. Louis for S.S. Norway, Anything Goes for M.S. Seaward, and Grease for M.S. Westward. Also books Las Vegas-style revues and singers revues on these and four smaller

ships. Cabaret and novelty acts booked, as well as illusionists. Also hires technical staff. Major audition tours twice each year; New York in autumn and January. Performers with resumes on file will be notified about auditions. Contracts for six months.

JOHN-JAMES PRODUCTIONS, INC.
435 W. 57 St., Suite 16F
New York, NY 10019
President: John Manzi;
Vice President: James Avery
Produces Broadway variety-type shows (usually casts of four) in association with Bramson Entertainment for clients including American and Royal Cruise lines. Casts high-energy singers and dancers (including tap). Accepts pictures, resumes, audio and video tapes.

MCL PRODUCTIONS
401 W. 56th St., #5G
New York, NY 10019
(212) 586-0739
Producer: Chip Lavely;
Associate Producer: Patricia Froncek
Produces Broadway, Hollywood, Decades, Baggy Pants, and Las Vegas-style revues; magic shows; star packages. Shows booked directly with lines including American Hawaii Cruises. Accepts pictures, resumes, and tapes. Holds three open calls per year. Also accepts video and audio tapes, and arranges private auditions based on these submissions. Contracts talent for a minimum of four months.

MILLER-REICH ENTERPRISES
1922 N.E. 149th St.
North Miami, FL 33181
(305) 949-0227
Producer: Leonard Miller;
Casting Director: Mary Ann Delany
Books dancers and singers for Carnival Cruise Lines, Royal Caribbean Cruise Lines, and cruise ships in Finland. Produces lavish, Vegas-style shows as well as Broadway concepts. Auditions held mostly in New York and

other major U.S. cities at least six times yearly, and in London two or three times yearly. Long-term contracts (6-12 months) are with Miller-Reich Enterprises. Accepts pictures, resumes, tapes, videos, and C.V. Also accepts resumes from technical staff.

PETER GREY TERHUNE PRESENTS
Box 715, Cape Canaveral, FL 32920
(407) 783-8745
Co-Producers: Peter Grey Terhune/Cathy Abram Terhune
Produces custom revues, shows for cruise lines, industrials, resorts. Average talent contract is for five months. Accepts pictures, resumes, and tapes. Auditions in New York, Nashville, and several locations in Florida, at colleges and universities. Seeks singer/dancers with wholesome appearance. Shows booked by Bramson Entertainment or independently with cruise lines.

SPOTLIGHT ENTERTAINMENT
555 NE 15th St., Suite 16B
Miami, FL 33132
(305) 358-4305
Owner: Barry Ball
Books all types of acts for most major lines: comics, mimes, puppeteers, novelty acts (jugglers, comedy jugglers, magicians, and especially multi-instrumentalists). Contracts range from one week to several months. Accepts videotapes only, accompanied by pictures and resumes.

WEST WALL PRODUCTIONS
275 Central Park West, Suite 1-G
New York, NY 10024
President: Denise Padgett
Produces Broadway-style revues for lines with varying itineraries, including the Caribbean, South America, Scandinavia, and the Mediterranean. Seeking strong singer/dancers, usually for six-month contracts. Announces open calls in Back Stage; accepts pictures, resumes, and tapes.

ENTERTAINMENT DIRECTORS

Many cruise lines hire entertainment directors to handle bookings for their ships. The responsibilities of this position vary from line to line, from season to season. They may book talent either directly or through agents. Even if you have written the cruise agents and producers on the preceding list, it might be wise to contact those cruise lines which interest you. The following list was gathered from several established cruise agents, producers, and lines. The Cruise Lines International Association (500 Fifth Ave., New York, NY 10110) was also contacted. CLIA boasts 34 members, but not all of them hire performers. The following lines regularly seek and provide entertainment for their patrons.

ADMIRAL CRUISES
1050 Caribbean Way
Miami, FL 33132
(305) 539-6000
Hires novelty acts; singers. Director of Entertainment: Peter Compton.

AMERICAN HAWAII CRUISES
550 Kearny St.
San Francisco, CA 94108
(415) 392-9400(312)-466 6000
Submit entertainment inquiries to: Personnel Department, 604 Fort St., Honolulu, HI 96813.

CARNIVAL CRUISE LINES
3655 N.W. 87th Ave.
Miami, FL 33178-2428
(305) 599-2600
Hires entertainer/cruise director, staff personnel, entertainers, musicians. Address pictures, resumes, and tapes to Tom Lacey. Musicians, contact Steve Smith, music supervisor.

CELEBRITY CRUISES
900 Third Ave.
New York, NY 10020
(212) 223-3003
Entertainment Consultant: Douglas Ward
Hires singers, dancers, cabaret acts, magicians, jugglers, and all varieties of musicians. Accepts pictures, resumes, and tapes.

COMMODORE CRUISE LINE
800 Douglas Rd.
Coral Gables, FL 33134
Books musical revues through Alford Productions, Inc. (see Cruise Agents and Producers). Regarding other entertainment, send inquiries to: Pia Lang, Director of Hotel Services, Commodore Cruise Lines.

COSTA CRUISE LINES, NV
World Trade Center
80 S.W. 8th St., Suite 2700
Miami, FL 33130-3097
(305) 358-7325
Vice President of Entertainment:
Felice Campagna;
Assistant Vice President: Suzel Iglesia
Casts dancers, choreographers, magicians, novelty acts, vocalists, and groups. Italian cruise line sailing worldwide. Accepts pictures, resumes and videotapes.

CROWN CRUISE LINE
Box 3000
Boca Raton, FL 33431
(407) 392-4655
Kennedy Enterprises (President: Ray Kennedy) is Crown's exclusive, in-house producer.

Crown's flagship, the Monarch, features Sophisticated Ladies and three original musical revues; the Viking Princess, a day-tripper, offers two revues; soon to be launched is the Crown Majesty. All three ships cruise the Caribbean. Kennedy seeks singer/dancers and a specialty female tap dancer for contracts ranging from four to five months. Send pictures, resumes, and video tapes to his attention at Crown Cruise Lines.

CRYSTAL CRUISES
2121 Ave. of the Stars, Suite 200
Los Angeles, CA 90027
(213) 785-9300
Vice President of Entertainment: Cliff Perry; Artistic Directors: Gretchen Goertz, Kathy Orme; Musical Director: Bret Bullock.
Produces Broadway-style shows in-house. Musicians and bands should contact Bullock directly at (702) 363-5815. Perry casts solo entertainment (singers, pianists, harpists, etc.), and specialty acts. Perry also seeks sound and lighting technicians, stage managers, and video programmers. Goertz and Orme cast production singers and dancers. Contracts vary in length: musicians—four months; singers—six months; dancers—one year; solos: negotiable. Holds auditions for singers and dancers in West Coast cities including Los Angeles, San Francisco, and Las Vegas. Accepts pictures, resumes, and video tapes from solo and specialty acts.

CUNARD LINE
555 Fifth Ave.
New York, NY 10017
Books through Jean Ann Ryan Productions, Garry Brown Associates, Spotlight Entertainment, Hanna Owen Entertainment Agency, and Bramson Entertainment Bureau. In-house, Cunard's Entertainment Manager Brian Beaton seeks especially comics and specialty acts (jugglers, mimes, Liberace- or Peter Nero-type pianists). Contracts run from 7-12 days. Accepts pictures and resumes. Do not send tapes.

DELTA QUEEN STEAMBOAT COMPANY
30 Robin Street Wharf
New Orleans, LA 70130
(504) 586-0631
Director of Entertainment: W. Chad Mitchell; Entertainment Manager: Tracey Schreiber
Hires performers directly, including musicians (especially banjo, ragtime, piano). Singers who dance and specialty acts perform staff or managerial duties as well. Contract is usually one year with rotation. Accepts pictures, resumes, and tapes.

FANTASY CRUISES
5200 Blue Lagoon Dr.
Miami, FL 33126
(305) 262-6677
Entertainment Director: John Perrino
Hires singers, dancers, cabaret acts, magicians, jugglers, and all varieties of musicians. Accepts pictures, resumes, and tapes.

HOLLAND AMERICA LINE
300 Elliot Ave. West
Seattle, WA 98119
(206) 281-3535
Books through a variety of agencies, including Bramson Entertainment Bureau.

NORWEGIAN CARIBBEAN LINE
95 Merrick Way
Coral Gables, FL 33134
(305) 447-9660
In-house production department (Jean Ann Ryan Productions) produces revues. Also books shows produced outside and variety acts. Hires through open auditions, agents. Accepts pictures, resumes, tapes. Variety performers should contact Sue Carper, Manager of Entertainment.

OCEAN CRUISE LINES
1510 S.E. 17th St.
Ft. Lauderdale, FL 33316
(305) 764-3500
Bookings made only in Paris. Call 011-331-49-24-4200.

PREMIER CRUISE LINES
400 Challenger Rd.
Cape Canaveral, FL 32920
(407) 783-5061
Casts through independent producers for themed musical revues. Also books cabaret artists, mainly comedians and novelty acts. Submissions of promo material accepted; send Attn: Jim Flynn, Entertainment Director

PRINCESS CRUISES
10100 Santa Monica Blvd., Suite 1800
Los Angeles, CA 90067
(213) 533-1770
Director of Entertainment: Billy Hygate
Cruises to Caribbean, Mexico, South America, Alaska, Mediterranean, and South Pacific. Hires vocalists, comedians, duos, trios, magicians. Also produces in-house revues. Accepts tapes (audio and VHS) and resumes.

REGENCY CRUISES
8880 N.W. 20th St., Suite M
Miami, FL 33172
(305) 592-2933
Entertainment Director: Paul McEvoy
Hires production groups, dancers, comedians,

novelty acts. Casting through independent producers, agents, or direct submissions. Entertainers double as cruise staff.

ROYAL CARIBBEAN CRUISES, LTD.
1050 Caribbean Way
Miami, FL 33132
(305) 539-6876
Production Supervisor: Robin Cahill.
Produces revues in-house. Cast size ranges from 10-16 and features singer/dancers, singers, dancers, adagio. Contracts are for 6 months. Annual major audition tour goes to 6-10 cities, including New York, Los Angeles, and Chicago. Prefers live audition, but accepts pictures, resumes, and videotapes.

ROYAL CRUISE LINE
One Maritime Plaza, Suite 1400
San Francisco, CA 94111
(415) 956-7200
Hires vocalists, cabaret performers, bands, variety acts, and fully produced revues through Bramson Entertainment (see Cruise Agents and Producers). Does no direct hiring.

ROYAL VIKING LINE
95 Merrick Way
Coral Gables, FL 33134
(305) 447-9660
Director of Cruise Programs: Greg Von Seeger.
Hires variety and cabaret-type acts: comics, ventriloquists, classical artists, jugglers, vocalists, instrumentalists. Talent booked directly, as well as through agencies worldwide. Send materials to Morag Veljkovic, Manager of Entertainment.

SEAESCAPE, LTD
1080 Port Blvd., Port of Miami
Miami, FL 33132
(305) 377-9000
Hires singer/dancers for four different 45-minute revues. Two shows per day, six days per week. Entertainers live on ship with crew; four-month contracts. Uses in-house production department (see Cruise Agents and Producers). Send pictures, tapes and/or resumes to Entertainment Department. Do not call.

SUN LINE CRUISES
One Rockefeller Plaza, Suite 315
New York, NY 10020
(212) 397-6400
Entertainment Director: Tina Smith
Hires singers, dancers, dance groups, comedians, magicians. Cruises to Caribbean and Europe.

SUMMER STOCK: COMBINED AUDITIONS

BY JILL CHARLES

Combined auditions are the means by which many summer stock companies fulfill their casting requirements. These auditions are held at central locations in different parts of the country, and representatives, such as managers and producers, from various theater companies gather at the audition sites to audition and interview the performers and theater personnel they are going to need during the coming season.

Listed here are 22 locations where state and regional combined auditions are held for summer stock companies throughout the country. If you don't have an Equity card yet, and you've been frustrated at not being able to get auditions, now is your chance, since the bulk of representatives attending these regional combined auditions are from non-Equity companies. Do you double as a carpenter, costumer, or lighting designer? You may be able to parlay your technical skills into a full season somewhere with an acting/tech combination that will actually leave you with money in your pocket come Labor Day. This is a good time, too, if you have honed your special skills, like singing, dancing, stage combat, or juggling, to take advantage of some unique theatrical opportunities offered by outdoor dramas and Renaissance fairs.

So, look over the list below, and start applying for audition slots. Many of these auditions are nothing but "cattle calls," true, but it's an efficient way to be seen by many companies. Combined auditions also present an excellent opportunity to test your audition technique, which is also a good reason for trying to get to more than one audition.

COMBINED AUDITION PROCEDURES

In general, this is the way combined auditions work: you write to the given address, usually several months in advance of the audition, and request an application form. When you receive your application, you fill it out and return it with an application fee. If your application is early enough, and you are not screened out (screening is usually based on a minimal level of experience), you will be given an audition time. At callbacks, after the audition, if the company likes your work, you will be: (1) scheduled for a second audition to take place at a future date; (2) offered a job then and there; or (3) contacted later for another audition or with a job offer.

Directors, designers, stage managers, management persons, and technicians are usually interviewed at separate times from the performers' auditions. There are various mechanisms for doing this, but the first step is always the application, and the organization running the combined auditions will take it from there.

Many of the auditions listed here are regional auditions, run by a state or regional theater organization. Some require that you be a resident of, or attending school in, the state or region holding the auditions. You may have to join the regional organization to be eligible to participate in the auditions. Many of these regional auditions are held as a part of that regions' annual conference. You should write several months in advance of the auditions, as most of them have deadlines for receiving the application of at least one month beforehand.

Audition rosters fill up quickly, so even if your application is made by the deadline date, you still are not guaranteed an audition. If you don't get an audition, sometimes you can be placed on a waiting list; or you can stand by at the audition in the hope that there will be a last minute opening.

At a typical combined audition you will encounter 30 to 50 producers and directors. With so many persons involved, and because of the strict time limitations on auditions that this imposes, it is crucial to come into the situation well-prepared in all respects. The following guidelines are directed toward the special problems presented by these auditions.

1. Follow directions. Read the application carefully and fill it out correctly. Because of space and time limitations, all applications are not accepted, and incomplete applications are usually rejected automatically.

2. Research the companies. Along with your audition notification, you should receive a tentative list of the companies for whom you will be auditioning. Find out what these companies are all about and then gear your audition pieces toward those companies that you are interested in. Prepare a classical piece if you are auditioning for a Shakespearean troupe, or a song and dance routine if you are trying to get into a musical comedy company.

3. Be well-prepared. You should know your pieces thoroughly at least two weeks before the audition. Never make the mistake of performing a monologue that you learned the night before at an audition. That's a guaranteed way of going up on your lines.

4. Photo/resumes. Take a good supply of 8 x 10 photos and resumes to the audition. Make sure that vital statistics are up-to-date and accurate, especially your contact phone number.

5. Sheet music. Sheet music must be in good condition and clearly marked for the accompanist. Not all accompanists can transpose music at sight, so it is especially important that your music be in the right key.

6. Dress. Dress as you would for any audition. Present yourself as a person, not as the character you are performing. Wear something flattering that makes you feel good. The mistake women most often make is to wear a leotard or something revealing; the mistake men most often make is to underdress, to wear old jeans and a T-shirt.

7. Audition introduction. The way you enter, look at the auditors, and say your name and the title and character of the piece you're doing are as important as the audition itself. Don't explain the piece; be yourself.

8. Be professional. Your manner should demonstrate confidence, competence, and a pleasant personality. Take the time to be nice to those whom you meet, from the people at the registration desk, to the timekeepers, to the gofers, to the company representatives, to your colleagues.

9. Attitude. Remember that the auditors are not your enemies. They are there to cast their seasons, and they want you to be good. Keeping this in mind will help you to approach the audition with a positive attitude.

10. Callbacks. Try to make it to any and all callbacks. If time restrictions or scheduling prevent you from attending, contact any company you are interested in and try to set up another appointment. When you are speaking with a company that has shown some interest in you, get as much information as you can about what they are offering. Make written notes. Combined audition weekends are chaotic events, and details of important meetings and conversations can be difficult to recollect; written notes will prove to be an indispensable source of reference once you return home.

———

ORGANIZATIONS OFFERING COMBINED AUDITIONS

The following organizations sponsor combined auditions. When writing to request an application, include a #10-size SASE.

BAY AREA GENERAL AUDITIONS
Sponsored by: Theatre Bay Area
Attended by: San Francisco and
Bay Area companies
Auditions: early February
Place: rotates throughout Bay Area
Eligibility: no residency requirement, but non-members of TBA must pay fee; application is published in January issue of *Callboard*.
Contact: Theatre Bay Area
657 Mission St., Suite #402
San Francisco, CA 94105
(415) 957-1557

EAST CENTRAL THEATRE CONFERENCE
Attended by: professional, educational, and community theaters in DC, DE, MD, NJ, NY, PA
Auditions: early to mid-February
Place: rotates among member states
Deadline: early to mid-January
Eligibility: Equity and non-Equity, students from university training programs
Fee: $20 students; $50 professionals; $10 processing fee only for AEA members
Format: two contrasting monologues or one monologue and one song (bring recorded music on cassette tape, ECTC provides tape deck); two-and-a-half-minute time limit; design/tech interviews conducted as well.
Contact: Wayne Bond
Dept. of Speech and Theatre
Montclair State College
Upper Montclair, NJ 07043

GREAT LAKES THEATRE CONFERENCE (GLTC)
Each of GLTC's five member states (IL, IN, MI, OH, WI) holds its own auditions; these are included in this list. After an individual has registered for auditions in his/her own state, membership fees in other conference member states will be waived.

ILLINOIS THEATRE ASSOCIATION
Auditions: early March
Place: Chicago location
Contact: Mr. Wallace Smith,
Executive Director
Illinois Theatre Association
1225 W. Belmont
Chicago, IL 60657
(312) 929-7288

INDIANA THEATRE ASSOCIATION
Auditions: early February
Place: various Indiana colleges
Deadline: usually in January
Eligibility: applicant must be a member of a professional union, or be recommended by a professional director; applicants under 17 years of age must attend a screening.

Fee: $15 state residents; $25 out-of-state
Format: singing or non-singing; two-minute limit; interviews for tech/design/management.
Contact: Judy Giesting
Indiana Theatre Association
Butler University Theatre
400 Sunset Ave.
Indianapolis, IN 46208

LEAGUE OF RESIDENT THEATRES
LORT Lottery Auditions
These are eligible performer auditions which are held twice a year in New York City for the fall/winter and spring/summer seasons. Since there are more applicants than available audition slots, selection is made by lottery. There are also interviews for stage managers. LORT theaters are required to attend by Equity.
Contact: AEA, 165 West 46th St., New York, NY 10036, (212) 869-8530

MICHIGAN THEATRE ASSOCIATION
Statewide Professional Theatre Auditions
Auditions: late February/early March
Place: rotates throughout state
Deadline: early February
Eligibility: at least 18 years of age or college sophomore
Fee: $30
Format: two contrasting monologues; two-minute total time limit; (applicant may add 16 bars of song after time limit); optional dance auditions; tech interviews arranged.
Contact: Michigan Theatre Association
Box 726
Marshall, MI 49068
(616) 781-7859

MID-AMERICA THEATRE CONFERENCE AUDITIONS
Attended by: companies from IA, IL, KS, MN, MO, ND, NE, SD, WI
Auditions: mid-March
Place: rotates among member states
Deadline: early February (if audition slots are available after the cut-off date, later applicants will receive time slots on a first-come, first-served basis)
Eligibility: no residency requirement
Fee: $27.50 includes registration fee and access to audition or interview
Format: two minutes, with or without song; pianist provided; bring music in the correct key; singing/dancing auditions are held at the end of each day; interviews for tech and design positions held as well.
Contact: Glenn W. Pierce
MATC Auditions
Dept. of Theater & Film
University of Kansas
Lawrence, KS 60045
(913) 864-3511

MIDWEST THEATRE AUDITIONS

Sponsored by: Conservatory of Theater Arts, Webster University
Attended by: 60 companies
Auditions: mid-February, three days
Place: Loretto-Hilton Theatre, Webster University, St. Louis, MO
Deadline: early January
Eligibility: no residency requirements; non-Equity application form signed by an instructor or director; dance calls are only open to actors who have auditioned previously that day; AEA members may audition and should request application.
Fee: $20, non-Equity actors; $20 for design/tech applicants
Format: two minutes to present one or two pieces; at least one must be non-musical, although musical pieces are encouraged; pianist will be provided; callbacks same day; bring at least 20 copies of resumes (photo/resumes for callbacks only).
Contact: Peter Sargent, Coordinator
Midwest Theatre Auditions
Webster University
470 E. Lockwood
St. Louis, MO 63119

MONTANA SUMMER THEATRE AUDITIONS

Attended by: approximately 6-8 companies
Auditions: February or March
Place: rotates throughout Montana colleges
Registration: on day of auditions
Eligibility: non-Equity; no residency requirements
Fee: $25
Format: three minutes for two contrasting pieces and 16 bars of a song (Note: at least three of the companies are looking specifically for musical talent).
Contact: Kim DeLong
Carroll College Theatre Dept.
Benton Ave.
Helena, MT 59601

NATIONAL DINNER THEATRE ASSOCIATION

Auditions: mid-March
Place: rotates among states (usually East and Midwest)
Deadline: late February
Eligibility: Equity or non-Equity; 18 years of age or older; applications screened to 300 maximum.
Fee: $15 or $20 late fee
Format: one-minute monologue; 16-bar song is optional; technicians can send resumes to be made available to producers.
Contact: NDTA Auditions
c/o David Pritchard
Box 726
Marshall, MI 49068
(616) 781-7859

NEW ENGLAND THEATRE CONFERENCE (NETC)

Attended by: approximately 75 companies from across the country, but primarily from New England and East Coast
Auditions: mid to late March
Place: Tufts University, near Boston
Deadline: early February
Eligibility: non-Equity; college students must be 18 years of age or older and their application form must be signed by an instructor or director (about 1,350 applications are received; 700 applicants are auditioned).
Fee: $20 for NETC members, $30 for non-members; NETC membership fee $15 for students, $25 for non-students.
Format: two audition rooms run concurrently—one for acting, one for acting/singing/dancing; two-minute auditions; tech and staff auditions are held one of two afternoons; Equity auditions are held in late summer, organized by StageSource, 1 Boylston Pl., Boston, MA 02116. (No phone calls.)
Contact: Marie L. Philips, Exec. Sec'y.
NETC
50 Exchange St.
Waltham, MA 02154

NEW JERSEY THEATRE GROUP

An association of the state's professional (AEA) theater companies, NJTG sponsors a Job Fair for interns and entry-level tech and management staff, held in April or May (no auditions). For more information, write (after Jan. 1) to:
Laura Aden, Executive Director
New Jersey Theatre Group
Box 21
Florham Park, NJ 07932
or call (201) 593-0189

NORTHWEST DRAMA CONFERENCE

Attended by: various companies from WA, OR, AK, ID
Auditions: early February (part of regional theater conference)
Place: rotates throughout colleges in Northwest
Deadline: varies; write for information
Eligibility: non-Equity
Fee: modest
Format: two contrasting pieces; five minutes maximum; bring photo/resume.
Contact: George Caldwell, Coordinator
Drama Dept.
Washington State University
Pullman, WA 99164-2432

OHIO THEATRE ALLIANCE

Attended by: 47 companies
Auditions: mid to late February
Place: Columbus, OH
Deadline: mid to late January
Eligibility: must be OTA member, must be pre-registered, Equity or non-Equity
Fee: $20; OTA membership fee $10 for students, $25 for non-students (all fees must be paid by money order or certified check).
Format: two minutes; must bring own accompaniment tape and player, if singing; callbacks same day; interviews for tech and management; no separate dance auditions.
Contact: Fran Bay, Executive Director
OTA
504 N. Park St.
Columbus, OH 43215

OUTDOOR DRAMA AUDITIONS

Sponsored by: Institute of Outdoor Drama
Attended by: 14 to 18 companies from GA, IL, IN, KY, MN, NC, NY, OH, OK, TN, TX, WV; majority are non-Equity, some AEA; most casts number about 50; seasons run 12 to 14 weeks.
Auditions: mid- to late March
Place: University of North Carolina at Chapel Hill
Deadline: early to mid-March
Eligibility: auditions are limited to 200 pre-registered applicants who must be at least 18 years of age and who have had previous theater training or credits; a statement of support from a teacher or director is required.
Fee: $15, non-refundable
Format: actors, one-minute monologue; singers, one-minute prepared number (accompanist provided); dancers, group warm-up led by choreographer, combinations using modern, ballet, and folk choreography; tech, individual interviews.
Contact: Auditions Director
Institute of Outdoor Drama
CB 3240, NCNB Plaza
University of North Carolina
Chapel Hill, NC 27599-3240
(919) 962-1328

ROCKY MOUNTAIN THEATER ASSOCIATION SUMMER THEATER AUDITIONS

Attended by: companies in CO, ID, MT, UT, WY
Auditions: January or February (part of RMTA's "Festivention")
Place: rotates among states
Deadline: early January, or register at Festivention
Eligibility: application must include recommendation from faculty member or home institution

Fee: $10 student membership fee to join RMTA, plus $5 registration fee for Festivention; audition fee is $20 students, $25 non-students up to two weeks before Festivention date; then add $5.
Format: acting—four minutes, two contrasting monologues; musical—six minutes, two monologues plus 16 bars of song; accompaniment provided; tech/design/staff interviews.
Contact: Gladys Crane
Dept. of Theater & Dance
Box 3951, University Station
Laramie, WY 82071

SOUTHEASTERN THEATRE CONFERENCE

Attended by: about 90 companies from AL, FL, GA, KY, MS, NC, SC, TN, VA, WV
Auditions: first Wednesday in March
Place: rotates throughout states
Eligibility: students must pass state screening; forms may be obtained from college theater department in the early fall; screening takes place in the fall at state theater meetings. Students and non-Equity professionals write directly to SETC for application form.
Deadline: February 1 (SETC also holds AEA and non-Equity auditions in September; application deadline is August 15)
Fee: students—$15 membership, $15 registration, $10 audition fee; professionals—$30 membership, $30 registration, $10 audition fee.
Format: one and a half minutes for acting and singing; one minute for acting only or singing only; dancers audition on Thursday evening and the following Friday and Saturday; callbacks are on the evening of the same day; audition briefings are held at 9 AM on the day of the audition; administrative and tech interviews are also held during these dates, through the Job Contact Service. Jobs are listed monthly in the Job Contact Bulletin that is distributed to members.
Contact: Marian Smith, SETC
506 Stirling St.
University of North Carolina at Greensboro
Greensboro, NC 27412

SOUTHWEST THEATRE ASSOCIATION

Attended by: companies from AR, LA, NM, OK, TX
Auditions: mid to late~ January
Place: usually at a Texas college
Deadline: early January
Eligibility: Equity and non-Equity
Fee: ranges from $15 to $20, depending on membership status in SWTA
Format: actors, one and a half minutes; bring 20 to 25 photo/resumes for callbacks; dancers, a choreographer will teach a routine; technicians/administrators should bring portfolio for interview (three minutes).

Contact: Paul Baker
Route 1, Box 139
Waelder, TX 78959-9729
(512) 540-4279

STRAW HAT AUDITIONS
Attended by: about 30 companies, mainly from the Northeast
Auditions: late March or early April
Place: New York City
Deadline: two to three weeks before auditions (appointments usually fill up earlier)
Eligibility: open to all non-Equity performers; some screening; no stand-bys or walk-ins; staff/design open to all.
Fee: $40 for performers; $20 for design/tech/staff
Format: performers have two minutes to present two contrasting pieces, one of which may be a song—accompanist provided; there are a limited number of non-singing appointments available; producers are given a bound, indexed book of performers' photo/resumes in order of appearance; callbacks are posted hourly; staff/design interviews Thursday afternoon.
Contact: Straw Hat
Box 1226
Port Chester, NY 10573

UNIVERSITY/RESIDENT THEATER ASSOCIATION NATIONAL UNIFIED AUDITIONS (U/RTA)
U/RTA is an organization of professionally-oriented university and resident theaters. These auditions may lead to summer positions with resident theater companies, or to acceptance into a graduate program at member universities. Auditions are open to candidates in all areas of theater. There are two stages to the auditions.
1. Preliminary Screening Auditions. Applicants must be nominated by faculty/staff of a college/university, and must send in the required form and recommendation by the middle of November. Preliminary screening auditions are held in early January in fourteen cities around the country. A panel of judges makes written evaluations of each presentation (candidates are later mailed copies), and selects candidates to attend final auditions.
2. Final Auditions. If selected, applicants audition at the most convenient location (New York City; Evanston, IL; Long Beach,

CA), on a weekend in February or early March. Applicants are seen by members of the U/RTA schools and guest theaters (there is no guarantee that every member will attend each site). No firm offers are made until after the last weekend of final auditions. Acting auditions are limited to four minutes; other auditions are eight minutes (the application form has detailed instructions about all presentations). For information, please write to: University/Resident Theater Association, Inc. 1560 Broadway, Suite 801, New York, NY 10036

VERMONT ASSOCIATION OF THEATRES AND THEATRE ARTISTS
Attended by: about 12 to 15 companies
Auditions: mid-March
Place: Burlington, VT area
Deadline: two weeks before auditions
Eligibility: Vermont residents and college students preferred; if space available, NH, MA, and NY applicants will be seen; NYC and Boston actors are discouraged from attending.
Fee: $10 for VATA members, $20, non-members; design/staff/tech fees are $5 for VATA members, $10 for non-members.
Format: performers have three minutes to present two contrasting pieces or one monologue and one song—accompanist provided; tech/design/staff interviews at the end of the day.
Contact: VATA Auditions
Box 93
Dorset, VT 05251

WISCONSIN THEATRE AUDITIONS
Attended by: about 24 companies
Auditions: February
Deadline: pre-registration recommended by Feb. 1
Eligibility: non-Equity, no residency requirements
Fee: $15
Format: two and a half minutes for actors; three minutes for actor/singers; interviews for tech/design/staff.
Contact: Wisconsin Theatre Auditions
Continuing Education for the Arts
Room 726, Lowell Hall
610 Langdan St.
Madison, WI 53703

BUSINESS THEATER

BY BILL ERVOLINO

o you act? Sing? Dance? Write? Stage manage? Do you want to work on your craft and make some good money in the process? Would you like to work side by side with some of the most creative people in the business? Would you like to be part of a big-budget production, one with the kind of capital behind it that utilizes state-of-the-art production techniques? If your answer to any of these questions is yes, then business theater—or "industrials"—may be for you. Industrial shows offer valuable training and experience in your chosen field. They pay well. And if you work in them, you will be working in the world's most advanced technology.

Larry Katen, the business representative at Actors' Equity for Off-Broadway productions, business theater, and workshops, is high on business shows and the opportunities they offer to a wide variety of acting professionals. "I don't know why more actors don't pursue them," he says. "They have become pretty open and have a good record in terms of affirmative action and non-traditional casting. I think everyone's impression of industrials used to be tall, WASPy blondes, but it's not like that at all. Today, industrials encompass a broad section of the population. And there are many opportunities for actors, singers, dancers, and spokespersons. The performers do not get seen by the general public, casting directors, or agents, but the pay is great."

The current business theater contract between Actors' Equity and the Producers' Guild (an organization of industrial producers), provides minimum weekly salaries of $804 for actors, $1,135 for stage managers, and $926 for assistant stage managers. The salaries for periods of seven days to two weeks are $1,006 for actors, $1,408 for stage managers, and $1,155 for assistant stage managers. For periods lasting less than a week, actors receive $287 for the first day and $144 for each day thereafter; stage managers are paid $402 for the first day and $201 for each day thereafter; assistant stage managers receive $330 for the first day and $165 for each day thereafter.

Because of the high rate of pay, many performers and technicians view industrial shows as an ideal way to tide themselves over while they continue to focus on more artistic goals. There are, however, writers and performers who object to working in business theater—they don't want to have anything to do with dressing up like a tube of lipstick and singing "A Kiss Is Still a Kiss" or jumping up on a piano and tap-dancing during a 20-gun salute to Egg McMufffins. Nevertheless, many artists do derive artistic satisfaction from working in this medium. According to Joan Marshall, head of Contempo Communications, a producer of industrial shows, and a past president of the Producers' Guild: "For performers, business theater is a lot like getting a commercial. It's not what you do for your art, but it's a way of using your art to put a roof over your head. It's an outlet for your talent, it provides a good income and some people actually find the creative challenges very stimulating. It's almost like writing a sonnet in that you are forced into a form that has certain restrictions. If you look at it that way, as many people do, it becomes a growing experience."

Sal Rasa, who is director of concept development for Maritz Communications in Manhattan as well as a composer, is an eloquent spokesman for the artistic merits of the form. "Theater has always been society speaking to itself about itself," Rasa says. "Rather than see theater possibilities dwindle to a few existing facilities, we should open it up. Yes, we do put on shows for sales meetings, awards ceremonies, and business meetings, but we are also attempting to go further and attack real corporate issues." One of Rasa's projects, for example, was directing a video presentation on AIDS in the workplace for the Equitable Life Insurance Company. "Projects like this," he continues, "allow us to bring an almost journalistic and dramatic approach to real issues in the corporate world."

Rasa insists that "industrials truly represent the producers of today, and for serious, theatrically minded people to avoid this arena is foolish. What we do in terms of entertainment is to create shows from start to finish. We don't specialize in star packages or ready-made acts. We create theater. We are really attempting to bring quality theater to the industrial world, and this is important because our corporate clients have supported the arts enormously in this country. I don't see why they can't enjoy some of it in their own corporate sphere."

REINVENTING THE "INDUSTRIAL"

There was a time when industrial theater stood for slick auto pageants or lavish, Broadway-type extravaganzas touting the latest trends in the fashion industry. But cars and fashions have changed a lot in the past 20 years and so has business theater. According to Joan Marshall, who was instrumental in changing Equity's classification to Business Theater, "'industrial' is not what our basic business is about." She maintains that "there is presently an enormous amount of this kind of theater being done and it can run the gamut."

Today, just about every major corporation in America relies on some form of theater to spice up its business meetings, motivate its sales forces, reward its top employees, or familiarize its staff with new products. And these products can run the gamut, too, whether they're as innocent as a new ruffled potato chip or as imposing as a new jetliner. Patty Soll, vice president of production and staging at Caribiner, Inc., notes that in either case, the shows built around these products can be as incredible as the client wants them to be.

Soll, whose clients have included Mobil Oil, IBM, Ford, and State Farm

Insurance, recalls a particularly unusual show put together by Caribiner's London office: "The client was British Airways and they were looking to reveal a new plane to their people. The show was held in an airplane hangar and the audience was in seating that was designed to move up and over so that the plane could be revealed.

"Firms with the kind of funds required to put together such spectacular displays don't seem to mind spending the money. To them, a good show is an investment—something that supports their business. And whether that means using laser lights or fan-dancers, they're willing to go the distance."

As Buck Heller—formerly senior producer and creative director of business productions at Radio City Music Hall, and now president of Heller Creative Inc.—explains it, "If you wanted to persuade someone to buy a car, just showing the tires might not sell the product. But if the whole product is well-lit and pretty, the sale is easier. A person spending five straight hours in a meeting room might not retain important information: a show breaks up all the information and makes it easier to swallow. Slides, film, video, live entertainment, guest speakers, and breakout seminars are some of the ways this can be done."

While different agencies will approach an industrial assignment in different ways, there is one constant—they need talent. A show could be a take-off on the traditional Broadway musical, with pertinent new lyrics written into well-known show tunes, or it could be a mix of comedy and drama, incorporating the latest in video technology and light effects. Whatever direction a production may take, the need for writers, performers, and technicians remains.

The New York-based Weiss-Watson company uses its own writers for industrial productions, but it does hold open calls for cast members. Spokesman Philip Weiss describes an industrial show his firm put together for the Philip Morris Company. "This particular show had two performances," Weiss notes, "one in Chicago for the Wholesale Grocers Association, and the other in Orlando, Florida for the National Association of Tobacco Distributors. It was a 40-minute live musical show with a 10-piece orchestra, a cast of 12, and a magician. The primary theme of the show was that profitability is not an illusion."

The two Philip Morris shows were basically the same production with slight changes made to reflect the different needs of the grocers and the tobacco distributors. "We used the same cast for both shows," Weiss says, "so they had the opportunity to travel. We auditioned and rehearsed in New York but used local musicians in Chicago and Orlando. The set traveled with us and we had a union designer, a union light designer, and professional video-tape people for the video interludes."

As for the cast, Weiss says, "We put casting announcements in the trades and the performers came down to audition. The cast loved doing it and Philip Morris is a terrific company to work for. They treated the cast like all-stars, with hospitality suites and so on. It was a terrific relationship. The cast got to work together for about six or seven weeks. They did two actual performances plus one videotaped performance for which they were paid."

The cast also had the opportunity to work with some top-notch talent. The director for the Philip Morris productions was Crandall Diehl, whose 30 years of credits include directing Rex Harrison on Broadway in *My Fair Lady*, Siegfried and Roy at the Frontier Hotel in Las Vegas, and staging numerous editions of The Greatest Show on Earth for Ringling Brothers. The Philip Morris show's musical director, Liza Redfield, "was the first female director ever on Broadway," reports Weiss. "She did *The Music Man* and a couple of productions for the New York Shakespeare Festival. She has also done 17 musicals on tour and has performed as a jazz pianist."

In preceding years of the Philip Morris shows, the stars included Patrick Quinn, who appeared on Broadway in *A Day in Hollywood/A Night in the Ukraine* and at Palsson's in *Forbidden Broadway*; Barbara Marineau who played Nellie Forbush in the recent national tour of *South Pacific*; and Leslie Feagan, who was in the original cast of *Anything Goes* at Lincoln Center Theater.

NON-EQUITY PRODUCTIONS

The Philip Morris shows are pretty much the standard fare in modern industrials. They're also light years away from the type of productions that Nancy Lombardo concocts. A comedienne, writer, and actress, Lombardo fashions shows for company heads whom she describes as being tired of the same old thing. These are non-Equity productions and Lombardo makes every effort to make them as unconventional as possible.

"One I really loved doing," the actress recalls, "was a show we did in Puerto Rico for Pfizer Pharmaceuticals. The entire cast was dressed up as waiters and waitresses. The audience was made up of about 40 of Pfizer's top executives, and they had no idea what was going on. We came out speaking in Spanish and gave the worst service they had ever had. And this was at the Caribe Hilton, so they were particularly horrified. At one point, for example, I brought out all their crabmeat salads. Then I left, waited until they'd all had a bite and then came back and told them in Spanish that the fish was bad. They were panicked. Plus, they were seated on the floor, Japanese-style, and we were stepping all over them. At one point I accidentally spilled a drink on one of the women but by that time she was so upset she stabbed me with her fork. Then, two other actors, Michael Schaeffer and Jane Brucker, both started flirting with the same guy. It was hysterical. We tormented them like this for about 45 minutes and then, afterwards, told them that we had been hired by the company to do this to them. Then we went into our show, which consisted of sketches and musical numbers with Pfizer products incorporated into the material."

The audience was so impressed with the show, they later hired Lombardo and one of her cast members, Joe Perce, to "get even" with the Pfizer executive who had hired the actors in the first place.

Lombardo describes her industrial projects as "high-concept comedy," and says her cast members must be well versed in improv as well as acting and singing. "For me," she explains, "versatility is the key. The more an actor can do, the better. When I look at a resume, for example, I'm especially interested in special skills—things a person can do that are beyond the norm."

REQUIREMENTS FOR THE JOB

Knowing how to break-dance isn't a requirement for most industrial work, but it certainly doesn't hurt. In fact, the more versatile you are, the better your chances are of finding work in business theater. In addition to acting ability, most industrial producers are looking for performers who can also sing and dance.

Can you juggle, perform magic tricks, or do you have a ventriloquism routine? There's always a need for specialty acts, according to Joan Marshall. "Not for their own sake," she says, "but we appreciate all kinds of techniques that can be worked into our concept or theme." In other words, make sure you communicate these special talents to a potential employer. You never know when they might be the hook that snares you the job."

According to Larry Katen at Actors' Equity, "You also have to be a quick study. It's a special talent and a lot of wonderful actors who can't work quickly have had problems in industrials. You have to be quick." Sal Rasa agrees: "The difference between industrials and legit theater is that there are no previews, no second chances. Things have to be right in a very short period of time."

TYPECASTING

As for type, well, the field is wide open. Although industrial work was at one time restricted to handsome leading men and bosomy showgirls, the addition of more theatrical pieces into industrial productions has led to a growing need for real people who look like real people. Most corporations are interested in making presentations that reflect either their consumers or their employees. As Caribiner's Patty Soll puts it: "For chorus work, the cast needs to look as attractive and all-American as possible. That really hasn't changed. But there are many book shows being produced, and these types of shows will always need characters and types."

One thing producers do look for is performers who can convey a corporate image. This doesn't necessarily mean you have to look like Joe or Jane Yuppie. It just means that you should be clean, manicured, and perhaps look a little more "professional" than you might for a regular audition. Your hair and make-up should be on the conservative side. Your clothes should also look suitable for an office situation. As Buck Heller explains it: "The producers and directors are theatrical folks, but the client sitting next to us may not be that astute. They have to be comfortable seeing you. They shouldn't have to imagine what you're going to look like onstage. Your appearance is very important."

ETHNICITY

Most corporations are anxious to present shows that reflect the diversity of the general population (as well as their own pool of employees), and actively seek out minorities for their industrial productions. Notes Joan Marshall: "Ethnic types are definitely becoming more and more important in business theater. And we are certainly noticing more diverse audiences: more women, more blacks, more Hispanics. In terms of consumers, in fact, the Hispanic market is the one that is growing the most rapidly. As a result, there has been a sharp increase in clients specifically requesting more ethnically diverse performers."

"Our clients have no ethnic quotas," says current Producers' Guild president, Gene Bayliss. "They say, 'make sure that you consider everybody equally.' We're out to get the best talent there is, regardless; that's what our clients want us to do."

For the record, the agreement between the Producers' Guild and Actors' Equity Association specifically spells out casting obligations with respect to affirmative action as follows:

"Integration is acknowledged to be a goal of Actors' Equity Association and the Producers' Guild. Each production shall be integrated with Equity ethnic minority actors, to the best of the producer's ability.... Recognizing the need for expanding the participation of ethnic minorities and women in the artistic process, the Producer will support a flexible and imaginative casting policy known as non-traditional casting. Non-traditional casting shall be defined as the casting of stereotypical roles (e.g., company executive, manager, salesman, spokesman, consumer, etc.) with ethnic minority and women actors.... Periodic meetings will be held between representatives of Equity and the Producers' Guild, Inc., to evaluate and monitor the implementation of this policy."

UNSCRIPTED PERFORMANCES—IMPROV

Interestingly, there are a growing number of companies who are finding that an evening of unscripted material can be just as valuable to them as more traditional forms of industrial theater. Katha Feffer, creative director of For Play, a New York-based improvisational group, says that the demand for improv artists in industrials is on the upsurge. Caribiner vice president Mike Meth agrees: "I've used improv acts, ventriloquists, and other specialty acts and think they can bring something special to a show. I don't like gratuitous things—it has to have a reason for being there—but I've seen a lot of improv recently, and it has worked quite nicely. There are a lot of improv groups out there and it can make things a little easier for a producer because you're buying a package. You've got built-in chemistry."

For Play once developed an industrial show for Vista International. As Feffer relates, "It was a training program for different personnel from the company on how to make working conditions better for employees. The meeting involved lots of communications seminars and problem-solving seminars, and the night we were there, they had a full program that involved theater games which concentrated on communication."

Feffer says her group was well received by the employees. "At the beginning of the evening we asked members of the audience for five topics which related to their business relationships—topics like miscommunication, and so on. We started our show off with a scenario of an office meeting in which everyone thought they were talking about the same thing, but were in fact, talking about different things. The audience enjoyed it, and at the same time we were able to make valid points that related to their jobs."

Prior to the show, Feffer says she spent three hours with Vista executives discussing problems the company was trying to solve. She was also briefed on office gossip and nicknames for key employees. "They provided us with all sorts of tidbits we could incorporate into the show," Feffer says, "and we worked them in wherever we could."

The folks at Vista, Feffer notes, "really understood what we were doing and worked with us to put together a great show. They didn't tamper with our material. They had a great stage, a great sound system. They even had someone come in that morning and make sure the piano was tuned for us. Plus— and this is usually the biggest problem—they made sure that our show did not coincide with dinner."

THE INDUSTRIAL REVOLUTION

The many professionals who have joined the ever-growing industrial revolution will tell you, for the most part, much the same thing, that business theater has been good to them. It has given them the opportunity to work, grow, and to make valuable new contacts. It could do the same for you. For further information regarding business theater, contact Actors' Equity Association at (212) 869-8530, the Producers' Guild at (212) 721-2729, or consult the audition notices in *Back Stage*.

BUSINESS THEATER PRODUCTION COMPANIES

The following is a list of current members of The Producers' Guild. Most of the production companies listed are signatory with the current Actors' Equity Association agreement governing employment in business theater. The guild office is located at 230 West End Ave., Suite 15A, New York, NY 10023, (212) 721-2729. There are also a number of additional companies, not members of the guild, that also produce business theater shows. Among them are Carabiner, Inc. 16 W. 61 St., NYC, 10023, (212) 541-5300; Imero Fiorentino Associates, 33 W. 60 St., NYC, 10023, (212) 246-0600; Radio City Music Hall Productions, 1226 Ave. of the Americas, NYC, 10020, (212) 632-4000; and Weiss-Watson, Inc., 1140 Ave. of the Americas, NYC, 10036, (212) 753-9800. Some business theater producers cast via agencies, some from submitted pictures and resumes, and some through casting directors.

ARMSTRONG WORLD INDUSTRY, INC.
Box 3001
Lancaster, PA 17604
(717) 396-4203

BUSCH CREATIVE SERVICES CORP.
5240 Oakland Ave.
St. Louis, MO 63110-1436
(314) 289-7883

THE CHARTMAKERS, INC.
33 W. 60th St.
New York, NY 10023
(212) 247-7200

COMART ANIFORMS KLP
360 W. 31st St.
New York, NY 10001
(212) 714-2550

CONCEPT NEW YORK, INC.
156 Fifth Ave., Suite 725
New York, NY 10010
(212) 741-1122

CONTEMPO COMMUNICATIONS, INC.
29 E. 10th St., 5th fl.
New York, NY 10003-6147
(212) 777-0600

CORTEZ/SEIDNER, INC.
227 E. 56th St.
New York, NY 10022
(212) 753-6600

DEPOSITORY TRUST COMPANY
7 Hanover Sq., 25th fl.
New York, NY 10004
(212) 709-1602

FLYING FINISH PRODUCTIONS
13 Washington Rd.
Woodbury, CT 06798
(203) 263-2752

GENE BAYLISS
16 Burritts Landing
Westport, CT 06880
(203) 227-7521

GINDICK PRODUCTIONS, LTD.
21 E. 40th St., Penthouse
New York, NY 10016
(212) 725-2580

INTERGROUP MARKETING & PROMOTION
10 W. Long River Rd., Suite 2
Bloomfield Hills, MI 48013
(313) 433-5200

THE KENWOOD GROUP
222 E. 44th St., 9th fl.
New York, NY 10017
(212) 986-4540

JACK MORTON PRODUCTIONS
641 Ave. of the Americas
New York, NY 10011
(212) 727-0086

MARITZ COMMUNICATIONS CO.
120 W. 45th St.
New York, NY 10036
(212) 819-9100

MARITZ COMMUNICATIONS CO.
1000 Town Center Blvd., Suite 1100
Smithfield, MI 48075
(313) 948-4543

MEETING ENVIRONMENTS, INC.
9 E. 19th St.
New York, NY 10003
(212) 677-3500

MICHAEL BROWN ENTERPRISES
335 E. 50th St.
New York, NY 10022
(212) 759-2233

MICHAEL CARSON PRODUCTIONS
250 W. 54th St., 10th fl.
New York, NY 10019
(212) 765-2300

RW VIDEO, INC.
4902 Hammersley Rd.
Madison, WI 53711-2614
(608) 274-4000

VISUAL SERVICES, INC.
2100 Woodward Ave., Suite 100
Bloomfield Hills, MI 48013
(313) 644-0500

INDUSTRIAL FILMS

BY MIKE SALINAS

Thousands of performers have given shape and direction to their careers by working in the little-known field of industrial and educational films. Although a good many performers assume that industrials are boring and consist mostly of non-union work, these are misconceptions which, for the most part, are not valid. While it is true that some of the films are dull beyond description, the work itself can be interesting and extremely valuable for both beginning and accomplished performers.

Industrial films are regulated by the trade unions; both the Screen Actors Guild and the American Federation of Television and Radio Artists have union jurisdiction over industrials. Joan Greenspan, national director of industrial organizing at SAG, attests to this by saying, "many people are not aware we have contracts for our members to cover these films. Actors should become acquainted with them." Indeed they should. Union figures indicate that this field grew last year by about 10 percent, and there is every indication that that kind of growth will continue indefinitely.

An industrial film helped Scott Geyer land a starring role in the Home Box Office sit-com "First and Ten." Geyer knew he was right for the role and felt that he was close to being cast for the part. But something seemed to be getting in the way. Finally, after a number of auditions, he offered the producers a tape of an industrial film he'd shot a couple of years earlier. He figured that even though the role he had played (a linoleum installer) was very different than the part for which he was being considered (a pro football player), it would still give the executives an opportunity to see how he looked on camera, and that it might help his chances. He was right. In fewer than 24 hours he had been cast for the role of the quarterback in "First and Ten."

WHAT ARE INDUSTRIAL FILMS?

According to the SAG handbook on industrial films there are two kinds of industrials. One kind, called Category I films, are defined as those "programs designed to train, inform, promote a product, or perform a public relations function, and are exhibited in classrooms, museums, libraries, or other places where no admission is charged." High school assembly films (on hygiene, drug abuse, how to use a slide rule, and so forth) are typical Category I films. Their counterparts in the business world are produced by corporations for the purposes of bolstering productivity and morale among their employees and to foster product knowledge.

Category II industrial films look more like commercials and are "intended for unrestricted exhibition to the general public," according to the SAG handbook. Rather than being shown on the airwaves, however, they must be shown "at locations where the product or services are sold, or . . . at public places such as coliseums, railroad stations, air terminals, or shopping centers." This category includes videotapes created as promotional giveaways and "point-of-purchase" video demonstrations.

Some industrial films consist of little more than a single person droning into a camera, but the best ones are patterned after such proven formats as music videos, television dramas, or situation comedies. Industrial filmmakers believe that when dealing with complex problems like sexism or racism on the job, they are more likely to achieve their goal by imitating television, since generations that grew up with this medium are accustomed to seeing difficult issues introduced, discussed, and settled in 28 minutes. Other industrials emulate documentary films and/or news programs, and many of them go to great lengths to recreate the look and feel of the great television features, including stylish camera techniques and extensive music scores. The great bulk of industrials produced today, however, usually employ about a half-dozen contract players to act out vignettes, plus a spokesperson or narrator to drive home the all-important moral.

The main difference between a contract player and a spokesperson according to Joan Greenspan is that a "'spokes' is one whose part is substantially in monologue, performing the preponderance of the script." Union scale for a contract player for one day's work on a Category I film is $333, whereas the spokes will make an additional $273, for a total of $606—but only for the first day. Beyond that, scale reverts to $333. For a Category II film, the figures are a little higher: $414 for a contract player and $717 for a spokes.

For a three-day contract player, the scale is $837 (or $1,032 for a Category II film), and a weekly player gets $1,168 (or $1,447 for a Category II film). For spokespersons, those rates are supplemented by the same one-time surcharges as above. Extras receive $111 per day, except in special circumstances (if they do a "silent bit," or if they are a photo double, they stand to make more money), and an off-camera voice-over day player makes $273 for the first hour's work and $79 for every subsequent half-hour. These rates are in effect through April 30, 1993.

Performers are usually required to provide their own costumes in industrials, for which they are paid a cleaning allowance of $15 per outfit, per two-day period "or part thereof," by the producer. They are also paid for traveling to an overnight location, and are given a meal allowance and single room accommodation. All rates are increased for weekend or holiday work.

INDUSTRIAL FILM BENEFITS

Industrials offer benefits other than just paychecks. Performers are frequently able to obtain a videotape of the performance and may have an opportunity to get their union cards. Industrial films offer good opportunities for beginning actors, too, who may be able to pick up a non-speaking role like playing the part of a doorman or a clerk.

Character actors who have been frustrated in their attempts to get even minor roles on soaps may find industrials a good source of "bread and butter work." Moreover, corporations producing these films are eager to represent their companies as multi-ethnic, so a fair number of blacks, Hispanics, and Asians are able to find work in this field, often as spokespersons.

One of the greatest benefits for inexperienced performers is that industrials offer the opportunity to gain precious on-camera experience in relatively relaxed surroundings. Industrial film shoots are usually pretty calm (a far cry from the chaos of a television taping or the pressures of full-scale big-budget moviemaking), and are less constrained by time than commercials. Therefore, industrial films present an excellent way to learn the craft and mechanics of filming.

AUDITIONS—THE INDUSTRIAL FILM IMAGE

The first step for actors who want to audition for industrial films is to study the corporate look in America today. Since most of the films are set in business environments, from boardrooms to loading docks and all levels in between, it is necessary to have a feel for the people who work in these places. What distinguishes a middle-management type from a senior manager? How do men and women in corporate America dress? How do they speak? The answers to these questions can provide guidelines for the way performers should look and sound when they arrive at their auditions, and how their industrial film resume photo should look.

According to Salli Frattini, former manager of production services at Zink Communications, a leading industrial production house, "For men, the look is more and more casual." However, she elaborates, casual in an industrial film means "still in a tie, but with the jacket off and the shirt sleeves rolled up." Also, she says, there are more women in corporate videos these days, and for them "the look is now more business executive than secretary. For a casting session, they should wear a skirt, a nice blouse, and maybe a jacket. But the look is less conservative and more stylish than it used to be; it's not all bow ties and little high collars anymore."

Of course, for blue-collar characters—loading dock supervisors or linoleum installers—a suit is hardly a necessity. For these roles, actors should dress exactly as they would for a commercial audition. But for jacket-and-tie roles, an actor should wear something that typifies the corporate image. One way to dress for success at an industrial audition, is to wear a classic blue pinstripe suit, recently cleaned and pressed. Bring eyeglasses if you wear them.

SPECIAL SKILLS

Performers with technical, medical, or electronic expertise are advised to list it among other special skills on their resumes. The ability to breeze through a script full of complicated assessments of cycles-per-nanosecond or meticulously detailed descriptions of eye-surgery techniques will not fail to impress agents and casting directors of industrial films. Similarly, prior experience operating specialized machinery, like forklifts, may come in handy and should be listed as a special skill.

The majority of successful industrial performers have never had real experience in the fields portrayed in the films; what the very best spokespersons *do* have is an authoritative attitude and a clear speaking voice (and a blue pinstripe suit or two, of course). Some are very good looking, but a high percentage are only average looking; they range in age from mid-20s to mid-60s, with the majority somewhere in the middle.

As the field of industrial films continues to expand, more jobs are available for both novice and experienced industrial performers of all ages. "Work begets work," says one agent, "and when you've cracked the field, it's naturally easier to get the next job." And the fact is that industrials can be remunerative and can go a long way toward paying monthly bills while performers continue to work toward super-stardom, or more esthetically satisfying career goals.

CABARET

BY BOB HARRINGTON

The world of cabaret provides performers with a milieu that is unique in the entertainment industry. The cabaret stage is usually small, and contact with the audience is intimate. To attract a following, a performer must possess that special personal characteristic called charisma. Even so, the most charismatic entertainers still know that it is not always easy to fill a house.

The difficulty of bringing in an audience is one of the most troublesome problems facing cabaret artists. Whether a headliner or a novice, all cabaret entertainers share this problem. Reputation and good publicity can cushion established stars against those nights when performer and musicians outnumber patrons, but even big names find themselves occasionally playing to sparsely populated rooms. For beginners the problem increases almost immediately after opening night. Once Aunt Rose and all the folks from the office have attended the big debut, who will show up for the next performance? Walk-in business cannot be relied upon—in most clubs accessible to new acts it is negligible. Audiences simply will not go to see an unknown act.

There are ways, however, to build an audience, though most performers are surprisingly uninformed on the subject. Many entertainers are remarkably naive. They expect the club to provide the audience and believe that good reviews will cause audiences to magically appear; or they think people will just somehow find out about them and plunk down a cover charge. The opposite is true. No matter who you are, if you want an audience, you're going to have to go out and get one, and you're going to have to work at it until you reach a level of success which allows you to hire someone else to work at it for you. You may think that big stars are able to sell out houses on the strength of their names. But when you see Barry Manilow or Patti LaBelle break box office records, you're seeing the results of a publicity blitz and hype that cost big bucks; you're seeing good management and good press relations; and you're seeing the product of years of self-promotion. It takes a monumental effort to become and remain a star, and no one is above the effort.

If you're determined to become a star, keep in mind that the first step to stardom is building an audience. A performer who fills a room never lacks bookings, and eventually attracts the right attention. And, you can approach building an audience the same way you would approach locating customers in any other business: logically, methodically, and with a plan in mind. What follows are some of the things you should be doing and some advice on how to do them to the best effect.

MAILING LISTS

After you have decided to try a club act, the first step is to build (and maintain) a mailing list. Sit down and write out the names and addresses of everyone you can think of who might be interested in what you're doing. Every friend, co-worker, and relative goes on your mailing list, and you work from that core. Adding to and updating this list must become a number one priority, for how you add to your mailing list will, in many respects, determine how successful you become. After you've composed your initial list, buy a little spiral note pad. Keep it with you at all times, and jot down the name and address of any person who expresses an interest in what you are doing.

Determined performers treat their mailing lists with reverence. They use computers in some instances, and work on it for hours every week. They will add names to their lists constantly. No one walks out of one of their performances without being spoken to, thanked, and if willing, listed. They pass little guest books around before every show. The names they collect during their first run help turn their second run into sell-outs. These performers place mailing list cards on every single table when they perform, and remind the audience of this during the performance.

You can also take a creative approach to building a mailing list. Katha Feffer of the improvisational troupe, For Play, brought the group to the Duplex from Oregon. They knew no one in the city. She built a mailing list from people back home who had friends and relatives in New York. She took yearbooks from Oregon colleges and culled out the names of the students who were from New York. She traced Oregonian graduates who had moved to New York. She invited practically everyone who had ever been passed through Oregon to see For Play—and this became her core list.

The actual mechanics of preparing a mailing list depend largely on your finances and organizational ability. A personal computer, particularly one with the capability of running off mailing labels, is, of course, ideal. The right software will make your mailing list easy to access and update, and you can use it to identify different groups within the list for targeted mailings. Even a basic system, however, can cost a lot of money; money which might be put to better use elsewhere at the beginning of a career. A computer is, after all, nothing more than an elaborate and efficient filing system, and you can do almost as well on your own. A simple, unalphabetized running list will do in a pinch when you're still addressing fliers by hand, but index cards quickly become essential. You can add to your file by simply slipping in the cards filled out by patrons at your shows. Another advantage to using index cards is that you can make notes on them to show who is responding to your mailings as you cross-reference with the people filling out new cards or signing guest books at your shows. This helps you eliminate the dead wood. Keep it simple—name, address, and zip code, affiliation if pertinent, and underneath just pencil in a date of attendance. Cards can also be rearranged by zip code quickly and easily, which simplifies things when you take them in to have address labels made.

When you are ready to have mailing labels made from your handwritten or typed list, get two copies of each address made and simply paste the extra addresses onto individual cards—the result is an instant file. You can use the same method to update your list when you're working from names scrawled on cocktail napkins, matchbook covers, and the backs of envelopes. Business cards can be taped or stapled directly to your index cards.

Those are the main details of building and maintaining a mailing list. As you can see, it's a lot of work—but it pays off. If you scrupulously keep your mailing list it will, like Mae West's diary, someday keep you.

PHOTOGRAPHS

There are pros and cons to spending heavily on good headshots for cabaret, but a good photograph can turn out to be a valuable asset. It's true that the major dailies don't like headshots, but they almost never run pictures with reviews anyway so that's not a major concern. Headshots are used in *Back Stage*, *Nightlife Magazine*, *Michael's Thing*, and other publications that cover cabaret. They are also useful for fliers, postcards, and posters.

But the headshot must be good—and that means distinctive, attractive, and slickly professional. It is not unusual for an editor to put a blurb together or ask a writer to do a piece only in order to use a particularly attractive picture. It is possible to garner an extraordinary amount of extra publicity just because of the quality and beauty of photographs. Comics who can come up with especially amusing or interesting photos will also benefit.

If you're not particularly photogenic, don't get photos taken until you can afford the best. It's amazing what a good photographer can do, and it's probably a good thing that performers aren't covered by the "truth in advertising" laws. But a bad job is worse than useless. Grainy, unflattering, blurry, or bland photographs reflect poorly on you as a performer and are of no help in getting you any publicity.

FLIERS, POSTCARDS, POSTERS, AND ADS

A flier is essential. It is your calling card to the world of cabaret so let it represent you as a polished professional and not as a rank amateur.

Fliers designed for cabaret should be neat, clean, and simple. A headshot or publicity photo as the centerpiece, a club logo, and basic information is all that is required. Later, you may add quotes from reviews or even entire reviews (if appropriate) when you get them. It's better to spend a few dollars to get a good, basic flier professionally made (you can use this over and over by changing the dates) than to use a photocopy machine, typewriter, or crayons. Fliers can be run off on standard paper, folded in three, labeled, and mailed. They can also be distributed in piano bars, at places of employment, or anyplace that will help.

If you can afford the additional cost, postcards are an effective means of publicizing your show. For one thing, you can't throw one in the garbage without seeing who it's from. For another, postcards imply a certain amount of success and status just because they're more expensive—which is, of course, the down side—they're expensive. Generally, the guidelines for putting together a cabaret postcard are the same as they are for cabaret fliers. Keep it simple.

Posters are probably a waste of time and are certainly not cost-effective. A moderate poster campaign costs close to $1,000 and you'll never recoup that in cover charges. Posters rarely bring in much new business. All they do is notify people who already know who you are that you're around again. You can do the same thing more effectively with a good mailing list and a few well-placed ads.

What posters do accomplish is to let people in the business know that you really mean it, and again, they imply a certain status and success. If the club pays for the posters, go ahead and have them printed up. If not, don't bother unless your primary purpose is to increase your prestige and visibility within the business.

Taking out ads can cost a small fortune and have no effect whatsoever on your audience if you don't place them correctly. For an unknown, the only affordable and sensible place for an ad is in the trade papers, where agents, colleagues, and other performers will see it. After you're established, and your name has been around a while, you can explore more elaborate forms of advertising.

The best way to get an ad in a paper is to find work in a club that advertises its performers on a regular basis. Most clubs will also see to it that you get listed in those publications that provide free listings. Keep your eyes open and get a feeling for the kinds of ads that work for the various clubs and performers. It doesn't work the same way for everyone. Sometimes huge ads in newspapers are not at all effective. There are many factors that determine the effectiveness of an ad, including the demographics of the publication, the day of the week, the time of performance, the type of act, and what the ad looks like.

NEWSLETTERS AND THE PERSONAL TOUCH

Performers who have a devoted, regular following might consider sending out a newsletter. If you go this route, make sure that your newsletter is interesting and informative; don't inundate your fans with homey little notes. Some performers use newsletter-type mailings to share items of special interest. This could consist of good reviews, articles of interest about them or about cabaret in general, or could describe an award or citation they've just won, and might include a short personal note. Such an approach is effective, tasteful, and appropriate. It also makes people feel that you're really trying to stay in touch. Newsletters that are filled with obviously manufactured information, on the other hand, are not effective and may be annoying.

The personal touch cannot be underestimated when it comes to building and maintaining a steady following. Smart performers make personal contact with everyone who comes to see them. Be accessible, be friendly, say thank you and get the names for your mailing list. It's hard to greet dozens of people and repeat yourself over and over without sounding phony. Learn how, because if you are successful in cabaret, you'll be greeting hundreds of people and repeating yourself over and over. So now is the time to cultivate a good memory for names and faces. If you are casually acquainted with a person, or if you get the feeling that the person is expecting more than a perfunctory thank you, make an effort to personalize the interchange. You don't have to get into a major conversation, and you can always excuse yourself to greet other people. Countless performers muff a chance to turn a first-time patron into a steady regular by projecting the wrong attitude. In cabaret, all performers, stars included, are accessible. Big names like Julie Wilson, Margaret Whiting, and Kaye Ballard still try to meet everyone who comes to one of their shows. That's one of the reasons why they're such well-loved personalities. And it's no coincidence that they also work steadily.

DEALING WITH THE CRITICS

The easiest (but not easy) publicity to get comes from critics. Critics have followings, just like performers, and their reviews can help you build an audience. A good word from a critic can also be immensely supportive and helpful to your career in other ways. Good reviews guarantee the support of the critic's publication, status within the cabaret community, and a clear validation of your talents as a performer. Such reviews can interest agents, get you jobs, and attract other critics. Reviews appearing while you're still performing can sell out your show, or at least increase your audience (and mailing list).

A review, however, can blow you out of the water, emotionally and careerwise, if it is a bad one. The biggest and most common single mistake made by performers is to invite critics to their shows before they are ready to be reviewed.

The best advice you're going to get is from the club owners, operators, and booking managers. They don't want bad reviews any more than you do. If they're not encouraging you, take the hint. You're asking for trouble if you pressure a club owner or press agent into inviting a critic. It is not unheard of for an owner or press agent in that situation to gleefully give in and let the performer take his or her richly deserved lumps. Use your head—the people who run the club have every reason to want you to be reviewed if you're good enough. If they're not bending over backwards to get the critics out, there's a hidden message in there for you. Don't be in such a hurry.

If you decide you are ready to face the critics, and you're getting some encouragement from objective sources, then you must decide *which* critics you want to come. *Do not think you are ready for every critic in town.* Here again, the club staff can help you. If you don't know who's who, they will. Even if you're good enough, you have to go about this carefully. You don't want a major newspaper reviewing a short one-week run that will have a much longer run later on. They won't review you again no matter how much they like you, and even a rave from the *Times* has little appreciable audience effect when your appearance has already ended. The quotes look good on your fliers and publicity, but yesterday's reviews can be as dead as yesterday's news when it comes to drawing an audience. Plan your campaign.

In reality, critics are much more aware of what's going on and far more selective than you probably think they are. If you're good enough to be reviewed by the top critics, they probably already know about you. Critics rarely see anyone they haven't already gotten at least some input on, though they occasionally respond to a particularly interesting letter or personal contact. But mostly, critics rely on feedback from club owners, press agents, bookers, waiters and waitresses, other performers, and audience members.

Critic Stephen Holden of the *New York Times* cites the following considerations that help him decide whom to review: "I rely on publicists and on word of mouth," Holden says. "I also trust club owners. I know what to expect in different clubs and what level of professionalism to expect." To some critics, professionalism is a major factor in determining their decision to review. Others, however, will knowingly see a rank beginner. Stephen Holden will not. Holden suggests that performers "try to have some sense of whether they're really ready to be reviewed—usually they're not." Critics are also influenced by other critics' reviews (keep in mind that this is a double-edged sword), and you can build a press kit that will help you attract the major critics by building on previous reviews.

Assuming that you're ready, and that you've chosen the critics you think you're ready for, the object now becomes getting them in to see you. If you or the club you're working at has a press agent, leave it in their hands. If not, write a letter or send a flier. Every critic is different. A personal letter influences some, others prefer working off monthly club schedules and fliers. But if you choose to write, don't try to be cute. Just write a sincere letter explaining why you want the critic to see you; don't try to dazzle the critic with clever *bons mots*. Avoid stridency or boastful claims and keep in mind that critics know their field, are aware of who's who, and are basically just looking for information on who's doing what and where.

Every critic operates the same way—the standard arrangement is complimentary covers and no check for drinks or food. Some clubs have a two-drink comp limit, which isn't unreasonable. But I suggest you make it your business to find out if the critic you've invited has had *three* drinks and then make sure your critic doesn't get a check for the third drink. Some clubs will comp dinners for some critics but not others, and some clubs won't comp anything but the cover. For the most part, critics know which clubs are doing what and will act accordingly. But mistakes do happen. Every critic occasionally gets a check by mistake, or gets billed without having been informed that club policy does not include comps. This can create bad feeling for the performer and for the club, and it's your responsibility to take care of this in advance. The unwritten rule is that the critic is your guest unless the club policy is otherwise. And that's something you should be aware of from the start. Some clubs have written into their contracts that critics are the guests of the club. Other clubs handle the whole thing informally, and have well-developed relationships with individual critics. It is the policy of some clubs, though, to bill the performer for a critic's tab. One performer learned to her dismay that she owed a club $1,000 for food and drinks supplied to critics and agents whom she thought the club was comping. Know what you're doing before you start mailing out invitations all over town.

Most critics scrupulously avoid wearing out their welcome by running up big tabs and resent it when a club bills a performer for their dinner and drinks. Nevertheless, it is your responsibility to make arrangements for *your* critics in accordance with the policy of *your* club. Mistakes can cost you *and* the club a great deal of good will.

You'll usually find out when a critic has accepted an invitation to see you, though sometimes a club will invite one and not tell you to avoid making you nervous. If you want to keep critics happy, provide them with a play list of the songs you'll be doing, including lyricist and composer. And make sure this information is accurate. If the critic coming uses photos (and again, you should know this), have one available. A short press release is all right, but don't load a critic down with tons of irrelevant facts. Always include contact information (for both yourself and the club you are performing at) in your invitation to critics.

There are probably dozens of reasons why a review may not run, the most obvious one being considerations of space in the newspaper. After a review has run, thank you notes are optional. No critic expects them, but all critics like them when they're thoughtfully done. They don't even have to be in response to a rave review. If a critic says something that moves you to write, then write. But never write to complain or argue, even if you think a critic is 100 percent wrong.

If you use a portion of a review in your publicity, make sure it is representative of what was actually said. You may fool some people lifting one good word or sentence out of a negative review, but you'd better believe the critic will hear about it. If you do quote, use the critic's name and not just the publication in which the review appeared.

SHOW BUSINESS IS GOOD BUSINESS

They call it show *business* for a reason. Your chance of succeeding will be greater if you master both the business and the artistic side. No one will take care of business for you in the beginning, and the more you learn at the start, the less likely it is that someone will take you for a ride later on. As in any endeavor, hard work and training will pay off if you keep at it. Stardom may or may not come to you, but if you have the art and you take care of business, you'll always have an audience to play to.

CABARET ROOMS

Below is a selective, up-to-date listing of cabaret rooms across the country. In general, these venues present acts and revues. Others, where noted, are not strictly "cabaret," preferring to emphasize, for example, jazz. When contacting the booking agent, be sure to check club policy (auditions, appointments, open-mike nights); and ask about publicity arrangements and whether or not an accompanist is provided.

NOTE: MAC (Manhattan Association of Cabarets and Clubs) members are denoted with an asterisk.

NEW YORK CITY

ADAM'S RIB
1340 First Ave.
New York, NY 10021
(212) 535-2112
Contact: Joe Holloway (212) 929-4950

*THE BALLROOM
253 W. 29th St.
New York, NY 10001
(212) 244-3005
Contact: Mario Obando (mail only)

*BIRDLAND
2745 Broadway
New York, NY 10025
(212) 749-2228
Contact: Mark Morganelli

THE BITTER END
147 Bleecker St.
New York, NY 10012
(212) 673-7030
Contact: Ken Gorka

BLUE ANGEL
323 W. 44th St.
New York, NY 10036
(212) 262-3333
Contact: James Cione (212) 262-1111

*CAFE CARLYLE
35 E. 76th St.
New York, NY 10021
(212) 744-1600
Contact:Rene Peyret

CATCH A RISING STAR
1487 First Ave.
New York, NY 10021
(212) 794-1906
Contact: Louis Faranda

*DANNY'S SKYLIGHT ROOM
at Danny's Grand Sea Palace
346 W. 46th St.
New York, NY 10036
(212) 265-8133
Contact: John Britton

*DON'T TELL MAMA
343 W. 46th St.
New York, NY 10036
(212) 757-0788
Contact: Sidney Myer (212) 265-0001

*THE DUPLEX
61 Christopher St.
New York, NY 10014
(212) 255-5438 (call after 4 pm)
Contact: Collette Black
(212) 989-3015 (1-4 pm)

*EIGHTY EIGHT'S
228 W. 10th St.
New York, NY 10014
(212) 924-0088
Contact: Erv Raible

*55 GROVE STREET CABARET
at Rose's Turn
55 Grove St.
New York, NY 10014
(212) 366-5438
Contact: Sidney Myer (212) 265-0001

5 & 10 NO EXAGGERATION
77 Greene St.
New York, NY 10012
(212) 925-7414
Contact: Robert Mergler or Keith Lane

*FORTUNE GARDEN PAVILION
209 E. 49th St.
New York, NY 10017
(212) 753-0101
Contact: Alvin Mass

HAMBURGER HARRY'S
145 W. 45th St.
New York, NY 10036
(212) 840-0566
Contact: Carmine DeSena

THE IMPROVISATION
358 W. 44th St.
New York, NY 10036
(212) 765-8268
Contact: Silver Friedman

*J's
2581 Broadway, 2nd fl.
New York, NY 10025
(212) 666-3600
Contact: Judy Barnett
(Jazz only)

*JEWEL BOX
323 W. 44th St.
New York, NY 10036
(212) 262-3333
Contact: Jim Cione (212) 262-1111

*JUDY'S RESTAURANT CABARET
49 W. 44th St.
New York, NY 10036
(212) 764-8930
Contact: Rich Hendrickson

KELLY'S
46 Bedford St.
New York, NY 10014
(212) 929-9322
Contact: Vera Dunkle

LA MAMA CABARET
74A E. 4th St.
New York, NY 10003
(212) 475-7710
Contact: Ellen Stewart or Meryl Vladimer

L'OMNIBUS de MAXIM'S
680 Madison Ave.
New York, NY 10021
(212) 751-5111
Contact: Monty Zullo

*STEVE McGRAW'S
158 W. 72nd St.
New York, NY 10023
(212) 362-2590
Contact: Nancy McCall

MICHAEL'S PUB
211 E. 55th St.
New York, NY 10022
(212) 758-2272
Contact: Gil Weiss
(Established musical acts only)

MONKEY BAR
at Hotel Elysee
60 E. 54th St.
New York, NY 10022
(212) 753-1066
Contact: Pat Norell (212) 265-0943

*MOSTLY MAGIC
55 Carmine St.
New York, NY 10014
(212) 924-1472
Contact: Imam

NILE
327 W. 44th St.
New York, NY 10036
(212) 262-1111
Contact: Jim Cione (212) 262-1111

*THE OAK ROOM
at the Algonquin Hotel
59 W. 44th St.
New York, NY 10017
(212) 840-6800
Contact: Kate McGrath

*CABARET! at
The Russian Tea Room
150 W. 57th St.
New York, NY 10019
Produced by Don Smith
(212) 265-0947
Contact: Andrew Freeman

*RAINBOW & STARS
30 Rockefeller Plaza, 65th fl.
New York, NY 10020
(212) 632-5000
Contact: Eddie Micone (212) 632-4000

*SWEETWATERS
170 Amsterdam Ave.
New York, NY 100123
(212) 873-4100
Contact: Copper Cunningham/Dee

*TATOU
151 E. 50th St.
New York, NY 10022
(212) 753-1144
Contact: Couri Hay

*TOWNHOUSE
236 E. 58th St.
New York, NY 10022
(212) 754-4649
Contact: Nicholas Pavlik

*UPSTAIRS AT GREENE STREET
105 Greene St.
New York, NY 10012
(212) 925-2415
Contact: Marlo Courtney or Leah Sutton

WESTBETH THEATRE CENTER CABARET
151 Bank St., New York, NY 10014
(212) 691-2272
Contact: Jane MacPherson

WILSON'S
201 W. 79th St.
New York, NY 10024
(212) 769-0100
Contact: Leah Sutton

CALIFORNIA

BACKLOT CABARET THEATRE
657 N. Robertson Dr.
Los Angeles, CA 90069
(213) 659-0472
Contact: Scott Forbes

CARLOS 'N CHARLIE'S
8240 Sunset Blvd.
Los Angeles, CA 90046
(213) 656-8830
Contact: Bernice Altshul

CINEGRILL
Hollywood Roosevelt Hotel
7000 Hollywood Blvd.
Hollywood, CA 90028
(213) 466-7000
Contact: Jan Walner

GARDENIA
7066 Santa Monica Blvd.
West Hollywood, CA 90038
(213) 467-7444
Contact: Toni Rolla

PLUSH ROOM
York Hotel, 940 Suttcr St.
San Francisco, CA 94109
(415) 885-6800
Contact: Herb Leigh

ROSE TATTOO
665 N. Robertson Ave.
Los Angeles, CA 90069
(213) 854-4455
Contact: Linda Gerard

VINE ST. BAR AND GRILL
1610 Vine St.
Los Angeles, CA 90028
(213) 463-4375
Contact: Ron Berinstein
(Jazz, blues, swing, r&b)

ILLINOIS

GOLD STAR SARDINE BAR
680 N. Lake Shore Dr.
Chicago, IL 60611
(312) 664-4215
Contact: Bill Allen

MASSACHUSETTS

CLUB CABARET
209 Columbus Ave.
Boston, MA 02116
(617) 536-0966
Contact: Joseph McAllaster
(Send tape, no calls)

REGATTA BAR
Charles Hotel, Harvard Sq.
Cambridge, MA 02138
(617) 937-4020
Contact: Walter Music Mgt., (617) 876-8742
(jazz)

SCULLERS
400 Soldiers Field Rd.
Brighton, MA 02180
(617) 783-0811
Contact: Joe Anderson

THEATRE LOBBY
216 Hanover St.
Boston, MA 02113
(617) 227-9872
Contact: Sain Jerris

PENNSYLVANIA

ODETTE'S
Box 127, S. River Rd.
New Hope, PA 18938
(215) 862-2432
Contact: Bobby Egan

STAND-UP COMEDY

BY BILL ERVOLINO

Most successful stand-up comedians have known they were funny since childhood. They were class clowns or practical jokers. Richard Belzer, who was abused as a youngster, used to tell his mother jokes to keep her from hitting him. Howie Mandel pulled so many practical jokes in high school he was constantly on the brink of being expelled.

But not all class clowns grow up to be professional comedians. Until recently, in fact, stand-up comedy never seemed like much of a career option. Even back in the 1970s, when the club scene first began to mushroom, comedy was a risky business—hardly the kind of occupation you'd brag about to your fiancee's parents. The world of comedy was dominated by performers who had started out in vaudeville: folks like Milton Berle, George Burns, and Bob Hope.

A few things happened in the 1970s that changed the entire scene. A whole new batch of comic daredevils began to emerge, performing comedy that was risky, irreverent, and scathingly, wonderfully hip. Those of us who tuned in that night in 1975 when *Saturday Night Live* discovered an incredibly talented group of off-the-wall comedians who called themselves The Not-Ready-for-Prime-Time Players. Some had done stand-up previously; all had received serious comic training in sketch or improv troupes. And they swiftly redefined comedy for a generation that had very little in common with Berle, Burns, and Hope.

Other acts to come out of this period were Steve Martin, Robin Williams, and a virtual gaggle of high-energy comics with kitschy routines that seemed to teeter dangerously over the edge. Simultaneously, more established comedians were finding tremendous success on television and in films. Woody Allen won an Oscar for *Annie Hall*; Joan Rivers was becoming a household name; and comedy in general was becoming more aggressive, acerbic, and youth oriented.

By the mid-1980s, the burgeoning club scene had emerged as the ideal place to discover new talent for films, sitcoms, talk shows, cable television, and even commercials. Just take a look around you. In addition to Martin, Williams, Allen, and Rivers, stand-up is the vehicle that first brought us Bill Cosby, Eddie Murphy, Roseanne Barr, Whoopi Goldberg, Billy Crystal, Arsenio Hall, Rodney Dangerfield, and a host of other huge names who went on to establish themselves, royally, in other media.

In the late 1970s, aspiring stand-up comedian Robert Wuhl paid a visit to Rodney Dangerfield. "I walked into his club, went to his dressing room and said 'Rodney, I have a couple of jokes for you.'" Wuhl performed the material in the best Dangerfield impression he could muster—he even tugged, Rodney-style, at his tie—and waited quietly for the verdict.

"Rodney told me he hated the impression," Wuhl recalls, "but he bought the jokes." Before long, other comedians began buying Wuhl's jokes, too. And studios started looking at his scripts. And he sold a pilot. And he became a writer and story editor for a series (*Police Squad*). And then. . .he started all over again.

Wuhl returned to stand-up. He was booked onto the "Tonight Show." And "Late Night with David Letterman." Oh yes, and then there was the mega-hit *Batman*, in which Wuhl played a nosy reporter competing with Michael Keaton for the attentions of Kim Basinger.

Although most people don't know Wuhl by name, he has established himself, as a performer and a writer, in just about every medium open to him. He works steadily, makes lots of money, and seems genuinely content with every twist and turn his comedy career has taken.

BEING DISCOVERED

For Wuhl and countless other talented performers, "being in the right place at the right time" meant performing in a comedy club in the 1980s. Aside from teaching them how to handle themselves onstage and how to develop their sense of comic timing, it put comedians in a spotlight, one in which their talents were observed by some of the most influential people in show business.

That tradition continues today. Talent scouts from MTV, HBO, Showtime, Fox, "The Tonight Show," "Arsenio Hall," and "Late Night with David Letterman" continue to prowl stand-up venues looking for great, undiscovered talent. Lately, however, the job has been getting tougher and tougher.

Today, being an undiscovered comedian means you've probably never found your way to a big city. There are now so many opportunities for comics on television that newcomers are gobbled up as soon as they they've got a workable routine. Some shows, produced by the club owners themselves, have eliminated the middle man (or scout) altogether. New York clubs such as Caroline's and the Comic Strip all have their own weekly television shows, as does The Improv. And many of the smaller suburban clubs have weekly shows on their local cable access channels. Turn on your TV, flip through the channels, and—at any time of the day or night—you're likely to find somebody standing at a mike, telling a few jokes. On weekends, you'll probably see several. Stand-up, for better or worse, is everywhere.

From a business standpoint, try looking at it this way: the unemployment rate among actors is somewhere in the vicinity of 96 percent. Among comics, however, it's virtually nil. If a comic is any good at all, she's working. And if she's working, she has an excellent shot at being discovered—and landing more work as a result of it.

"It's a situation that is accelerating at a very rapid pace," observes Cary Hoffman, owner of Stand-Up New York, "and one which is altering stand-up tremendously. We're seeing comics today developing cleaner, more generic acts—television acts. They are also much more concerned with their acting abilities. A lot of them are even taking acting classes. By now, they are all familiar with the story of how Carl Reiner came into the Comedy Store and discovered Robin Williams. To many of them, stand-up has become a quick steppingstone to television and films."

New York's Catch a Rising Star owner Richard Fields agrees: "We have close to 100 performers appearing regularly at Catch, but I'd say only two or three of them see stand-up as a long-term goal. The rest are waiting to be discovered. And, while they wait, they can earn $30,000 to $75,000 a year. Our management company currently handles some acts—people who are not major stars—who are earning two to four thousand per week."

Many of the clubs aggressively pursue casting people, inviting them to stop in, have a drink and sample that night's acts. "Casting people call us all the time," Cary Hoffman notes, "and yes, we do pursue them. The comedy clubs are now viscerally connected to films and just about every other medium. ABC, for example, has a pilot development program, and they are always in the clubs looking for people to build pilots around. They *want* comics."

TAKING COMEDY SERIOUSLY

The club surge, once considered a fad within the entertainment industry, began being taken very, very seriously. The annual Manhattan Association of Cabaret awards, held every March in New York City, includes a generous smattering of comedy and musical comedy categories. Another annual event, the televised American Comedy Awards, is produced by "Laugh-In" creator George Schlatter, and generally pulls healthy ratings. And the Just for Laughs Festival, an annual gathering of comedians from the U.S., Canada, and Europe, has become an important international event every July in Montreal.

One press conference at Montreal's Delta Hotel during the 1990 festival brought together Tom Freston, the president of MTV; Charles Joffe, the producer of Woody Allen's films; Marty Klein, the manager of Steve Martin, Rick Moranis, John Candy, and Steven Wright; Buddy Morra, manager of Robin Williams and Billy Crystal; Robert Morton, producer of "Late Night with David Letterman"; Ted Robinson, vice-president in charge of comedy for ABC in Australia; and Steve Hewitt, the senior vice president at Showtime. (How would you like to do five minutes before that little congregation?)

DEVELOPING A PERSONA

If you've already decided to try your hand at stand-up, the next thing you have to figure out is what you're going to do while you're standing there. What are you going to say? How are you going to say it? Will you tell jokes? Stories? Play different characters? Wear funny glasses? Use props? Or just go out there and be yourself?

Props? Characters? Clearly, different things work for different comics. And, since audience tastes tend to vary, finding what works for you can often be a complicated procedure of trial and error.

"The first night I went out onstage," Joy Behar recalls, "I did a character called Sadie Catalano. She was an Italian woman from Brooklyn who told all the news in the community. So I went out there and did it, and I had a great, great set. I was so shocked. I was so nervous I can't tell you. But they [the audience] were hysterical. People were pounding the table, they were so hysterical. Even people who weren't Italian. Then, I did the same act again for a different crowd. . . and it died."

Although Behar still uses her Sadie Catalano character occasionally, she eventually decided to be more like herself onstage. Her reasoning? "In stand-up you have to be able to react. You have to ad-lib. And sometimes, with a character, that just doesn't work. For me it was just too limiting."

Like Behar, Angela Scott recommends honesty onstage. An accomplished comedienne, Scott is regularly seen in comedy clubs. She is also a regular warm-up act for series such as *The Cosby Show* and has even been a booking agent for comedy shows in which she has also performed. "It's important to do what feels good to you," she notes, "no matter what anyone says. If you aren't true to yourself, the audience isn't going to buy it."

This is not to say that a character won't work onstage. Gilbert Gottfried has found tremendous success working in character. So has Judy Tenuta, Steven Wright, and Emo Philips. But, as so many well-known comics have proven, it is hardly something that is necessary for success.

CREATIVITY AND EXPERIENCE

Think *you've* got what it takes to go out there and make people laugh? Perhaps you do. If your friends think you're funny and your relatives think you're funny and the people you work with think you're funny. . . well, there's a good chance you really are funny. It doesn't mean, however, that you're ready to walk out onto a stage and keep people laughing for twenty minutes. You still need an act.

Lucian Hold, who books acts for New York's Comic Strip, generally auditions some 30 new acts per month. "We have a call on the first Friday of every month for new comics," Hold explains, "and, of the 50 to 60 who show up, we draw numbers for about 30 of them. Those comics whose numbers are drawn are then invited back and added into our schedule. Our Mondays are audition nights, and that is when they perform. Those who do well are then invited back."

What does Hold look for in a new comic? "I like to be surprised and I like to be made to laugh," Hold says. "That's the combination. I like to see something new or different in the character or the way the joke is written. I always tell people to be original. Avoid material written by other people. And, if your friends tell you that you remind them of someone, whether it's Robin Williams or Steven Wright or whoever it is, deal with that before you come in. Try to make the act your own."

An additional piece of advice: "Don't steal material. Some auditioners will come in here using material that's been lifted from someone else's act—something they've seen in a club or on a Showtime special. Never do it. I may not recognize the material right away. But someone else will, somewhere along the way."

If you're clever enough to write your own material, smooth enough to pass your audition, and funny enough to get regular bookings, you're just about on your way. But you're still going to be lacking one extremely important ingredient: experience.

Before she began finding regular bookings, Angela Scott performed in New York with a comedy troupe called the Kitchen Table, which included, at one time, filmmaker Robert Townsend. "We performed everywhere," Scott laughs. "In Washington Square Park, on Sixth Avenue, in Central Park, at festivals, fairs, and anywhere else we could. And that means weddings, bar mitzvahs, in your living room, and anywhere else you can grab people's attention. It's important. It's the kind of thing that helps you to get ready to walk out there and make people laugh."

In addition to honing your skills in the fine art of coping with a crowd, your live experience, whatever it may be, will also help you to define your onstage persona and sharpen up your material.

Lucian Hold's final piece of advice to aspiring stand-ups: "Observe other comics. Watch them on TV. See them live. Go to the clubs. Study the craft."

HITTING THE CLUBS

If you want to be a pastry chef, you study in Paris. If you want to be a stand-up comic, you study in New York. The club scene in Manhattan, much like this city's legitimate theater, is extensive, varied, and—as far as the entertainment industry is concerned—important. As just about any comedian will tell you, New York's audiences are tough, discerning, and hipper than most. For those reasons, you'd be wise to go into the New York clubs as often as possible, see what other comics are doing, and observe how the audiences react and what they are reacting to. (Realize, however, that unless you're a big name, the money you'll make in the New York clubs is minute; for lesser-known acts, "on the road" is where the money is.)

There are several sources of information which can answer any additional questions you may have concerning a career in stand-up. One is the Professional Comedians Association, a group that describes itself as a "watchdog organization for comedians, protecting their rights in just about every avenue."

The trade publication *Comedy USA Newswire* bills itself as "the first trade publication to take funny business seriously." For a year's subscription send $40 to: *Comedy USA Newswire*, 401 E. 81st St., New York, NY 10028.

An amusing and informational glimpse into the current world of stand-up appears in the book *Comic Lives* (Fireside Books) by Betsy Borns. The book contains interviews with 30 top comics as well as booking agents, club owners, and television executives.

COMEDY CLUBS

Information for the following list of comedy clubs in New York, Chicago, and Los Angeles was gathered by the Professional Comedians Association. The PCA is a service and information organization of professional comedians, with nearly 1500 members nationwide. To contact the PCA: 581 Ninth Ave., Suite 3C, New York, NY 10036; (212) 643-5233.

NEW YORK

BOSTON COMEDY CLUB
82 W. 3rd St.
New York, NY 10012
(212) 956-6000
Booker: Jocelyn Halloran

CATCH A RISING STAR-NYC
1487 First Ave.
New York, NY 10019
(212) 794-1906
Booker: Louis Faranda

CHRISTOPHER'S SUPPER CLUB
3501 Quentin Rd.
Brooklyn, NY 11234
(718) 336-6432
Booker: George Tassone

COMEDY CELLAR—NEW YORK
117 MacDougal St.
New York, NY 10012
(212) 254-3630
Contact: Bill Grundfest

COMIC STRIP—NEW YORK
1568 Second Ave.
New York, NY 10028
(212) 861-9386
Booker: Lucien Hold

DANGERFIELD'S
1118 First Ave.
New York, NY 10021
(212) 593-1650
Booker: Caroline Zebrowski

EAGLE TAVERN
355 W. 14th St.
New York, NY 10011
(212) 924-0275
Booker: Tim Andre Davis

GRANDPA'S—STATEN ISLAND
106 New Dorp Plaza
Staten Island, NY 10306
(718) 667-4242
Booker: Tony Camacho

UPSTAIRS AT GREENE STREET
105 Greene St.
New York, NY 10012
(212) 925-2415
Booker: Leah Sutton

IMPROVISATION (ORIGINAL)
358 W. 44th St.
New York, NY 10036
(212) 765-8268
Booker: Silver Friedman

JIMMY'S COMEDY ALLEY
4729 Bell Blvd.
Bayside, Queens, NY 11361
(718) 631-5055
Booker: Caroline Zebrowski

NEW YORK COMEDY CLUB
915 Second Ave.
New York, NY 10022
(212) 273-9289
Booker: Noel Murphy

PIPS
2005 Eammons Ave.
Brooklyn, NY 11235
(718) 646-9433
Booker: Seth Schultz

STAND-UP NEW YORK
236 W. 78th St.
New York, NY 10024
(212) 595-0850
Booker: Cary Hoffman

TICKLES
8901 Third Ave.
Bay Ridge, Brooklyn, NY 11209
(718) 836-8973
Booker: Rick Morgan

TRUBBLES
46 E. 29th St.
New York, NY 10016
(212) 213-2131
Booker: Margaret Ost

VILLAGE GATE
160 Bleecker St.
New York, NY 10012
(212) 475-5120
Booker: Raphael D'Lugoff

CHICAGO

BARREL OF LAUGHS
10345 S. Central Ave.
Oak Lawn, IL 60453
(708) 499-2969
Booker: Bill Brady

CATCH A RISING STAR—CHICAGO
Hyatt Regency
151 E. Wacker Dr.
Chicago, IL 60601
(312) 565-1234
Booker: Bob Hillman

CATCH A RISING STAR—OAK BROOK
Hyatt Regency
1909 Spring Rd.
Oak Brook, IL 60521
(708) 573-7888
Booker: Naomi Reed

COMEDY COTTAGE—ROSEMONT
9751 W. Higgins Rd.
Rosemont, IL 60018
(708) 698-2584
Booker: Ed Hellenbrand

COMEDY WOMB
8030 W. Ogden Ave.
Lyons, IL 60534
(708) 442-5755
Booker: Mark Shufeldt

FUNNY BONE—SCHAUMBURG
1725 Algonquin Rd.
Schaumburg, IL 60173
(708) 303-5700
Booker: Jerry Kubach

FUNNY FIRM
318 W. Grand Ave.
Chicago, IL 60610
(312) 321-9500
Booker: Len Austrevich

IMPROVISATION—CHICAGO
504 N. Wells
Chicago, IL 60610
(312) 782-6387
Booker: Budd Friedman

LAST LAFF—LISLE
Holiday Inn Crown Plaza
3000 Warrenville
Lisle, IL 60532
(708) 505-1000
Booker: Jay Berk

LAST LAFF—ROSEMONT
6350 N. River Rd.
Rosemont, IL 60018
(708) 823-5233
Booker: Jay Berk

WACKOS
6317 W. Roosevelt Rd.
Berwyn, IL 60402
(708) 749-9225
Booker: Joni Byford

WHO'S ON FIRST
684 W. North Ave.
Elmhurst, IL 60126
(708) 833-3430
Booker: Denise Mix

ZANIES—CHICAGO
1548 N. Wells St.
Chicago, IL 60610
(312) 337-4027
Booker: Bert Haas

ZANIES—MT. PROSPECT
2200 S. Elmhurst Rd.
Mt. Prospect, IL 60056
(708) 228-6166
Booker: Bert Haas

ZANIES—PHEASANT RUN
Pheasant Run Resort
North Ave.
St. Charles, IL 60174
(708) 513-1761
Booker: Bert Haas

LOS ANGELES

COMEDY LAND
Anaheim Plaza Hotel
1700 S. Harbour Rd.
Anaheim, CA 92802
(714) 957-2617
Booker: Kelly Jones-Craft

COMEDY & MAGIC CLUB
1018 Hermosa Ave.
Hermosa Beach, CA 90254
(213) 372-1193
Booker: Jimmy Miller

COMEDY STORE—HOLLYWOOD
8433 W. Sunset Blvd.
Hollywood, CA 90069
(213) 656-6225
Booker: Jim Davis

ICEHOUSE
24 N. Mentor Ave.
Pasadena, CA 91106
(818) 449-6542
Booker: Bob Fisher

IGBYS
11637 Tennessee Pl.
Los Angeles, CA 90064
(213) 477-3553
Booker: Jan Smith

IMPROVISATION—IRVINE
4255 Campus Dr.
Irvine, CA 92715
(714) 854-5455
Booker: Budd Friedman

IMPROVISATION—LOS ANGELES
8162 Melrose Ave.
Hollywood, CA 90046
(213) 651-3625
Booker: Budd Friedman

IMPROVISATION—SANTA MONICA
321 Santa Monica Blvd.
Santa Monica, CA 90401
(213) 394-8664
Booker: Budd Friedman

L.A. CABARET COMEDY CLUB
17271 Ventura Blvd.
Encino, CA 91316
(818) 501-3737
Booker: Ray Bishop

L.A. CONNECTION COMEDY THEATER
13442 Ventura Blvd.
Sherman Oaks, CA 91423
(818) 784-1868
Booker: Kent Skov

LAFF STOP—MONTCLAIR
9365 Monte Vista
Montclair, CA 91763
(714) 624-7867
Booker: Howard Trussman

LAFF STOP—NEWPORT BEACH
2122 SE Bristol
Santa Ana, CA 92707
(714) 852-8762
Booker: Howard Trussman

LAUGH FACTORY
8001 Sunset Blvd.
W. Hollywood, CA 90046
(213) 656-8860
Booker: Michelle Dunphy

LONG BEACH COMEDY CAFE
49 S. Pine
Long Beach, CA 90802
(213) 437-6709
Booker: Francine Osborn

SHENANIGANS
6471 Westminster Ave.
Westminster, CA 92683
(714) 898-2058
Booker: Ken Sands

AFTERWORD: ACTORS AWARE

BY ANDREA WOLPER

"**M**any people are eager to become actors, announcers or models. Unfortunately, those who seek careers in these fields are easily victimized by false promises of money and stardom." Those words, from a pamphlet published by the New York State Department of Law's Consumer Fraud Division in cooperation with AFTRA, aren't only for the kid fresh off the farm; they're for anyone pursuing a career in the performing arts.

If you think you can never be victimized, think again. There are people who have been ripped off and don't even know it. They've given their time or money or hard work to phonies, and gotten little or nothing in return. Certainly you have to take chances; everything about this business—from classes to auditions—is a gamble, and anybody can get taken if the circumstances are right. When you want something badly enough, it's not hard to talk yourself into believing people who say they can get it for you.

Competition being what it is, most actors and models hear "no thank you" so often that a "yes" is like manna from heaven. Something comes along and maybe you have your doubts, but what the heck—something's better than nothing, right? Maybe. In order to distinguish between the worthy investments and the shady deals, it is necessary to remember that most legitimate operations are governed by laws, union regulations, or at the very least, time-honored traditions.

PERSONAL SAFETY

This is a funny business. Deals aren't always cut in offices during regular business hours. Making contacts, schmoozing, pursuing friendships are all part of the game. Add the pressure to be easy-going and ever-so-agreeable (because if they don't *like* me they might not *hire* me), plus the fact that sexuality is a salable commodity, and you've got a confusing, potentially dangerous mix.

Think twice if a director, producer, or anyone else asks to interview you in a hotel room or apartment. As an alternative, suggest a coffee shop or hotel lobby. If you meet resistance, forget the whole thing. Yes, there are exceptions: some people do work out of their homes. But the basic rule of thumb is, "don't go." Even if you recognize the person's name, ask around: maybe someone else has had an experience—good or bad—with him or her. If you're uncertain about a situation, ask questions. If the person is vague about the project or refuses to answer appropriate questions, or seems dishonest or unprofessional, it's not worth following through.

Don't assume people have all the answers just because they say they do. If you find yourself in a situation that feels dangerous or illegal or like a scam, leave. Say you want to think about it, or that you have another appointment. If you have even a suspicion of danger, forget for the moment the job, the money, the career. Think about your safety and well-being, and get out.

AGENTS AND MANAGERS

There are certain divisions of labor in the performing arts and modeling businesses, and it's important that you know the differences, the overlaps, and who does what. Agents must be licensed by the state, and are entitled to collect commissions of no more than 10 percent after you've been paid for your work. ("Modeling agencies" are technically "model management" firms, and commissions generally are in the 10-15 percent range.) Casting directors are paid by the production companies, studios, or whomever hires them, and never by the talent. Personal managers aren't licensed, and though their commissions are not fixed, 15-20 percent is the norm.

By law, agents and managers are not permitted to make promises of employment, nor may they accept advance fees or retainers. They may recommend, but should not insist upon, particular photographers, teachers, and so on.

Sometimes, people with nebulous or even non-existent ties to the business call themselves managers. Even if they're not after your money or your body (maybe they just want to be in show biz), you must determine whether such a relationship will benefit your career. Is the person in a position to advise you, to make you known to agents and casting directors? Remember that in order to help shape and promote your career, a personal manager should be familiar with your talents and abilities.

According to Joseph Rapp, president of the National Conference of Personal Managers/East Coast, a legitimate manager does not send out your headshots *for a fee*, or coach you *for a fee*. A legitimate manager works on commission. Coaching may be part of your working relationship, and a legitimate manager may recommend photographers and help you make selections from contact sheets. A legitimate manager may ask clients to chip in (say, $25 a month) to help cover expenses, but does not ask for large fees up front.

If you want to check the credentials of a manager, call the Conference of Personal Managers (see chapter on Personal Managers). Membership standards are high, so you can be pretty confident that a member is trustworthy. On the other hand, not every legitimate manager is a member. Still, the people at NCPM will do what they can to help you. You can also call the Better Business Bureau in your city and ask if any complaints have been registered against the person in question.

PICTURE THIS

You've seen those "MODELS! ALL TYPES! EARN TOP $$$! NO EXPER. NEC!" ads that run in the daily papers, and you probably know that some of them are placed by people who will try to sell you expensive classes or photographic services, or convince you to pay a registration fee, all the while leading you to believe they run legitimate modeling firms.

Some advertisers are pretty clever, so it isn't always easy to spot the fraudulent ads. Be cautious when you see promises of high pay, or the words "no experience necessary," which usually translate to mean "amateurs wanted." Why? Because amateurs are less likely to know the ins and outs of the business and are easier to victimize.

If you're the parent of young children, you may receive letters suggesting your kids try modeling, or see ads for seminars on child modeling. If you respond, you'll probably be invited to spend hundreds of dollars on photographs. You should know that legitimate talent and modeling agencies do not provide photographic services (though they may refer you to photographers), nor do they require expensive photos of babies and toddlers. Instead, send snapshots to licensed agents and personal managers who handle young people. If they're interested, they will ask you to bring your child in for a meeting, at which time the agent or manager can advise you further.

Kids under age five aside, models do need pictures. But no reputable model management company (modeling agency) will charge you for test shots. Eileen Ford of Ford Models explains that prospective new models are put in touch with photographers so that test shots may be taken; you can also hook up with photographers who are building their own portfolios or trying new ideas. The model pays for film expenses—that's all. When you're ready to hire a photographer for headshots or composites (this goes for actors, too), get several names and take a look at their work. If any agent or manager pushes you to shoot with one particular photographer, take care: he or she will probably get a kickback; who knows what you'll get?

If you're considering paying to have your picture placed in a book or "talent register," do some investigating. If you're being represented by a reputable modeling agency, this is a legitimate expense. But anyone can put together a book and advertise on TV or in newspapers. The question is, who's going to look at that book? Before your spend a penny, call some agents or casting directors and ask them if they know of and utilize the book in question.

SCHOOL SMARTS

The New York State Education Department (Laws, section 5001-f) mandates that schools that provide instruction in modeling or announcing must be licensed. However, according to Ron Long of the Department's Bureau of Proprietary School Supervision, "even licensed schools engage in improper conduct, especially in the modeling industry."

Your first step when considering such a school should be to call the

Department of Education to find out if the school is licensed and if there have been any complaints. Long also urges that people "go to the school and ask for a list of former students they can talk to. Or go and speak to current students who are near the end of the program. If the school resists, walk away."

Music, dramatic art, and dance schools are exempt from licensing, which means anybody can hang out a shingle and open shop. Since dance and music classes usually can be paid for on a per-class basis, you can try a class or two without risking too much. Acting instruction, however, generally requires a more substantial commitment of time and money. When seeking any kind of performance or modeling instruction, your best course of action is to ask people whose work you admire where they study. The peers you trust and respect are your best sources of information.

Be wary of anyone who tries to pressure you into enrolling in a school or class. Run the other way if you hear promises of employment if you enroll. If you respond to what appears to be a casting notice or help-wanted ad, and it turns out to be bait to attract students, do what *A Chorus Line*'s Morales did: go find another class!

WHERE TO GET HELP

If you've been the victim of a scam or fraudulent practices, there are numerous agencies you can turn to. To investigate the reputation of any company, start with the Better Business Bureau, which can tell you if complaints have been registered or other inquiries made. To find out if a school is properly licensed, contact the Licensing Bureau of the State Department of Education.

If you have trouble collecting pay, start by writing letters, calling, and visiting the person or company that owes you the money. You can try making such a pest of yourself that they'll pay up just to get rid of you. You can threaten, as one actor did, to publicize the company's "slow pay tactics in the craft unions and trade press." If your own efforts don't produce results, you can turn to the Better Business Bureau and any appropriate union and/or professional associations. In the end, you may have to file suit in Small Claims Court.

If you've been ripped off by a company that disappears after having received your money, or have been defrauded in any way, contact the Better Business Bureau, the State Attorney General's Office Bureau of Consumer Fraud and Protection, and the Federal Trade Commission. If the scam involved *any* use of the U.S. Postal Service, contact the Mail Fraud Division.

If you've been subjected to sexual abuse or harassment, notify the Better Business Bureau, the State Division of Human Rights and/or the City Commission on Human Rights, and the sex crimes unit of your local police department, as well as any appropriate talent, trade, or professional unions or associations.

In New York City, the Department of Consumer Affairs has appointed a liaison to investigate complaints about fraudulent practices by agents and personal managers in the entertainment industry. Complaints examined by the department include: unlicensed activity, charging consultant fees or high photography and print-book fees, and improper withholding of an artist's monies or other property.

While Equity, SAG, and AFTRA members are advised to contact their union representatives before calling Consumer Affairs, non-union performers with complaints against agents or managers should write directly to: Pam Hamilton, Entertainment Industry Liaison, City of New York Department of Consumer Affairs, General Counsel's Office, 80 Lafayette St., #4, New York, NY 10013.

To be prepared for any such unpleasantness, always keep copies of contracts or other agreements, and of any correspondence between yourself and the party with whom you have a dispute.

POINTS TO REMEMBER

It's really hard to know what to do when you want something so badly—when every job seems to turn on how other people respond to your talents, your personality, your looks. The very nature of the business requires that you put your trust in people you may not know, from photographers to teachers to agents to directors. So take care of yourself. Make sure you understand all information sheets or legal documents given you. Learn how to ask questions in a way that makes you comfortable, and seek explanations of anything that isn't clear. Ask to see reviews, resumes, credentials; ask if you can audit a class or speak to students before you enroll. Ask friends and colleagues if they know anything about the person or company in question. Ask *yourself* if it feels right.

Don't be afraid to ask for a written contract if none is offered. Look, anyone who would fire you because you insist on a professional contract is doing you a favor. Remember that acting, modeling, and/or dancing is your profession; if it means holding out until the good guys recognize your genius, then hold out.

Learn to read between the lines of casting notices. If an ad specifies "model types," make sure there's a good reason for it. Ditto "no experience necessary," which may mean that the people who placed the ad simply prefer not to comply with accepted standards of professional behavior. Never pay a producer, director, or anyone else for a script or for the privilege of auditioning.

Don't accept for a minute that posing for pictures or having sex with somebody is the only way to get a job. Your sex life is your business, but don't think that having sex will guarantee you a part in a movie. It may work in some cases, but how do you know it'll work in yours?

Remember that the agent, manager, director, producer, or whatever in front of you isn't the last one on earth. Ask yourself if this person is someone you'd want to know under other circumstances. Remember why you went into this field in the first place—it certainly wasn't to suffer and throw money away, was it?

While it's probably safe to say that the majority of folks you run into are honest and well-meaning, the con artists and the merely incompetent can be very clever. They know that what you want is tied up with a great deal of ego and emotion. Of course you want to believe anyone who says you're great, you're talented, I can hire you; in this business, one can't hear those things too often! Just keep your wits about you. Be sure that when you go to auditions and meetings, you take more than your picture and resume. Take all of *you* with you—your brains and intuition, your instincts, and your confidence and self-respect.

CONTRIBUTORS

Jonathan Abarbanel serves as a theater critic for *North Shore Magazine*, Chicago correspondent for *Back Stage* and the *Dramatists Guild Quarterly*, and executive director of the new Foundation of the American Theatre Critics Association. His articles have appeared in *American Theatre, Stagebill, TheaterWeek*, and *Variety*, and he has written special material for CBS and PBS, award-winning TV and radio advertising, and industrial film/multi-image scripts. He also is a playwright/librettist and has been a literary manager for several Midwest theaters.

John Allen wrote and published the *Summer Theater Guide* and the *Regional and Dinner Theater Guide* from 1982-1990. He also authored *The New Equity Audition System* in 1988 and his essays occasionally appear on the "McNeil/Lehrer Newshour." His career started in radio; in 1975, a series of programs he developed won an Iowa Arts Council Award and he's hosted a radio interview program where his guests included Aaron Copland, Studs Terkel, and Hubert Humphrey. He left radio for theater in 1979 and has performed extensively. He also performs in and manages Interborough Repertory Theater, a Brooklyn-based theater company which he and his wife founded in 1986.

Jill Charles is the founding artistic director of the Dorset Theatre Festival, an Equity company which produces summer seasons at the Dorset Playhouse in Dorset, Vermont. She also developed and continues to edit the nationally distributed *Summer Theatre Directory, Regional Theatre Directory*, and *Directory of Theatre Training Programs*. She taught for 10 years in both conservatory and liberal arts college theater departments; her last position was at Williams College in Massachusetts. She has directed over 40 productions, in Dorset and elsewhere. She recently authored *The Picture/Resume Book*, with theatrical photographer Tom Bloom.

Maureen Clark is an associate director of the Riverside Shakespeare Company in New York City, and has served the company as a teacher, director, verse coach, and casting consultant. Among numerous other Riverside projects, she directed the Joseph Papp summer parks tour of *The Taming of the Shrew*; *Love's Labour's Lost* for the "Sunday in the Park with Shakespeare" series; and *Macbeth*. She has also directed and acted professionally at numerous theaters in New York, Boston, and Denver.

Bill Ervolino is the television editor for the *Bergen Record* and a columnist and critic for *Back Stage*. He has written for the *New York Times*, the *Daily News*, and was the comedy critic and an entertainment writer for the *New York Post* for several years. His articles have appeared in *Vogue, Entertainment Weekly, The Hollywood Reporter*, and numerous other publications. In 1986 his first play, *The Lights on Walden Court*, was co-winner of the Jane Chambers Playwriting Award and was subsequently produced Off-Off Broadway.

Rorri Feinstein currently works as a comedian. She appears at clubs in New York, as well as in Chicago and San Francisco. Her theater credits include a season at The Adirondack Playhouse, productions in Los Angeles, and numerous Off-Off-Broadway shows in New York. Behind the camera, she has worked as an extras casting director on several feature films, and has worked on commercials doing script/continuity, production coordination, and production managing. She is a native New Yorker and holds an MFA in acting from UCLA.

Marje Fields has been at the head of her own agency, Marje Fields, Inc., since 1968. Her full-service agency represents writers as well as performers in TV, theater, film, and commercials. Prior to opening her own agency, she worked with Charles B. Tranum, a talent agency specializing in commercials. Before that, she worked at Air Features, where Frank and Anne Hummert wrote and produced the *original* soap operas. Ms. Fields is currently the president of the National Association of Talent Representatives, the trade organization which represents agents with SAG, AFTRA, and Equity.

Victor Gluck currently writes features for *Back Stage* and reviews for the *New York Native*. He's writing has also appeared in *Our Town, New York Guide/Wisdom's Child, Stages*, the *Shakespeare Bulletin, Downtown Manhattan, The East Side Express*, and *The Brooklyn Spectator*. He was the dramaturg at the Soho Repertory Theatre from 1980-1990, and has given literary advice to Manhattan Punch Line and the Hudson Guild. His plays *Amouresque* and *Arabesque* were produced as a double bill by the Quaigh Theatre in 1981. In that year he was also a Critic Fellow at the National Critics Conference of the Eugene O'Neill Theater Center.

Phyllis Goldman is a dance reviewer and feature writer on dance for *Back Stage*. She has also contributed to *Elle, Interview*, American Express's *Departure Magazine*, and writes regularly on theater personalities for the *New York Forward*. She has worked as a professional dancer, a teaching assistant to Lee Theodore at the American Dance Machine Training Facility, and as a choreographer for regional theater and television. She holds a BS degree in education with a major in dance from Ohio State University. She is currently at work on her first screenplay about, oddly enough, what goes on in the ballet world.

Bob Harrington is the cabaret critic for the *New York Post, Back Stage*, and the *Bergen Record*, and theater and cabaret editor for *Long Island* and *New York Nightlife* magazines. His series of educational articles on the business of cabaret in *Back Stage* garnered him a coveted Manhattan Association of Cabarets MAC Award in 1986. He is currently on the board of directors of the Outer Critics Circle, the Manhattan Association of Cabarets and Clubs, and the Society of Singers, he is also a member of the Drama Desk, and an American Theatre Wing Tony voter. He has written on cabaret and its stars for a variety of other publications, including the *Chicago Tribune* and the *Hearst Syndicate*.

Pat Hilton is a freelance writer specializing in the entertainment field. Interview subjects have included John Huston, Orson Welles, and George Burns, as well as a myriad of contemporary young stars. Work positions have included the editorship of *Beverly Hills People* and writer for syndicated columnist Marilyn Beck.

Michele LaRue is the associate editor for *Back Stage* and has been a contributing editor since 1985 for *Theatre Crafts* magazine, specializing in architecture, stage, and costume design. Her multifaceted career includes a life on stage as actress—notably in her one-woman show *The Yellow Wallpaper*—and behind the scenes as a researcher, writer, consultant, and special projects director. She is a member of Equity, SAG, AFTRA, and is a trustee of The East Lynne Company, the country's only theater company specializing in 19th-century American plays.

William M. Lynk's background includes over 15 years in the educational system, business field, talent management, writing profession, and entertainment areas. He has produced and directed a number of television commercials, radio spots, and video tapes; he currently assists with public relations and advertising at the Carousel Dinner Theatre in Akron. He is the national exectuive director of the American Dinner Theatre Institute, and writes about the activities of these dinner theaters in his monthly column in *Back Stage*. He is in the process of writing a book on the dinner theater industry.

Frank Meyer is currently managing editor of *Agent & Manager* magazine. He has spent his entire career in the communications field, as columnist, reviewer in print and on radio and television, radio talk show producer and host, public relations account executive, and newspaper executive, working in the U.S., Europe, and the Middle East, and even served a very brief stint as an agent. Meyer started with *Variety* as a Miami Beach stringer and worked his way up to managing editor, leaving the paper after more than 25 years. He has written many freelance articles, including a number for *Back Stage*.

Toni Reinhold is a features and entertainment writer, an investigative reporter, and an internationally syndicated columnist. An award-winning journalist, she began her career at age 17, stringing for WHN Radio News, WNBC Radio News, and the *New York Daily News*. In 1978, Toni joined the Murdoch organization as a staff reporter for the *Star* and performed stand-in shifts at the *New York Post*. In 1985, she signed with United Features Syndicate to write two weekly entertainment Q & A columns, and a year later added a third column. Ms. Reinhold is a regular contributor to such publications as *Back Stage*, *Redbook*, and *Woman's World*. She is also an author, most recently of *Untamed—The Autobiography of the Circus's Greatest Animal Trainer* (William Morrow & Co.).

Mike Salinas has worked in all aspects of theater, all around the world: as three-time stage manager of the European bus-and-truck tour of *West Side Story*; as a New York City talent agent; as a sound and light technician in Los Angeles; as the founding editor of *TheaterWeek*; and as the author of *Back Together Again*, the musical version of William Wharton's novel *Birdy*, with music by Curtis McKonly.

Fred Silver is currently an associate professor and voice teacher. A protege of the late Richard Rodgers, his shows include *For Heavens Sake*, *Hannah*, *Like It Is*, *Exodus and Easter*, and *In Gay Company*; his latest musical, *Good Little Girls*, originally produced by Lucille Lortel, is optioned for New York production. He created nightclub acts for Kaye Ballard, Lynne Carter, and Hermione Gingold, and wrote "The Age of Elegance" for Nancy Dussault and Karen Morrow. "Twelve Days After Christmas," written for Carol Burnett, has sold over a million copies. He is the author of *Auditioning for the Musical Theater*, published by Newmarket Press and Penguin Books.

Don Snell is an actor who recently moved to Los Angeles after starring in the film *For Immediate Release*, which received the 1990 FOCUS Award. He has played recurring roles on several daytime dramatic shows, including *All My Children*, *As the World Turns*, and *Days of Our Lives*. For the last four years, Don has worked both sides of the camera: he is the marketing director for Corporate Productions Inc. of North Hollywood; his clients include IBM, Exxon, and Philip Morris. The 42-year-old comedian balances the two careers by having a very good wardrobe. Other acting credits: *Alice*, *Places in the Heart*, *How I Got That Story*, *Rise and Shine*.

Michael Sommers is a feature writer and theater reviewer for *Back Stage*, and a contributing editor to *Theatre Crafts International* and *Lighting Dimensions*. He writes about theater and design for a number of magazines ranging from *Stagebill* to *Elle Decor*. His book on American stage costume will be published in 1992.

Rob Stevens lives in Hollywood and serves as a theater critic for *Frontiers* and as the "West Coast Stages" columnist for *Back Stage*. He has covered theater in Los Angeles since 1973 and reviews an average of 150 plays yearly. His reviews and feature articles have appeared in numerous publications in Los Angeles and New York. He is a member of the Los Angeles Drama Critics Circle and the American Theatre Critics Association. He presents the annual Robby Awards for "distinguished achievement in theater."

Thomas Walsh is a senior editor at *Back Stage* and has been with the company in numerous roles since 1986. He was a sports writer and editor for nearly five years with Sterling's Magazines, Inc., New York, and is the author of two recreational sports books for children. He has worked in an editorial capacity for many places, from SportsChannel to *Cosmopolitan* and *Back Stage/SHOOT*, and his subjects have ranged from professional hockey and major-league baseball to country music and UFOs. He remains determined to one day check out EPCOT Center for himself.

Andrea Wolper works as both an actor and a freelance writer. She has written for a variety of publications including *New York Woman$* and *In Fashion*, and since 1983 has been a frequent contributor of feature articles to *Back Stage*. Her "Actors Aware" article was nominated for the 1989 William H. Donaldson Award for Editorial Achievement, and her city-by-city resource guide to the acting profession will be published in 1992.

LIST OF ADVERTISERS

Back Stage Handbook for Performing Artists
Adv. Production Manager:
Claudia Griffiths

Back Stage Publications
Adv. Sales Manager:
Scott Berg
Production Director:
James Contessa
Publisher: Steve Elish
VP/Group Publisher:
Howard Lander